BASIC CHRISTIAN

CONVICTIONS

by

EDMUND G. KAUFMAN, PH.D., LL.D., D.D.

President Emeritus, Bethel College,
North Newton, Kansas

Published by
Bethel College
North Newton, Kansas 67117

Printed in USA

Mennonite Press, Inc.
North Newton, Kansas

FOREWORD
AND ACKNOWLEDGEMENTS

THIS VOLUME IS INTENDED AS AN INTRODUCTORY DISCUSSION OF THE Christian Faith. In 1932 when the author began serving as president of Bethel College, the curriculum committee of the school suggested that as a Christian college, Bethel should offer a course in Basic Christian Convictions for upper-level students. This was based upon the general observation that students coming to college with immature religious ideas often become confused in their religious thinking by courses in the natural and social sciences as well as in the humanities and philosophy. As a result they are then inclined, either to hang on to their pre-college religious concepts, or else cast aside all interest in religion as infantile and irrelevant. The course in Basic Christian Convictions for upper-level students was to help them re-evaluate and reintegrate their thinking in this important area in the light and meaning of their total college experience.

For many years it has been the privilege of the author to conduct classes of upper-level college students in this general area at Bethel College and at other institutions in America and abroad. A college community with alert students and faculty provides a stimulating atmosphere for considering various religious viewpoints. In this process student and teacher can profit greatly and one is eternally grateful for such learning and fellowship opportunities. Former students have repeatedly expressed the wish that the author would put his thinking in this general area into writing. The attempt to do that is herewith gratefully undertaken.

Theological thought has undergone many changes in the past and today is subjected again to critical analysis and examination due to more advanced biblical scholarship, scientific and philosophical developments, as well as closer contact with other world religions. However, this is not a book by an expert for other experts. There is a considerable gap between specialized theological and popular religious books. Theologians tend to provide scholarly volumes that are understood by comparatively few, namely, by other experts. On the other hand popular religious books often are in the form of sermons or discussion of religious questions. Both types have a place and value but do not altogether meet certain needs. There is a place for middle ground discussion of the Christian faith which is the purpose of this volume.

Since the subject matter of this volume relates to a number of areas and as it is difficult for one individual to be conversant with them all, the author is grateful that each of the following individuals has been willing to read one chapter in manuscript form and make corrections and suggestions:

Harold H. Gross (Ph.D., Iowa State), Professor of Philosophy and Religion, Bethel College, North Newton, Kansas, Chapter I. "Religion and the Religions";

Alvin Beachy (Th.D., Harvard), Professor of Bible and Religion, Bethel College, Chapter II. "God, Our Father";

Lloyd L. Ramseyer (Ph.D., Ohio State), President Emeritus, Bluffton College, Ohio, Chapter III. "Creation, God's Handiwork";

Henry A. Fast (Ph.D., Hartford), Emeritus Professor of Bible and Christian Education, Bethel College, Chapter IV. "Man, His Majesty and Misery";

William Keeney (Ph.D., Hartford), Academic Dean, Professor of Bible and Religion, Bethel College, Chapter V. "Jesus Christ, Lord and Savior";

Henry Poettcker (Th.D., Princeton), President and Professor of New Testament, Canadian Mennonite Bible College, Winnipeg, Chapter VI. "The Holy Spirit and the Trinity";

Cornelius Krahn (Th.D., Heidelberg), Professor of Church History, Bethel College, Chapter VII. "The Kingdom and the Church";

Jacob J. Enz (Ph.D., Johns Hopkins), Professor of Old Testament and Hebrew, Mennonite Biblical Seminary, Elkhart, Indiana, Chapter VIII. "The Bible: the Story of Reconciliation";

Cornelius J. Dyck (Ph.D., Chicago), Professor of Historical Theology, Mennonite Biblical Seminary, Elkhart, Indiana, Chapter IX. "The Christian Hope";

David C. Wedel (Th.D., Iliff), Former President, now Associate Director of Development, Bethel College, Chapter X. "The Christian Life."

A number of persons have also given time and energy to go over the entire manuscript and make corrections and suggestions. These are:

Robert S. Kreider (Ph.D., Chicago), President and Professor of History, Bluffton College, Bluffton, Ohio, who also wrote the "Preface";

Erland Waltner (Th.D., Eastern Baptist), President and Professor of Bible, Mennonite Biblical Seminary, Elkhart, Indiana, who also wrote the "Introduction";

my son, Gordon D. Kaufman (Ph.D., Yale), Professor of Systematic Theology, Divinity School, Harvard University;

my daughter, Karolyn K. Zerger (A.B., Kansas Wesleyan), Kindergarten Teacher, Salina, Kansas;

Duane Friesen (Th.D., Harvard), Professor of Bible and Religion, Bethel College, North Newton, Kansas;

and my wife, Edna R. Kaufman (Ph.D., Ohio State), Professor of Home Economics, Bethel College, North Newton, Kansas.

The many helpful suggestions made by various individuals were much appreciated, although not all of them could be incorporated. Naturally, the author alone is responsible for any mistakes or omissions.

The author also wishes to thank the following publishers for permission to quote from their various works cited below:

Beacon Press, Boston, for quotations from Fred Gladstone Bratton's *A History of the Bible*, 1959;

Cambridge University Press, New York, for quotations from C. H. Dodd's *The Bible Today*, 1947;

Charles Scribner's Sons, New York, for quotations from William A. Brown's *Christian Theology in Outline*, 1921; *Robert E. Hume's The World's Living Religions*, 1959; and Reinhold Niebuhr's *The Nature and Destiny of Man*, 1941;

Division of Christian Education of the National Council of Churches of Christ in the U.S.A. for quotations from *The Revised Standard Version of the Bible*, copyrighted in 1946 and 1952 by them and published by Thomas Nelson & Sons, New York, 1952;

Harper & Row, New York, for quotations from L. H. DeWolf's *Theology of the Living Church*, 1953; Harry E. Fosdick's *A Guide to Understanding the Bible*, 1938; A. Eustace Haydon's *Man's Search for the Good Life*, 1937; H. R. Niebuhr's *Radical Monotheism and Western Culture*, 1960; Pierre Teilhard de Chardin's *The Divine Milieu*, 1960; and *The Phenomenon of Man*, 1961;

John Wiley & Sons, Inc., New York, for quotations from John R. Platt's *The Step to Man*, 1966;

The Mennonite Publishing House, Scottdale, Pa., & Faith and Life Press, Newton, Kansas, for quotations from *The Mennonite Hymnal*, 1970; and *The Mennonite Encyclopedia*, 1955;

Prentice-Hall, Inc., Englewood, N.J., for quotations from Kee, Young, & Froelich's *Understanding the New Testament*, 2nd edition, 1965;

Religious Education Association, New York, for quotations and graphic reprints from W. C. Bower's article "Trends in Psychology of Religion," in *Religious Education*, January, 1928, Vol. XXIII, No. 1 issue;

The World Federalist, USA. Inc., Washington, D.C., for a quotation from their Bulletin, Oct., 1968.

The author also wishes to express sincere gratitude to the Schowalter Foundation, Newton, Kansas, who along with others, helped make it financially possible to publish this volume. Bethel College as the publisher and The Mennonite Press as the printer, also deserve grateful mention for their respective contributions in this whole undertaking.

In work of this nature it is impossible to make adequate acknowledgement of all the sources used or to mention all persons who have been helpful. Hence to those mentioned as well as to the many not mentioned the author is grateful indeed. Most of all he is indebted to his wife, who, in spite of many responsibilities in home and community, gave invaluable assistance in innumerable ways and constantly stood by with kind encouragement to persevere to the final completion of the task.

Not everybody will agree with the point of view and interpretations here presented. Some will think it too conservative, others will consider it too liberal. The writer is a firm believer in the Christian faith but recognizes different ways of interpreting and expressing these convictions. This volume is sent forth with the hope and prayer that many might find it helpful toward personal growth in and dedication to the Christian faith and life.

EDMUND G. KAUFMAN

PREFACE

As I read these pages a picture of thirty years ago came into focus in my inner eye: a low-ceilinged basement classroom, drab walls in need of redecoration, an ill-lighted room for the 7:30 morning class three mornings a week. Although most of us were Mennonite students, we were diverse: a former missionary in the Far East, an athlete soon to enter the coaching career, a minister's daughter, a chemist to be, a future social worker, another who would become a teacher in a Bible school, and others.

The course was Basic Christian Convictions and the teacher was the then President of Bethel College, Dr. Ed. G. Kaufman. This was my first introduction to the study of theology. It was exciting fare he served us—some of us very conservative and critical, some of us proud of our new-found learning and prone to blurt out our unbeliefs.

I remember Dr. Kaufman less for his answers than for his questions, less for his lectures than for his intense class discussion which he generated, less for his declarations of his theological belief than for his invitations to further inquiry. Ed. G. Kaufman as a teacher probed, questioned, encouraged, exploded with bursts of enthusiasm, and even sometimes shocked his students. A tingle of pedagogical electricity pulsated through these class sessions. His course was one of those courses at Bethel which was widely discussed. The issues of man and God, Christ and the Spirit, sin and salvation were terribly important issues and intriguingly discussible.

Perhaps his most important contribution was his method of compelling us to get off the fence of indecision and to declare ourselves in writing on each theological question. Now, in this volume, the teacher, too, declares himself in writing.

As one of the hundreds of students stimulated by this encounter with the course, Basic Christian Convictions, I greet with appreciation the publication of this volume. He helped us to see theology as a study to be treated with high seriousness — "the queen of the sciences." In a sense, he confirmed the importance of theology simply by the act that as a busy college administrator he took time to lead us in the study of Christ and His Kingdom — the great issues.

Ed. G. Kaufman brought to that basement classroom a rich background of experience of mission service in China and doctoral studies in religion and sociology, and all this being conditioned by the sobering wear and tear of college administration. This volume reflects his classroom experience over several decades of college teaching. We gather here a sense of a unique Mennonite mind at work on theological questions — seeking and probing, widely read, searching for analogy and illustration from a wide range of intercultural experiences.

The author makes no claim of being a systematic or a biblical theologian in the classical sense. However, theological study has been his continuing concern for more than half a century. For those of us who studied theology with Dr. Kaufman in that basement classroom, one finds something extra in this volume. Since those days Dr. Kaufman has taught college and seminary students on other campuses, including a black college in the South and universities in Egypt and India. Not the least of the new dimensions reflected on these pages is a father's continuing dialogue with his theologian son, Dr. Gordon D. Kaufman, now on the faculty of the Divinity School of Harvard University. A father studying theology afresh under the stimulating guidance of an able son reminds one of the line of the poet, "The child is father of the man."

I read this book, *Basic Christian Convictions,* with gratitude— written by one of the master teachers of our brotherhood and about the most important subject of human inquiry—theology.

ROBERT KREIDER,
President, Bluffton College,
Bluffton, Ohio.

INTRODUCTION

MARTIN E. MARTY HAS CHARACTERIZED THE AMERICAN RELIGIOUS situation of the past decade by observing that the beginning of the 1960's were marked by "religious revival," the middle of the decade by "religious renewal," whereas the beginning of the 1970's is best described as a time of "religious revolution." However one may choose to describe religion in America, clearly, changes are taking place. Manifestly the study of religion continues to occupy a major place in contemporary scholarship. This is evident not only by the large volume of books on diverse aspects of religion which continue to pour from the world's printing presses, but also by the establishment of departments of religion in many major public universities in the last decades. For a time in the recent past it seemed that this kind of study was the special province of the church-related liberal arts college. Subsequently, the interest in the study of religion has become much more widespread.

With this growth of scholarly interest in religion, there has come a tendency toward specialization. Most scholars seem to fix on some one facet of the whole large world of religion and probe its many ramifications. Concerned about depth, many scholars sacrifice comprehensiveness. Specialization in religious studies has its values but also its weaknesses. It is far too easy to lose broad perspectives in the search for some small nugget in the large dimensions of religious reality. Perhaps one reason that for many modern men "God is dead," is precisely that they have lost their perspectives in the search for reality.

While some would argue that religion is no longer relevant to a world in which man has "come-of-age," the current scene raises profoundly the question of how "mature" modern man has come to be; whether, indeed, he is able to decide and act as an enlightened and rational being; and whether he is really able to make do without the transcendent in his life. A revival in America of keen interest in the occult, in Eastern religions, in astrology, and in spiritualism bear testimony to a fundamental need of modern man for that which is beyond himself.

In the context of this situation, the book, *Basic Christian Convictions,* by Edmund G. Kaufman, can be welcomed as a comprehensive synthesis in outline. It brings together the studies and experiences of the author over a period of several decades. It includes many of the ideas and insights which this missionary-teacher-administrator has shared with his many students through the years. It reflects his broad interest in world religions, stimulated by his teaching experience in China, Egypt and India. His scholarly interests in philosophical and sociological studies shine through at many points. Basically, however, he writes as one who is concerned about the Christian faith, seeking to express what this means for contemporary man.

This volume is not an attempt at a "systematic theology." The Author does not claim to have undertaken the awesome task of re-casting the Christian faith into some new form. What he does is to set before the reader, even as he did before his students, first a quick panorama of world religions and then move on to examine the salient aspects of the Judeo-Christian faith. While seeking to maintain a certain objectivity in the handling of his materials, his own commit-ment to biblical faith centered in Jesus Christ and His reconciling love, comes through.

While the Author has been a lifelong leader in the General Con-ference Mennonite Church, the materials which he has brought to-gether in this volume are far from sectarian. This, in fact, is likely to be a criticism of the book, namely that it does not sufficiently reflect the Author's own Anabaptist-Mennonite background. It would ap-pear that he has deliberately pursued a posture of objectivity and thus has generally avoided to allow this book to become a "credo." This concern for objectivity has much to commend it in a time when the subjective has been overly glorified.

To his former students, his book will be a welcome compendium, bringing back many experiences and learnings of former days. To those who do not know the author, this will serve to introduce them to the breadth of his interests and the comprehensiveness of his con-tinued studies in matters of faith through the years. For still others this volume can serve as significant source material, an aid to further research, and a basis for study of how Christian faith has been ex-pressed and taught by an esteemed mentor who has helped many eager students make their way from a naive, simplistic faith to a more intelligent and aware understanding of Christian discipleship.

Precisely in a time when the sense of history has become dim for many, this volume, quoting sources across many decades and thus reflecting dynamic developments in religious thought over a longer period of time, has singular significance.

Moreover, many volumes in the area of religion generally, or on Christian faith in particular, are designed to be read primarily by professionals. This book, on the other hand, can and ought to be read by many nonprofessionals. Its language and its approach, as well as its structure, make it useful to the person who has not had special theological training but who is seeking to understand better what it is that Christians believe in the context of the larger world of religion.

For putting these materials together in this way and thus making them available to former students and to many others, the author has placed all deeply in his debt.

ERLAND WALTNER,
President, Mennonite Biblical Seminary,
Elkhart, Indiana

CONTENTS

CHAPTER I

RELIGION AND THE RELIGIONS

And he made from one every nation of men to live on
all the face of the earth, having determined allotted
periods and boundaries of their habitation, that they
should seek God, in the hope that they might feel after
him and find him. Yet he is not far from each one of
us, for 'In him we live and move and have our being'
. . . 'For we are indeed his offspring' (Acts 17:26-28).

THEOLOGY IS PRECEDED BY RELIGION, AS BOTANY IS PRECEDED BY
the life of plants. Hence, religion is the reality of which theology is
only the study. Religion along with art and philosophy has always
been one of the chief interests of mankind. Religion is the chief characteristic that differentiates man from all other creatures. No tribe
has ever been found without some form of religion. Throughout the
history of man religion has been his preeminently noble characteristic.

Religion is part of man's adjustment to the world to achieve a
better life. On the lower levels this ever-present quest expresses itself
in search for food and shelter, and on higher levels in search for social,
intellectual and spiritual values. This has always been a double
search in which God is searching for man; but He has also implanted
a hunger in man which in turn expresses itself in man's searching for
God. Man has gradually but increasingly become conscious and
aware of this double search.

A. THE GROWTH OF RELIGION[1]

Authorities tend to think that primitive man considered nature as
widely diffused power. To this, his reaction was characterized by a

---

1. G. F. Moore, *Birth and Growth of Religion,* Scribners, 1923; H. H. Titus,
Living Issues in Philosophy, Am. Book Co., 1964, Chapter 23; Homer W.
Smith, *Man and his Gods,* Little Brown & Co., 1956; J. B. Noss, *Man's Re-*
ligions, Macmillan, 1969; E. W. Hopkins, *Origin and Evolution of Religion,*
Cooper Square, 1969.

sense of awe. This indefinable, mysterious power (mana), was thought of as permeating everything but often more concentrated in individuals or things and so manifesting itself in extraordinary persons, special things, or unexpected events. It was responsible for catastrophes, diseases, and other good and evil events. It brought about the increase in plants, animals, and human beings, as well as their death. It gave skill to the warrior, the hunter, and the craftsman. It worked in the rain, the lightning, and the thunder as well as in the waves of the sea and the growth of plants. It might break out anywhere and at any time. It was thought of as power, sheer unpredictable power.

1. *Animism*

At a later stage in the development of religion, nature was thought to be filled with spirits. This is called animism. The trees, brooks, clouds, stars and other objects are thought to be dwelling places of spirits. Primitive man gradually projected his own experience into objects around him. Animism involves the notion of a soul, and so is not regarded as purely primitive as this could only have been achieved after considerable reflection. In animism it is thought that the spirits can be influenced in various ways, such as: by taboo, magic, totemism, and fetishism.

At a later stage the spirits are thought to move about and are more free. There are spirits of objects and dead ancestors. There is the angry spirit of thunder, the busy spirit of the wind, the weeping spirit of the rain, the gentle spirit of the river, the mysterious spirit of the woods, the restless spirit of the ocean, the wandering spirit of the ancestor, and many others. These spirits are worshiped and appealed to for guidance and help. It is assumed that primitive man's experience of dreaming had much to do with developing the idea that every object has a spirit that can leave the body even as man seemingly does in sleep when he dreams.

2. *Pantheism*

Pantheism identifies the universe as a whole with God. It denies a separate existence of God from the universe. Often an extreme form of mysticism goes with pantheism, holding that the divine One is the only true reality. All is God and God is all. Pantheism holds that God exists, not as a person, but as manifested in the material universe and in man. Hinduism is an example.

3. *Polytheism*

When the spirits are given names and are thought of in terms of personalities we have polytheism, meaning the belief in many gods. Spirits are elevated to the status of gods and are thought of as dwelling above and beyond the world inhabited by man. With the gradual change from tribal to national life a transition to polytheism in religion also takes place. Now the gods are considered to have human faculties and passions. All sorts of stories or myths about the gods, the world, man and other beings, arise and develop into an elaborate mythology. Mythology is not a religion but rather an interpretation or sort of primitive theology of the then current religion.

4. *Henotheism*

When one god is gradually elevated above others we have henotheism. So Zeus became supreme among the Greek gods, and Jupiter among the Roman gods. Henotheism recognizes other gods but considers one supreme over others. The early Hebrews recognized Yahweh as their God, but also thought of Baal as the god of the Canaanites. It took a long time for them to recognize Yahweh as the one and only God in the universe.

5. *Dualism*

Dualism is the doctrine that the universe is under the domination of two opposing forces—one good and the other bad—God and Satan. Zoroastrianism is an example with *Ahura Mazda* the personification of light, truth and the good, and his twin brother *Angra Mainyu* the personification of darkness, evil and the lie. These brothers are pitted against each other in perpetual warfare. To help him in the struggle, the one brought forth many angels such as order, wisdom, health and immortality. These good angels in turn were aided by a host of sub-angelic beings; while in opposition the opponent created a legion of evil demons who manifest themselves in filth, chaos, disease, and death. Man must choose between these two powers, and everything he thinks or does is on one or the other side of the struggle. The Hebrews, during the Babylonian captivity, were greatly influenced by this dualistic Zoroastrianism.

6. *Monotheism*

Monotheism is the belief in the existence of only one God. Abraham (about 1500 B.C.) and Moses (about 1200 B.C.) are usually considered the pioneers of monotheism. Although today many would claim to be monotheists, the general masses have always found it difficult, as indicated in the Old Testament, fully to accept monotheism and to live according to its implications. If there is only one God, the question naturally arises as to what kind of being is He? The prophets insisted on *Ethical Monotheism*, that God loved righteousness and hated injustice, that He is an ethical, spiritual, and universal being, interested in goodness, purity, mercy, justice, and truth. Jesus in His teaching, His life, and death taught and demonstrated that God is Love. This idea has been difficult for mankind to fully grasp and apply socially.

Love of the neighbor is required in every religion, but in polytheism and henotheism my neighbor is the one who is near me and in my-interest group. In both instances the counterpart of neighbor love is the requirement to hate the enemy. In radical monotheism my neighbor is my companion, and though he is my enemy, the requirement still is to love him.

In radical monotheism God alone is the ultimate object of trust and loyalty, and sacredness must be denied to any other being. There are no special times, places, persons, communities, as more representative of the One than others. No sacred groves, temples, kings, priests, or days are more representative of Him in whom all things live and move and have their being.

The counterpart of this secularization is the sanctification of all things. Now, every day is the Lord's; every nation is a holy people; every person is sacred and made in His image; everything, on earth, in the heavens, and in the sea is His creation; the entire universe and the infinity of space is His temple filled with His glory. This recognition is the basis of a transformed ethics and religion. Even Western civilization is still far from fully living according to radical ethical monotheism.[2]

Although there are some general stages discernible in the growth of religion, there is no definite line of development through which all religions must go. The stages of development usually are related to the stages of civilization and culture of a people. Religion, as other social phenomena, has its ups and downs and does not necessarily follow a definite line of unbroken progress. There may be times of arrested development or even decadence.

---

2. *Hastings Bible Dictionary, article,* "Development of Hebrew Religion"; H. Richard Niebuhr, *Radical Monotheism and Western Culture,* Harper, 1960.

B. Patterns of Religion[3]

There are dead and living religions. A dozen or more developed religions have passed away although they left their mark on others that survived. Among them are: the ancient religions of Egypt, Babylonia, Assyria, Mexico, Peru, of the Phoenicians and Hittites, Mithraism, and Manichaeism of Asia Minor, the religions of ancient Greece and Rome, and those of Celtic and Teutonic peoples of Europe.[4]

Eleven organized living religions exist today all of which are over 500 years old. Asia was the birthplace of them all. According to the place of origin they fall into three groups: Those originating in South Asia (India); those originating in East Asia (China, Japan); and those originating in West Asia (Palestine, Persia, Arabia).

1. Religions Originating in South Asia (India)

Listed historically, religions originating in India would include Hinduism, Jainism, Buddhism, and Sikhism.

(a) *Hinduism* (436,745,000 adherents)[5]—Hinduism is the religion of divine immanence and an hereditary social structure or caste system. There is no definite founder identifiable. The Aryan invasion of India between 1500 and 2000 B.C. brought Hinduism with it. During the centuries, six different types of Hinduism developed. (1) *Early nature worship* before 1,000 B.C. with the *Four Vedas* (Books of Knowledge) as the scriptures, and prayer as the means of salvation. (2) *Priestly Hinduism* (1000-800 B.C.) with the *Brahmanas* as scriptures, and priestly sacrifice as means of salvation. The horse-sacrifice took a whole year and 609 horses. (3) *Philosophic Hinduism* (800-600 B.C.), with the *Upanishads* as chief scriptures, and meditation on Atman (self) as part of Brahma (God) bringing salvation from reincarnation. (4) *Legalistic Hinduism,* with the *Laws of Manu* (250 B.C.) as scripture, and ritualistic ceremonies as means of salvation from reincarnation. (5) *Devotional Hinduism,* considering the *Bhagavad Gita* (about 1 A.D.) as chief scripture, and for salvation, Krishna's emphasis on doing one's duty as a caste member

---

3. E. W. Hopkins, *Origin and Evolution of Religion*, Cooper Sq., 1969; R. E. Hume, *The World's Living Religions*, Scribners, 1959; John B. Noss, *Man's Religions*, Macmillan, 1969; Huston Smith, *The Religions of Man*, The American Library, 1958.

4. Hume, *Ibid.*, p. 13.

5. Statistics for religions are taken from *The World Almanac*, 1972, p. 391.

even to the point of killing relatives in war time. (6) *Popular Hinduism,* based on *Puranas* as scriptures (1-250 A.D.), with variety and vagueness of belief, much idolatry, worshiping Brahma the Creator, Vishnu the Preserver, Siva the Destroyer, Rama, Krishna, Kali, and thousands of others in many temples, pilgrimages to rivers and mountains, with numerous ceremonies and festivals.

The historic castes are: (1) Brahmans—priests and intellectuals, (2) Kshatriyas—rulers and warriors, (3) Vaisyas—farmers and artisans, (4) Sundras—servants, and (5) outcastes and untouchables, to which about 100 million of India's present vast population belongs. In time, over two thousand sub-castes developed. Castes are mutually exclusive, with hereditary occupation, and no intermarriage nor even eating with each other. With India's independence, in 1947, castes were outlawed; but being deeply ingrained in custom and culture, it will take generations to abolish them.

Features of Hinduism are: the caste system; reverence for Vedas; belief in Karma (reincarnation); Brahma is all and all is Brahma; salvation from reincarnation by merging of self with Brahma through prayer, sacrifice, meditation, ritualism, and devotion, thereby avoiding rebirth.

(b) *Jainism* (about 2,000,000 adherents)—Jainism began as a reform movement of Hinduism and was founded by Vardhamana Mahavira (599-527 B.C.), the son of a rich Rajah in northeast India. At age 30 he made the "Great Renunciation," left his wife and child to seek salvation by asceticism, giving away his wealth, plucking out his hair, neglecting his body, and spending much time squatting in deep meditation. At age 42 he gave up the solitary life and became an ascetic teacher. He won many monk followers and died at age seventy-two.

He opposed the Brahman priests, the *Vedas,* animal sacrifice, and the caste system. He denied existence of any gods, condemned worship and prayer, but stressed suppression of the body to achieve Nirvana (salvation by absorption into Brahma). After his death he was worshiped as God and Savior.

Jain scriptures are the *Angas,* written about 200 years after the founder. Two important sects of Jainism are the "White-clad" and the "Sky-clad" (clothed and naked), accommodating to the northern and southern climate. The chief virtues are mendicant asceticism and non-injury (Ahimsa). All life is sacred. A cloth screen is worn over the mouth lest a gnat is swallowed. The ground is swept as they walk lest a worm is stepped on. Gnats, worms, etc., in reincarnation,

6

may be dead ancestors or relatives. Five Sacred Vows are: to abstain from all killing, lying, stealing, sex, and all attachments (including love and hate).

Jain means "overcomer." Both Hindus and Moslems have persecuted Jains and gradually they have gone back to temples, idolatry, polytheism, caste, and are slowly being reabsorbed by broadminded Hinduism.

(c) *Buddhism* (176,920,000 adherents)—Siddhartha Gautama (560-480 B.C.) born about 100 miles north of Benares was the only son of a rich Rajah. He was greatly disturbed by human misery and suffering. One day, riding in the royal park, he saw an old man, a sick man, a dead man, and a wandering beggar. To solve the riddle of suffering he made the "Great Renunciation," left his wife and child, became a monk, studying the *Vedas,* meditating, and wandering about as an ascetic for six years in search for an answer to suffering. At last after forty-nine days of desperate ascetic meditation under a Bodhi (Fig) tree the "Great Enlightenment" came to him. Now he became an itinerant monk, preaching self-discipline and ethical self-culture until his death at eighty.

The "Four Noble Truths" of Buddha (The Enlightened One) are: (1) All existence involves suffering; (2) All suffering is caused by indulging desires; (3) Therefore, all suffering will cease upon suppressing all desire; (4) However, while still living one must follow the "Noble Eight-fold Path" of *right* belief, aspiration, speech, action, livelihood, endeavor, thought, and concentration. As water runs downhill, as fire is hot, and as ice is cold; so good produces good and evil produces evil. Karma (The Law of the Deed) is supreme, inescapable, impersonal justice, automatic, and needs no God, sacrifice, ceremony, prayer or priesthood. Buddha opposed Hindu gods, sacrifice, and caste. He urged *not to* kill, steal, lie, commit adultery, use intoxicants, and to avoid bodily pleasure. The world and the self are illusions (Maya). Nirvana (heaven) is achieved by extinction of consciousness when being ceases as when a light is extinguished or a drop of water is lost in the ocean. The blissful detachment from the world and the self, stops the cycle of rebirth.

Buddhist scriptures are the *Tripitaka* (Three Baskets); (1) Discipline Basket, rules of behavior; (2) Teaching Basket, discourses of Buddha; (3) Metaphysical Basket, doctrinal expositions. Hinayana Buddhism (Lesser Vehicle) spread to Southeast Asia, preserving monasticism and regarding Buddha as the great teacher of escape from misery. Mahayana Buddhism spread to the North and the

Far East, stressing salvation by contemplation and Buddha as divine savior. In India it has largely been reabsorbed by Hinduism but it is strong in the Far East (China, Japan, Tibet, etc.). It has spread high ethical concepts of tolerance and nonviolence.

(d) *Sikhism* (9,000,000 adherents)—The youngest of the eleven living religions, Sikhism (Disciples of the One True God) was founded by Nanak (1469-1538 A.D.). He was born thirty miles south of Lahore, the capital of the old Punjab. His father was a Hindu in the employ of a Muhammadan feudal lord. This Hindu-Muhammadan relationship puzzled him. At twenty-six, he left his wife and two children for the forest, where, after years of meditation, he was told in a vision, "My name is Brahma and you are the divine Guru (Teacher)." After this "call" he went home and announced his intention to combine Hinduism and Muhammadanism.

At thirty-seven, Guru Nanak, with a Muhammadan servant as musician, went on a missionary journey. For twelve years they preached and sang the gospel of "Discipleship to the One True God" as they wandered about. Later journeys were made to southern India including Ceylon, then to Kashmir, the Himalayas, Mecca in Arabia, and Bagdad in Iran. In the efforts to syncretize, the Hindu ideas of Karma and Transmigration were kept; but the *Vedas,* caste, idolatry, and infanticide were dropped. From Islam, the monotheistic idea of God with his special Guru, extreme reverence of scriptures, worshipful repetition of the deity's name, a powerful militaristic church-state, Amritsar as their Mecca, a sense of fatalism, and other similarities were adopted.

Sikhism had ten successive Gurus, ending with Govind Singh in 1708 A.D. The scriptures are writings of various Gurus, called *Granth* (The Book), containing meditations on God and exhortations on life. It has over 1,500 large pages in six different languages.

Under Muhammadan persecution, Sikhism increasingly developed into a military theocracy. All Sikhs were required to take the name Singh (Lion), let beard and hair grow which is kept under a turban, and undergo baptism as they join the congregation Khalsa (The Pure). Today they are a people of large physique and aggressive spirit in northern India.

2. *Religions Originating in East Asia* (*China, Japan*)

Listed historically these religions would include Taoism, Confucianism, and Shintoism. In China religion is more a code of conduct than a mystic concept of divine power. Underlying China's faiths are the rituals of primitive folklore, the worship of nature, and ancestor worship. Out of this background came Taoism and Confucianism, which later were interwoven with Mayahana Buddhism to form Chinese philosophy.

(a) *Taoism* (54,324,000 adherents)—There are few recorded facts about Lao-tze (604-517 ? B.C.), the founder of Taoism. Lao-tze means "Old Boy." Legend says he was born when eighty years old with a long white beard, from the side of his mother, joyfully clapping his hands for he had come to proclaim the TAO (The Way of the Gods). Lao-tze became curator of the imperial museum at Peking and was renowned as a scholar and sage. Later he resigned from this post and after a period of meditation, withdrew from society and journeyed westward. Eventually he came to an outpost of the empire. The gate-keeper recognized him and begged him to write down his philosophy before leaving China. In a few days Lao-tze composed the *Tao-Te-King,* the essence of classical Taoism. Having written his 248 Chinese characters, he went on his way over the mountain pass, never to be seen again.

Lao-tze stressed the relationship between Heaven, Earth, and Man, forming an indivisible unity. If man obeys natural laws, there is tranquillity; if he transgresses, disaster follows. The harmony between Heaven, Earth, and Man is governed by two forces. One is male (Yang), active, violent, engendering fire, tempest and earthquake; the other is female (Yin), passive, benign, causing the flow of the rivers and the cycles of the seasons. Although seemingly opposites, they are essentially in accord. Together they are good and necessary for the order of the universe. Above these two is the Tao (The Way), the creative, corrective, and integrative force of the universe. It coordinates Yang and Yin. Salvation lies in resigning oneself to the Tao and becoming an instrument of its will. Among all religions, Taoism comes nearest to Christ's teaching—to return good for evil. Some 268 parallels have been listed between the Tao-Te-King and the New Testament.[6] The emphasis of the Tao (Way) reminds one of the many references to the "Way" in the New Testament.

However Taoism has a pathetic history. Gradually its mysticism degraded into polytheism, demonology, witchcraft, and superstitious fraud conducted by many priests with a pope as head. Modern educa-

---

6. H. E. Hume, *The World's Living Religions,* Scribners, 1959, p. 140.

tion and science should do much to purify and enhance the noble qualities of this religion.

(b) *Confucianism* (371,587,000 adherents)—Confucius (551-479 B.C.), born and buried in the province of Shantung, was the founder of this religion. More details of his life are in the *Analects* than are known about any other founder of a religion. He was the youngest of eleven children. His father died when he was three. He married at nineteen and had one son. Being a good student himself, he started a school which, in thirty years, grew to some three thousand pupils. At fifty-one he was appointed Assistant Superintendent of Public Works of Shantung and rapidly advanced to Chief Justice of the province. His phenomenal success in promoting peace and order caused jealousy and intrigue among others, so at fifty-five he resigned to give himself to itinerant preaching of administrative social reform. From age 68 to his death at age 72 he devoted himself to writing. His disciples mourned his death for three years.

Later appreciation for Confucius became very extreme. Already in 195 B.C. the emperor worshiped at his tomb with animal sacrifice. In 555 A.D. separate temples for his worship were ordered at the capital of every prefecture. A magnificent temple was also erected in his honor at Peking. Here for 1,200 years, twice annually, the emperor conducted services with animal sacrifice and great ceremony. Similar services were also held, twice a year, by local officials in cities down to the third rank, numbering some 1,500. All this required over 60,000 animals annually. Gradually, by government decrees, Confucius was raised to equal rank with the deities of Heaven and Earth.

The scriptures of Confucianism are the *Six Classics* that he edited and compiled, including one original volume *Spring and Autumn* which he himself composed, and the *Four Books* of his sayings and other material compiled by his disciples. He considered himself a transmitter and not an original thinker. Among religious founders he is, however, unique in that he was also an author.

From these sources there emerged the system of ethics by which the Chinese lived for more than twenty centuries. The fundamental principle here is social propriety or reciprocity. The Confucian formulation of this system is based on *Five Human Relations*, considered to be fundamental to good society, which are: that of ruler and subject; parent and child; husband and wife; older and younger brother; friend and friend. Each relationship is based on duty and piety, bound together by the "Golden Rule" stated negatively; "What you do not want done to yourself, do not do to others." He held to the existence of a spiritual world but discouraged belief in a personal God and the practice of prayer. He stressed the middle-road of wisdom, propriety, reciprocity, benevolence, righteousness, studiousness, moderation, calmness, and fortitude. These are covered by three hundred rules of ceremony and three thousand rules of behavior.

Confucianism has no separate priesthood and yet his teachings became the state-religion, and his writings, the basis for civil examinations for all government offices until 1905. It was not until 1915 that the newly established Republic of China discontinued the worship of Confucius along with Heaven and Earth.

Taoism emphasizes the study of nature; Confucianism, the study of man; Taoism teaches that by submitting to nature, harmony among men results; Confucianism, that, by promoting harmony among men, harmony with nature results; Taoism is romantic, vague, intuitive, and mystic; Confucianism is formal, orderly, rational, and humanistic. Later Buddhism introduced gods in human form, prayer, and a priesthood. Together with nature and ancestor-worship this complex has moulded Chinese culture and life for more than two thousand years.

(c) *Shintoism* (69,662,000 adherents) —Japan received much of its civilization from China. Shintoism is the Chinese "Shen" (Gods) and "Tao" (Way), meaning "The Way of the Gods." Earliest religion in Japan was nature worship. Later, reverence for the imperial house was added. This combination made for national stability and furnished the basis for the longest reigning dynasty in history.

In 712 A.D. a book appeared called *Kojiki* (Record of Ancient Matters). This was followed in 720 A.D. by another one, called *Nihonji* (Chronicles of Japan). Here the history of Japan and the imperial line are traced back to the very beginnings. Here we also read of the divine beings, "Izanagi" and his wife "Izanami," together producing the Japanese Islands and the Japanese people. Among many gods is the great sungoddess, Amaterasu-O-Mikami, ruling the heavens as the highest divinity in the pantheon. It was her grandson, Jimmu Tenno, who assumed the rule of Japan in 660 B.C. and began the long line of divine Mikados. These scriptures contain many legends and poems indicating the divine origin of the Japanese Islands, the Mikado, and the people. The *Nihonji* refers to 80 myriad deities and the *Kojiki* to 800 myriads. Both male and female gods in these scriptures are born, wed, get sick, vomit, weep, kill, steal, die, rise again, etc. In fact, their morals are lower than that required of the Japanese people themselves.

After 500 A.D., Taoism, Confucianism, and Buddhism spread from China to Japan and intermingled with the indigenous religion. Complete acceptance of the divine Mikado was built up gradually. The Imperial Rescript on Education, October 30, 1890, promoted the demand of unquestioned devotion to the Mikado. In time, State-Shintoism came to be regarded as a patriotic cult in which all Japanese were to share, regardless of their religious beliefs. Japan's military success in World War I greatly advanced Mikado worship. However, on New Year's Day after the military defeat of Japan in 1945 (World War II), Emperor Hirohito issued an Imperial Rescript disavowing his own divine nature and that of the Japanese people. Such a revolution, naturally, at first results in widespread atheism, and only time will tell what the religious future of Japan will be.

3. *Religions originating in West Asia* (*Palestine, Persia, Arabia*)

Four living religions had their origin in West Asia. They are Judaism, Zoroastrianism, Muhammadanism, and Christianity.

(a) *Judaism* (13,537,000 adherents) —The Jews think of Abraham (1500 B.C.?) as their father, but Moses (1200 B.C.?) is usually considered the founder of Judaism. The central belief of Judaism is ethical monotheism as expressed in the *Shema* (Confession) repeated daily: "Hear, O Israel, Yahweh, our God is One" (Deuteronomy 6:4). Yahweh revealed himself progressively beginning with Abraham and Moses and on through the prophets, including scribes and rabbis. Israel was chosen by Yahweh to be His special servant in bringing all mankind to the knowledge of Him. Yahweh's will for man relates to all of life, all people, all places, all times, to the individual, the family, the community, the nation, and the world. Truth, justice, humility, faithfulness, and loving-kindness are highly regarded.

The Jewish scriptures include the Old Testament (the Pentateuch, the Prophets, and the Writings). Oral interpretations of the Pentateuch (or Torah) are the *Mishna,* and further interpretations of it are the *Gemara.* In the sixth century both the *Mishna* and *Gemara* were also written out and called the *Talmud.*

The family is central in Judaism. The height of family ritual is on the Sabbath, beginning Friday evening and lasting twenty-four hours. On the Sabbath, strict Jews do not work, write, telephone, travel, touch money, etc. Some Jewish holy days are: *Rosh Hashanah,* the

Jewish New Year; nine days later, *Yom Kippur,* the day of Atonement, a 24-hour fast; *Passover,* in March or April, recalls the liberation from Egyptian bondage; *Purim,* in February or March, in memory of the biblical Queen Esther; and *Hannukkah,* the Feast of Lights, in November or December, celebrating Jewish victory over the Syrians in the second century B.C. when the Temple lights were again rekindled.

Religious instruction begins at age five. At thirteen, a boy celebrates Bar Mitzvah (Son of the Commandments), assuming adult religious duties. Girls also get religious instruction early. Intelligence and education are very highly regarded. At present there are three divisions in Judaism: (a) "Orthodox," which is strict in ritual-observances, dietary laws, the Sabbath, and looks for the coming Messiah; (b) "Conservative," observing Rabbinical traditions less strictly; and (c) "Reform" Judaism, having made many alterations in old practices but stressing the ethical teachings of the prophets and works toward the coming of the Messianic age, encouraging cooperation with liberal Christians.

Today Judaism has no priesthood. The rabbi is a teacher. The synagogue, originating in the Babylonian captivity, is still the central institution of worship. Judaism's God is one of hope. He created the world to fit man for the Kingdom of Heaven. Life is God's gift to be lived according to His will. The Jews were the first to bring ethical Monotheism into sharp focus. Today they are located mostly in Israel, Russia, Europe and North America.

(b) *Zoroastrianism* (138,000 adherents)—The founder of Zoroastrianism was born in Persia not later than 600 B.C. At age thirty he felt called into the presence of *Ahura Mazda* (God of Light), who appointed him as His prophet. It took ten years to win the first convert, but with the conversion of the king, Vistaspa, others of royal blood joined and the masses followed. In holy war the Persian armies conquered their neighbors, including Babylon in 539 B.C. thereupon helping the captive Jews to return to Palestine. The Persian armies pushed on toward Europe, resulting in the Greek-Persian wars (480-330 B.C.) and ended in complete victory of Alexander the Great

Of all non-biblical religions, Zoroastrianism has the closest connection with our Bible. It is not mentioned by name, but the kings of Persia, who were Zoroastrians, are mentioned in eight books of the Old Testament: (II Chronicles 36:22-23; Ezra 1:1; Nehemiah 2:1; Esther 1:3; Isaiah 44:28; 45:1; Daniel 9:1; 10:1; 11:1; Haggai 1:1; Zachariah 1:1). Artaxerxes and Cyrus are repeatedly spoken of rather favorably. Isaiah refers to Cyrus as the Lord's "anointed" and as His "shepherd." In Matthew's Gospel the wise men from the East, Magi, whom some identify as Zoroastrian priests, were of the first to see the newborn Jesus at Bethlehem. Some scholars hold that in the Babylonian captivity the Jews took on some ideas and beliefs from them, such as an elaborate angelology, the idea of Satan and demonology, bodily resurrection, final judgment, a future savior (Soshyout), and the final victory of the God of light and truth (Ahura Mazda) over Satan the force of evil, darkness, and the lie (Angra Mainyu).

This ethical dualism expresses itself in struggle of a good but finite God against all forces of evil. Every individual has a definite part on the side of the one or the other with good or bad thoughts, words, and deeds. According to their scriptures, the *Avesta,* at the end of time comes the final judgment when the wicked will be sent to hell for purification and the righteous taken to heaven. Finally, however, God's victory will be so complete that even Satan will be converted and hell will be renovated to become an entrance hall to heaven.

In the seventh century the Muhammadans conquered Persia, and nearly exterminated Zoroastrianism. Today Zoroastrians are found mostly around Bombay, India, where they are a comparatively small but rather wealthy group, representing some of the most public-spirited and philanthropic citizens of India. Commonly, they are thought to be fire and sun worshipers, which they however deny by pointing out that the sun and fire are only symbols of Ahura Mazda, the God of light, truth, and purity.

(c) *Muhammadanism* (493,012,000 adherents) —Muhammad was born at Mecca, Arabia, in 570 A.D. As a youth he served as camel caravan-driver for a rich widow, Katija, whom he later married. In her employ he traveled in Syria and Palestine, mingling with Jews and Christians. One night he slept in the cave under the rock in the Temple at Jerusalem and had an experience in which he was taken up to the seventh heaven where Allah (God) commissioned him as His prophet. Upon his return to Mecca, he proclaimed Allah as the only God, denounced idolatry, to which the people objected, and in 622 he had to flee to Medina. This year of the Hegira (Flight) has been adopted as the beginning of the Muhammadan calendar.

In Medina he set up the rule of Allah with himself as dictator, and Islam (those who submit to Allah and his prophet) became a military

14   BASIC CHRISTIAN CONVICTIONS

theocracy. Mecca capitulated and soon all Arabia was conquered. Now, Mecca became his headquarters and emissaries were sent to the rulers of Greece, Persia, Egypt, and Abyssinia demanding abolition of idolatry and acceptance of his faith, by the sword. He died at age sixty-two in the arms of Aisha, the favorite wife in his harem of eleven.

The *Koran* is the Moslem sacred book. Soon after Muhammad's death compilations of the prophet's life and teaching appeared. About a decade later the third caliph, Othman, ordered an official revision to be made and all previous compilations to be destroyed. The Koran has 114 chapters and is a little smaller than our New Testament. It contains some Arabic traditions, Zoroastrian ideas, as well as Old and New Testament material. The Koran is basic for Islamic law, including rules for diet and hygiene, for marriage and divorce, and penalites for crime. It forbids worship of images and no likeness of Muhammad exists. Moslem art is floral and geometric without pictures of people or animals.

Muhammadanism's six basic beliefs are:
    (a) There is only one God, Allah.
    (b) Belief in angels; good ones intercede for believers with Allah, evil ones are devils seeking to mislead.
    (c) Belief in the Koran.
    (d) Belief in the prophets, twenty-two from the Old and three from the New Testament are named in the Koran, including Jesus, but Muhammad is the last and greatest of them all.
    (e) Belief in Judgment when believers go to Paradise and the wicked to Hell.
    (f) Belief in Divine Decrees—the predestination of everything.

The "Five Pillars" of the faith are:
    (a) To repeat the creed every day: "There is no God but Allah and Muhammad is his prophet."
    (b) Prayer—five times a day, kneeling, facing Mecca.
    (c) Almsgiving—offerings to Allah range from feeding beggars to giving money for public institutions.
    (d) Fasting—during the month of Ramadan, from sunrise to sunset, in self-examination and gratitude to Allah.
    (e) Pilgrimage to Mecca—at least once in a lifetime, but if impossible, then help a substitute to go. At Mecca the pilgrim participates in many ceremonies. This pilgrimage (Hadj) entitles one to be called Hadji and to wear a white arm band, indicating sanctity.

Today there is a reawakening in Islam. In spite of many sects, Muhammad's birthday is celebrated in all Moslem countries. Whirling Dervishes are dancing mystics who exorcise evil spirits. "Purdah," keeping women in seclusion or shrouded and veiled is slowly passing. Moslem mission-work is expanding, especially in Africa. Perhaps the strongest attraction is that Muhammadanism practices what Christianity preaches—namely equality. All Moslems are brothers under Allah.

(d) *Christianity* (924,274,000 adherents).—Christianity is the religion of the love of God and love of man as revealed in Jesus Christ. Since this volume deals mainly with Christianity, we shall not discuss it further here.

4. *General Characteristics of Religions*

(a) *Major Religions in Order of Origin*[7]

Name	Birth of Founder	Founder	Deity	Main Present Location	Scriptures	Millions of Adherents
Hinduism	1500 B.C.	None	Brahma	India	Vedas	436
Judaism	1200 B.C.	Moses	Yahweh	Many Countries	Old Testament	13
Shintoism	660 B.C.	None	Nature-Gods	Japan	Kojiki, Nihongi	69
Zoroastrianism	660 B.C.	Zoroaster	Ahura Mazda	Persia and India	Avesta	1/5
Taoism	604 B.C.	Lao-tze	The Tao	China	Tao-Te-King	54
Jainism	599 B.C.	Mahavira	None; now founder	India	Angas	2
Buddhism	560 B.C.	Buddha	None; now founder	Far East	Tripitaka	176
Confucianism	551 B.C.	Confucius	Heaven, or founder	China	Classics	371
Christianity	4 B.C.	Jesus	Father-God	World (?)	Bible	924
Islam	570 A.D.	Muhammad	Allah	Moslem Countries	Koran	493
Sikhism	1469 A.D.	Nanak	True Name	India	Granth	9

(b) *The Main Teachings of the Eleven Major Religions*

Religions originating in South Asia (India) are: *Hinduism* with its reflective genius, emphasizing salvation from rebirth by merging with divine immanence; *Jainism* stressing salvation from rebirth by asceticism; *Buddhism* practicing peaceful, ethical self-culture to be saved from rebirth by suppressing all desire and so merge with divine immanence; and *Sikhism* attempting to syncretize Hinduism and Muhammadanism, emphasizing discipleship of the one true God.

---

7. Based on Hume, *Ibid.*, p. 2. Statistics from *The World Almanac*, 1972, p. 391.

BASIC CHRISTIAN CONVICTIONS

With the exception of Sikhism, these religions have a negative outlook on life. To be saved from reincarnation the self must so completely merge with the Divine All so that successive rebirth does not take place anymore.

Religions originating in East Asia (China, Japan) are: *Taoism* with its mysticism and effortless spontaneity in submitting to the divine Way; *Confucianism* stressing humanism, social propriety and reciprocity. Harmony and peace is a chief objective. The *Shintoism* of Japan was an ethnocentric state-religion including nature and emperor-worship.

Religions originating in West Asia (Palestine, Persia, Arabia) are: *Judaism* requiring obedience to the self-revealing righteous and only God; *Zoroastrianism* with its dualistic struggle, pressing for choice and action on the part of man in this struggle between good and evil; *Islam* stressing the absolute sovereignty of Allah and requiring submission to this divine potentate and his prophet Muhammad; and *Christianity* with dynamic responsibility expressed in the love of God and the love of man as revealed in Jesus Christ. With the exception of Zoroastrianism these religions are monotheistic. All four of them are aggressive and action oriented. Evil is to be overcome, either by force or by goodness and love. All of them have a militaristic history. Muhammadanism today has the second largest number of adherents of all religions and Christianity has about twice as many adherents as any other one religion. Muhammadanism, Buddhism, and Christianity are the three most missionary-religions today.

(c) *General Characteristics of Historic Religions*

Certain aspects appear regularly in all living religions and evidently indicate fundamental needs deeply rooted in the nature of man, which all religions take into consideration and try to meet.[8] Among these characteristics are the following:

God's Sovereignty and Grace. Man's finitude lies at the heart of the religious impulse. Man simply is not in full control and so feels dependent. This feeling of dependence drives him toward simplicity, coherence, and oneness. All this issues in the theological concept of God and His sovereignty, and sustains the germ of the concept of grace. God's gift not only makes life possible but also sustains it.

---

8. Huston Smith, *The Religions of Man,* Harper, 1958, p. 101 ff.

Authority. The problems and solutions of man's religious life are as complicated as those of health and government. Attention to these problems will naturally raise some persons beyond the masses in their capacity to understand and deal effectively with the human spirit. Due to simple respect for the competence of such leaders, priests, prophets, and teachers, they are considered authoritative in this area and their advice is sought.

Ritual, Ceremonies and Prayer. Ritual may have been the cradle of religion. Ethics and theology came later. Celebration of any kind calls for ceremony where the individual and the group can participate. Rhythm, song, words and activity are necessary in this performance. Birds fly in formation, monkeys fall into rhythmic activity, cows walk in procession, and man also needs ritual and movement in which he can lose and find himself in motion with his group in religious activity. Prayer has grown from simple appeals for help to elaborate ceremonies emphasizing ritual and meditation.

Tradition. Of all forms of life man is least governed by instinct. This gives him freedom for innovation and advancement but also makes his position more precarious. The lessons learned by his ancestors through trial and error are not automatically available to man through his genes but must be transmitted consciously by each generation through the chain of culture. If one link of this chain fails to pass on the wisdom of the fathers, the human venture will be set back many centuries and has to begin all over again. Of all cultural institutions transmitting the wisdom of the past, religious tradition is one of the strongest.

Institutions, Organizations, Holy Places and Times. In seeking contact with, and securing divine help, certain rites and ceremonies are developed. To perform and promote these ceremonies, organizations and institutions come into being. This naturally calls for definite locations and certain times. Hence, holy places such as temples, and sacred times as the Sabbath, become important. Furthermore, organizations, institutions, sacred places and times are a help to promote and carry out programs of a religious and social nature.

Scripture and Creed. In time, religious history and doctrine are written out for the instruction of others and to be preserved for future generations. Gradually the best of these writings are considered sacred and inspired scriptures, while the doctrinal statements of faith are accepted as infallible creeds. Thus scripture and creed become an integral part of the various religions.

Mystery and Speculation. Life and religion are full of mystery. This mystery often gets mixed up with magic and superstition, with the occult, uncanny, and the supernatural. Always naturalists arise and complain about this credulity. Religion deals with the infinite and the beyond as well as with the here and now. Thought and reason cannot be excluded from religion. Man wonders about nature, God, man, and their relation to each other. This wonder expresses itself in speculations which can never be proven but undergoes changes and advancement as intelligence increases. Understanding grows, but will never solve all mysteries.

All living religions point to the Infinite. Paul Tillich writes:

> In the depth of every living religion there is a point at which the religion itself loses its importance, and that to which it points breaks through its particularity, elevating it to spiritual freedom and with it to a vision of the spiritual presence of the ultimate meaning of man's existence.[9]

All living religions point up the finitude of man and his need for the Infinite. There is the old story of the emperor who kept a servant whose sole duty was repeatedly to say, "Remember, you too are mortal." Man is finite and all religions are an expression of his search for the Infinite, of whom Paul says:

> "Yet he is not far from each one of us, for 'In him we live and move and have our being'. . . 'For we are indeed his offspring' " (Acts 17:27-28).

All Religions undergo change. Religion deals with matters of eternity, ultimate truth, and final values. But man is finite, and in these rapidly changing times, when we are increasingly becoming ONE WORLD, the great problem is to maintain a balance between progress and social identity. If progress is too fast, the social identity of a people disintegrates and confusion is the result. Religion is the core of the social identity of a people. To retain this social identity there must be a continuity of the best of the past with progress toward a better future. The educational system of a people is the main force in helping to maintain a proper balance between progress and retaining their social self-identity. Christian mission schools have served as a catalyst in this process of change. They have been among the most important shock troops in this modernization process by constantly stimulating reformulation of belief and practice in the

---

9. *Christianity and World Religions,* Columbia Univ. Press, 1963, p. 97.

light of the total worth and meaning of life. Not all Western contacts with other peoples have been constructive, but the missionary efforts of the Christian church have been a positive and constructive force affecting all areas of life, including the course of historical development with its cultural, political, economic, educational and other social changes taking place in our contemporary world.[10]

C. The Nature of Religion

The scientific study of religion may be said to have had its rise near the middle of the eighteenth century with the publication of *The Natural History of Religion by* David Hume (1711-1776). Since then there have been various ways of thinking about religion and trying to define it. Like time, religion is hard to define. It is more than can be embodied in a definition. J. H. Leuba (1868-1946) offered some fifty definitions from about that many authors.[11] Some have thought of religion in connection with only one phase of life, such as the intellect, the emotions, or the will, etc. Others thought of it only in individual or social terms.[12]

1. *The Intellectual Approach*

The German philosopher, Georg W. F. Hegel (1770-1831), held that religion is absolutely true knowledge. "Religion is the region of eternal truth."[13] The anthropologist, Edward B. Tylor (1832-1917), thought of religion as "the belief in spiritual beings," derived from animism.[14] Max Mueller (1823-1900) says "Religion is a mental faculty or disposition, which . . . enables man to apprehend the infinite."[15] Herbert Spencer's (1820-1903) reference to the "Unknowable" falls in the same class, and G. J. Romanes agrees that religion is a "department of thought having for its object a self-conscious and intelligent Being."[16]

---

10. Robert N. Bellah, ed., *Religion and Progress in Modern Asia,* Free Press, 1965, pp. 168 ff.
11. *A Psychological Study of Religion,* 1912, see index.
12. E. D. Soper, *The Religions of Mankind,* Abingdon, 1921, pp. 16-26; W. C. Bower, "Religious Education and Psychology of Religion" in *Religious Education,* January 1928, p. 7ff.; E. J. Jurji, *The Christian Interpretation of Religion,* Macmillan, 1952, pp. 1-5.
13. *Philosophy of Religion,* Speirs and Sanderson translation, I. p. 90.
14. *Primitive Culture,* 1871, Vol. I., p. 383.
15. *Introduction to the Science of Religion,* 1882, p. 13.
16. *Thoughts on Religion,* p. 21.

Basic Christian Convictions

2. *The Emotional Approach*

Friedrich Schleiermacher's (1768-1834) famous definition of religion is in terms of the emotions. He held that religion "is neither thinking or acting, but intuition and feeling."[17] Or again, "The essence of religious emotions consists of the feeling of absolute dependence."[18] August Sabatier says religion "rests upon a feeling of dependence which every man experiences with respect to universal Being."[19] John McTaggart in a similar statement says: "Religion may best be described as an emotion, resting on the conviction of a harmony between ourselves and the universe at large."[20]

3. *The Voluntaristic Approach*

The German philosopher Immanuel Kant (1724-1804), in considering religion, stresses the will. He thinks of "religion as the recognition of all duties as divine commands." Matthew Arnold similarly says, "Religion is morality touched by emotion."[21] Professor J. H. Leuba (1868-1946) considers "that part of human experience in which man feels himself in relation with powers of a psychic nature, usually personal powers, and makes use of them . . . it is therefore a part of the struggle of life."[22] J. B. Pratt also considers religion as "the attitude toward the Determiner of Destiny."[23]

4. *The Worship Approach*

Allen Menzies says: "Religion is the worship of higher powers from the sense of need."[24] A. S. Geden concludes that "Religion is best described as consisting in worship."[25] William Newton Clarke has a short statement: "Religion is the life of man in his superhuman relations."[26] William Adams Brown (1865-1943) approvingly quotes this statement by Clarke, and then expands on "superhuman relations" by saying:

> That is, his relation to the power on which he feels himself dependent, the authority to which he deems himself responsible and

---

17. *The Nature of Religion*, pp. 29, 57.
18. *On Religion*, p. 106.
19. *Outline of Philosophy of Religion*, p. 21.
20. *Some Dogmas of Religion*, p. 3.
21. *Literature and Dogmas*, 1873, p. 46.
22. *A Psychological Study of Religion*, p. 52.
23. *Religious Consciousness*, pp. 2, 3.
24. *Studies in Religion*, Scribners, 1914, p. 13.
25. *Studies in Religions of the East*, Kelly, London, 1913, p. 53.
26. *An Outline of Christian Theology*, Scribners, 1914, p. 1.

the unseen being with whom he is capable of communion. In the ideal of religion, dependence, responsibility and spiritual communion belong together.[27]

5. *The Psychological Approach*

The study of the psychology of religion was greatly stimulated by Professors Starbuck and Coe in 1899 and 1900. In the former year Starbuck published his *Psychology of Religion,* and in the latter year George A. Coe came out with his *Spiritual Life.* William James (1842-1910) in his *Varieties of Religious Experience,* which he later followed by *The Will to Believe,* speaks of religion as:

> The feelings, acts, and experiences of individual men in their solitude, as far as they apprehend themselves to stand in relation to whatever they may consider divine.[28]

These psychological studies tended to center religion in the conative aspects of experience as the matrix from which emerge one's value judgments, criticism, and organization at the conscious level.

6. *The Escape Approach*

The most widespread criticism of religion is based on positivism which rejects, on the one hand, all belief in metaphysics or in reality beyond natural phenomena; and, on the other hand, tries to explain religion in natural terms of psychological or sociological nature and does not think it necessary to invoke the idea of God or any transhuman reality to account for religion. The positivist view gets strong support from the theories of Sigmund Freud (1856-1939). He has made great contributions by showing how irrational some of our beliefs are and that we accept them because of deep unconscious drives that demand satisfaction. So he concludes that religion is merely a mechanism of escape from the unwelcome experiences of life, fabricated below the threshold of consciousness. For Freud the idea of God is simply the projection of the human father image, which the religious man still needs for protection and shelter because of his immaturity. "Religion is an opiate of the people" is one point of view.

It must be admitted that superstition and religion are often mixed and confused with each other. But the fact that astronomy had its origin in astrology and chemistry in alchemy does not invalidate

---

27. *Christian Theology In Outline,* Scribners, 1921, p. 29.
28. *Varieties of Religious Experience,* Longmans, N.Y., 1913, p. 31

astronomy and chemistry. As man matures, the true and the false will be separated. And only as man participates in the realities of religion can this be done. After all, the "truth of the pudding lies in the eating thereof." Religious faith, far from fragmentizing personality, is actually a most powerful stabilizing and unifying factor. Many students of religion today have turned away from Freud's negative valuation of religion. They rather go along with Carl G. Jung in acknowledging religion as a positive factor in integrating and strengthening personality. The religious experience is far more complex and difficult to deal with than any other type of human experience. As man's intelligence increases and his achievements advance, he will become less superstitious but more really religious. The psychological study of religion (including psychiatry, psychotherapy, and psychoanalysis) has important contributions to make toward more fully understanding religion.[29]

7. *The Value Approach*

Religion has also been defined without reference to higher powers, but as stressing the conservation of values. Harold Hoeffding was a pioneer in this value approach. Already in 1906 he identified religion with man's valuational attitude. He wrote: "The conservation of values is the characteristic axiom of all religion."[30] In 1910 Edward Scribner Ames and Irving King came out with their respective studies: *The Psychology of Religion* and *The Development of Religion,* both arriving at much the same conclusion: that religion deals with conservation of values. They especially emphasized social values, not in static but in dynamic terms. Ames states: "Religion is the consciousness of the highest social values." And again: "The religious cconsciousness . . . is just the consciousness of the great interests and purposes of life in their most idealized and intensified forms . . ."[31]

---

29. Alfred Adler, *Understanding Human Nature,* Fawcett Library, 1957; Gordon W. Allport, *The Individual and His Religion,* Macmillan, 1951; Victor E. Frankl, *Man's Search for Meaning,* Washington Square Press, 1966; Erich Fromm, *Psychoanalysis and Religion,* Yale University Press, 1956; Carl G. Jung, *Psychology and Religion,* Yale Univ. Press, 1938; Everett Dean Martin, *The Mystery of Religion,* Norton, 1924; Albert C. Outler, *Psychotherapy and the Christian Message,* Harper, 1954; P. W. Pruyser, *A Dynamic Psychology of Religion,* Harper, 1968; David E. Roberts, *Psychotherapy and a Christian View of Man,* Scribners, 1950.
30. *Philosophy of Religion,* Macmillan, 1916, p. 10.
31. *Psychology of Religion,* Houghton Mifflin, 1910, p. vii., 297.

Conceiving religion in terms of value also found expression in Professor Stratton's writings, "Religion is the appreciation of an unseen world . . . and . . . whatever seems clearly to be moving toward such appreciation or returning from it . . . better described as man's whole bearing toward what seems to him Best and Greatest."[32]

The concept of religion as related to values is more inclusive than some other approaches. It considers religion as not only related to one phase of life but including the entire being of man. E. D. Soper points out that,

> Religion consists of a number of elements. It is a relationship of conscious dependence on higher powers; it makes a demand on the whole of man's life, intellect, emotion, and will; it is both individual and social; it is worship, yet it is more than worship; and it conserves all the values which give worth and meaning to human life.[33]

While H. Richard Niebuhr has a still longer descriptive statement:

> Religion means both piety—a personal relation to divine powers —and also the great historic combinations of doctrine, ritual, organization, and common ethos that we encounter in Christianity, Judaism, Mohammadanism, Buddhism, Confucianism, Taoism, Shintoism, etc. . . . They are movements in human history; they are more or less close-knit communities. In them encountering drives, needs, feelings, traditions, doctrines, and practices which, though derivative from many sources, have been brought more or less under the influence of certain powerful convictions or attracted toward certain magnetic centers.[34]

Paul Tillich's statement is concise but very inclusive:

> Religion as ultimate concern is the meaning-giving substance of culture, and culture is the totality of forms in which the basic concern of religion expresses itself. In abbreviation: religion is the substance of culture, culture is the form of religion. Such consideration definitely prevents the establishment of a dualism of religion and culture.[35]

A. Eustace Haydon uses two short and descriptive statements of religion as titles of his books, namely: *The Quest of the Ages,* Harper,

---

32. *Psychology of the Religious Life,* 1911, p. 343.
33. *The Religions of Mankind,* Abingdon Press, 1925, p. 25.
34. *Radical Monotheism in Western Culture,* Harper, 1960, p. 49.
35. *Theology of Culture,* Oxford Univ. Press, 1959, p. 42.

1929, and *Man's Search for the Good Life,* Harper, 1937. Although these titles are short they nevertheless indicate religion as seeking value in broad and inclusive terms:

> All elements that enter into any religion have some bearing upon the values central to the group ideal of living. It is possible to speak of three phases of the religious complex: The ideal of satisfying life; the values are won; and the extra-human powers which help or hinder in the quest. That is to say, a religion has an ideal, a cult or ceremonial, and a theology. And the history of any religion might be written by following any one of these three threads. The driving force always is in the life-hunger of earth-oriented man and woman.[36]

> It took many generations of the scientific study of religions to shift the emphasis from belief, first to include cult and practical behavior, then to give central importance to the social quest for values and the creative new modes for each new age. Religion becomes the thread of meaning on which the ages of human history are strung. . . . The religious drive is more important than all its products of theology and cult. It is simple and elemental. It is man's search through the changing ages for the values that make our common earthly life glad and beautiful and good . . . The task of religion is to make the shared quest for the good life the controlling, unifying center of the human life process . . . The task demands a mobilization of intelligence to give religion embodiment in a culture which will make the values of an abundant life available to all men . . . There will be one test for every phase of culture and civilization—does it help to realize the possibilities of human nature for joy, beauty, comradship, and creative power? . . . Hope for the future burns with a brighter flame as men, aware of the meaning of the religious quest, turn from dreams of perfect worlds to take up once more the practical task of actualizing the good life for man on earth.[37]

D. RELIGION AS RE-EVALUATION OF ALL OTHER VALUES

Already in 1916 G. A. Coe differentiated the evaluating process in religion from other forms of valuation. Religion, he points out, is not identified with any one set of values as such but rather a total "desire within desire" directed toward the integration of life as a whole which is constantly undergoing reconstruction. This process involves the idealization, completion, unification, and conservation

---

36. *The Quest of the Ages,* p. 6.
37. *Man's Search for the Good Life,* pp. 78, 79, 83, 246, 254.

of all values of life. At this point all values of life are fused into a total worth and meaning of life as such. To quote:

> A revaluation of values that both makes us individuals and organizes us into society . . . think of it as the value of values, that is the value of life organizing and completing, or seeking a destiny.[38]

This whole idea is developed further by W. C. Bower who points out that value arises in the *gap* between the ongoing conative activity and the end toward which it is moving, through delay, suspense, and uncertainty. In proportion that this *gap* is caused by delay and uncertainty, in that proportion the end is lifted sharply into consciousness and the *gap* is filled with the most powerful emotions. Hence:

> . . . religion involves an emotional attitude toward values, an intellectual criticism of them, and a tendency to act with reference to them . . . This makes possible a clear insight into the interrelation of the conative, affective, and intellectual aspects of the total process of a unified religious experience.[39]

1. *Illustrated by Graphic Figures*

An important implication of this view is the manner in which all experience enters into the content and pattern of religious concepts. The rootage of religious concepts in human experience Bower represents by the graphic Figure No. 1 below. The areas of human interest and activities, such as economic, social, intellectual, ethical, aesthetic, etc., are represented by ellipses. Their interrelatedness is indicated by their overlapping as they approach the point of convergence. Thus no area can be altogether isolated from the others. The intellectual experience has its social, ethical, economic, and aesthetic aspects and the influence of the same, and these, in turn, help to understand and appreciate it. This is also true of all other specialized areas of experience.

> But it is at the central point of fusion, where all particular values whatsoever are integrated into a total meaning and worth of life, that the religious experience arises. It is in this central area of fusion, as suggested in Figure 2, that God as the central and fundamental reality of the universe appears. It is at the point of the reference of all particular experiences to God that any experience takes on religious quality.[40]

---

38. *Psychology of Religion,* Univ. of Chicago Press, 1916, pp. 68, 70.
39. W. C. Bower, "Psychology of Religion," in *Religious Education,* Jan., 1928, p. 11.
40. *Ibid.,* p. 14.

Figure I   Figure II

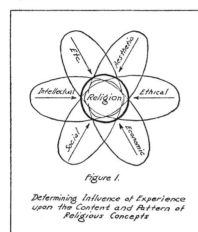

Figure 1.

Determining Influence of Experience
upon the Content and Pattern of
Religious Concepts

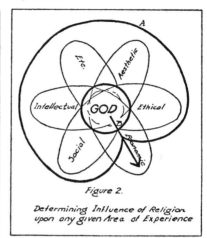

Figure 2.

Determining Influence of Religion
upon any given Area of Experience

Figure 1 indicates that religion is not just another interest or activity along with other such interests and activities—economic, social, ethical, intellectual, etc. Religion is the central, or re-evaluating value of all other *values,* and it is influenced by all these other *values* as indicated by the arrows in Figure 1.[41]

In Figure 2 this central area of religion, God, or supreme value in the light of the total worth and meaning of life including all areas, as indicated by circle "A" re-evaluates each separate area of activity and interest as indicated by line "B" in Figure 2. So here the arrow points outward from the center. This manifold and constant operation indicated by both Figures is important to the concept of religion as the re-evaluation of all other values in the light of the total worth and meaning of life as interpreted in terms of its relation to God.

When religion reacts upon any one particular area, it does not simply feed back into that area what that area first fed into the central area of fusion, but rather the total fused influence of all other areas combined. Not only do the expanding experiences and activities of life influence our concept of God, but in turn our concept of God also influences every area of interest and activity of our life. This relation of our religion (or supreme value, or God-concept, all indicated by the center of the diagram) as our special interests and

41. *Ibid.,* p. 14 (used with permission).

activities is reciprocal, and serves as a powerful reconstructing influence both ways.

This central point of integration and reference gives insight and helps us understand that mystifying problem as to why religious concepts, including the concept of God, are different in various social groups having different economic, intellectual, social, ethical, and aesthetic backgrounds. Also, why religious concepts, including the idea of God, change in history within the same group as their economic, intellectual, social, and other values change. The content and pattern of religious ideas are derived from these areas of interest, experiences and values. By referring the various interests and values to God at the center they receive their religious quality.

2. *The Ancient Hebrews as Example*

This process of change, Bower points out, is illustrated in the history of the ancient Hebrews. Here one can see how the specialized interests, activities, and values of a people feed into the central core and determine the pattern of their religious concepts, including their God concept.

In the early nomadic and pastoral period their social organization was based on a tribal and kinship level. Here they naturally thought of Yahweh as the God of the tribe, coexisting with gods of neighboring tribes and moving with them as a tribal shepherd-God from place to place as they sought more fertile pastures for their flocks (Psalm 103).

In the period of conquering Canaan, their entire pattern of life changed and became militaristic. The shepherd Yahweh of the desert-and-the-flocks became the Yahweh of hosts and a God of war, going before His people in military conquest and victory (Psalm 18:33-42).

In the period of settlement and nation-building the pursuit of agricultural life called for new qualities in Yahweh. These functions had formerly been carried on by the Baals of the dispossessed people. In the history of religion, when one people conquers another, the functions of the dispossessed deities are absorbed by the god of the conquering people. This assimilative process helps to understand the conflict between the prophets of Yahweh and the prophets of Baal. As this process went on, Yahweh also became the God of rain, sowing, and harvest (Psalm 65:9-13).

During the later period of international conflict between Egypt and Assyria, the writing prophets emerged. In this tense and dangerous situation of world conflict in which Israel found itself, the time was psychologically ripe for Israel finally to see Yahweh as the universal, ethical, spiritual, and the only living God (Isaiah 41:24).

When the structure of their nation finally fell to pieces and crumbled, as they were in captivity, the individual for the first time emerged in personal and responsible relation to Yahweh. This fundamental note was first expressed by the prophets of the exile. "Each man who eats sour grapes, his teeth shall be set on edge" (Jeremiah 31:30; Ezekiel 18:1-4).

In each stage of development the content of the concept of God is supplied by the interests and activities of the group and the religious quality of the changing experience is derived from the total meaning and worth of life as interpreted in terms of its relation to Yahweh. This makes religion an intense reality and deepens the sense of God's self-disclosure as the more adequate concepts emerge in the moving current of the life-process. For a fuller discussion of the development of the Yahweh concept in Israel see Chapter II.

Naturally the content and pattern of our present religious concepts are also undergoing change in the light of the growing experience of modern life. The findings of science as to the structure and age of the universe, the creative processes of our industrial economy, the democratic ideal of our society, the growing recognition that the world and mankind are one, and other changes in our total experience, greatly enlarge our concept of God. They place Him at the center of mankind's struggle, longing for understanding, fellowship, and strength, in the high pursuits of life.

3. *A Modern Factory as Example*

In a factory, Bower points out, the economic interest too often determines the fused content of religious concepts at the center. But if the reciprocal influence of religion is felt upon the economic interests, every other specialized-interest-area will influence the economic area also. The intellectual area will feed new values back into the total process. As a matter of human consideration and even economic advantage, excessive speed and undue long hours will be eliminated, exposed machines will be protected, worker's compensation and sanitary conditions will be affected. The social-interest-area will feed back into the economic process the consideration of workers as humans and not only as "hands," and call attention to society's needs and not only factory profits. So also the ethical and aesthetic interest areas will feed back into the factory process ethical and aesthetic considerations and insist that products be not merely profitable but also useful and beautiful. Production will be more humanized and the whole plant will be set in a framework of beauty and joy for workers and society as a whole. This converging of different interests and values upon the economic area in the process takes on new significance in the light of the total worth and meaning of human life which would not happen when isolated from other interest areas. See line "A" in Figure 2.

4. *The God Centered Life*

Another function of religion is the transformation of the specialized areas as they are fused at the center. At this point God emerges in human experience. What is fed back from the center is more than the sum total of all other values. In this glowing center all values are fused and a new and intense quality is added to experience, as the bringing together of two units of hydrogen and one of oxygen results in a new product, namely that of water, which did not exist before and which disappears when it is decomposed. When a number of individuals separately consider a problem, the result is not the same as if they meet as a committee and each one makes his contribution to an integrated solution of the problem. So also in religion, at the point of fusion of experience in terms of its relation to the total, a new quality appears that was not present previously in separate experiences. Once the result of this fusion has arisen, it is more and different than the mere sum of all of them. In this new and central core of experience the fundamental reality of the universe becomes most intense and meaningful. To quote Bower again:

> It is in relation to God who there discloses himself that meaning and worth of life are raised to their nth degree of significance. The emergence of God gives more than a heightened significance to the sum of all other areas of interests feeding back into any particular area of experience, represented by the encircling line "A" in our figure; it gives a new and unique quality to experience in every area of life. This unique and dynamic influence is indicated in Figure 2 by line B.[42]

E. SUMMARY AND CONCLUSION

In this chapter we have considered various aspects of religion under four subheads: The Growth of Religion; Patterns of Religion; The Nature of Religion; and Religion as Re-evaluation of all other Values. Now to some significant conclusions.

---

42. *Ibid.*, p. 18.

1. The Importance of Personality

Conceiving religion as the process of re-evaluating all other values in terms of one supreme value, places great emphasis on persons. Value has no meaning apart from persons. Only persons, so far as we know, are capable of becoming conscious of these value-ends and of organizing their resources for their attainment.

> And since religion is conceived in terms of the integration of all values whatsoever into a total meaning and worth of life, it is only possible for the quality of experience that is religious to arise within the experience of persons.[43]

These considerations also have far-reaching implications concerning the nature of ultimate reality itself. Is this world primarily a world of things or a world of persons? The fact that our world is intelligible only to intelligent beings, indicates that throughout its thus-far-explored areas, an intelligence greatly beyond our comprehension is at work in the universe. But reality itself would seem to lie closer to the drives of our older, vital, and practical experience than to our more recently acquired intelligence. Our yearnings for the realities that make life satisfying at its highest levels, determine what is most real to us. So in the last instance reality would root in our values. The highest values we possess are personal values, and the highest expression of personal value is personality itself. This would lead to the interpretation of ultimate reality in terms of a Supreme Person whose highest function is the same as the function of personality: namely, Creator and Preserver of Values.

2. Every Person Has a Supreme Value Which Is His God

If religion is considered as re-evaluation of all other values in the light of the total worth and meaning of life, then no human being is without religion or a god of some kind. Even atheists have values and a supreme value whereby they re-evaluate all other values. This supreme value, then, is their god. This also applies to people whose supreme value is wealth, power, pleasure, the nation, or a form of government, etc. These items then are their gods. Jesus said:

> "For where your treasure is, there will your heart be also . . . No one can serve two masters; for either he will hate the one and love the other, or he will be devoted to one and despise the other. You cannot serve God and mammon" (Matthew 6:21, 24).

---

43. *Ibid.*, p. 13.

In other words, no one can have two supreme values but every person has one supreme value and that is his god. The Christian, of course, is one whose supreme value is "the God and Father of our Lord Jesus Christ," and who re-evaluates every other value in the light of that supreme value. So we turn to the next chapter, "God, Our Father."

FOR FURTHER READING ON RELIGION AND THE RELIGIONS

Bach, M. S. - *Major Religions of the World,* Abingdon, 1970.

Bahm, A., World's Living Religions, Ill. Un. 1971.

Burtt, E. A. - *Man Seeks the Divine,* Harper, 1957.

Bellah, Robert N. - *Beyond Belief,* Harper & Row, 1970.

Bliss, E. A. - *The Future of Religion,* Watts, 1969.

Cassels, L., *Faiths Men Live By,* Doubleday, 1971.

Durkheim, E. - *Elementary Forms of Religious Life,* Free Press, 1963.

Edwards, G. L. - *Religion and Change,* Harper, 1969.

Eliade, Mircea - *Patterns of Comparative Religion,* Sheed & Ward, 1958.

Fromm, Erich - *Psychoanalysis and Religion,* Yale University Press, 1950.

Hopkins, E. W. - *Origin and Evolution of Religion,* Cooper Sq., 1969.

Hume, R. E. - *The World's Living Religions,* Scribners, 1959.

Katigawa, J. M. - *Modern Trends in World Religions,* Open Court, 1959.

Kaufman, G. D. - *God the Problem,* Harvard University Press, 1972.

Kraemer, H. - *Why Christianity of All Religions?,* Westminster, 1962.

Noss, J. B. - *Man's Religions,* Macmillan, 1969.

Neill, S. - *Christian Faith and Other Faiths,* Oxford, 1961.

O'Collins, - *Man and His New Hopes,* Herder & Herder, 1969.

Potter, C. F. - *Great Religious Leaders,* Simon & Shuster, 1958.

Pruyser, Paul W. - *A Dynamic Psychology of Religion,* Harper, 1968.

Radhakrishman, C. - *East and West,* Harper, 1956.

Severy, Merle, editor, *Great Religions of the World,* National Geographic Soc., 1971.

Shapley, E. - *Science Ponders Religion,* Appleton, 1960.

Smith, Huston - *The Religions of Man,* New American Library, 1958.

Smith, H. W. - *Man and His Gods,* University Library, 1956.

Tillich, P. - *Christianity and World Religions,* Columbia U. Press, 1963.

Toynbee, A. - *Christianity Among the Religions of the World,* Scribners, 1957.

Waring, E. G. - *Friedrich Schleiermacher on Religion,* Unger Pub. Co., 1955.

Weber, Max - *The Sociology of Religion,* Beacon Press, 1963.

Widgery, A. B. - *What Is Religion,* Harper, 1953.

Williams, D. R. - *World Religions and the Hope for Peace,* Beacon Press, 1951.

CHAPTER II

GOD, OUR FATHER

"Blessed be the God and Father of our Lord Jesus Christ" (I Peter 1:3).

THE CHRISTIAN IDEA OF GOD AS OUR FATHER HAS A LONG AND interesting history, beginning with the Hebrew Yahweh and gradually leading up to the "God and Father of our Lord Jesus Christ," and from there on through Christendom to the present.

The concept of God is the most important influence in history. The reality of God and man's idea of God are not the same. Man's concept of God has been influenced by many factors and undergone many changes. The reality of God and the word, *God,* are also different. The word is only the symbol of the reality for which the word stands. The meaning of words change. Often the same word carries different meanings in different periods of history. The English word "let," for example, has completely reversed its meaning since Shakespeare's day. When Hamlet cries out, "I will slay the man that *lets* me," he means he will kill whoever tries to stop him, which is just the opposite of what *let* means today. Social change often alters the meaning of words.

A. THE YAHWEH-CONCEPT IN THE OLD TESTAMENT[1]

The Old Testament reflects a long period of deepening and enlarging spiritual experience and insight. The early concepts, mixed with primitive faiths gradually change so that, between these origins and the messages of the prophets, a remarkable development is

---

1. See E. Kautzsch: "Religion in Israel," III. iii, 2, Hastings' *Dictionary of the Bible,* Extra Volume, p. 645 ff.; W. F. Albright, *Yahweh, and the Gods of Canaan,* Doubleday, 1968; W. F. Albright, *The Archaeology of Palestine,* revised, Pelican Books, 1960; G. E. Wright, *God Who Acts,* SCM Press, 1962; B. W. Anderson, *Understanding the Old Testament,* Prentice-Hall, 1957.

indicated. Seen from one side it would indicate human achievement and discovery; seen from the other side it is divine self-revelation.

The early Hebrew view of God developed in the social context of an essentially nomadic people. Only for relatively short periods did they have a homeland of their own. These settled periods were usually less creative than the times when they were on the move. The escape from Egypt, the wandering in the wilderness, the occupation of Canaan, the Babylonian captivity, the return to Palestine, were events in which their faith was developed.

1. *Yahweh of Mount Sinai* (about 1200 B.C.)

It is clear that the Fathers of Israel (about 1900 B.C.) Abraham, Isaac, and Jacob were believers in one God, but the name "Yahweh" for this one God began with Moses (about 1200 B.C.) according to Exodus 3:14, 15. Between Abraham and Moses there was a considerable span of time, and one would expect some development. We read that "Moses was instructed in all the wisdom of the Egyptians" (Acts 7:22). This learning may well have included the Babylonian code of Hammurabi (1728-1686 B. C.?) which is so similar to the Ten Commandments of Moses. He certainly also was acquainted with the famous Egyptian Pharaoh Ikhnaton (Amenhotep IV), (1370-1353 B.C.), who had promoted a religious revolution in Egypt by introducing a kind of monotheism based upon the worship of the sun as the symbol of the one and only God Aton. However "Yahweh" of Moses was not the sun or whom it might symbolize, but rather the Creator of the sun and the entire universe. Moses is considered to have been the architect of Hebrew Monotheism, with the central idea that a single righteous God is at work in the social and natural order. The prophets, each with his particular emphasis, all constantly refer to Moses as the original and final authority.[2] This is indicated by the impressive fact that *The Exhaustive Concordance of the Bible,* by James Strong, 1890, contains over 800 references to Moses.

When Moses was facing the burning bush in the desert and was asked to go back to Egypt and lead the children of Israel out of their bondage to freedom he hesitated, and in fear asked for the name of the one who was sending him.

---

2. W. F. Albright, *From the Stone Age to Christianity,* Johns Hopkins Press, 1946, "Moses and Monotheism," pp. 196-207.

God (Elohim) said to Moses, "I AM WHO I AM." And he said, "Say this to the people of Israel, 'I AM has sent me to you.'" God (Elohim) also said to Moses, "Say this to the people of Israel, 'The Lord (Yahweh), the God (Elohim) of your fathers, the God (Elohim) of Abraham, the God (Elohim) of Isaac, and the God (Elohim) of Jacob, has sent me to you': . . ." (Exodus 3:14-15).

At various stages Israel used different names for God. El Elyon, Elohim, El Shaddai, and of course, most often, Yahweh. One illustration of daring willingness to move on to new names, when the situation called for it, we have in the following quotation.

And God (Elohim) said to Moses, "I am the Lord (Yahweh). I appeared to Abraham, to Isaac, and to Jacob, as God Almighty (El Shaddai), but by my name the Lord (Yahweh) I did not make myself known to them" (Exodus 6:2-3; cf. Genesis 4:26; 17:1).[3]

After the Exile, the Jews again changed their name for God. Disturbed by the debasement of the name Yahweh, which was considered too holy for everyday use by everybody, they began to use the term Adoni (Lord) which is still used today in their synagogues.

There are indications that it was in connection with the Exodus from Egypt that the name Yahweh was first used for the God of Israel. Moses, a believer in Yahweh, led his fellow Israelites out of the Egyptian bondage, and at Sinai they and Yahweh made their covenant with each other based on the Ten Commandments. Yahweh may have been a former deity of Judah (Exodus 3:16-18), but Moses seemingly first came upon Yahweh at the "Mountain of God" (Exodus 3:1ff.). The special attachment of Yahweh to the mountain made it hard for Israel later to conceive that He was going with them in the wilderness. Repeatedly it is stated that it was only the angel of Yahweh that accompanied them (Exodus 23:20-23; 32:34; 33:1-3).

Later Joshua commanded the people to "put away the gods which your fathers served beyond the River (Euphrates) and in Egypt; and serve Yahweh" (Joshua 24:14). Commonly the prophets also

---

3. B. W. Anderson, *Understanding the Old Testament,* Prentice-Hall, Inc., 1957, p. 25. This is the Revised Standard Version, excepting that the original names Elohim, Yahweh, and El Shaddai are added in parenthesis to enable the reader to become more vividly aware of the development of the concept of the Divine in Old Testament times. In this section on the Old Testament, then, Yahweh is used for Lord in various scripture verses.

BASIC CHRISTIAN CONVICTIONS

associated the Yahweh relationship with Exodus (Hosea 12:9; 13:4; Jeremiah 2:1-2; Ezekiel 20:5).

The so-called Kenite theory holds that Moses, fleeing from Egypt to the wilderness, joined himself to the Kenites, a Midianite tribe, probably related to Israel and living in the desert close to Sinai. Moses married into this tribe. His father-in-law, Jethro, was "the priest of Midian" (Exodus 3:1). Moses joined his wife's clan and became a devotee of Yahweh, the Kenite god (Exodus 18:1-12; Judges 1:16). Jael, a Kenite woman and worshiper of Yahweh, smote Sisera (Judges 5:24-27). The son of Rechab was a Kenite supporting Jehu in the revolt against Ahab (II Kings 10:15-18; I Chronicles 2: 55). Even in Jeremiah's time, the Rechabites put the Hebrews in Jerusalem to shame in their devotion to the laws of their fathers (Jeremiah 35).[4]

The close association of Yahweh with Sinai (also called Horeb), as a mountain-god is indicated repeatedly. Deborah pictured Yahweh as coming with thunder and power from Sinai to help His people (Judges 5:4-5). Elijah, discouraged in his struggle for Yahweh, fled to "Horeb the mount of God" (I Kings 19:8). Repeatedly Yahweh is spoken of as coming from Sinai (Deuteronomy 33:2; Habakkuk 3:3; Psalm 68:7-8). Repeatedly Yahweh is saying, "I am the God of your father, the God of Abraham, the God of Isaac, and the God of Jacob" (Exodus 3:6, 15, 16; 4:5), but it was in the covenant at Sinai that the faith of Israel in Yahweh as their God came to a fuller expression.

2. *A Tribal, Storm- and War-God*

This *mountain-God* of Sinai had various characteristics. In early times he was thought of as a *tribal* deity who loved and protected Israel and hated Israel's enemies. Even the covenant said, "I will be an enemy to your enemies, and an adversary to your adversaries" (Exodus 23:22).

He was a *storm-god,* associated with violent expressions of nature's power. When the liberated clans from Egypt had their first meeting with Him, as well as in later battles, there was much tumult of nature:

> The smoke thereof ascended as the smoke of a furnace, and the whole mount quaked greatly (Exodus 19:18; 20:18). The earth trembled . . . the mountains quaked . . . from heaven fought the stars . . . The torrent Kishon swept them away (Judges 5:4, 5,

---

4. For the Kenite Theory see T. J. Meek, *Hebrew Origins*, pp. 86 ff.

20, 21). The adversaries of Yahweh shall be broken to pieces; against them will be thunder in heaven (I Samuel 2:10). Yahweh thundered with a mighty voice on that day against the Philistines, and threw them into confusion (I Samuel 7:10). He came swiftly on the wings of the wind. He made darkness his covering . . . Before him there broke through his clouds, hailstones and coals of fire . . . he flashed forth lightnings, and routed them (Psalm 18: 12-14).

He was a god of *war*. In the Song of Moses we are told that "Yahweh is a man of war; Yahweh is his name" (Exodus 15:3). In the day of Joshua when "the sun stood still" . . . "Yahweh fought for Israel" (Joshua 10:13-14). When David defied Goliath, he said, "I come to thee in the name of Yahweh of hosts, the God of the armies of Israel" (I Samuel 17:45). Reference is even made to *the book of the Wars of Yahweh* (Numbers 21:14). We read:

> He trains my hands for war, so that my arms can bend a bow of bronze . . . I pursued my enemies and overtook them; and did not turn back till they were consumed. I thrust them through, so that they were not able to rise; they fell under my feet. For thou didst gird me with strength for the battle; thou didst make my assailants sink under me. Thou didst make my enemies turn their backs to me, and those who hated me I destroyed . . . I beat them fine as dust before the wind; I cast them out like mire of the streets (Psalm 18:34-42; see also Psalm 144).
>
> Yahweh will have war with Amalek from generation to generation (Exodus 17:16). "Now go and smite Amalek, and utterly destroy all that they have; do not spare them, but kill both man and woman, infant and suckling, ox and sheep, camel and ass . . ." Then Samuel said, "Bring here to me Agag the king of the Amalakites". . . And Samuel hewed Agag in pieces before the Lord in Gilgal (I Samuel 15:3, 32, 33).

One way to secure Yahweh's help in battle, they believed, was to promise Him the sacrifice of captured property and persons (Numbers 21:1-3). So jealous was Yahweh thought to be of this loot of war, that when at Jericho, tabooed property was secreted, his wrath was ruinous (Joshua 7). When Ahab spared the life of the king of Syria, Yahweh is pictured as demanding "therefore your life shall go for his life" (I Kings 20:42). It took a long time to outgrow this primitive war-god concept. In fact, it has not even been outgrown by Christians today.

Primitive people think of their gods in human terms. Yahweh was thought to have hands, feet, face, eyes, nose, ears and the like. Gradually these references came to be thought of symbolically. Even today we use such terms. In fact, man being finite and God infinite, symbolical human language is the only way man can express himself regarding infinite matters. Originally, however, such terms were no doubt taken literally. Yahweh walked in the Garden of Eden in the cool of the day and talked with Adam (Genesis 18:1ff.). He visited with Abraham and made a covenant with him (Genesis 15:18). He wrestled with Jacob (Genesis 32:24-30). Various sacrifices were "a pleasing odor to Yahweh" (Leviticus 1:9; 2:9; 3:16). He wrote the law on stone tablets "with his own finger" (Exodus 31:18). When Moses asked Yahweh,

> "I pray thee, show me thy glory" ... the Lord said, "Behold, there is a place by me where you shall stand upon the rock; and while my glory passes by I will put you in a cleft of the rock, and I will cover you with my hand until I have passed by; then I will take away my hand, and you shall see my back; but my face shall not be seen" (Exodus 33:18, 21-23).

In spite of the command, "You shall make for yourself no molten gods" (Exodus 34:17), there was the golden calf (Exodus 32:4). Micah, the Ephraimite, had an image of Yahweh (Judges 17:3-4); Gideon made one out of captured gold (Judges 8:24-27); David's wife Michal had an image of some kind to help protect David (I Samuel 19:12-16); and "Rachel stole her father's household gods" (Genesis 31:19). Not only was Yahweh portrayed in images, but He was also thought of as having very human emotions, such as hate, jealousy, vindictiveness, and regret for mistaken decisions (Genesis 6:6; 8:21). The prophets, however, objected to all this, took a firm stand against it and expressed Yahweh's displeasure with it (Amos 5:21-24; Hosea 8:4-6, 13; Isaiah 1:1, 13).

3. *The Ark and Divine Mobility*

One important difference between Yahweh and gods of Israel's neighbors was His mobility. The early nomadic life of Israel provided the necessary social setting for the emergence and development of Yahweh's mobility. The Ark of the Covenant in all details, such as rings and staves to carry it, the cherubims of gold and the mercy seat above it, were built for mobility. This was also true of the movable tent-like tabernacle to house the ark with the altar, various vessels, candlesticks, and other utensils (Exodus 25: 10-40). The ark became the visible symbol of Yahweh's presence as well as the vehicle for His mobility. Where the ark was, He was (Numbers 14:41-45). At the crossing of the Jordan it played an important role (Joshua 3:15-17; 4:11). At the fall of Jericho the ark had its place (Joshua 6:11 ff.). It was a calamity for Israel when the

Philistines captured it, and an occasion for great rejoicing when it was again restored (I Samuel 4:5, 6).

King David respected it and considered it the abiding place of Yahweh. When it was brought to his capital, Jerusalem, he and his people danced with joy before it (II Samuel 6:2-5; 12-15; I Chronicles 13:3-6). Being thought of as holy, its presence also carried certain risks with it (I Chronicles 13:9-13). This mobility differed from Egyptian sphinxes and Babylonian ziggurats, which were places for localized deities. As Israel moved into new territory, Yahweh not only moved with them but even "went before them by day in a pillar of cloud to lead them along the way, and a pillar of fire to give them light, that they might travel by day and by night." (Exodus 13:21).

4. *Syncretism in Canaan* (1200-900 B.C.)

An important change in Israel's view of Yahweh developed as they settled in Canaan. The need for the war-god was still there as they occupied the land and tried to exterminate the natives. However, this was an agricultural land, and the fertility deities that gave the increase in grain and herds were Baal and Ashtoreth. Extermination of the natives was not possible and so accommodation resulted.

Yahweh was hard and disciplined, a sponsor of self-control and social solidarity. The gods of agriculture and fertility have uniformly been licentious. When two cultures are so close together they will inevitably influence each other. That some licentious, fertility-sexual practices were accepted by the Jews is clear (II Kings 23:7; Hosea 4:13-14). Even Yahweh worship under the likeness of bulls was set up at Dan and Bethel by Jeroboam (I Kings 12:26-29). Gradually the local agricultural Baals and Ashtoreths seemingly were widely accepted.

> They built for themselves high places at all their towns, from watchtower to fortified city; they set up for themselves pillars and Asherim on every high hill and under every green tree, and there they burned incense . . . as the nations did whom Yahweh carried away before them. And they did wicked things, . . . and they served idols, of which Yahweh had said to them, "You shall not do this" (II Kings 17:9-12).

When Queen Jezebel sponsored Melkart, the Baal of Tyre, that again aroused the advocates of Yahweh. The translation of economic class struggle into religious conflict was the crux in this conflict. Underneath it all was the fierce hostility between two economic and cultural systems. The Amorite lords and nobles hated and feared the equalitarian practices of the Hebrew nomads, and the Israelites with equal revulsion despised the city-dominated social order with its private ownership of land and water (I Kings 17:19). Elijah championed Yahweh as the God of the old folkways of Israel, and by now also of rain and agriculture. Seven thousand in Israel who had not yet bowed to Baal were with him in the opposition against new customs of luxury and inequality represented by the nobles and Queen Jezebel and Baal Melkert with selfish wealth, wicked commercialism, and social injustice (I Kings 19:18). Elijah supported Naboth against Ahab with his luxurious court and conscription of shepherds and farmers for military service, but mounting taxation and moral decay were threatening the ideals of nomadic brotherhood and social justice (I Kings 21).

That the agricultural functions were gradually taken over by Yahweh is clear from the agricultural festivals, such as: the Feast of Unleavened Bread, and the Feast of Harvest. At last it was Yahweh and not some fertility god, who sent the rain, gave the blessings of increase in grain and herds and even taught them methods of farming.

> Thou visitest the earth and waterest it, thou greatly enrichest it; the river of God is full of water; thou providest their grain, for so thou hast prepared it. Thou waterest the furrows abundantly, settling its ridges, softening it with showers, and blessing its growth. Thou crownest the year with thy bounty; the tracks of thy chariot drip with fatness . . . The pastures of the wilderness drip, the hills gird themselves with joy, the meadows clothe themselves with flocks, the valleys deck themselves with grain, they shout and sing together for joy (Psalm 65:9-13).
>
> Give ear, and hear my voice; harken, and hear my speech. Does he who plows for sowing plow continually? does he continually open and harrow his ground? When he has leveled its surface, does he not scatter dill, sow cummin, and put in wheat in rows and barley in its proper place, and spelt as the border? For he is instructed aright; his God teaches him.
>
> Dill is not threshed with a threshing sledge, nor is a cart wheel rolled over cummin; but dill is beaten out with a stick, and cummin with a rod. Does one crush bread grain? No, he does not thresh it for ever; when he drives his cart wheel over it with his horses, he does not crush it. This also comes from the Lord of hosts; he is wonderful in counsel, and excellent in wisdom (Isaiah 28:23-29).

5. *The Yahweh of the Holy Land*

Gradually, Yahweh came to be thought of in connection with the territory of His people. When David had to take refuge in Philistine cities, hardly twenty-five miles from Bethlehem, he complained, "They have driven me out this day that I should have no share in the heritage of Yahweh, saying, 'Go, serve other gods.' " (I Samuel 26:19). Jonah is pictured as taking a ship to another country that he might flee "from the presence of Yahweh" (Jonah 1:3, 10). When Naaman, the Syrian, was healed by Elisha, he carried "two mules' burden of earth" from Israel's land back to Damascus so that even in a foreign country he could stand on it and worship the God of Israel (II Kings 5:17).

When one was in other lands, one would naturally worship other gods. So Ruth is pictured as changing gods when she passed from Moab to Bethlehem, although the two places were only about 30 miles apart (Ruth 1:6). Even in Jeremiah's time, to be exiled from the Holy Land was interpreted as being forced to worship other gods.

> 'Therefore I will hurl you out of this land into a land which neither you nor your fathers have known and there you shall serve other gods day and night' (Jeremiah 16:13).

When the Northern Kingdom fell, in 721 B.C., the Assyrian monarch settled strangers in Samaria who did not fare so well since they "didn't know the law of the god of the land." So a priest was provided to "teach them the law of the god of the land" (II Kings 17:24-33).

The international royal marriages also had their influence on the Yahweh-concept. We read:

> Then Solomon built a high place for Chemosh the abomination of Moab, and for Molech the abomination of the Ammonites, on the mountain east of Jerusalem. And so he did for all his foreign wives, who burned incense and sacrificed to their gods (I Kings 11:7-8).

So if Chemosh and Molech can be worshiped at Jerusalem, presumably Yahweh can also be worshiped in Moab. Gradually, gods were intermingled across boundaries, and a change of land did not necessitate a change of gods.

As a mountain-god, Yahweh controlled thunder and lightning and was associated with the sky. The story of Jacob's dream of the heavenly ladder (Genesis 28:12-13), as well as the story of the tower of Babel where Yahweh jealously protects His heavenly dwelling from the invasion of men, indicates the extension of Yahweh's sovereignty far above the mountain to the sky (Genesis 11:1-9). Later the Psalmist speaks of Yahweh as:

He who sits in the heavens . . . Yahweh has established his throne in the heavens, and his kingdom rules over all (Psalm 2:4; 103:19).

Solomon at the dedication of the temple exclaims: "Behold, heaven and the highest heaven cannot contain thee; how much less this house which I have built!" (II Chronicles 6:18). Gradually, Yahweh was not limited to the Holy Land.

6. *Yahweh of the Pre-Exilic Prophets* (750-586 B.C.)[5]

About two hundred years before the Babylonian Captivity the early writing-prophets emerged and emphasized a shifting of emphasis from ceremonies and sacrifices to ethical obedience. Stressing the faith of the Fathers they were not innovators. *Amos* proclaimed the need of personal and national obedience to a righteous Yahweh, otherwise worship is an abomination to Him (Amos 2:6, 7; 3:1, 2; 4:1-5).

> I hate, I despise your feasts, and I take no delight in your solemn assemblies . . . Take away from me the noise of your songs; to the melody of your harps I will not listen. But let justice roll down like waters and righteousness like an ever flowing stream (Amos 5:21-24).

Hosea added to this uncompromising justice of Yahweh, the earliest declaration that God really loves human beings. Through his distressing experience of his faithless wife, whom he could not forget and still loved, he came to the conviction that Yahweh also loves persistently and is ready to forgive the repentant sinner, though he will also punish.

> For I desire steadfast love and not sacrifice, the knowledge of Yahweh, rather than burnt offerings (Hosea 6:6). How can I give you up, O Ephraim! How can I hand you over, O Israel! How can I make you like Admah! How can I treat you like Zeboiim! My heart recoils within me, my compassion grows warm and tender, I will not execute my fierce anger, I will not again destroy Ephraim; for I am Yahweh and not man, the Holy one in your midst, and I will not come to destroy (11:8-9). "So you, by the help of Yahweh, return, hold fast to love and justice" (12:6).

---

5. Max Weber, *Ancient Judaism,* The Free Press, 1952; also E. Voegelin, *Israel and Revelation,* Louisiana Univ. Press, 1956; J. M. P. Smith, *The Prophets and their Times,* Revised by W. A. Irwin, Univ. of Chicago Press, 1965.

Isaiah began his work with a vision of majestic holiness of Yahweh. "Holy, holy, holy is Yahweh of hosts; the whole earth is full of his glory." (Isaiah 6:3). Amidst the distressing national and international problems, Isaiah emphasizes the moral content and practical application of their inherited faith. Yahweh's chief interest is not in ceremonial sacrifices, but in righteousness, redemption, and peace (Isaiah 8:19-20; 28:7-22).

> Bring no more vain offerings; incense is an abomination to me . . . I will not listen; your hands are full of blood. Wash yourselves; make yourselves clean . . . cease to do evil, learn to do good; seek justice, correct oppression; defend the fatherless, plead for the widow (Isaiah 1:13, 15-17).

Isaiah also pictured a glorious future of peace, in spite of inevitable punishment.

> It shall come to pass in the latter days . . . He shall judge between the nations, and shall decide for many peoples; and they shall beat their swords into plowshares and their spears into pruning hooks; nation shall not lift up sword against nation, neither shall they learn war any more (Isaiah 2:2, 4-5; also Joel 3:10; Micah 4:3).

Micah also rejects the idea that Yahweh would necessarily protect Hebrew material interests and insists with Isaiah that He is a God of peace (4:3-4) but that, as a moral being, would punish Israel, even with the hand of other nations, for their unrighteousness. He summarizes what Yahweh demands in these words:

> He has showed you, O man, what is good; and what does Yahweh require of you but to do justice, and to love kindness, and to walk humbly with your God? (Micah 6:8).

Jeremiah in bitter personal sorrow learned the healing consciousness of fellowship with Yahweh. He emphasized Yahweh's concern for the individual as shown in His renewing influence in the heart of man.

> "In those days they shall no longer say: 'The fathers have eaten sour grapes, and the children's teeth are set on edge.' But every one shall die for his own sin; each man who eats sour grapes, his teeth shall be set on edge . . . after those days, says Yahweh: I will put my law within them, and I will write it upon their hearts; and I will be their God, and they shall be my people . . . for they shall all know me, from the least of them to the greatest, says Yahweh; for I will forgive, their iniquity, and I will remember their sin no more" (Jeremiah 31:29-30; 33-34).

This opened the way for personal, active monotheism and was the basis for a missionary interpretation of religion (Jeremiah 12:14-17).

The other pre-Exilic prophets, Zephaniah, Nahum, and Habukkuk, all preached a similar message of judgment and hope. The pre-Exilic nationalistic concept of Yahweh had to be overcome.

> "Am I a God at hand, says Yahweh, and not a God afar off? Can a man hide himself in secret places so that I cannot see him? says Yahweh. Do I not fill heaven and earth? says Yahweh" (Jeremiah 23:23-24).

Gradually Yahweh was universalized, spiritualized, and as an ethical being identified with righteousness. To be unrighteous was in itself idolatry (Jeremiah 25:5-7). But there still was a long and tragic road ahead before ethical monotheism became the common property of the people.

7. *Yahweh of the Prophets in Exile* (586-539 B.C.)

To us, who grew up with ideas of divine unity and omnipresence, there is no difficulty in worshiping the one and only God in many places, but to people beginning with the presupposition that there are many gods, as did the early Hebrews, having many places of worship, tended to keep the idea alive that there are many gods.

Hence, the prophetic movement, represented in Deuteronomy, meant to make the oneness of God real to the people by introducing the practice of daily repetition in family worship of the watchword:

> "Hear, O Israel: Yahweh, our God is one Lord; and you shall love Yahweh your God with all your heart, and with all your soul, and with all your might" (Deuteronomy 6:4-5).

To help along in this emphasis naturally, a program of suppression of the local shrines was instituted along with the establishment of an exclusive, centralized worship in the temple of Jerusalem (II Kings 23: 6, 8).

With the destruction of the Northern Kingdom in 721 B.C., Yahweh's land was restricted to Judah and the unification of His worship in Jerusalem. All of this helped symbolize the unity of Yahweh. But now, with the Babylonian captivity, this unity was utterly destroyed. The Psalmist, in anguish, expressed his feeling "As with a deadly wound in my body, my adversaries taunt me, while they say continually, 'Where is thy God?' " (Psalm 42:10).

We have here a wonderful example of transmutation of tragedy into gain which was an achievement of the later prophets. They used the disaster of Zion and the destruction of the temple as a means to spiritualize and universalize the idea of Yahweh.

Jeremiah's Yahweh was not confined to Palestine or the temple.

He wrote a letter to his brethren in exile declaring the availability of Yahweh anywhere at any time, indicating that this exile experience was meant for their good.

> "For I know the plans I have for you, says Yahweh, plans for welfare and not for evil, to give you a future and a hope. Then you will call upon me and come and pray to me, and I will hear you. You will seek me and find me; when you seek me with all your heart, I will be found by you, says Yahweh" (Jeremiah 29: 11-14).

Isaiah, however, was the great spokesman in the Exile for Yahweh and monotheism. As for other gods he has Yahweh say:

> "Behold you are nothing, and your work is nought; an abomination is he who chooses you . . . Before me no god was formed, nor shall there be any after me. I, I am Yahweh, and besides me there is no savior, . . . I am the first and I am the last; besides me there is no god, . . . My hand laid the foundation of the earth, and my right hand spread out the heavens, when I call to them, they stand forth together." (Isaiah 41:24; 43:10-11; 44:6; 48:13).

It is important to note that the prophet is not saying all this about a god of a victorious people but of a humiliated and defeated people in exile. It was in the depths of national ruin that the prophet maintains his confidence in the sole existence and absolute power of Yahweh. Had he done this in victory of his people, that would be understandable, but the significance lies in the fact that the prophet does this in the face of seeming triumph of Babylonian idols and the evident defeat and ruin of his own, Yahweh's people.

In Isaiah's judgment, it was not the Babylonians nor their gods who had triumphed over Judah and Yahweh, but it was Yahweh himself who had launched Nebuchadnezzar and his army against Judah to execute His righteous judgment on His own chosen people. This was a moral victory. The dominant motive behind it was the faith that Yahweh's social justice would conquer. This is clearly indicated in the great passages on the suffering servant where Isaiah indicates that the one and only Yahweh, cares for all mankind and mercifully purposes salvation not only of the Jews but, through them, of all people. This is monotheism at its best and highest. Judah is to be Yahweh's servant.

> "I have given you as a covenant to the people, a light to the nations, to open the eyes that are blind, to bring out the prisoners from the dungeon, from the prison those who sit in darkness. I am Yahweh, that is my name . . ." (Isaiah 42:6-8).

> "You are my servant, Israel, in whom I will be glorified . . . It is too light a thing that you should be my servant to raise up the tribes of Jacob and to restore the preserved of Israel; I will give you as a light to the nations, that my salvation may reach to the ends of the earth." (Isaiah 49:3, 6; see also chapters 52 and 53).

This is universal, ethical monotheism of the righteous Yahweh purging and preparing His chosen people through the fires of suffering in Exile to be used as an instrument and servant in His hand for the salvation of all mankind.

Ezekiel, another prophet with his people in exile, taught that this hard experience was not merely a penalty, but also a means of purification and discipline. Proceeding on the basis of Jeremiah's individualism, he stresses personal responsibility and opportunity before Yahweh, irrespective of heredity: "Behold all souls are mine; the soul of the father as well as the soul of the son is mine; the soul that sins shall die" (Ezekiel 18:4). Indeed, Yahweh himself would put a new heart into the sinner (Ezekiel 11:19; 36:26). He also brought great encouragement to the people with his sketch of the new community and temple (Chapters 40-48). He meant to organize religious worship so thoroughly as to insure the blessings of Yahweh. However, the focus of this picture was again upon ceremonial details centering at Jerusalem.

> "Therefore thus says the Lord God (Yahweh Elohim): No foreigner, uncircumcised in heart and flesh, of all the foreigners who are among the people of Israel, shall enter my sanctuary" (Ezekiel 44:9).

So Ezekiel became the father of narrow Judaism who, after the Exile, were called Jews.

8. *The Post-Exilic Development* (539 B.C. - 100 A.D.)

After the capture of Babylon by Cyrus, in 539 B.C. the Jews were permitted to return to their home in Palestine. A considerable number accepted the privilege. The great desire on the part of many to go back and rebuild their temple and city was only natural. Under the leadership of Zerubbabel, and Joshua, a second temple was completed in Jerusalem and in 516 B.C. regular worship was renewed.

Later, under the leadership of the Governor, Nehemiah, the city of Jerusalem was also rebuilt. Soon after, under Ezra the Scribe, the movement begun under King Josiah some centuries earlier, to have people live more nearly in accord with the law of Moses (as reformulated in *Deuteronomy*) took on new life. The Priestly Code, completed in Ezra's Exile days he now took with him from Babylonia to Palestine, and with Governor Nehemiah's aid persuaded the people to accept it. The aim was to inspire greater respect for and loyalty to Yahweh, but its method was again to stress externals, ceremonial purity, rites and sacrifices, Sabbath observance, and a vast number of details growing into an elaborate scheme of legalism overshadowing the spiritual side of religion.

In Babylon, and the wretched years thereafter in the restored community at Jerusalem, Israel faced a precarious struggle for sheer existence. Naturally, they felt compelled to magnify their distinctiveness in order not to be absorbed by surrounding paganism. The same Exile which on the one hand released Israel's faith from old dependencies to universalize it, on the other hand also encouraged them to stress their peculiarities to prevent their assimilation into the life of Babylon. Ezekiel in exile dreamt of a future church-state of Zion centered in the temple, governed by the priests of Yahweh, and distinguished by ceremonial peculiarities. Post-exilic Judaism presents no unanimous picture. Monotheism again was mingled with old tribal deities, racial prejudices, and even national hatreds, encouraged by Nehemiah the Governor and Ezra the Priest.

On the one hand there was the book of Esther, clearly indicating Jewish nationalism. On the other hand there were the books of Ruth and Jonah with their appeal against racial prejudice. On the one hand is the concept of Yahweh before whom men cry:

> Remember, O Yahweh, against the Edomites the day of Jerusalem, how they said, "Rase it, rase it! Down to its foundations!" O daughter of Babylon, you devastator! Happy shall he be who requites you with what you have done to us! Happy shall he be who takes your little ones and dashes them against the rock! (Psalm 137:7-9).

On the other hand there is Yahweh saying:

> In that day Israel will be the third with Egypt and Assyria, a blessing in the midst of the earth, whom Yahweh of hosts has blessed, saying, "Blessed be Egypt my people, and Assyria the work of my hands, and Israel my heritage" (Isaiah 19:24-25).

In other words the Yahweh concept of Judaism was something of a paradox. He was both national and universal, the God of a special people but also of the universe, at home in a special temple and yet accessible to everyone anywhere through prayer, pledged to the ultimate victory of His people and yet the savior of all mankind. In Isaiah's great chapters on the suffering servant, this paradox is resolved but not even all prophets agreed with that, some insisting

Jerusalem will still be the necessary center of the future monotheism, as for example:

> "And Yahweh will inherit Judah as his portion in the holy land, and will again choose Jerusalem" ... And Yahweh will become king over all the earth; on that day Yahweh will be one and his name one . . . And if any of the families of the earth do not go up to Jerusalem to worship the king, Yahweh of hosts, there will be no rain upon them. (Zechariah 2:12; 14:9, 17).

The long-run future, however, belonged to the prophets with greater insights who left the smaller ideas of a narrow Judaism behind. Gradually, for Israel, the loss of the Ark, the destruction of the Temple, the demolition of Jerusalem, along with the defeat of the homeland and the experience of captivity, all helped more completely to divest the Yahweh concept of any racial and geographical limitations. Increasingly, the prophetic concept of Yahweh as the spiritual, ethical, and universal creator and controller of the universe and history, who nevertheless was one of nearness, mercy, love, and peace for all mankind, became more and more acceptable.

B.   The Concept of God In The New Testament

There is quite a gap between the Old and the New Testament which cannot be covered here. Our discussion must be limited to a short treatment of the Transition from the Old to the New Testament, "The God and Father of our Lord Jesus Christ," and The Apostolic and Early Christian Concept of God, as indicated in the New Testament.

1.   *The Transition from the Old to the New Testament.*

In the Old Testament, God is often spoken of as a king, while in the New Testament He is more often referred to as Father. In the Old Testament He is more a God of Justice, while in the New Testament He is more a God of Love and Peace. In the Old Testament at first, He seems to have been referred to as "the God of your fathers." For example, in the passage where God meets Moses at the burning bush, the phrase, "God of your fathers," is used three times (Exodus 3:13-16; cf. Gen. 15:2; I Chronicles 28:9). Later by the prophets God is occasionally spoken of as the "Father of Israel" (Jeremiah 3:4, 19; 31:9; Isaiah 63:16; 64:8; Malachi 1:6; 2:10). The Psalmist speaks of Him in more personal terms as "Father of the fatherless" (68:5; cf. 69:26) and "As a father pitieth his children, so Yahweh pities those who fear him" (103:13). But in general, with the exception of a few prophets, the Old Testament never entirely gets beyond a nationalistic and racial view of Yahweh.[6]

As one passes into the New Testament, one is aware of a fresh view of God and individual experiences with Him. One of the main causes that brought about this difference, no doubt, was the expulsion of the Christians from temple and synagogue. The early Christians were Jews who had found the promised Messiah in Jesus but otherwise expected to remain Jews. When driven out of synagogue and temple, this disrupted their religious framework. Christians were an outlawed group and regarded as aliens by the Jewish community. The theological effect of all this was far-reaching. God, for them, now lost all national and racial entanglements. Now He became the truly universal God with no local temple or chosen people to limit Him. Now He was worshiped by people of all tongues, races, and nations on equal terms, for in Christ "there cannot be Greek and Jew, circumcised and uncircumcised, barbarian, Scythian, slave, free man, but Christ is all, and in all" (Colossians 3:11).

Not only was there complete separation of church and synagogue, they also met for worship on the first day of the week instead of the last. The original language of the New Testament was Greek, while that of the Old Testament was Hebrew. The New Testament concept of God, therefore, is a universal one as Peter put it:

> "Truly I perceive that God shows no partiality, but in every nation any one who fears him and does what is right is acceptable to him" (Acts 10:34).

This freeing of the God-concept from the Old Testament restrictions also opened the Christian mind to the influences of religious ideas of the Greco-Roman world of their day. The Alexandrian Jews, among them such thinkers as Philo (c. 20 B.C.-A.D. 50), were already greatly influenced by Hellenistic thought. Although the Old Testament was at first the only Bible available to Christians, Alexandrian Judaism had long since shown that it could also be interpreted in Greek thought forms. In general, Christians found it easier to persuade Gentiles than Hebrews, which helped to promote that larger mental hospitality and later led to overwhelming influence of Greek thought on Christian theology. Furthermore, the Greek language was in current use everywhere, the Old Testament was already translated

---

6. See Paul Ricoeur, "The Father Image" and Herbert Bronstein, "Yahweh as Father in Hebrew Scriptures," articles in *Criterion,* Divinity School, University of Chicago Press, Vol. 8, No. 1, Autumn-Winter 1968-1969.

Basic Christian Convictions

into Greek, and most of the New Testament writings were originally produced in Greek.

In the opening words of the Fourth Gospel we are introduced to the Greek Logos—the outgoing eternal God of creation and salvation. This Logos was proclaimed to be "the true light that enlightens every man . . ." (John 1:9). This was Greek stoic and Neo-Platonic doctrine. The first verses of John's Gospel would not have been unfamiliar to the people in Ephesus or Athens of that day, although they probably would have hesitated to identify the Logos with Jesus.

It, therefore, cannot be said that the New Testament just takes over the Old Testament idea of God.[7] The God concept of the New Testament is the eternal Spirit of Love accessible everywhere to everybody without any special ritualistic requirements, who was supremely revealed in Jesus Christ.

2. *"The God and Father of our Lord Jesus Christ"*

The personality of Jesus was the major creative force that made the difference between the ideas of God in the two Testaments. In His thinking Jesus was the natural successor of Hosea, Jeremiah, and Isaiah of the Exile. Monotheism was not only stressed as to its cosmic significance but more especially as to its moral implications. His God was ethical, spiritual, universal, a God of grace, forgiveness, and love, as well as judgment. He demanded not ritual conformity but moral sincerity, and brotherly conduct. In dealing with His people's heritage Jesus did not practice wholesale acceptance but thoughtful selectivity. This selectivity really resulted in a new emphasis amounting to quite a different idea of God.

His intention was not so much to maintain faith in one God as over against other gods, but rather to emphasize the moral meanings of monotheism as over against the legalism of the Pharisees. He thought of God as judging men by their acts to others. What men thought, would automatically be expressed by what they did or left undone, as in the case of the last judgment scene:

> "Come, O blessed of my father, inherit the kingdom prepared for you from the foundation of the world; for I was hungry and you gave me food, I was thirsty and you gave me drink, I was a stranger and you welcomed me, I was naked and you clothed me, I was sick and you visited me, I was in prison and you came to me' . . . 'Truly, I say to you, as you did to it to one of the least of these my brethren, you did it to me.' " (Matthew 25:34-36, 40).

---

7. K. S. Latourette, *A History of Christianity,* Harper, 1953, "Marcion and the Marcionites," pp. 125-136.

Jesus thus universalized God's requirements, regardless of race or nation. At first even the disciples could not follow as they could not yet fully understand. The later development of an international and interracial Christian faith was the logical outcome of the way Jesus thought of God.

God was very real in the personal experience of Jesus. The disciples were deeply affected by the spiritual fellowship of Jesus with His Father God. His God was not only revealed by the words He used but especially by the life He lived. So they asked Him to teach them to pray even as He did (Luke 11:1). Jesus often spoke of "My Father" and now He teaches His disciples to pray to "Our Father," and in conversation with them He often referred to "Your Father."

Various writers of the New Testament were so impressed by the intimate relationship of Jesus and the Father that they repeatedly referred to "The God and Father of our Lord Jesus Christ" (I Peter 1:3; I Corinthians 1:3; 2 Corinthians 1:2; Ephesians 1:3; Colossians 1:3). Upon the lips of Jesus Abba (Papa, Daddy) meant more than any name for God ever meant before (Mark 14:36; Romans 8:15; Galatians 4:6). So ardently did it issue from the depths of His being that it communicated itself to His followers with such forceful reality that it introduced a new and transforming epoch in the life of the human spirit.

Jesus continued the prophetic opposition to sacred places and holy homelands. Naturally, the Zealots did not like this as they felt it their mission to help save the homeland from the pagan Romans. Jesus repeatedly spoke of the future destruction of the temple and the city of Jerusalem. In the transfiguration story He does not allow His disciples to build permanent living quarters.

The God of Jesus cared and was concerned even about the everyday needs of His children on earth.

> "Therefore I tell you do not be anxious about your life, what you shall eat or what you shall drink, nor about your body, what you shall put on . . . Look at the birds . . . your heavenly Father feeds them. Are you not of more value than they? . . . Consider the lilies of the field . . . if God so clothes the grass of the field . . . will he not much more clothe you . . . your heavenly Father knows that you need them all" (Matthew 6:25-33; cf. Matthew 10:29-31).

Jesus thought of God as being aware of alms given in secret and knew about particular human needs before they were expressed in words:

52   BASIC CHRISTIAN CONVICTIONS

> "Beware of practicing your piety before men . . . when you give alms, do not let your left hand know what your right hand is doing, so that your alms may be in secret; . . . And when you pray . . . go into your room and shut the door and pray . . . and your Father who sees in secret will reward you. And in praying do not heap up empty phrases, . . . for your Father knows what you need before you ask him" (Matthew 6:1-8).

Jesus thought of God as a forgiving Father, but whereas forgiveness is a two-way affair and cannot be received by an unforgiving heart, he emphasized that only "if you forgive men their trespasses, your heavenly Father also will forgive you" (Matthew 6:14).

There are pre-Christian and extra-Christian references to God as Father. The Greek Zeus was thought of as the great Father. Plato in his *Timaeus* refers to the Father and maker of the universe. In the Hindu *Vedas*, Brahma is spoken of as the Father of all things. Old Testament references have already been cited. But in Jesus we have at least four absolutely new notes regarding God as Father.

First, there is a very personal relationship with God as Father. Repeatedly, he addresses God as "My Father," "Our Father," "Your Father." All this is very personal and intimate whereas pre- and extra-Christian references to God as Father referred to this relationship only in very general terms as Father of the universe or of Israel as a people.

Second, the Father-love revealed in Jesus Christ is a gracious, unmerited, outgoing, seeking agape-love, that not only welcomes the sinner when he comes back but actually goes out to seek him as in the parables of the lost coin, sheep, and son, pictured in Luke 15. A Jewish scholar points out:

> Surely this is a new note, something which we have not yet heard in the Old Testament . . . or in the Talmud . . . The virtues of repentance are gloriously praised in the rabbinical literature, but this direct search for and appeal to the sinner are new and moving notes of high import and significance.[8]
> The Rabbis, too, taught that God welcomed the sinner on his repentance. But to seek out the sinner, and instead of avoiding the bad companion to choose him as your friend in order to work out his moral redemption, this was, I fancy, something new in the religious history of Israel.[9]

---

8. Montefoire, *The Synoptic Gospels,* Macmillan, 1909, II, p. 985. Quoted by J. S. Shaw, *Christian Doctrine,* Philosophical Library, 1954, p. 32.

9. Montefoire, *Some Elements of the Religious Teaching of Jesus,* Macmillan, 1910, p. 57, Quoted by J. S. Shaw, *Christian Doctrine,* Philosophical Library, 1954, p. 32.

Third, a distinctive note in the thought of Jesus about God as Father is that it was a revelation made not merely through His words and teaching, but above all through His life and conduct. The best indication of the picture Jesus had of God was His own character and life. He was convinced that He came into the world to reveal the Father. Repeatedly He says that He was "sent" by the Father (John 5:24, 30, 36, 37; 8:16; 12:49). When Jesus told His disciples about His going back to the Father and indicated that they knew the way,

> Thomas said to him, "Lord we do not know where you are going; how can we know the way?" Jesus said to him, "I am the way, and the truth, and the life; no one comes to the Father but by me. If you had known me you would have known my Father also; henceforth you know him and have seen him." Philip said to him, "Lord, show us the Father, and we shall be satisfied." Jesus said to him, "Have I been with you so long, and yet you do not know me, Philip? He who has seen me has seen the Father; how can you say, 'Show us the Father'? Do you not believe that I am in the Father and the Father in me? The words that I say to you I do not speak on my own authority; but the Father who dwells in me does his works. Believe me that I am in the Father and the Father in me; or else believe me for the sake of the works themselves" (John 14:5-11).

There is a great difference between merely proclaiming a new truth and acting it out in one's life. Jesus acted out, embodied, incarnated His new teaching about God as Father-love with and in His own life of gracious, compassionate, and self-sacrificing regard for the least, the last and the lost. As "he went about doing good" (Acts 10:38) He was the revelation of God as Father-love and especially on the cross praying for those who crucified Him.

Fourth, the most unique way that Jesus emphasized the idea of God as Father-love was by His unique Act and Fact and Event of incarnation, crucifixion, resurrection, ascension, and outpouring of the Holy Spirit, however these may be interpreted. This whole Act of God "reconciling the world to himself" (II Corinthians 5:19) vividly pictures this new idea of God as Father-love. Kierkegaard calls this the "Scandal of Particularity." Here the Universal became individual and particular, the Eternal became temporal and historical. "The Word became flesh, and dwelt among us . . . full of grace and truth." (John 1:14).

3. *The Apostolic and Early Christian Concept of God*

The early Christians were Jews and as such were familiar with the Old Testament ideas of God. They had great respect for their ancestral faith and regarded their new experiences as fulfillment of its promises. The newness of this Father concept of God is unmistakable when we remember that in the Old Testament the term Father for God occurs less than twenty times, whereas in the New Testament, Mark uses it four times; Luke, fifteen times; Matthew, forty-two times; and John, one hundred and two times. Evidently the designation of God as Father was rather rare among early Christians, but became increasingly common during the redactional period of the New Testament. No doubt, the use of the Lord's Prayer was an influence in this direction. The acceptance of the Father-designation is complete in John, but may be traced back as far as Matthew, in the so-called prayer of Jubilation:

> "All things have been delivered to me by my Father; and no one knows the Son except the Father, and no one knows the Father except the Son and any one to whom the Son chooses to reveal him" (Matthew 11:27).

To the early Jewish Christians, Jesus was the Messiah. All this was at first associated with Him as "the son of David." However, when the gospel was carried from the Jewish to the Gentile world, the term "Messiah" was exchanged for the term "Christ" which had more meaning to the Gentiles. Gradually "Jesus the Christ" became shortened into "Jesus Christ." In Paul's Epistles, the title "Lord" is used as this title was current in Greek culture and religious practice. So when the Jewish name "Yahweh" was translated into Greek the word "Lord" was used. This finally developed into the title "The Lord Jesus Christ."

> For although there may be so-called gods in heaven or on earth—as indeed there are many "gods" and "lords"—yet as for us there is one God, the Father, from whom are all things and for whom we exist, and one Lord, Jesus Christ, through whom are all things and through whom we exist (I Corinthians 8:5-6).

This development came to its climax in the interpretation of Jesus as the "Logos," the eternal Word of God. Jewish thought was already familiar with this idea in their word "Wisdom." So here was a word that could serve as a medium of thought ready for Christian use in interpreting Jesus and which would identify him with the divine realm. Paul preached:

> the gospel of the glory of Christ, who is the likeness of God (II Corinthians 4:4) . . . the image of the invisible God, the first-born of all creation (Colossians 1:15).

GOD, OUR FATHER   55

The writer of Hebrews speaks of Him as the one who "reflects the glory of God and bears the very stamp of his nature . . ." (Hebrews 1:3). And John says of him "In the beginning was the Word (Logos), and the Word was with God, and the Word was God" (John 1:1). In the New Testament then the idea of God came to be measured and determined by what Jesus taught, was, and did.

The effect of considering Jesus as divine was of far-reaching influence on the Christian conception of God, making the character of Jesus central in the concept of God. In Christian thinking God became Christlike. When the early Christians thought of the divine they thought of Jesus. This meant that God's care of and concern for individual persons was emphasized as it never was in the Old Testament.

In the Old Testament both God and good men are pictured as hating sinners. Now God is pictured as merciful, forgiving, and intent on saving the sinner. Jesus commanded "Love your enemies and pray for those who persecute you, so that you may be sons of your Father who is in heaven; . . ." (Matthew 5:44-48; cf. Romans 5:8). God was still ruler of history with the right of the potter over the clay (Romans 9:21) but the directive control of the Most High now is thought of as "according to the eternal purpose which he has realized in Christ Jesus our Lord" (Ephesians 3:11). The main attribute of God came to be considered the kind of agape-love that was found in Christ. Paul entreats:

> by the meekness and gentleness of Christ (II Corinthians 10:1)
> . . . though he was rich yet for your sake he became poor, so
> that by his poverty you might become rich (II Corinthians 8:9).
> Bear one another's burdens, and so fulfil the law of Christ
> (Galatians 6:2). Put on then, as God's chosen ones, holy and
> beloved, compassion, kindness, lowliness, meekness, and patience,
> forbearing one another and, if one has a complaint against an-
> other, forgiving each other; as the Lord has forgiven you, so you
> also must forgive (Colossians 3:12-13).

This centrality of agape-love in Paul's thought of Christ was naturally also carried into his concept of God who loves us so much that nothing can separate us from His love (Romans 8:38-39). And as for John the result of Christ's influence on his God concept is plain when he says "God is love, and he who abides in love abides in God, and God abides in him" (I John 4:16). Obviously something new had entered into the old concept of God through the personal influence of Jesus. Old frameworks of thought were taken over

56 BASIC CHRISTIAN CONVICTIONS

from Jewish tradition and new ones added from Greek culture, but for Christians the picture in all of them was Jesus Christ.

But we must go farther than even this. The center of the New Testament is not so much an idea as a deed. In Christ, God had done something for the world. Both the Gospels and the Epistles are engaged in the presentation of a crucial deed which was the very hinge of history on which depends the world's and each individual person's destiny. The early Christian idea of God cannot be fully understood apart from this deed which God had done in Christ.

God is a righteous and loving doer of mighty acts and history is a process under His sovereign will in which He performs His mighty acts. History is the workshop of God. And the church is the chosen vehicle for His purpose. In the Old Testament one of His mighty acts was the deliverance of Israel from Egypt, and in the New Testament God has sent His Son into the world and what "many prophets and righteous men longed to see . . ." (Matthew 13:17) had now come to pass. In the coming of Jesus, God had done the supreme and saving deed for man's salvation.

The New Testament idea of God roots back into this deed wherein,

> God shows his love for us in that while we were yet sinners Christ died for us (Romans 5:8). Darkness is passing away and the true light is already shining. (I John 2:8). To all who received him, who believed in his name, he gave power to become children of God (John 1:12). When the time had fully come, God sent forth his Son . . . that we might receive adoption as sons (Galatians 4:4-5; cf. John 1:12; Romans 8:14, 15; Matthew 5:45; Ephesians 1:5).

Jewish monotheism stood for the existence and sovereignty of one God. Christianity was developing new dimensions in its monotheism by thinking of the Father as revealed in the Son and made immediately available to the believer by the indwelling Spirit. Paul expressed this enriched idea of God in the benediction "The grace of the Lord Jesus Christ and the love of God and the fellowship of the Holy Spirit be with you all" (II Corinthians 13:14). The early Christians could not express about God all they wanted to say in the terminology of the old monotheism. They saw themselves dealing with God in three special ways—as cosmic Creator and Father, as incarnate Savior and Lord, and as the indwelling Spirit of Power. All this is suffused with a sense of mystery. All this indicated to them the manifoldness of the Father's approach to man. Paul was attempting to express the ineffable—"O the depth of the riches and wisdom and knowledge of God! How unsearchable are his judgments, and how inscrutable his ways!" (Romans 11:33).

4. *Summary of the Growing Biblical God Concept*

The idea of God has greatly changed through the centuries. Different human situations called for different needs to be met and the God concept gradually changed accordingly. This development has been summarized as follows:

> Beginning with a storm god on a desert mountain, it ends with men saying, "God is spirit, and those who worship him must worship in spirit and truth" (John 4:24).
>
> Beginning with a tribal war god, leading devotees to bloody triumph over their foes, it ends with men seeing that 'God is love, and he who abides in love abides in God, and God abides in him' (I John 4:16).
>
> Beginning with a territorial deity who loved his clansmen and hated the remainder of mankind, it ends with a great multitude out of every tribe and tongue and people and nation, worshipping the universal Father (Revelation 5:9).
>
> Beginning with a god who walked in a garden in the cool of the day or who showed his back to Moses as a special favor, it ends with the God whom 'no one has ever seen' (John 1:18) and 'in him we live and move and have our being' (Acts 17:28).
>
> Beginning with a god who commanded the slaughter of infants and sucklings without mercy, it ends with the God whose will it is that 'not . . . one of these little ones should perish' (Matthew 18:14).
>
> Beginning with a god from whom at Sinai the people shrank in fear, saying, "Let not God speak with us, lest we die," (Exodus 20:19; Deut. 5:25) it ends with the God to whom one prays in the solitary place and whose indwelling Spirit is our unseen friend.
>
> Beginning with a god whose highest social vision was a tribal victory, it ends with a God whose worshippers pray for a worldwide kingdom of righteousness and peace.[10]

C. The God Concept In Christendom

Having traced the concept of God in the Old and the New Testament we now come to the further development of this concept in Christendom. This is a long period of time and we must restrict ourselves to a brief discussion under the following subheads: The Greek Influence; The Reformation; Modern Thought; The Influence

---

10. Harry E. Fosdick, *A Guide to Understanding the Bible,* Harper, 1938. p. 54.

58   BASIC CHRISTIAN CONVICTIONS

of Science; The Impact of Industrialism; Current Social Mobility; and A Suggested Definition of God.

1. *The Greek Influence.*

Greek philosophers identified God with the absolute. By absolute was meant ultimate reality lying back of all phenomena and binding the various elements of experience into a unity. God is thought of in an abstract and transcendent way as standing over against the universe and acting upon it through intermediate beings like the Demiurge or the Logos, but himself remaining apart from its finite and imperfect life. This abstract conception of God helped emphasize the unity, spirituality, and rationality of God. The Christian idea of God gradually filled the same place in the universe which was assigned by philosophy to whatever was considered to be ultimate. What the materialist attributes to matter, the idealist to spirit, the pessimist to blind force, the Christian attributes to "the God and Father of our Lord Jesus Christ." He is the ultimate and the absolute.

The Greek Philosopher tended to eliminate all finite limitation of the God idea and then concluded that the abstraction remaining was perfect. God then was conceived as beyond human comprehension, infinite, eternal, unchangeable, and incomprehensible. These are all characteristics that emphasized the contrast between man and God, leaving aside love, pity, and patience which express kinship between God and man. The center was shifted from the historic Jesus to the eternal Word or Logos consubstantial with the Father.

From the Greek church fathers this concept was taken to the Latin church by Augustine. From Roman Catholicism through the schoolmen it also entered Protestantism. With this absolutism also went the idea of God as arbitrary will, considering Him a being of unrestricted choice and bound by no law but His own good pleasure.

2. *The Reformation*

Reformers thought of God as bound by his own nature to punish sin and so uphold righteousness and justice. In place of arbitrary will, which could remit penalty, they put immutable will, requiring punishment equal to guilt. Hence atonement was considered to be the only way open to God to forgive sin. The contradiction of immutable will and unrestricted choice, Calvinism sought to reconcile by attributing omnipotence, holiness, and justice to the nature of God, and love and mercy, on the other hand, were considered as matters of God's will. God must be just, it was thought, but He may or may not be merciful as He chooses. In this dualism God's being is robbed of the inner constraint of redemptive love, although He is still free to exercise love by grace, which however must also be given a new meaning.

Side by side with the abstract and negative attributes derived from contemporary philosophy somehow Christian thinkers tried to make room for the ethical and spiritual qualities which are so central in the Christian faith. What cold logic ruled out, living piety supplied; and redemptive love was expressed in God's fatherly forgiveness and so grace was kept alive.

3. *Modern Thought*

Modern theology has again brought into prominence the ethical and spiritual qualities so central in the thought of Jesus about God. For the abstract Absolute and the arbitrary Will, it substitutes the "God and Father of our Lord Jesus Christ" and points out that in His wise, holy and loving character we have the reality which philosophy calls the Absolute. Modern psychology of personality helped to overcome the supposed opposition between freedom and law; while modern philosophy renewing the emphasis upon the immanence of God, opens the way to include the concrete features of the Christian conception of God.

Now, it is held that it is not will but character that is fundamental for our conception of personality. The person is most truly free, whose will is most completely dominated by consistent moral purpose. Character denotes consistency in moral purpose, and law is its most effective means of expression. In the revelation that Jesus gives us of God we go behind His acts, to the character which finds expression through His acts. Instead of thinking of ultimate reality as most abstract, we are coming to think of it as most concrete. Thus the Absolute becomes teleological, the goal of progress. The qualities which Christian faith finds central in God become those most needed to explain the actual facts of life. Thus the religious interest which makes Christ central in Christian thought and faith is to be interpreted by life's highest, and not its lowest forms. This gives Jesus Christ the central position in Christian faith and life.[11]

4. *The Influence of Science*

The influence of science on religion in general and on the concept of God in particular has been very far reaching. Gradually, however,

---

11. W. A. Brown, *Christian Theology in Outline,* Scribners, 1921, pp. 85-93.

contemporary theologians have managed to integrate the findings of cosmology, genetics, anthropology, and other scientific areas so that today the anguished struggle between religion and science, even though it has not altogether subsided, nevertheless is not nearly so militant as it was in former days.

The geologist pushed the earth's origin many millenniums back beyond the calendar assumed in the Old Testament. The biologist traced evidences of human life back into the caves, jungles, to the remains in the rock formations, and possible origin in the sea. The astronomer and the astronaut punctured the notion of a heaven up in the skies. The psychologist, sociologist, and psychiatrist made personality and society ever more mysterious. But gradually western thinkers on the whole tended to accept the authority of science even to the point of rejecting or re-interpreting almost everything in the Bible that can not be justified on scientific findings.

More recently, however, many Christian thinkers have been having second thoughts. Scientific materialism seemingly went from triumph to triumph, but remained unprepared for possible atomic disasters, the nuclear disturbances, and the computerized inhumanity that would litter its own future pathway if it is to be considered as having the ultimate answers. Gradually the mechanistic "billiard ball" conception of the universe has been greatly affected by the findings of the new physics, biochemistry, psychosomatic medicine, psychotherapy, and other scientific research. Much of this has been forcing mind or spirit back into the picture.

With mind or spirit once admitted as something more than secondary phenomenon, it becomes of crucial importance to distinguish between mind that can view reality as "accidental collocations of atoms" and the divine Mind or Spirit described by Paul as "the mind of Christ." Where God had formerly been rejected as an unnecessary hypothesis, He now is becoming an increasingly needed source of ultimate meaning and value, which otherwise seemingly would be draining out of human history.

Men like Niels Bohr, Werner Heisenberg, Albert Einstein and others have come forth with principles of "uncertainty, indeterminacy, and relativity" which have revolutionized physical science and ushered in the nuclear age. The very universe itself has turned against the old science, and there is now developing a new philosophy of science. Science, is taking on a new modesty. Finding facts is no guarantee for power to give value. Either science must enlarge its scope or else subordinate facts to a higher authority. It must deal with other relations and not only with mechanistic connections. We have been disillusioned by the use to which science can be put and learned that it can also be a false Messiah and a curse as well as a blessing. Man needs, not only cool scientific detachment and objectivity, but also a fierce commitment to unprovable faith, passionate hope, and dedicated love for God and man.

Reality now is found in the realm of relationships and the God concept is increasingly being set free from mere anthropomorphism. Spirit, soul, life, truth, goodness, peace, and love are taking on new meaning and more reality. If science concerns itself with the questions of "What" and "How" and religion seeks answers to the questions of "Who" and "Why" these two disciplines will not only continue to understand each other better but also make unprecedented contributions to the welfare of mankind.[12]

5. *The Impact of Industrialism*

We are living in an age of the technician, the scientist, the social planner, and the political revolutionary. Now it is in this context that the term God must acquire meaning and reality. Truth is functionally unified in this industrial age by bringing different specialities to bear on concrete problems and perplexities.

All cultures use symbols which are drawn from some aspect of social life. When people think of God in occupational context, they call Him "shepherd." When they think of Him in a political setting they call Him "king." When they think of Him in family relationship they call Him "father." Changing structures of society inevitably result in using different symbols for God. To continue calling Him "shepherd" in an industrial society might suggest that God's name and His reality have merged in the thinking of people to such a degree that He might slip out of existence if the name was changed. On the other hand to call Him "chief engineer," or "grand architect," in an industrial society would at first seem rather irreverent also.

In those earlier societies of the tribe and family relationship, authority was predominantly horizontal. In modern technical culture, the authority pattern is neither of a horizontal kinship variety nor

---

12. See Werner Heisenberg, *Physics and Philosophy: The Revolution in Modern Science,* Harpers, New York, 1958: For a shorter discussion see *Living Issues in Philosophy,* Fourth edition, by Harold H. Titus, American Book Co., New York, 1964, pp. 107-120; also *Science is a Sacred Cow,* Anthony Standen, Dutton, Everyman Paperback, New York, 1958; *The Science Myth,* Magnus Pyke, Macmillan, New York, 1962.

of a vertical pattern. These are replaced by more of a working team pattern. In industry it is the team of scientists that work together on a research project. The tribal setting of work groups is patterned by familial connections, while the modern industrial work groups are more task oriented. Team relationships at work tend to be of a different character than family connections. While in a society of city culture marked by individualism, God would be thought of more in an "I-Thou" relationship. The relationship is one of confrontation.

God is one who has authority over me. In the more primitive familial type He is more a part of the family, and the family a part of Him. In modern industrial society with the team experience the relationship becomes more one of alongsidedness, or an "I-You" relationship. It derives from work that is done together on a co-operative basis. This "I-You" relationship will influence the God concept. Already in many places one hears, especially younger people in their prayers, addressing God not as "Thou" but as "You."

In Jesus, God was willing to take His position of working within the group, of washing His fellows' feet and even of needing someone to carry His cross. Paul in Galatians, chapter four, hints at an "I-You" relationship when he speaks of the relationship as not that of a child or slave, but rather that of a son and heir. This would imply that the strictly vertical relationship of a father to a minor child is discarded for the adult relationship between a grown man and his father. This would indicate that the relationship of man to God comes from the work they do together and find joy in the partnership.

God wants man to be interested not only in Him but especially in his fellowman. In Jesus the religious quest is answered. Here man is freed to serve and love his neighbor. "Truly, I say unto you as you did it to one of the least of these my brethren, you did it to me" (Matthew 15:40). Industrialization, with men working side by side, could and should in the end help promote the brotherhood ideal with God as a co-worker for the good of all.

6. *Current Social Mobility*

Technical industrialization brings about conditions that cause people to be on the move much more than they were in the preceding rural era. In those days most folks had their particular piece of ground to take care of and extract their living from, hence had to, more or less, stay put. This has radically changed in modern industrial society when people of necessity move from city to city to find work for which they are qualified by virtue of their particular training and experience. All this makes for a high degree of social mobility.

Beginning as far back as Abraham who "obeyed when he was called to go out . . . not knowing where he was to go" (Hebrews 11:8), this tradition of mobility continued later in the release from Egyptian bondage, in the wilderness wanderings, in the Babylonian captivity, and finally even during the early Christian persecution. They knew that ". . . here we have no lasting city, but seek the city which is to come" (Hebrews 13:14).

The belief of Christians in the Resurrection and the Ascension is evidence of their refusal to allow their Lord to be localized and spatially restricted. Jesus is not a local deity but the Lord of History. Jesus said He is "the way" and the early Christians were known as the people of "the way." (Acts 9:2; 18:26; 24:14).

The Christian life as a journey repeatedly appears in Christian history, from St. John of the Cross to Dante's *Divine Comedy,* to Bunyan's *Pilgrim's Progress,* to Kierkegaard and more recently to Dietrich Bonhoeffer. Too often this idea has been individualized whereas the earlier visions were of a people moving together.

The church's social position after Constantine, led to a de-emphasis of this stranger and pilgrim motif. The church gradually made itself at home in the culture of its day as the Israelites did in the time of the monarchy. The temptation always has been to fashion a sacred civilization and transmute the Gospel into a Baal culture. This also happened in medieval times when Christendom was spatialized and became the religion of Western Europe.

The historical, universal, non-spatial genius of the Christian faith was not even recovered during the Reformation. The Reformation movement was mainly concerned with a reshuffling within Christendom, with the exception of the persecuted Anabaptist wing. Only with the missionary movement of the nineteenth century, and the ecumenical movement of the twentieth, did Christianity gradually again realize that this notion of a static Christendom was not really Christian. Today the secularization of so-called Christian countries, the appearance of non-Western churches in Asia and Africa, the renewed emphasis on eschatology in *The Theology of Hope* while continuing *The Search for a Usable Future* will all help to bring about a reawakening and rededication of Christians to *The Future of God*.[13]

Mobility can be dangerous and may indicate an unwillingness to

---

13. Jurgen Moltmann, *The Theology of Hope,* Harper, 1965; Martin E. Marty, *The Search for a Usable Future,* Harper, 1968; Carl E. Braaten, *The Future of God,* Harper, 1969.

take on responsibility. But on the whole, mobile people are less tempted than the settled ones to demote God into a local Baal. They will not so easily idolize a town, a nation, or a political structure as the definite and clear expression of how things have been and should remain. They will be more willing to change and move on.

Jesus was born during a journey, spent part of His childhood in exile, later was driven out of His home town and himself declared that He had no place to lay His head. In His "Great Commission," He calls upon His followers to "Go therefore and make disciples of all nations . . . teaching them to observe all that I have commanded you; and lo, I am with you always, to the close of the age" (Matthew 28:19-20).

7. *A Suggested Definition of God.*

The dictionary says that a definition is "a brief explanation of the exact meaning of a term." To define something is to say what is essential of the thing defined, which will not apply to anything else. A definition is a symbolic fence built around the item defined that excludes all nonessentials and includes all essentials of the respective item. Hence it is a very audacious, in fact an impossible undertaking, for a finite mind to attempt to define the infinite God. But even so by way of description and explanation the effort may be helpful. A meaningful descriptive definition of the Christian idea of God is given by W. A. Brown:

> God is the personal Spirit, perfectly good, who creates, sustains and orders the universe according to the wise, holy and loving character and purpose revealed in Jesus Christ; and who, through his Spirit, indwelling in man, is ever at work in the world, calling men out of their sin and misery into the kingdom of God, and by His redemptive grace, transforming individuals and society into the likeness of Christ. The name which best expresses his character, and which, since Christ, has become the characteristic Christian name for God, is Father.[14]

This statement contains three fundamental elements in the Christian idea of God. (1) It emphasizes personality in the highest ethical form. "God is the personal Spirit, perfectly good." (2) It stresses absoluteness. It is God "who creates, sustains and orders the universe . . ." He is the one and only supreme being on whom everything depends. (3) It describes God's character and His relation to the

---

14. W. A. Brown, *Christian Theology in Outline*, Scribners, 1921, pp. 98-99.

universe in terms of the revelation of Christ. What He does is done "according to the wise, holy, and loving character and purpose revealed in Jesus Christ." It is this third item which gives the definition its distinctively Christian character. The Jewish and Moslem religions also emphasize absoluteness in their idea of god, but the Christian religion conceives of God's personality and absoluteness in terms of the revelation we have in Jesus Christ, and that differentiates it from other religions.

This statement also indicates the Christian view of the relation between God and man. It includes the effects which God's Spirit had and still has on human life. According to the Christian idea it is God's nature to impart himself in sacrificial love as revealed in Jesus Christ. The historic Christ and the Holy Spirit belong with the Father into the Christian thought of God. The statement further states that God through His Spirit "is ever at work in the world . . . transforming individuals and society into the likeness of Christ." So we have here indicated not only what kind of being God is, but also what He has been and is now doing, as well as how He is operating, namely in the spirit "revealed in Jesus Christ." "Through His Spirit he is ever at work calling men out of their sin and misery into the kingdom of God." This Christian idea of Him is best expressed as "The God and Father of our Lord Jesus Christ" (I Peter 1:3). As His children we are to cooperate with Him in promoting His Kingdom here on earth.

D. ON KNOWING GOD

There always have been differences of opinion as to the possibility of knowing God. Even in scripture we find those who doubt if God can be known. For example, Job laments:

> Oh, that I knew where I might find him, that I might come even to his seat! I would lay my case before him and fill my mouth with arguments. I would learn what he would answer me, and understand what he would say to me . . . Behold, I go forward, but he is not there; and backward, but I cannot perceive him; on the left hand I seek him, but I cannot behold him; I turn to the right hand, but I cannot see him . . . Therefore I am terrified . . . for I am hemmed in by darkness, and thick darkness covers my face (Job 23:3-5, 8-9, 15-17).

Job did not doubt God's existence, he only complained that he could not be found. One might say that he looked for God in the wrong place, for the wrong reason, and with the wrong concept of God in

BASIC CHRISTIAN CONVICTIONS

mind. But nevertheless, he looked and God honored his looking. We read,

> Then the Lord answered Job out of the whirlwind: "Gird up your loins like a man; I will question you, and you declare to me. Will you even put me in the wrong? Will you condemn me that you may be justified?" (Job 40:6-8).

After God asks Job a few questions about nature and the universe, about life and death, Job repentantly exclaims:

> "I have uttered what I did not understand, things too wonderful for me, which I did not know . . . I had heard of thee by the hearing of the ear, but now my eye sees thee; therefore I despise myself, and repent in dust and ashes" (Job 42:3, 5-6).

On the other hand the Psalmist felt that it is not a question of finding God, but rather altogether impossible to get away from Him. He declares:

> O Lord, thou hast searched me and known me! Thou knowest when I sit down and when I rise up; thou discernest my thoughts from afar. Thou searchest out my path and my lying down, and art acquainted with all my ways. Even before a word is on my tongue, lo, O Lord, thou knowest it altogether. Thou dost beset me behind and before, and layest thy hand upon me. Such knowledge is too wonderful for me; it is high, I cannot attain it. Whither shall I go from thy spirit? Or whither shall I flee from thy presence? If I ascend to heaven, thou art there! If I make my bed in Sheol, thou art there! If I take the wings of the morning and dwell in the uttermost parts of the sea, even there thy hand shall lead me, and thy right hand hold me. If I say, "Let only darkness cover me, and let the light about me be night," even the darkness is not dark to thee, the night is bright as day; for darkness is as light with thee (Psalm 139:1-12).

1. *God As Person*

The stress of Jesus on the personal characteristic of God is necessary to really know God. God as only Ultimate Reality would be a vague, impersonal power, or if he were only an abstract idea like the First Cause, we might accept these concepts intellectually but He would have little relevance to our lives and would not provide us with much real meaning and understanding of life. The Greek philosophers thought of God as the First Principle, whereas Israel's prophets described God as a righteous Lord. Both the intellectual and the experiential approach are important.

Part of God's nature must be known and understood through the mind. God is rational, not irrational. His power is operative within His intelligence or purpose. He is the Prime Mover, the First Cause, the Divine Mind of the universe; but He is also more and beyond that a Personality. By this is meant that He can be experienced by other persons. If God is Love then He can best be known by man through experience. Love as an abstract idea is rather meaningless and powerless. But Love experienced is something very potent and meaningful. So when we say that God is personal we are merely trying to say that God can be experienced personally by man. God is personal in the sense that love is personal. He is like a Father and so can be known by His children. The New Testament stresses this personal side of God—of course as God, He may also be more than merely person, but not less. The word super-personal has been used to indicate this.

2. *Levels of Knowing*

There are different ways of knowing anything or anybody. Perhaps we should say different levels of knowing. For example some years ago in China the writer had a very severe case of oriental smallpox. Here too there are different levels of knowing possible. Just to *hear* people talk about smallpox is rather superficial, but nevertheless something can be learned in that way. To *read* about smallpox you would learn more and what one would learn would probably be more accurate also. To *see* somebody that actually has smallpox would give one an even more vivid impression. Doctors hear, read, study, and even see patients that actually have smallpox. However, actually experiencing and having smallpox oneself is still a different matter and will give knowledge of it in a different way.

Or, let us take a person like Dr. Albert Schweitzer. One way of learning about him would be to listen what folks who knew him have to say about him. That would be learning by *hearing*. Another method would be to *read* reports others have written, or books he himself has written. This would be a higher level than the first one. A third level would be to *see* and *hear* him speak in person. This would certainly give us information and impressions that the first two methods could not give. But the best way to really know Dr. Schweitzer would be to *live* with him and *share* his mind, his work, and his concerns.

So there are also different ways of knowing God, not only knowing about Him. One can *hear* other people talk about Him in Christian homes, schools or churches. Or one can *read* about Him in the Bible and other Christan literature. Or one can *see* Him or His work in the wonders of nature and in the lives of parents and other good people, in the history of Israel, the church, and of mankind as a whole. However, really to know God personally one must open one's life to Him, really *live with Him, share* His work, His purpose, and His concerns as portrayed by Jesus Christ and His Spirit.

3. *Commitment Necessary*

In John's Gospel we are told "If any man's will is to do his will, he shall know whether the teaching is from God or whether I am speaking on my own authority" (John 7:17). And again John quotes Jesus as saying, "And this is eternal life, that they know thee the only true God, and Jesus Christ whom thou has sent" (John 17:3).

Yes, hearing, reading, and seeing all will help, but the supreme test after all is experiencing God in one's own personal everyday life. The existence of God can not be absolutely proven by our finite minds, or He would not be God. Reason will help but can only give us intimations. Finally one must go beyond reason and in faith commit oneself to Him. Only by opening one's life to Him and sharing His life and concerns for persons and society will one experience God and be satisfied.

One can only learn to float on water as one lets go and commits oneself to it. The patient can only be healed as he commits himself to the surgeon and is willing even to become unconscious before the operation takes place. "God is love" (I John 4:8, 16) as revealed in Jesus Christ, but He only becomes a reality for us as we commit ourselves to Him in childlike faith and confidence.

E. SUMMARY AND CONCLUSION

In this chapter on "God, Our Father" we have considered: The Growing Yahweh Concept in the Old Testament; The Concept of God in the New Testament; The Concept of God in Christendom; and a section On Knowing God.

Only as we increasingly commit ourselves to "the God and Father of our Lord Jesus Christ," and so more fully share His concern for individual persons and human society, will we also be given more light, courage, power, joy, peace, and love, constantly to serve Him better and more effectively promote His Kingdom.

Albright, W. F., *Yahweh and the Gods of Canaan,* Doubleday, 1968.

Anderson, B. W., *Understanding the Old Testament,* Prentice-Hall, 1957.

Argyle, A. W., *God in the New Testament,* Lippincott, 1966.

Baillie, John, *The Sense of the Presence of God,* Scribners, 1962.

Barth, Karl, *Call for God,* Harper, 1967.

Braaten, C. E., *The Future of God,* Harper, 1969.

Buber, Martin, *Eclipse of God,* Harper, 1952.

Burkill, T. A., *God and Reality in Modern Thought,* Prentice-Hall, 1963.

Cauthen, K., *Science, Secularization and God,* Abingdon, 1968.

Cochrane, A. C., *The Existentialist and God,* Westminster, 1956.

Dewart, L., *Theism in a World Come of Age,* Herder & Herder, 1966.

Edwards, D. L., *The Honest to God Debate,* Westminster Press, 1963.

Farmer, H. H., *God and Men,* Abingdon, 1957.

Gilkey, Langdon, *The Renewal of God-Language,* 1968.

Grant, R. M., *Early Christian Doctrines of God,* Va., U., 1966.

Guthrie, H. H., *God and History in the Old Testament,* Seabury, 1960.

Hartsborne, C., *Philosophers Speak of God,* Univ. of Chicago, 1953.

Jenkins, D. E., *The Christian Belief in God,* Westminster, 1965.

Jenson, R. W., *God after God,* Bobbs-Merrill, 1969.

Johnson, A. R., *Israelite Conception of God,* Verry, 1961.

Kaufman, G. D., *Systematic Theology,* Part I, Scribner's, 1968.

Keys, Donald, ed., *God and the H-Bomb,* Bellmeadows, 1961.

Lewis, C. S., *The Christian Idea of God,* Macmillan, 1945.

Macquarrie, John, *God and Secularity,* Westminster Press, 1967.

Phillips, J. B., *Your God is too Small,* Macmillan, 1953.

Robinson, J. A. T., *Honest to God,* Westminster, 1963.

Soper, D. W., *God is Inescapable,* 1959.

von Balthasar, H. U., *The God Question and Modern Man,* Seabury, 1967.

Wright, G. E., *God Who Acts,* SCM Press, 1962.

Wolf, W. J., *Man's Knowledge of God,* Doubleday, 1955.

CHAPTER III

CREATION, GOD'S HANDIWORK

"The heavens are telling the glory of God; and the firmament proclaims his handiwork" (Psalm 19:1).

VARIOUS ANSWERS HAVE BEEN GIVEN TO THE QUESTION OF HOW TO explain the existence of the universe. The distinctiveness of the Christian view of God and His relation to the universe can be better understood and more appreciated when considered in contrast to other views on this question.

Besides primitive ideas of God and the universe we have Pantheism, identifying God with the universe; Dualism, where God and Satan are regarded as two antagonistic identities in the universe; Deism, emphasizing transcendence only and putting God beyond the reach of man; and Materialistic Mechanism, with the universe automatically going on according to cause and effect without any God at all. *Biblical Monotheism,* on the other hand, avoids all these extremes and insists on a cosmology that leaves God free as Creator, Preserver, and Director of the universe. Here God is free to find man and free to be found by man.

A.   THE BIBLICAL ACCOUNTS OF CREATION

The Hebrew view of creation is a very marked departure from other primitive views. It separates God from nature and distinguishes between man and nature. The Hebrews had contact with many cultures and freely borrowed from their mythologically-oriented neighbors, such as the Sumarians, Egyptians, Canaanites, Babylonians, and others, but they drastically modified what they borrowed.

In Genesis the sun, the moon, and the stars are called into being by God who puts them in the sky to light the world for man. They are not gods nor do they have any special power or control over man. They are creations of God and have no claim for any religious awe or worship. There are two creation stories in Genesis. The first one in Genesis 1:1—2:3 and the second one immediately following, beginning with Genesis 2:4 to the end of the chapter. These accounts are evidently designed to teach basic truths about creation. Let us briefly look at some of them.

1. *Nature not Magic*

The world within itself contains no explanation for its existence. Everything in the world depends upon something else. The tree depends upon seed, atmosphere, soil, sunshine, and each of these factors depend upon something else. The seed requires another tree to produce it, the soil comes from rock erosion, and so on. Nothing in the world, as we find it, is ultimate, it is all dependent upon something else. So we read, "In the beginning God created" (Genesis 1:1).

2. *The Creator Transcends Creation*

God transcends creation. He is beyond the natural processes of nature. He called nature into being. His relation to creation is one of freedom, not one of necessity. Each of the creation stories begins with emphasizing the fact that God is the creator. "In the beginning God created the heavens and the earth" (Genesis 1:1), and ". . . the Lord made the earth and the heavens" (Genesis 2:4). Throughout both accounts it is repeatedly stated that "God said," "God made," "God caused," "God formed," "God finished," and other such phrases, all indicating that God transcends creation.

3. *Creation Was Good*

God is good and His creation was good. Six times we read "And God saw that it was good" (Genesis 1:4, 10, 12, 18, 21, 25). And when it was all finished, with man also there, we read it was "very good" (Genesis 1:31). In some religions, nature is considered neutral or even evil and a curse, hence it is important to note that here it is considered good and a blessing. The material world is good but it can be misused.

4. *Man, the Crown of Creation*

Man is the crown of creation but, he nevertheless, is also a creature. He is not only differentiated from the rest of creation but is also to be distinguished from God. He is between God and the rest of creation. God is the creator and man is a creature, but not quite like the other creatures. In a real sense, he is also a creative creature made in the "image of God" and is a "living being" different from other creatures.

In Hebrew tradition the giving of names was important and had great meaning. So here every beast and bird was brought before man to see what he would call them; "and whatever the man called every living creature that was its name" (Genesis 2:19). In other words, man shares with God in creation. Man is neither to reverence nature nor to ravage it. His task is to tend it and make use of it and so assume the responsibility assigned to him by his creator to "subdue" it and have "dominion over" it, "to till it, and keep it."[1]

see class notes

5. *Order and Progress*

These creation stories are permeated with a sense of order and progress. Beginning when everything still "was without form and void, and darkness was upon the face of the deep, and the Spirit of God was moving over the face of the waters and God said 'Let there be light . . .'" and then He "separated the light from the darkness" calling the one "Day" and the other "Night," "And there was evening and morning, one day" (Genesis 1:1-5). From here on through, each day a special step in the picture as a whole is presented until man appears on the sixth day "and on the seventh day God . . . rested . . . from all his work . . . blessed . . . and hallowed it" (Genesis 2:3).

Admittedly the order may not be quite that indicated by modern science. But there is order, and there is purposive progress. This is not science nor history but symbolic oriental literature. The days of the early part of the story could not refer to twenty-four hour days for the sun does not come into the picture until the fourth day. Six times we are told "And there was evening and there was morning," indicating a certain day (Genesis 1:5, 8, 13, 19, 23, 31). A modern writer would have reversed this and said "there was morning and evening," but this ancient Hebrew was conscious that God moves from darkness to light, evening to morning, and not in the opposite direction. The purposive orderly progress here is from the void and darkness to order and light; to heaven and earth; to the sun, moon and stars; to vegetable and animal life; culminating in man made in God's image, as co-laborer with God.

The progression is from chaos toward cosmos, only the beginning is referred to, with great future potentiality of the entire creation, including man. The first story ends with man and the day of rest, while in the second story man enters the picture earlier, is placed in the garden, and ends with Eve being recognized by man as "bone of my bone and flesh of my flesh . . . and they became one flesh" (Genesis 23:24). The human family - God's Kingdom in miniature and potentiality.

---

1. For a fuller discussion of man see chapter IV.

✳ Man is not tied to nature by kinship. The lines of kinship in the Bible are temporal not spacial. Instead of reaching out to encompass animal and totem poles, they reach back to the stories of the fathers and forward to the fortunes of the children's children. The structure of Hebrew kinship is linear, historical and not cosmological. Nature is neither man's brother nor his god, as such it offers him no salvation. When he looks up to the hills, the Hebrew turns from them and asks "from where does my help come?" His answer is: Not from the hills but "my help comes from the Lord who made heaven and earth" (Psalm 121:1-2). In the Bible, neither man nor God is defined by his relationship to nature, which sets both of them free for history and makes nature available for man's use. Man is free to enjoy nature and delight in it. He is not a mere expression of nature, and nature is not a divine entity.

This world view provides an absolute precondition for the development of natural science. No real scientific breakthrough could have been possible without man being able to face the natural world unafraid. Wherever nature is thought of as an extension of man himself, or as the embodiment of the divine, the development of natural science, as we know it, is impossible and precluded. This means that the passing of many traditional religions is inevitable, or modern civilization in countries where such religions prevail is impossible.

The biblical creation stories are not philosophical speculations but expressions of religious faith in God as the Creator of the universe. The biblical account does not pretend to offer any explanation of the creative process, it simply declares that the stuff as well as the structure of the world has God as its author. Creation is not simply once-for-all-time, but in some real sense is a continuation. The creative process will not reach its goal until this present world is reshaped into "a new heaven and a new earth" (Revelation 21:1) wherein God's Kingdom will be more fully expressed. The world as it now is cannot be God's finished work of creation.

B. THE PROVIDENCE OF GOD

The Christian doctrine of Providence expresses the continued dependence of the world on God, and His continued active relationship to the world in the interest of the fulfillment of His ends, that He revealed in Christ. Providence can be thought of in two parts. One aspect would be His preservation of creation, and the other would be His directing it. It is difficult to think of God's preservation or sustaining creation aside from His directing or governing it. The two belong together and are included in the word Providence.

1. *Providence and History*

Providence is already implicit in the Genesis account of creation where man is made "in the image of God," as this implies potential development and growth of such a being. Providence implies a philosophy of history. The dominant Greek and Roman conception of history, as of Hinduism, is of a cyclical nature within which events repeat themselves resulting in an endless circular recurrence of things, without purpose and without goal. The Hebrew, on the other hand, had a linear view of history determined by a great ethical and spiritual God. This view found its most explicit and consummating expression in the life and teachings of Jesus Christ, according to which, there is over all a Fatherly purpose guiding history toward the accomplishment of His ends with men and nations for an ever fuller realization of His Kingdom. The Apostle Paul writes that even

> creation waits with eager longing for the revealing of the sons of God; for the creation was subjected to futility, not of its own will but by the will of him who subjected it in hope; because the creation itself will be set free from its bondage to decay and obtain the glorious liberty of the children of God. We know that the whole creation has been groaning in travail together until now; and not only the creation, but we ourselves, who have the first fruits of the Spirit, groan inwardly as we wait for adoption as sons, the redemption of our bodies. For in this hope we were saved (Romans 8:19-24).

Man is only relatively independent as he also is dependent upon divine Providence, however, not in a mechanical or slavish way. Man has a real but limited sphere in which he is to exercise rational foresight and control, a finite providence serving infinite Providence. But man is also able to turn against God and His Providence and treat Him as adversary, but man is not able to defeat God's purpose in the end. In this divine process the chosen people of the Old Testament, Jesus Christ, and the Church all have an important role to play. The world process is dependent upon God's Providence and adapted to ultimate ends while still respecting the existence of limited freedom of mankind.

God's creative, sustaining, and governing activity are in close relation to each other. He is above the world but also inwardly sustains the world. Thus He maintains the real existence of His creatures without surrendering His power to overrule them yet not violating their relative independence.[2]

2. *Concern for the Individual*

In the pre-Christian Jewish view God's interest was recognized as pertaining more to society as a whole than to the individual person. However, Jesus laid great emphasis on God's Fatherly providence including the individual, and not only the welfare of humanity in the mass. In the three parables of the Gospel according to Luke, chapter fifteen, Jesus speaks of the lost sheep, the lost coin, and the lost son, indicating this individual interest and love of God in a most striking and impressive way. On another occasion Jesus said:

> ". . . do not be anxious about your life, what you shall eat or what you shall drink, nor about your body, what you shall put on . . . Look at the birds of the air; they neither sow nor reap nor gather into barns, and yet your heavenly father feeds them. Are you not of more value than they? . . . Consider the lilies of the field, how they grow; they neither toil nor spin; and yet I tell you, even Solomon in all his glory was not arrayed like one of these. But if God so clothes the grass of the field, which today is alive and tomorrow is thrown into the oven, will he not much more clothe you . . . ? Therefore do not be anxious . . . your heavenly Father knows that you need them all" (Matthew 6:25-32).

God is interested in humanity as a whole, surely, but also in each person. It is only natural that there should be difficulties with this doctrine, especially in the light of modern science and the vastness of the universe. Even the Psalmist exclaimed: "When I look at thy heavens, the work of thy fingers, the moon and the stars which thou hast established; what is man that thou art mindful of him, and the son of man that thou dost care for him?" (Psalm 8:3-4). All this is difficult to comprehend. However, the expert librarian knows the individual books much better than a mere bookman, and the expert engineer knows the screws, bolts, pistons, levers, and details of a machine much better than the average mechanic. But these comparisons fall far short of the truth here referred to. The reality of God's individual care one can only come to appreciate through individual experience as the Psalmist suggested when he said: "O taste and see that the Lord is good! Happy is the man who takes refuge in him!" (Psalm 34:8).

---

2. W. M. Horton, *Christian Theology*, Harper, 1955, Chapter IV.

3. Cause and Effect

Experience and investigation indicate that there are certain principles being followed by God in the conduct of this world. The law of cause and effect is one of these principles. God is not arbitrary but regular and consistent in maintaining and directing the universe. Science accepts the principle of universality of law because it helps to explain things. Religion accepts it because it indicates something about God's character. God manifests himself through law, not in spite of it. Law is not a limitation but an expression of moral consistency of God's character. The same cause is followed by the same effect. Law indicates the regularity of God's working in nature.

This regularity is the very ground-basis of the development of rational life of mankind. Without it the universe would be a chaos and not a cosmos. No rational dealing on man's part, with nature or with fellowmen, would be possible without it. No results could be forecast. The reign of law or the uniformity of nature is thus not a limitation of the Divine working but, rather, a necessity for rational freedom of man. This also applies to the spiritual life. Paul writes:

> Do not be deceived; God is not mocked, for whatever a man sows, that he will also reap. For he who sows to his own flesh will from the flesh reap corruption, but he who sows to the Spirit will from the Spirit reap eternal life (Galatians 6:7).
> And Jesus said, "Are grapes gathered from thorns, or figs from thistles? So, every sound tree bears good fruit, but the bad tree bears evil fruit" (Matthew 7:16-17).

Here also, in the moral and spiritual realm, the purpose of God's working according to law and regularity is a beneficient one. This makes possible the formation of character and moral and spiritual development. This involves consequences for ill as well as for good. We cannot have the advantages of the reign of law without the possible disadvantages also. The possible disadvantages in the form of suffering by ourselves or others are involved in God's Fatherly providential working out His purposes by the method of law or uniform order.

4. Growth and Development

Another principle which God uses in directing the universe is growth and development. The scientific theory that expresses this is evolution. The astronomers see it in the slowly evolving formless chaos into a system of suns and planets. The biologist sees it in the organic world. The historian sees it in the story of humanity gradually emerging from barbarism into civilization. Paul writes:

Not that I already obtained this or am already perfect; but I press on to make it my own . . . I do not consider that I have made it my own; but one thing I do, forgetting what lies behind and straining forward to what lies ahead, I press on toward the goal for the prize of the upward call of God in Christ Jesus (Philippians 3:12-14).

Growth is possible only when some individuals advance faster than others and set new standards to which others later also gradually conform. Growth is not uniform. There are irregularities and even retrogressions. We are all influenced by others for good or evil. At times Providence uses one or a few individuals or even a nation to bless the many by getting them to move forward. Abraham and Moses were such persons. Greece helped promote intellectual and cultural development. Rome made its contribution by way of law and order. Israel led in moral and religious areas. Within each nation, however, there are certain individuals who lead out, ahead of the group, and thereby stimulate growth.

5. *Conflict and Cooperation*

Another method that God uses in His providential care of the universe is conflict and cooperation. Conflict may be observed in vegetable and animal life, as well as in human life. Of the countless numbers born, only a small portion survives and of these only a comparatively few reach maturity. Nature is full of struggle and conflict for existence and fuller life. Races which are weak have yielded to the stronger. The Christian, like other people, meets obstacles, inner and outer, and grows in overcoming them. Darwin made much of "Survival of the Fittest," and Nietzsche taught that "Might makes Right." In other words this principle can even become an excuse for abuse.

Cooperation is a much more sane and effective method than conflict, to promote the welfare of man in the providence of God. The stronger helping the weaker will even make the stronger a better person. Wealthy nations sharing their know-how and other resources with weaker nations on a cooperative basis, will promote the welfare of all to a much greater degree than mere conflict. Even, the strong cooperating with the strong, holds more promise for the good of each of them and the general welfare than does conflict. The Russian writer Peter A. Kropotkin has written specifically in opposition to some of Darwin's ideas, and made a real contribution in this area.[3]

---

3. *Mutual Aid: A Factor in Evolution,* N. Y., Knopf, 1917.

6. *Sacrificial Love*

In God's providential care and government of the world sacrificial love has an especially significant place. In animal life one sees the principle of sacrifice operating in motherhood. In man this instinct is transformed to a moral principle. In primitive society it too often is limited only to the family, the tribe, or even the nation. People are not isolated individuals whose interest can be separated from that of others. The attainment of one may mean the advancement of many, and the sacrifice of oneself in love may mean the blessing of all. This applies to the individual as well as to the group. In sacrificial love we have the means of social and individual progress.

Christ teaches this better way of willingness to accept suffering and sacrifice as the means of not only deepening love but even fuller self-realization. "For whoever would save his life will lose it; and whoever loses his life for my sake and the gospel's will save it" (Mark 8:35; cf. Matthew 10:39; 16:25; Luke 9:24). The importance of this principle is indicated by its repetition. Jesus has also demonstrated this principle by voluntarily laying down His own life and in love sacrificing His own self. He said: "For this reason the Father loves me, because I lay down my life . . . No one takes it from me, but I lay it down of my own accord" (John 10:17-18). Or consider the example we have not only in Jesus but in the Father himself, "For God so loved the world that he gave his only Son, that whoever believeth in him should not perish but have eternal life" (John 3:16). Sacrificial love is then the most important principle that God uses in sustaining and governing the world in His providence to promote His Kingdom among men.

C. Religion and Cosmology

The idea that is held of God will also determine the idea that is held of the universe and what the relationship is between the two. Although cosmology is not a religious subject, it is nevertheless based on certain philosophic and religious assumptions. Hence any revolutionary discovery of science may cause religious controversy. This happened in connection with the globular shape of the earth, its revolution around the sun, the circulation of the blood, the law of gravitation, the mutability of species, and other scientific discoveries. The conflict between science and theology became especially pronounced in connection with the Copernican, and Darwinian controversies.

1. The Biblical Cosmos

Biblical writers considered the earth flat and over arched by sort of an inverted bowl of the sky, in which the stars, the sun, and the moon wander over its surface in certain paths; with a reservoir of water above the heavens, and another one in the deep beneath the earth, by whose downpouring and upgushing the earth may be completely flooded (Genesis 7:11-12).

2. Aristotle and Ptolemy

This biblical view of the universe held sway for a long time but gradually gave way to the Aristotelian-Ptolemaic cosmology developed by a long series of scientific observations and discoveries in ancient Alexandria.[4] According to this theory the earth was the fixed center of the universe with the other heavenly bodies revolving around it.

By the thirteenth century Dante (1265-1321) and Aquinas (1225?-1274) had accepted this cosmology and found it congenial to the prevailing hierarchical patterns of their day. Hell, the most imperfect place, was thought to be located at the very center of the earth, and the earth was at the center of the universe, with all imperfections bounded by the sphere of the moon. From there on were thought to be rising degrees of perfection in concentric circles beyond the moon to the sun and the stars, each controlled by its own rank of guardian angels, till at last came the highest heavenly sphere of absolute perfection with God's throne consummating the whole.

3. Copernicus and Darwin

The revolution of Copernicus (1473-1543) rudely shocked the medieval world by displacing the earth and man from their central position and promulgating the theory that the earth and the planets revolve about the sun. However by the early eighteenth century such thinkers as Sir Isaac Newton (1642-1727) and Gottfried Wilhelm von Leibnitz (1646-1716) had reconciled their Christian faith with an acceptance of this system.

The modern idealistic movement in philosophy, from Immanuel Kant (1724-1804) through George Wilhelm Friedrich Hegel (1770 1831) and others, has generally accepted the Newtonian view of the external, phenomenal world, while subordinating all this to a spiritual, inner world that is half-hidden and half-revealed by its outward appearance.

---

4. Aristotle - a Greek Philosopher 384-322 B.C.; Ptolemy - a Greek-Egyptian mathematician, astronomer, and geographer of Alexandria 127-131 A.D.

Since Charles Darwin (1809-1892) and his evolutionary theory, Christian thought has been going through another major revolution in its world view. The results of this, are not yet fully clear.

4. *Recent Scientific Trends*

In more recent times, when to Darwinian fluidity are added Albert Einstein's (1879-1955) relativity, Werner Heisenberg's (1901-?) principle of uncertainty or indeterminacy, and Alfred North Whitehead's (1861-1947) concept of organism, and contributions of other scientists, there are new adjustments to be made which further change the Newtonian world view and make it more flexible and less absolute. At present the very foundations of science are undergoing radical change again. Now in subatomic investigations seemingly the experimenter cannot, as he did in classical experiments, hold certain factors constant while varying others. If this is the case it would have profound implications for the notion of cause and effect. Percy W. Bridgeman says that "seldom in the history of physics . . . has there been such a radical difference of fundamental outlook between the acknowledged leaders." Arthur Holly Compton (1892-1962) another outstanding physicist says that it is "no longer justifiable to use physical law as evidence against human freedom."[5]

In spite of various shifts in emphasis, Christian thinkers on the whole have always preserved a rather common view of God's relationship to the universe and man. God and nature are not one and the same, but two and they are different from each other. Both have real existence, however the universe having been created by God is dependent upon Him. He providentially sustains it and in His sovereignty will finally bring about His Kingdom as the consummation of it all.

D. MIRACLE AND PRAYER

Christians through the ages, have clung to the belief that Divine Providence is looking after all our needs. It is, however, obvious

---

5. Sidney Hook, ed., *Determinism and Freedom in the Age of Modern Science,* Collier Books, 1961, p. 57; Arthur H. Compton, "Science and man's Freedom," *Atlantic Monthly,* Oct. 1957, pp. 61-74; Werner Heizenberg, *Physics and Philosophy: The Revolution in Modern Science,* Harper, 1958; Anthony Standen, *Science Is a Sacred Cow,* Dutton, Everyman Paperback, 1958; Magnus Pyke, *The Science Myth,* Macmillan, 1962; Pierre Teilhard de Chardin, trans. *The Divine Milieu,* Harper, 1960, *The Phenomenon of Man,* Harper, 1961, *The Future of Man,* Harper, 1964.

that we are not kept from pain, sorrow and death. Still the Christian faith has always affirmed that the Heavenly Father does exercise a guiding providence over human affairs, including individuals as well as society in general. The God who holds all the heavenly spheres in their respective courses is the same God of whom Jesus said "even the hairs of your head are all numbered" (Matthew 10:30). This world is of God's own making, including so-called causal law. It would be preposterous to suppose that He is powerless to express His love for individuals and society in a world of His own making, and where persons everywhere express their particular concerns for each other every hour of the day.

1. The Problem of Causal Law

The concept of causal law is not a rigid framework but an abstraction, a formula or a set of relationships in accordance with which certain sequences occur. No law taken by itself defines the course of actual events. Every event represents the convergence of many forces and it would take a complex formula to fully describe the orderly ways of God in any one event. God is faithful to His ordered system. But the ways of "the Father of lights with whom there is no variation or shadow due to change" (James 1:17) also includes the constant concern and care of His children. Scientific knowledge gives no reason for doubting the faith that divine concern has room for effective expression within the order God established.[6]

Certainly God would not consider the physical system He has created as of more importance than the purpose for which it was brought into being. If His purpose originally was a loving concern to create persons and to commune with them so that they would choose to serve Him and share His fellowship, He hardly would let the orderly procedure of causal law prevent Him from doing what might be needed to achieve that purpose. Naturally such events would not happen often or the formulas of natural science would have no meaning at all. Moreover dependable causal law is important for the development of moral persons. Only in a world where God "makes his sun rise on the evil and on the good, and sends rain on the just and on the unjust" (Matthew 5:45) alike, can responsibility and character be developed. Hence God would not

---

6. L. Harold DeWolf, *A Theology of the Living Church,* Harper, 1953, p. 125. For "mysteries that defy the mind of man" see Edwards, Frank,- *Stranger than Science,* ACE Books, Inc., 1959.

lightly contradict the formulas by which He also intended men to predict and partially control events.

In any seeming contradiction of causal laws it need not necessarily be assumed that God has violated His system of governance over the world. As yet we do not know all of these physical laws or how they work. An event may seemingly contradict our knowledge of natural law as of a given time, but later scientific developments may completely eliminate the contradictions or even enable the prediction and control of them.

2. *Miracle*

For the believer, any event that helps him better to understand and see God is a miracle. God can use any event or experience to reveal himself more fully to an individual so that it leads to faith and so becomes a miracle for the person who meets God in that particular event. The same event may not be miraculous to an unbeliever; he will have some other explanation.

There is nothing in the universe, including causal chain, independent of God. Without Him the non-miraculous and the miraculous could not occur. An unusual event may become an occasion for greater faith, but that is not true of all unusual events. From the Christian point of view the significance of an event or experience is dependent upon the power it has to help a person to see and meet God. The Christian asserts that the Creator upholds and directs the universe at all times. Whether the events that occur seem as ordinary or extraordinary they happen because of the creative and maintaining power of God. But any event, routine or spectacular from our human point of view, can become the occasion for a larger vision of and greater faith in God our Heavenly Father.[7]

There is another aspect to miracle that should not be overlooked. The insight that law is universal is important but not as important as the deeper insight that it is only in human consciousness that we find law at all. Thus the supernatural receives its true meaning from the personal, and the false antithesis between natural and supernatural is dissolved. The supernatural is the natural, seen in its spiritual meaning. The natural is supernatural and finds its expression in forms that make possible the discovery of its real worth and meaning as the natural, for God is immanent in the world. As the super-

---

7. George W. Forell, *The Protestant Faith,* Prentice-Hall, Inc., 1960, pp. 125-126.

natural, God transcends the world as personality always transcends its own expression. The events of the most revealing significance are not those of mystery and unreason, but rather those that reveal the permanent principles that serve most to bring order and unity into life. Hence the supernatural must be sought not so much in the physical but rather in the spiritual aspect of the world.

Through personal experiences we discover order and beauty in the world as well as worth and meaning in life. It is through great personalities that we gain our most direct contact with the divine mind. And it is in personal experience that we find miracles in the religious sense. Wherever and whenever man is conscious of receiving new insight and power for communication with God that is a miracle in the religious sense. Outward events may be given supernatural significance only if it is thought that through them such insight and power have come to persons. If this be so, it is clear that miracles must be recurring in every truly religious life.[8]

3. *Prayer*

Prayer is meaningful if God is personal as Christ reveals Him. If we are His children, it must be possible for Him to speak to us and for us to hear Him. If this world is God's creation and in His providence, is under His continual care and interest, it must be possible for us to recognize Him by His present working as well as by His works of the past.

There is much misunderstanding and misinterpretation regarding prayer. What does it mean to pray? Do we know better than God what should happen and are we trying to give God advice? Prayer is not like sending an order to somebody who has to obey. This is a magical concept of prayer and there are religions where prayer is a form of magical incantation which can be used, it is thought, to make the gods do something that they apparently do not care to do. The prayer-wheel, the prayer beads, or the long repetition of phrases, even if amplified over the loudspeaker as in Moslem countries, are examples of this sacrilegious distortion of prayer.

The essential ingredients of Christian prayer are faith and sincerity. Perhaps our most sincere prayers are those uttered when we are in trouble. Such prayers are a real expression of our dependence upon God, as children are dependent upon their parents. As Christians we can and should speak with God about everything. He may

---

8. W. A. Brown, *Christian Theology in Outline,* Scribners, 1921, p. 229.

BASIC CHRISTIAN CONVICTIONS

not grant all our requests but still He will hear our prayers. Although He knows what we need, He still wants us to talk it over with Him as that is the way of personal fellowship. Prayer is the most profound and meaningful expression of fellowship.

Whenever the Bible speaks about prayer it speaks of the father-child relationship to which prayer gives active expression. There has never been a leader, a prophet, an apostle, or a saint who did not pray. In the person of Christ we find God's clearest word to man. He is not only the supreme miracle, He is also the supreme example when it comes to prayer. The final proof that any particular event is really communication between God and man, or vice versa, is the fact that it promotes and strengthens in persons the type of character which we see in Jesus Christ.[9]

E.   The Problem of Evil

The presence of evil in the world has been a great puzzle to man. How can God be good, loving, and all-powerful, with so much evil and suffering in the world? The Christian affirms that there is only one God and that the same God we meet in our personal experiences is also the creator of all that is. This relation of God to creation gives meaning to the universe. But there is the problem of evil which does not fit into this meaningful relation. The Christian holds that God is good, that He is almighty, and that evil is real. This presents a problem. The dilemma can be avoided if any one of these three propositions is denied. But that is not a satisfactory solution. There is no neat answer to this problem. The phenomena of evil can be divided into two categories, natural evil and human evil.

1.   *Natural Evil*

Natural evil originates in the order of nature. Among these would be tornadoes demolishing homes and crops, floods ruining property of the rich as well as the poor, earthquakes destroying cities and people living in them. Natural evil is destructive of human meaning, human accomplishment, and human values. Then there are also the so-called "blind alleys" of evolution, such as the dinosaurs which have perished completely. Or the various creatures that live on others and maintain themselves only at the cost of other living creatures. This may not be considered so bad but it also goes on in

---

9. See also section on prayer in Chapter X.

exactly the opposite direction where worms or other parasites live at the expense of the higher forms of life.

Another aspect of natural evil is the problem of pain and suffering, both human and animal. Some pain is necessary for the maintenance of our life and safety, but why should it continue after it has served its alerting function?[10]

Pain makes us jerk our hand from the hot stove or electric wire, but it continues long after this warning function is fulfilled. In some forms of cancer seemingly nothing can be done to relieve the pain of the victim until he is released by death. These aspects of nature over which we have no real control and which seem so contrary to the meaning of life are a deep mystery when it comes to the relation of God's providence for His creation and creatures.

2. *Human Evil*

Some evil results from human choice. There may also be some relation here to natural evil. Floods, for example, can often be traced to the exploitation of forests by an earlier generation. Generally however, human evil seems to be confined to human affairs, as for example, in war. Even though population pressure may help to set the stage for war, actual hostilities depend upon organized human endeavor. Even with worthy objectives of war, such as freedom or protection, there come such evils as mass killings, wholesale destruction, and a host of personal and social problems.

The man ignoring a stop sign on the highway may involve innocent parties along with himself in an auto accident. Or the person leaving the garbage container uncovered involves the neighborhood in a plague of flies. In these cases the effects arising from human choices extend beyond those immediately involved as victims. There is much human evil resulting directly from human choice, as in the case of lying, stealing, and murder. Both natural and human evil seems to be blind, chaotic, meaningless and does not conform to the patterns one would expect in a world created and controlled by a good and almighty God.

---

10. For an interesting and helpful discussion on the value of pain see: Dorothy Clark Wilson, *Ten Fingers for God,* McGraw Hill, 1965, dealing with a surgeon's quest to combat the ravages of leprosy in India by restoring the possibility to feel pain. As blind folks are helped by "seeing dogs," so lepers are helped by cats that keep away rats, so at night, they do not eat the fingers and toes of lepers who ordinarily feel no pain in affected parts.

3. Is Evil Needed to Promote the Good?

There are those who feel that evil and good are only relative and a contrast is needed in order to know the difference. One's appreciation of love is greater if one has also experienced hate, one can only know light by also knowing darkness. A good apple tastes better if one has also known a rotten or a sour one. Must one experience sickness to appreciate health? One's appreciation may be greater, but that the one is necessary to have, or even be conscious of the other, is questionable.

Others maintain that in order to achieve anything worthwhile in life certain inconveniences and hard work are necessary. In order to develop certain qualities of character one must go through experiences that require patience, courage, and faithfulness. According to this view, personal hardship is good training for higher character values. No doubt there is some truth in the statement that with courage, patience and endurance one can extract some good from many evil experiences. However that is not the same as to consider this the purpose of evil itself.

Another aspect of this point of view is that evil only appears as such from a short-range view, and that if the long-range view is taken the whole picture can be seen and the end is good. As an example, Alexander the Great's conquests are cited. They brought untold hardship and suffering as all wars do. Yet as a result a common language was spread over the then known world, making a later world peace possible and enabling the early Christian missionaries to be understood wherever they went. So, it is said, seen from the total results, Alexander's conquests were a good and not a bad thing. This is certainly not true of all evil. This argument really does not deal with present evil which is still evil even if ultimately some good may come from it.

4. Is Evil Punishment for Sin?

That evil is punishment for sin also has some truth in it. According to this view the good man prospers and the evil one fails and suffers. Thus, when tragedy strikes a "good" family their goodness is questioned and thought to be only superficial. In the Bible we have Job as a blameless friend of God, suffering loss of everything including his health. His friends insisted that he must be guilty of hidden sins and should repent. Job however refuses to accept the accusation although he finally finds no satisfactory answer. Nevertheless in spite of all the suffering he does not give up his faith in God and is sure that sin is not the final and full answer to suffering. When the disciples met a blind youth and asked Jesus:

> "Rabbi, who sinned, this man or his parents, that he was born blind?" Jesus answered, "It was not that this man sinned, or his parents, but that the works of God might be made manifest in him. . . ." (John 9:2-3).

Sin brings evil but not all evil can be traced to the sin of the respective persons suffering.

5. Is Evil the Work of the Devil?

One of the most popular answers to the question of evil is that it is the work of a host of demons, directed by the Devil himself, all trying to defeat God's purposes. Although in the end, God will be victorious, according to this view, nevertheless during this life God's good creation is twisted to produce suffering and evil of all kinds. Not only are there catastrophies caused by nature, but there are also the most subtle perversions of the best things in life. Spiritual pride can infect the heart of the saint. Human love can degenerate into licentiousness. There seems to be warfare going on between spiritual beings, God and the Devil.[11]

But there also are difficulties with this view. Is this a universe or a multiverse? Are we dualists or monotheists? To remain monotheists and account for the origin of the Devil, it is argued that he was created by God as an angel and later rebelled so now is fighting God and all His works. Jesus often speaks of Satan and the Devil. Saint Paul writes that,

> the man of lawlessness is revealed, the son of perdition, who opposes and exalts himself against every so-called god or object of worship, so that he takes his seat in the temple of God, proclaiming himself to be God . . . The coming of the lawless one by the activity of Satan will be with all power and with pretended signs and wonders, and with all wicked deception . . . (II Thessalonians 2:3-10).

Peter writes that,

> God did not spare the angels when they sinned, but cast them into hell and committed them to pits of nether gloom to be kept until the judgment (II Peter 2:4; cf. Jude 6).

But even all this does not explain the origin of Satan or the origin

---

11. See H. R. Niebuhr, *Radical Monotheism and Western Culture*, 1960, Harpers, ch. 2.

of this temptation to pride, that in the traditional view, made the angels fall. In fact if they are kept in "pits of nether gloom" and "eternal chains" the origin of all this basic and irrational evil in the world now is all the more a mystery.

6. *Is God Limited?*

Another answer to the origin of evil, stressed by Edgar Brightman and others, is that God is limited. God is good but He is unable always to make His goodness prevail. Plato (427-347 B.C.) also thought that the Demiurge was struggling to impress form and order on recalcitrant matter. Zoroaster (660-583 ? B.C.), the Persian religious leader, also held that two forces, incompatible and inherently antagonistic, existed from the beginning. The one was Ahura Mazda, Lord of Wisdom, the God of light, life, truth and goodness; and the other was Angra Mainyu, the Daeva of darkness, later becoming the Diu and finally, in English, the Devil. He is lord of darkness and the father of the lie. These two forces are thought to have myriads of assistants in the form of angels and demons. In the struggle finally the Lord of Wisdom will however win and even convert the other one.[12]

Brightman however insists that the limitation cannot be something outside of God, since everything has its origin in God alone.[13] Evil also is something within God, which He is trying to overcome. According to this view the whole natural order is a limitation on God to which He must conform. He cannot make a square circle, or a round triangle, or unequals equal, or truth false. So, while God would gladly end all earthly evil, this cannot be destroyed without also destroying the possibility of good. The very possibility of God achieving the good means also the possibility of evil. This only lays the problem within God and does not solve our question of its origin. Many would disagree with Brightman and insist that God is not subject to limitations other than those of His own choosing.

7. *Is Evil an Illusion?*

In a book entitled *Theodicy,* Gottfried Wilhelm von Leibnitz (1646-1716) a German mathematician and philosopher argued that God was perfect in power, wisdom, and goodness. But since God is

---

12. R. E. Hume, *The World's Living Religions,* Scribners, 1950, pp. 201-205.
13. Edgar S. Brightman, *A Philosophy of Religion,* Prentice-Hall, 1940, pp. 336-40.

good as a rational being He can only choose the best. Hence His creative activity results in the best possible world. God is limited in His freedom since He is under moral necessity and can only choose the best. Hence evil is only an illusion due to man's shortsightedness.

Pantheistic religions, that make everything God, tend to view the material world as something less than real and consider only the inner spiritual reality as real. They hold that since evil is so intimately related to the physical world one can escape it by concentrating on the inner life. This view goes beyond the idea that in the long run evil will seem to be good. Unless we train ourselves through spiritual disciplines we do not see things as they really are and so are deceived. This view holds that there is no objective reality to evil as such. Its appearance is only due to human shortcoming in apprehension. But this view gives no answer to the problem of evil other than to assert that it does not really exist and so does not matter. It does not help us to differentiate between delusion and reality. If evil is unreal, perhaps the whole world, and even God himself is also unreal.

8. *Evil Originates in the Will*

Most theologians are inclined to find the source of moral evil in man's will rather than in God or the structure of the universe itself. Man with modern science can do something to mollify natural evil and in some cases even eliminate it altogether. And with moral evil, which has its source in man's own choice of values, man certainly can reduce, although perhaps not altogether eliminate it with education and proper social guidance and development.

Already Saint Augustine (354-430 A.D.) held that the origin of human evil is located in the will.[14] Temptation has no influence, he argues, on a pure man but only on one who already desires evil. Even the serpent, in the suggestion to Eve to disobey God, would not have appealed to her had she not first already been envious of God. If evil is traced to fallen angels, then here too we are confronted with an evil will, that in its free choice decided upon an evil course. Moral evil is falling away from God. A failure to adhere to God produces evil and corrupts the natural order that was created good. God is never evil, it is man who goes contrary to God and produces evil. God is good, but man produces evil by abusing the good.

This is no complete or fully satisfactory answer. It does not even refer to natural evil but only human evil. The Genesis account indi-

---

14. Augustine, *The City of God*, XII-7.

cates how evil might have come into the world but not why. Ultimately evil means the perversion of what is good, perversion through willfull misdirection away from God.[15]

9. *The Christian Attitude Toward Evil*

What then is the practical Christian attitude toward evil although its origin and meaning cannot be fully solved? A Christian distinguishes between God's purposive and permissive will. God purposes only good, but having given man freedom He will permit him to indulge even in evil. Freedom of choice is necessary for development of character. And for choice to be real, there must be a number of possibilities, ranging from good to others not so good, and even evil. Only so can character be developed. In order to make this possible Paul Hessert lists four conditions that are necessary.[16]

First, there must be a dependable and stable environment in which to make human choices. This is the picture of the world of causal law. Our choices would have no meaning if one day a dropped ball would fall to the ground and another day it would soar into the air. Decisions require a stable background.

Second, as human beings we must have sensitivity to our natural environment. This sensitivity must be dependable. Sensitivity consists of smell, sight, taste, sound, touch as well as inner feelings. Man's sensitivity with his capacity to remember and anticipate is superior awareness. Sensitivity sufficiently stimulated gives pain. To eliminate pain, sensitivity would need to be eliminated, making us less than human.

Third, choices must have definite results and consequences. Decisions would mean nothing if outcome would make no difference. This means that if I make the wrong decisions then the result must be endured. Learning is itself the result of choice. Learning is an achievement and at times we must act in ignorance with the attendant possibility of evil outcome. Yet without the possibility of choice with some unknown possibilities of outcome, freedom would be impossible and unreal.

Fourth, there must be a community of persons responsible to each other. To become a human being in the full sense, a person must live

---

15. For a stimulating discussion on Evil see John Hick, *Evil and the God of Love,* Harper and Row, 1965.
16. Paul Hessert, *Introduction to Christianity,* Prentice-Hall, 1958, pp. 245-250.

in human society. The capacities for decision are only developed in human relations. Learning to speak, or the meaning of love, can only be acquired in society and are based upon personal decisions. Yet the fact that we are bound to each other in community as human beings, brings about conditions that sometimes result in suffering because of the choices that are being made.

These four items: a dependable world, our sensitivity, consequence of decisions, and human interrelatedness, Hessert points out, make possible the highest reaches of our spirits in response to God and the universe by providing the context for our freedom, but at the same time also make evil possible. Evil is not good, but it is good that we have the possibility of choice, and choice may result in evil. Why this is so we do not know, but choice is necessary for our development as responsible human beings.

It naturally follows then, that the Christian attitude toward evil is not to ignore it, or deny its existence, or to blame God or the Devil for it, but to do what we can to understand, control, avoid, and eradicate it. God created man to have "dominion" over the earth and that he might "subdue" it, all for the welfare and growth of man himself. So when a tornado arises the Christian attitude is not to try and placate some storm-god but to exert such measures of control and safety as are possible. This attitude of modern western science, namely to understand nature in order to control it, has very definite Christian roots. In the gospels Jesus is presented as struggling with demonic forces and overcoming them. Persons are restored to sanity and health by the superior power of God (Luke 11:14-23) and the disciples are asked to do the same (Mark 6:7). For the Christian there is only one ultimate power, and He is at work to defeat evil and bring suffering to an end. In this struggle human beings are called upon to cooperate. This gives meaning to human life with all its struggle.

If ultimate moral evil is the evil will, then the defeat of it depends upon the redemption of man. That evil will in man expresses itself in the perversion of his dominion over nature and directing it away from God. Evil is real, but not final - in the end God will overcome it. So the prophets picture the days when even war will be abolished.

> It shall come to pass in the latter days that . . . he shall judge between many peoples, . . . and they shall beat their swords into plowshares, and their spears into pruning hooks; nation shall not lift up sword against nation, neither shall they learn war any more; but they shall sit every man under his vine and under his fig tree, and none shall make them afraid; for the mouth of the Lord of hosts has spoken (Micah 4:1-4; cf. Isaiah 2:2-4).

And even the wild animals shall live in peace:

> The wolf shall dwell with the lamb, and the leopard shall lie down with the kid, and the calf and the lion and the fatling together, and a little child shall lead them. The cow and the bear shall feed; their young shall lie down together; and the lion shall eat straw like the ox. The suckling child shall play over the hole of the asp, and the weaned child shall put his hand on the adder's den. They shall not hurt or destroy in all my holy mountain; for the earth shall be full of the knowledge of the Lord as the waters cover the sea (Isaiah 11:6-9).

And then there is John's vision of the victory over all evil including death:

> Then I saw a new heaven and a new earth; for the first heaven and the first earth had passed away, . . . and I heard a great voice from the throne saying, "Behold, the dwelling of God is with men. He will dwell with them, and they shall be his people, and God himself will be with them; he will wipe away every tear from their eyes, and death shall be no more, neither shall there be mourning nor crying nor pain any more, for former things have passed away" (Revelation 21:1-4).

While eradication of evil is the long-term answer to this problem, something must still be said for those called to endure all sorts of evil in the present. Here Christianity holds that endurance in faith along with all possible efforts toward the elimination of evil is the only answer. Endurance can work for good in us. As Paul puts it:

> we rejoice in our sufferings, knowing that suffering produces endurance, and endurance produces character, and character produces hope, and hope does not disappoint us, because God's love has been poured into our hearts through the Holy Spirit which has been given to us (Romans 5:3-5).

Enduring evil with faith in God gives life a quality it could not have otherwise. To those, who are called to endure suffering, God offers the transformation that only faith can effect. Paul says:

> We know that in everything God works for good with those who love him . . . No, in all these things we are more than conquerors through him who loved us. For I am sure that neither death, nor life, nor angels, nor principalities, nor things present, nor things to come, nor powers, nor height, nor depth, nor anything else in all creation, will be able to separate us from the love of God in Christ Jesus our Lord (Romans 8:28, 37-39).

10. *Evil a Mystery*

There is always a great margin of mystery when we consider the ways of God. God would not be God if it was otherwise. When confronting actual pain and sorrow we can at best only "see in a mirror darkly" and can only "know in part" what God means to do for us (I Corinthians 13:12). Perhaps suffering could not fully serve its purpose for us if we could understand the whole meaning of it. Perhaps it is God's purpose that we should be perplexed, intellectually and practically, by the existence of pain, suffering and trouble. Perhaps their purpose is only served as long as we cannot be at peace with them. So we must have faith and struggle with them until we enter the heavenly city where sin has no place and all tears are wiped away.

F. SUMMARY AND CONCLUSION

In this chapter on the Universe we have considered the Biblical Accounts of Creation; the Providence of God; Religion and Cosmology; Miracle and Prayer; and the Problem of Evil. Although there are many aspects of the Universe that are a mystery to man, especially the problem of evil, the Christian can still sing in confidence and faith:

This is my Father's world,/ And to my listening ears,
   All nature sings, and round me rings,/ The music of the spheres.
This is my Father's world,/ I rest me in the thought
   Of rocks and trees, of skies and seas-/ His hand the wonders
      wrought.

This is my Father's world,/ O let me ne'er forget
   That, though the wrong seems oft' so strong,/ God is the ruler yet.
This is my Father's world,/ The battle is not done,
   Jesus who died shall be satisfied, and earth and heaven be one.

—Maltbie D. Babcock, *Mennonite Hymnary,* No. 48

FOR FURTHER READING ON CREATION

Ames, Gerald, - *The Earth's Story,* N. Y., The Educational Society, 1962.

Asimov, Isaac, - *The Wellsprings of Life,* London, Abelard-Shuman, 1960.

Bondi, Hermann, - *The Universe at Large,* N.Y., Anchor Books, 1960.

Barth, Karl, - *Creator and His Creature,* Allenson, 1961.

Bube, R. H., ed., - *Christianity and Science,* Eerdmans, 1968.

Bonhoeffer, D., - *Creation and the Fall,* Macmillan, 1965.

Calder, Ritchi, - *Man and the Cosmos,* Praeger, Inc., N.Y., 1968.

Clark, H. W., - *Genesis and Science,* Southern Pub., 1967.

Dobzhansky, Theo. G., - *Mankind Evolving,* Yale Univ. Press, 1962.

Dykema, B., - *In the Beginning,* Carlton, 1970.

Ferre, Nels F. S., - *Evil and the Christian Faith,* Harper, 1947.

Fitch, W., - *God and Evil,* Eerdmans, 1969.

Gilkey, Langdon, - *Maker of Heaven and Earth,* Doubleday, 1959.

Heuer, Kenneth, - *The End of the World,* Rinehart, 1953.

Hick, John, - *Evil and the God of Love,* Harper, 1965.

Kaufman, G. D., - "The Christian Understanding of the World," Part II, *Systematic Theology,* Scribners, 1968.

Lewis, C. S., - *The Problem of Pain,* Macmillan, 1944.

Lewis, Edwin, - *The Creator and the Adversary,* Cokesbury, 1948.

Messel, Harry, ed., - *The Universe and its Origin,* St. Martin's Press, 1964.

Morris, Henry M., - *The Twilight of Evolution,* Baker Book House, 1963.

Neville, R. C., - *God the Creator,* Univ. of Chicago, 1968.

Overman, Richard W., - *Evolution and the Christian Doctrine of Creation,* Westminster, 1964.

Pike, Nelson, ed., - *God and Evil,* Prentice-Hall, 1964.

Riseley, Loren C., - *The Firmament and Time,* Atheneum Press, N.Y., 1960.

Scheffezyk, L., - *Creation and Providence,* Herder, 1970.

Shapley, Harlow, - *Of Stars and Man* (Rev. Ed.), Beacon Press, 1964.

Teilhard de Chardin, Pierre, - *Hymn of the Universe,* Harper, 1965.

White, John F., - *Study of the Earth,* Prentice-Hall, 1962.

CHAPTER IV

MAN, HIS MAJESTY

AND MISERY

What is man that thou art mindful of him,
  and the son of man that thou dost care for him?
Yet thou hast made him a little less than God,
  and dost crown him with glory and honor.
Thou hast given him dominion over the works of thy
  hands;
  thou hast put all things under his feet

(Psalm 8:4-6; cf. Heb. 2:6-8)

MAN IS THE CROWN OF CREATION AND THE ABOVE WORDS INDICATE his majesty when compared to the rest of creation. Still, man has always been a problem to himself and his misery is deep and real. Man's nature is complex and his destiny is hard to foresee. He possesses great and wonderful potentialities but his failure to realize these to a greater degree causes much frustration and deep disappointment. As Paul puts it:

> I do not understand my own action . . . I can will what is right, but I cannot do it. For I do not do the good I want, but the evil I do not want, is what I do (Romans 7:15, 19).

How is this rational, language-using, tool-making, culture-producing, religiously-inclined, and worldly-minded being to be understood? He can be so humble and yet so lordly. From time immemorial man has asked himself: What am I? Where did I come from? Why am I here? Whither am I going? How can I determine my direction?

A. THE ORIGIN OF MAN

In Genesis we have two accounts of creation. The first one we find in Genesis 1:1--2:3, and the second one just following the first one, Genesis 2:4 ff. In both of these accounts man is portrayed as of divine origin. In both accounts man is considered above nature and capable of fellowship with his creator. We read:

So God created man in his own image, in the image of God he created him; male and female he created them. And God blessed them, and God said to them, "Be fruitful and multiply, and fill the earth and subdue it; and have dominion . . . over every living thing that moves upon the earth" (Genesis 1:27, 28).

And in the second account we read:

then the Lord God formed man of the dust from the ground, and he breathed into his nostrils the breath of life; and man became a living being (Genesis 2:7).

Through the body man is rooted in nature, "of the dust from the ground," but through his spirit he is raised above nature and related to the Creator himself, "in the image of God he created him." It is of interest to note that in the first creation account man enters the picture only on the sixth day, while in the second account man comes at the beginning, right after "the earth and the heaven," and after him come the plants and animals. As the crown of creation man was to "subdue" it and "have dominion" over "every living thing." God himself prepared the garden and put man into it "to till and keep it" (Genesis 2:15).

In the Christian faith the origin and future of man belong together. The presence of Christlike capacities and ideals in man indicates his kinship to the Heavenly Father. Indeed it is only when man is included in considering the origin of the universe that the full force of the evidence of its divine origin is also revealed. Only then do the intermediate steps of the creative process take on ethical and spiritual meaning. The recognition of man as a child of God applies to both the race and the individual. It is natural that historically the recognition of the divine sonship of the individual comes later than that of the sonship of the social group.

The body of man in material and structure is a part of the physical universe. It is composed of the same matter as the planet upon which it lives. It is subject to the common laws of physics, chemistry, and biology. It closely resembles the bodies of animals in general, and is classified among them. "You are dust, and to dust you shall return" (Genesis 3:19). Man cannot disown his kinship with the earth and the creatures that live upon it, as far as his body is concerned. Concerning this point we do well to consult the natural sciences.[1]

---

1. Alfred L. Kroeber, *Anthropology*, Hartcourt & Brace, 1923, pp. 93-94.

B. Various Views of Man

There are various views of man, such as: the economic man of Karl Marx, the psychological man of Sigmund Freud, the existential man of Sören Kierkegaard, the humanistic evolutionary view of man of Julian Huxley, and others.[2] We briefly consider three views.

1. *The Rationalistic View of Man.*

The rationalistic view of man, coming largely from Greece and Rome and revived again during the Renaissance, holds that what most distinguishes man is his rational capacity. For Plato and Aristotle reason is man's highest and noblest capacity and it is that part of him that is immortal. The ideal person is the wise man. Mind is the unifying and organizing principle in the world. Reason, they thought, is the pride and glory of man. The intelligent man is the virtuous man. To know the right is to do it. Vice is the result of ignorance. The aim of life is the perfection of reason in man and society. This classical view of man is optimistic but life seemed too brief for many to attain the goal. History, too, had little meaning for them, since it was viewed as a series of cycles and endless recurrences.

2. *The Naturalistic View of Man*

The naturalistic view of man is mainly a product of the natural sciences and considers him a part of the physical order of nature. From this point of view man is just one of the many animals on earth and is a part of the age-long process of evolution.

From the time of the early Greeks there always have been those who asserted that the higher forms of life, including man are merely more complex processes that can be explained by the same laws that govern matter and motion. While others assert that living organisms owe their characteristics to some special creative life principle, and that new forms or levels of life appear that cannot be explained by the previous level.[3]

3. *Judaeo-Christian Interpretation of Man*

The Judaeo-Christian interpretation of man affirms his divine origin. Man was created by God in His own image. He is a finite creature, weak and sinful. But he is also a spiritual being that tran-

---

2. Perry LeFevre, *Understanding Man*, Westminster Press, 1966.
3. H. H. Titus, *Living Issues of Philosophy*, American Book Co., 1964, pp. 143-147.

scends nature and is of infinite worth, having unlimited possibilities. Man was placed in a meaningful and purposeful universe. He transcends the natural conditions of life and does not become his real self until he devotes himself to the good and to God. As a free being he can resist obedience to and fellowship with God and give way to sensuality, injustice, selfishness, and pride, seeking to satisfy only human desire and power. Man falls into these errors when he fails to make God the center of his life.

According to the Judaeo-Christian tradition man is a creature of great worth and value. Each person is an end in itself, never to be used as a means. The right act produces the good and the good is that which promotes value for persons. The position that persons have great intrinsic value is what makes society possible and is at the roots of the democratic faith underlying western civilization. Man has moral freedom and responsibility. Love and social-mindedness are his as the supreme virtues. In Judaism, justice and group consciousness are stressed. In Christianity, the life of Jesus Christ is the supreme expression of creative good. The chief end of man, in the Judaeo-Christian view, is devotion to God and His cause.

4. *Optimistic and Pessimistic Interpretations*

Some are inclined to look upon man with glowing optimism, while others look upon him with dark pessimism. The stubborn realities of history remind us that complacent idealism and naive optimism are morally inadequate. The abiding mystery of iniquity is not only a surface blemish that education and modern civilization can abolish and overcome. Our generation is again rediscovering the abysmal depths of evil and is realizing that public enemy number one is not ignorance, or defective social environment, or heredity, but sin. Natural and fundamental goodness of man cannot be assumed, for under stress human beings will do the most terrible and evil deeds.

Demonic, irrational and savage forces in the individual human heart, as well as in society as such, have undermined the assumption of utopian humanism that man will gradually achieve perfection through inevitable progress. Human perfectability does not seem so simple as it once did. There is a tragic paradox in the world process to which Jesus Christ himself bears witness in His parable of the wheat and the tares:

> "Lest in gathering the weeds you root up the wheat along with them. Let both grow together until the harvest"; . . . (Matthew 13:29-30).

As our civilization makes progress, the difficulties and dangers accompanying it also make progress. With our extended mastery of nature we are not achieving a corresponding mastery of evil wills, lusts, boundless egotism as well as fears. Along with the automobile there comes slaughter on the roads. With aviation there come bombs. Chemical research also produced mustard gas. Increased education makes increasing good possible but also more terrible crime. Man's power to do more good, also gives him power to do more evil.

Man has great possibilities for good and evil. The good is united with the will of God so that morality and religion touch all phases of life. As Reinhold Niebuhr says:

> To the essential nature of man belong, on the one hand, all his natural endowments and determinations, his physical and social impulses, his sexual and racial differentiations, in short, his character as a creature embedded in the natural order. On the other hand, his essential nature also includes the freedom of his spirit, his transcendence over natural process, and finally his self transcendence.[4]

Blaise Pascal in his *Penseés* analyzes man as between the infinite bigness of the universe and the infinite littleness of its parts, sort of a middle being between nothing and everything. Yet this fragile and easily destructible being dominates the world that makes him seem so little. "Though the universe should crush him, he is still greater than the universe, for he would know that he is being crushed."[5]

This contradiction of man appears especially in his moral nature. Here greatness and meanness so contradict each other that he is both the glory and the shame of the universe. The natural sciences tend to classify man with the cosmic forces that determine his existence and finally reduces him to helpless and meaningless nonentity. While idealistic philosophy, stressing man's creative power of mind over matter, classifies him with, and elevates him to, the divine. In the face of cosmic determinism Immanuel Kant (1724-1804) reasserted man's freedom. And when Georg W. F. Hegel (1770-1831) sees the Absolute himself first coming to self-consciousness in man, Charles Darwin (1809-1892) so deeply humiliates man again. The truth lies somewhere in between the two extremes. Man is no mere speck on the planet earth, nor is he an immortal god.

---

4. Reinhold Niebuhr, *The Nature and Destiny of Man,* Scribners 1941, Vol. I; Human Nature, p. 270.
5. W. M. Horton, *Christian Theology,* Harper, 1955, p. 142.

BASIC CHRISTIAN CONVICTIONS

The extremely pessimistic and cynical view of man is rejected by the Christian faith. Absolute despair is pagan. One may despair of man, but the Christian never despairs of God and His grace.

The Christian position is not that of optimistic humanism, nor that of the pessimistic cynicism but rather that of biblical realism. Pessimism alone would be a pagan answer to a superficial optimism. Man is a creature but also more than a mere animal. He was created in the image of God with an awareness that he was to be a "son" and not a "bond-servant." But man has rebelled against God and so has become estranged. Unlike animals, man is a sinner. He can rise higher than the animals but also sink lower. The essence of sin is man's denial of his distinctive endowment. In pride he rebels against God and repudiates His purposes. The prodigal son, even among swine, still remained a son and did not become a swine. He can return to his father's house. He is not all good, nor all bad, but has great possibilities in either direction.

5. Integration of Scientific and Christian Views

Various attempts to integrate scientific and Christian views of man have been made. One such attempt is that of Teilhard de Chardin (1881-1955), a French Jesuit and distinguished paleontologist, whose writings the Catholic Church forbade publication during his lifetime, but who, since his death, has met amazing response from Christians as well as nonbelievers. Teilhard sought to provide a Christian interpretation of evolution. From early youth he gave himself to the study of science. In his fieldwork he made expeditions to China, Africa, and South America. He gave himself to developing a synthetic view of the world and of man in it which would hold together a scientific approach to nature and the development of mankind, with a Christian interpretation of the meaning of these phenomena. His understanding of man was finally a synthesis of his insights as a scientist and a Christian.[6]

Teilhard holds that the meaning of man can only be understood in relation to man's past, for "nothing is comprehensible except through its history."[7] Earlier development went on without conscious awareness of its participants, but now within the sphere of human development it is directly influenced by human awareness, reflection, and activity. Man is the only creature that finally is conscious and

---

6. Perry LeFevre, *Understanding Man*, Westminster, 1966, chap. 3.
7. Pierre Teilhard de Chardin, *The Future of Man*, Harper, 1964, p. 12.

knows that he is conscious. Evolution has become evermore complex and conscious at the social and cultural levels. Man knowing his past and present, can give some direction to his future. Hence there is ground for hope about the future. Teilhard says:

> Evolution is an ascent towards consciousness . . . therefore it should culminate forward in some sort of supreme consciousness.[8]

Christianity has brought into being a new state of consciousness, namely Christian love. This universal Christian love has been operative in practice. Although Christians at first were frightened by evolution, it can now be understood as a means of new and mutual vitality and enrichment for both Christianity and science. Something that cannot be said of other ancient world religions because of their incompatibility with modern scientific thought. The Christian now perceives that this God-directed evolution even offers man a wonderful means of feeling more at one with God and of giving himself more to God. God is above but also present in and through everything, creating and redeeming as He moves through the evolutionary process toward consummation.

> Jesus on the Cross is both the symbol and the reality of the immense labour of the centuries which has, little by little, raised up the created spirit and brought it back to the depths of the divine context.[9]

Thus Teilhard, as a Christian, claims a new perspective and understanding of man and his journey, not in conflict with evolution but rather one which discloses a deeper meaning of it all and in line with the Christian faith.

> Across the immensity of time and the disconcerting multiplicity of individuals, one single operation is taking place; the annexation to Christ of His chosen; one single thing is being made: the Mystical Body of Christ, starting from the sketchy spiritual powers scattered throughout the world.[10]

Christ is the "All-in everything; of the universe moved and compenetrated by God in the totality of its evolution."[11] To help along in this is the dignified vocation, meaning and fulfillment of man. According to Teilhard the Christian view of evolution throws light on both the origin and destiny of man.

---

8. Ibid., *The Phenomenon of Man*, Harper, 1961, p. 258.
p. 258.
9. Ibid., *The Divine Milieu*, Harper, 1960, p. 79.
10. *Ibid.*, p. 124.
11. *Ibid.*, p. 139.

C. The Spiritual Nature of Human Personality

1. *Some Differences Between Man and Animals*

Man is structured and functions much like some animals, but even so he has many characteristics that differentiate him from lower creatures. Some of these are:

(a) Man is of erect posture which frees his arms and hands for various other manipulations.

(b) The prehensile thumb with the rotating arm gives greater flexibility to the forelimbs of man than animals have.

(c) Man's large brain and more highly organized nervous system permit development of greater variety and more subtle behavior.

(d) Animals can scratch, bite, smell, and taste, but man can also handle and manipulate objects.

(e) Man's articulate speech and written symbols as language permit a greater degree of social and cultural development in man than in animals. Language is the instrument of personal and social communication.

(f) All this leads man to various inventions and cultural advances including the discovery of fire, metals, the wheel, machines, social organizations and institutions.

(g) By cooperation man develops larger and larger units in agriculture, industry, education, science, government and even religion. Social cooperation on this larger basis, including the whole human race, seems to be one of the conditions for the better life of the individual and society as a whole.

(h) Self-consciousness is an important human characteristic. Animals are conscious but not self-conscious. On this consciousness of self, conscience is based, leading to personal and social responsibility, making imagination, understanding, and creative foresight possible.

(i) The ability of reflective thinking and the power of generalization also distinguish man from the animal. Animals can form percepts but only man forms concepts which enable him to deal with the abstract. Reflective thinking enables him to retain memories and extend himself into the future and so live in a world of new meanings.

(j) Man has the power of choice and ethical discrimination. His conscience and his sense of "ought" make for restlessness but are also the hope of the future. Moral progress comes through creative individuals.

(k) Aesthetic appreciation is an important quality of man and enables him not only to appreciate beauty but also to create it. The range and depth of appreciation and insight are indicated by man's interest in art and the beautiful.

(l) Man is capable of faith in a higher power and worshiping the same. He prays, repents, forgives and asks for forgiveness. This religious tendency is intrinsic in human nature.

(m) Man's creativity finds expression in art, science, philosophy, and religion as he searches for truth, beauty and goodness and expresses himself in various ways in civilizations and cultures that he develops.

(n) Emil Brunner points out that the main point in all this is that man with all these abilities still wonders just who and what he himself is? Who asks all these questions that lie behind himself but is also conscious of himself and what he is doing? Man is both subject and object. This is a great torturing but also glorifying mystery to man himself as he contemplates his own being.[12]

2. Man's Quest for Value

At one time it was taken for granted that the chief distinction of man from other creatures was his possession of rational faculties. Later investigation indicated that man is dependent to a large degree upon subconscious, irrational emotional forces rather than upon reason. As a matter of fact, he often uses reason to justify certain emotional needs. On the other hand he also uses reason to make distasteful choices, as for example to undergo an operation for the sake of his health. Man using reason to aid and control emotion indicates that he is chiefly characterized by something more fundamental than emotion. Man is dominated neither by reason nor by emotion but by his quest for values. Not only is man sensitive to values but he also can expand his range of appreciation of values. Man being a value-obsessed creature is the reason why his life can become gloriously rich and creative but also dangerously sinful and destructive.

All living creatures appreciate values to some extent. The plant prefers sunshine to darkness, the dog inspects the bones offered him

---

12. Emil Brunner, *Man in Revolt*, Westminster Press, 1947, pp. 17-18; H. H. Titus, *Living Issues in Philosophy*, pp. 146, 150.

before making a choice, but only man's whole life is dominated by this quest for values. Man's sensitivity to values is superior to that of any other creature. The range of values that man appreciates is also far more extensive. Because of his sensitivity to values man makes decisions with past experience in mind and with a yearning for the fulfillment of future values in an ever-widening range of appreciation. The sense of value yields emotional satisfaction and expands the range of appreciation.[13]

Man spends his life seeking for values and may even sacrifice his life for such values as friendship, freedom, or family. One of the elements that goes into the structure of relationships that make for values is sensation such as pleasantness or the opposite. Other elements are meaningful ideas, memories, and associations. The development of such a structure of relationship making for values is clearly dependent upon man's sensitive organism, his environment, and the interpretation of these to make them meaningful and precious. From the Christian viewpoint, God is the creator and sustainer of value structures, even as He is of the natural world order which is necessary for the growth of values, and of man who is the carrier of values.

Values are grasped by man personally but he can only partially share this experience with his fellows. Every value is involved in an elaborate context of relationships from which it is abstracted and intuitively grasped as something of great worth. There is nothing in the nature of values that compels a person to pursue the values if he prefers to give himself to the quest of lower values.

The forming of connections of quality and meaning in an experience is a continuous process which lures one on for a maximization of the given experience. The music lover will return again and again to hear a Beethoven symphony for a greater fulfillment of the latent value in the music. Values of all kinds tend to develop greater and more involved interactions. This is the process of growth. Not all values do this to the same degree and different levels of values must also be distinguished. Hence the wise person may forgo lunch to visit an art gallery, or visit a sick friend rather than the art gallery. On the higher levels of value experience, the decision is made not

---

13. M. W. Boyer, *Highways of Philosophy,* Muhlenberg Press, 1949, p. 241. The value concept is emphasized in the second half of Chapter I and religion is defined as the process of re-evaluating all other values in the light of one supreme or central value—namely a person's God.

so much on the basis of quality as on the basis of meaning. Meanings are communicated by signs or language which will enhance the value of a given experience. Meanings are enhanced by social contact which stimulates the growth of meaning and value. That is why international and interracial contacts are necessary for the increase of values among mankind.

Values tend to become organized in the life of persons and the social group, and form a value-system which is the sum total of hopes and interests of the individual or the group. We all have our value-systems and are directed by them. We devote our lives to that end, which gives purpose and meaning to it. Different groups or nations developing different or even contrary value-systems would naturally come to conflict and war. Hence from the Christian point of view it is important that individual as well as group value-systems are constantly checked by the revelation of God in Jesus Christ so as to keep the value-systems from becoming stagnant and keep it growing toward that revelation.

Man is superior over nature in that he is a conscious discoverer of natural processes and to a degree even an intelligent molder and regulator of nature. The uniqueness of man, however, is indicated even more clearly in his position as a creator and carrier of values. Human beings alone of all creatures, are capable to discover and appreciate higher values. Man is willing to make great sacrifice and undergo extreme suffering in order to preserve what he considers the higher values. He not only cherishes and tries to maintain them, but also feels a sense of responsibility to share them with others.

3. Man as a Living Soul

The term "Soul" has been given various meanings. The naturalistic-biological view is that there is no soul and that man is no more significant than other organisms. This view holds that man is a carrier of values because his biological organism is more finely constructed which enables him to think and choose between values and appreciate complex situations as agreeable and worthful. This would mean that values are limited to those appreciated by the biological organism and so would regard material things as alone possessing value. But man is more than a biological organism, in fact on occasions he is even willing to sacrifice that biological organism for the sake of higher values. From the naturalistic viewpoint there is no reason why those having the power should not run roughshod over others in

BASIC CHRISTIAN CONVICTIONS

attaining these material values. Materialistic communism is an example of this.[14]

A second view considers the soul as not personal but a disembodied emanation of a world soul into which it is again absorbed at death. Hinduism is an example of this view. Mystics in all religions are inclined toward this position. This life is regarded as a school to free oneself from the delusions of matter and prepare oneself for re-absorption into God. In this view, values associated with active participation in the world are denied existence and meditation is stressed instead. Hence, man's search for values becomes a self-centered world-denying quest in meditation. Matter is considered essentially evil. Bodily health and material possessions are ignored. Spiritualists hold that they can get in touch with disembodied souls. But in fact, in this life there is no such strict division between body and soul. Man is dependent upon his body to sustain his efforts at grasping higher values and these can only be achieved when there is a broad basis of material values to support them.

A third tradition places emphasis upon the intellect and holds that man is immortal insofar as his intellect conquers the nonrational elements of his personality. The mind enables man to consider choices in a rational way and then act upon them. Besides ancient Greek philosophers, some western thinkers such as Rene Descartes (1569-1650) Baruch Spinoza (1632-1677) and Georg W. F. Hegel (1770-1831) emphasized the predominance of reason and mind over will and other aspects of human nature. However, not all men are equally gifted with reasoning ability and many do not have the opportunities to develop their mental capacity. Hence to identify the intellect with the soul or person has its difficulties. Wherever the mind is regarded as the dominant factor in the soul, a tendency toward intellectual snobbishness almost always arises.

A fourth position affirms that the soul of man is moral will and only the person of good deeds is immortal. If will is regarded as the vital element of the soul then its use will determine the status of the soul in time and eternity. This would mean conditional immortality, depending upon one's good deeds. Western philosophers who have held that the will is more important than the intellect were Imman-

---

14. For fuller discussion on man as a living soul and free will, see M. W. Boyer, *Highways of Philosophy,* Muhlenberg Press, Philadelphia, 1949, Chaps. 13-14. Also Victor E. Frankl, *Man's Search for Meaning,* Washington Square Press, 1965.

uel Kant (1724-1804), Johann Gottlieb Fichte (1762-1814), and Arthur Schopenhauer (1788-1860), although none of these necessarily identified the will with the soul. Where the will is considered as dominant, another type of snobbishness tends to arise. The Pharisees who prided themselves upon the observance of the religious rules and regulations were examples of such snobbishness.

A fifth idea, which is the Christian view, holds that the soul of man is the totality of his personality as it responds to God. In other words the soul is man's capacity for eternal life with God. Here the soul cannot be distinguished from the total personality. Human personality is a creator and carrier of values because of its ability to respond to the divine personality, God, who is the source of all values. So in the struggle of life, man is sustained by the faith that he is not alone in this quest and not limited to his own powers. In primitive times as well as in historic cultures men have felt the need for help beyond themselves to create and sustain the values they were interested in. In the conviction that God answers this appeal we have the emergence of ethical religion. Man becomes conscious that he must not be motivated alone by his own selfish desires but by God's revelation of higher values as contrasted with lower values. Hence in the Judaeo-Christian tradition obedience to the will of God is considered as essential for the realization of the highest values.

Man is a part of nature but also more, and above nature, besides, he can have contact with God who is other and greater than nature or man. As a carrier of values man is dependent upon nature but as a creator of values he is motivated by God, who is other than man or nature. For the fulfillment of values man is after all dependent upon God's gift of eternal life. The soul is not considered something disembodied and separate from the self. It is not something that we possess but an activity of God by which our personalities respond to His creative power in us. This capacity to respond to God is found in all men.

This is a revolutionary doctrine of the nature of man. It promises not only redemption in the life after death, but insists that God's Kingdom begins here and now in the growth of values in the heart of man and in the Christian community. Eternal life is an immediate possession for the Christian.

> Jesus said . . . "I am the resurrection and the life, he who believes in me, though he die, yet shall he live, and whoever lives and believes in me shall never die" (John 11:25-26).

Too often Christians allow the consciousness of their sinfulness to blind them to the power and love of God as the creator and sustainer of values. Man's sinfulness must not be ignored but it is more important to remember that Christianity is a God-centered religion as revealed in Jesus Christ. Modern civilization needs renewed faith in human beings as creators and carriers of value which will arouse an attitude of reverence toward the life of man and make it impossible to ignore or exploit the same. However, for man to become creator as well as carrier of values he must be a free agent.

The origin of the individual soul or the spiritual side of man's being and how it becomes a part of the person along with the body has been variously explained. One theory is that of pre-existence of the soul. This was held by Origen of Alexandria (c 185-c 254 A.D.). According to this theory the soul or spirit has existed before the present life, and at birth becomes united with the body for existence here on earth. Origen derived this idea from Plato's (427-347 B.C.) eternal nature of "Ideas." It appears again in John Locke's (1632-1704) theory of "innate ideas." To Origen, as in modern Hinduism, this was a practical way to account for the inequalities of the present life as due to good or bad deeds committed in a previous state of existence. This theory of pre-existence has little support in scripture and never found general acceptance in the Christian Church.

Another suggestion is called "the creationist view," according to which each individual soul or spirit is created by God and united with the body when it comes into existence by natural procreation.

A third suggestion is called "the Traducianist or Transmission" theory, according to which the whole being of man, (soul and body) is derived by natural process from the previous being of the parents as naturally propagated. Both of these two last views conserve the immediate and personal relationship of the individual spirit or soul to God. The latter view, however, assumes the organic oneness of the human race and makes room for the facts of spiritual as well as physical heredity and so appeals more to the modern scientific temper.[15]

4. *Man as a Creative Being of Freedom and Love*

Freedom must be distinguished from determinism on the one hand and indeterminism on the other hand. The determinist holds that

---

15. J. M. Shaw, *Christian Doctrine,* Philosophical Library, 1954, p. 124-115; L. H. DeWolf, *A Theology of the Living Church,* Harper, 1953, p. 158 ff.

there are no free choices at all and that our lives are completely determined by factors beyond our control. The indeterminist on the other hand holds that everything depends upon conscious choice and that our lives are only the result of personal choices regardless of heredity and environment. There is some truth in both points of view. Freedom lies between determinism and indeterminism. Man is only partly free not absolutely so. We can choose, but only within limits. Obviously our hereditary and environmental factors will set certain limits upon our freedom. We are creatures of time and location and these will also set certain limits to our choices.

Freedom denying Tendencies. Two tendencies have appeared in the course of history to negate the freedom of the will - religious fatalism and scientific determinism. Some deeply religious leaders in meditating upon the power of God and weakness of man, have come to the conclusion that God is not only the source and sustainer of values but also the only creator of the same and that man is an empty vessel into which God may or may not pour the values of redemption as He sees fit. This is predestination and a denial of man's ability to choose and make decisions.

Thomas Aquinas (1225-1274) an important thinker of the medieval church escaped this predestinarian tendency by emphasizing the importance of man's intellectual faculty or his ability to reason and decide. Martin Luther (1483-1546), the Reformation leader escaped this temptation by emphasizing God's grace as open to all men. "For by grace you have been saved through faith; and this is not your own doing, it is the gift of God" (Ephesians 2:8). John Calvin (1509-1564) the Swiss Reformer gave up the struggle and accepted religious determinism. Muhammadanism carries religious determinism to its extreme and affirms fatalism in all of life's experience.

Modern man is not so likely to deny freedom of the will for religious reasons but is more likely to do so on scientific grounds. Modern science is based on what are considered inexorable laws of cause and effect found in nature. As a result man's choices are thought to be determined by heredity, environment, economic forces, or subconscious urges. However, recent developments in the natural sciences leave room for a less rigid conception of these natural causal laws than was formerly thought possible, as was indicated in the preceding chapter.

Man as a Decider. Man is the most unpredictable of all creatures. There is as much justification to attribute this unpre-

       BASIC CHRISTIAN CONVICTIONS

dictability to freedom of the will as to predetermined laws of nature. Without freedom of the will no system of moral order as a basis for society could be established. Freedom of the will must be accepted in order to give ethics any consideration at all. No progressive civilization has ever been built upon a system that denies the freedom of the will. Civilization can only be considered satisfactory or unsatisfactory insofar as it provides opportunity for progress by orderly selection and preservation of the values of the past for the individual, as well as for society. All this involves choice and decision by man, implying freedom of the will.

As carrier and creator of values, man must make decisions regarding the type of community, state or governmental system, to which he cares to give his loyalty and support as the conservator of values; what kind of education will serve best as transmitter of values; and above all, the type of religious faith he is to accept and promote as most promising to bring fulfillment of values in time and eternity. Hence freedom of the will needed for these important decisions, is a very basic concept of the Christian faith.

All this does not mean that man is wholly free. His freedom is real but limited. By creating man in His own image, God endowed man with a share of His own freedom and called him to cooperate in the work of the unfinished creation and unfolding possibilities latent in God's creative purpose. Man is free to respond to God and cooperate with Him, but man can also refuse and this brings us to his revolt and sin.

The Danish religious thinker Sören Kierkegaard (1813-1855) did much to promote the idea of man as a free being, as a being of decision. For a human being to exist means to make decisions. Man must accept ethical alternatives of either-or, and reject false hopes held out to him by the comfortable both-and philosophy. Man is essentially alone. In his attempts to overcome this loneliness man sometimes makes decisions which are wrong which drive him to despair and an awareness of sin. Only from the depths of despair, holds Kierkegaard, can man appreciate the true nature of his being and the possibility of finding God as redeemer. God must be known inwardly, not objectively. Man's own inner need points to "Something Other" in answer to that need.[16]

---

16. Kierkegaard has written many volumes but his *Either-Or, Fear and Trembling, Stages on the Way of Life, The Sickness unto Death, Training in Christianity, The Gospel of Suffering, The Works of Love*, are among the most

Our highest capacity and ultimate significance for self-determination that we as human beings possess is the choice of the God we shall serve and worship and with how much purpose and conviction we shall do this. Our understanding of the purpose of life naturally guides our decision. What we shall live for we must decide for ourselves. This freedom to choose our God, or our religious freedom, will determine all our other choices. Hence religious freedom is of greatest significance for the development of man and human society as we purposefully move into the future.

Love is the motive necessary for constructive decisions. Freedom alone is not enough. Freedom to be creative must be centered by love to have the motivation necessary for the right choice. For this realization, growth is necessary as man does not appear on the scene as a finished product. He is meant to become a creative being of freedom and love.[17] He is born with this potentiality. Such becoming is the fuller realization of the image of God in man. To say that man's task is to become a creative spirit indicates the dynamic character of this task. Man is not a static entity but a becoming, growing, creative being. He is a dynamic process. When man ceases to become, he ceases to be. The direction of this becoming is to be toward an ever more creative being of freedom and love. But the direction is not an end point. It is a moving goal. Freedom and love reach out in ever widening circles. So the spirit is also a growing spirit.

This task of becoming also involves risk as it involves choice. Failure here leads to meaninglessness. To draw back in fear, or contentment means to withdraw into a static existence and final death. To become more of a creative person man must have a proper spirit. Without a chief purpose man has no unity nor consistency, and loses his self-identity. Persons without a central value shift with every wind of doctrine. There is no integration and finally their "name is Legion" (Mark 5:9; Luke 8:30). This internal unity is not a simple matter of forming stable and habitual patterns. It is rather the result of reflection on the need for a unifying intention, a stable system of values and an underlying life purpose. This singlemindedness is what

---

influential. He has not only influenced modern existential literary and philosophical writers such as Heidegger, Jaspers, Unamuno, Marcel and Sartre, but also the great religious thinkers of our day, such as Karl Barth, Emil Brunner, Rudolph Bultman, Paul Tillich, Reinhold and H. Richard Niebuhr, and others.

17. Perry LeFevre, *Understanding Man*, Westminster Press, 1966, p. 135 ff.

Kierkegaard calls "Purity of Heart." This coherence and creative unity includes the individual's view of himself and his own self-identity as related to his view of God and the world. Centeredness alone, however, is not enough. A bigot or criminal may also have a high degree of internal consistency but yet be incapable of freedom and love. *Need freedom, love, + unity (integration)*

Becoming fully human in the Christian sense, is a becoming which increases one's creative freedom and his capacity for love. Freedom is a relative matter - one has more or less freedom and is more or less in bondage. One can become a prisoner of one's past and one's guilt. Guilt is both a heritage and a contemporary presence. It may be the result of commission or omission where the web of relationship that nurtures, sustains, and restores human good has been hindered or not furthered. It is the result of violating of what man was meant to be. Freedom is reduced when inner conflict threatens the creative center of the person when duplicity and guilt warp the perception of self and reality. On the other hand, whatever helps to extend the range of human possibilities helps to increase creative human freedom.

Love intends the good of the other, but that does not exclude one's own good, for all good is social. For full creative maturity, love must be mutual and reciprocated. Reciprocated love by healing restores the freedom to love. God's love expressed in Jesus Christ is to move man to respond and turn toward God and creatively love Him with heart, mind, and soul.

Becoming a Christian, or a creative spirit of freedom and love, is growth in grace and is not automatic. Life is full of threatening possibilities and even tragedy. Becoming a creative being of freedom and love requires the maintenance of direction in face of opposition and even tragedy. Therefore the cross is a part of the Christian life. Active trust in God, or ultimate reality, makes it possible for man to keep his direction toward becoming a creative spirit of freedom and love. Christ, even in facing the cross, in trust still prayed "nevertheless, not as I will, but as thou wilt" (Matthew 26:39). That is why His followers see God in Him. The reality disclosed in His creative life and ministry was the answer to man's agelong searching, and in this reality alone can man ultimately place his trust. In the death of Jesus on the cross the first Christians came to understand and feel the creative power of healing and transmutation of tragedy. In their encounter with Jesus, they found themselves in the hands of a creative power not their own, which grasped and drew them beyond themselves, finally remaking them in its own image and thus empowering them for their mission in the world. And the Christian's mission in the world is to be God's helper.[18]

5. *Man as God's Creative Helper*

Man was brought into being to serve as God's creative helper. In Genesis, God forms the animals but does not give them names, instead He asks man to do this. Creation implies forming, separating and naming. The world does not come to man already finished. It comes partly confused and even formless, and man is to give it significance and meaning which arises out of their becoming a part of his projects and purposes. Name giving was an act of sovereignty and command. This is an exalted view of man. God does not merely insert him into the world with the names and relationship and meaning patterns already established. Man must fashion these himself. He is not only to discover meaning but also to originate it.

Creation is not completed by God, man is to work as God's partner and help bring order into chaos and make it into more of a cosmos. This means that creation is still going on and is really never altogether completed and finished.

The theology of Karl Barth has helped to differentiate God and man. By emphasizing that "God is wholly other" the implication is that man then is free to master and shape, to create and explore, to disobey and rebel but also to try and reach out to the ends of earth and beyond, to God himself. Barth's system does not denigrate the role of man but rather gives him an exalted position as the following quotation shows.

> It is apparent that the formula, God is everything and man is nothing . . . is not merely a shocking simplification but complete nonsense. By the grace of God man is not nothing. He is God's man . . . He is recognized as himself a free subject, a subject who had been made free once and for all by his restoration as a free covenant partner of God . . . We cannot say or demand and expect too much or too great things from man . . .[19]

Man is a fashioner and creator of meanings that in turn give direction to history. The Gospel does not expect man to return to a

---

18. For more detailed discussion on the Meaning of Man as Becoming a Spirit of Freedom and Love, see Perry LeFevre, *Understanding of Man*, Westminster Press, 1966, Chapter 9.

19. Karl Barth, *Church Dogmatics*, Edinburgh: T. & T. Clark, 1958, pp. 89, 90.

previous stage of development but rather to come to spiritual maturity. He is not to abandon his interest in the problems of this world but rather accept these problems as a gift and challenge for the solution of which he, with the help of God, has the responsibility. His mission is to help make this world a more acceptable place for the growth and welfare of mankind.

The older view of man as held by Thomas Aquinas (1225-74) was greatly influenced by Greek thought. Plato wondered how the words tree, dog, man, or horse, which are attached to different objects had any reality. Where was the "dog" or the "horse" of which all similar creatures on earth were merely copies? His answer was his "theory of Ideas." He asserted that the physical things we perceive are not real but only appearances of the eternal ideas. Ideas are eternal and creatures are only temporal expressions of the same. Or to put it another way: Names precede men, not vice versa. Hence for the Greeks man's role as creator of meaning was not significant. The world is not something to be shaped by man but rather something given and already finished and fixed for all time.

Only in more recent times have scholars broken away from these Greek concepts of a changeless objective order and come more to the Hebrew view that the ordered, objective and knowable world is not simply awaiting man's efforts to uncover it, but rather consider the meaningful ordering of the world itself to be a human enterprise and a responsibility which man is to undertake as God's partner. All this implies a different view of God, of the world, as well as of man.

By creating man in His own image, that is, with creative responsibility, man was to become a partner and co-laborer with God. Creation is a process not an act, and man is to help carry it on to greater height and a more completed form. There is no contradiction of the God and man concepts in this. God voluntarily limited himself to some degree to give man some needed freedom both to develop himself and to help in the creative process.

The absolute concept of God, of Platonic and Aristotelian origin is purely metaphysical. The Hebrew and biblical concept of God and man help to correct the Greek concept which in this day of science and pragmatism causes us so much trouble.

D.   MAN AS A SINNER

Sin is man's revolt against God. Turning away from the true God, man worships idols. In a sense all sin is a violation of the First

Commandment. "I am the Lord your God . . . You shall have no other gods before me" (Exodus 20:2-3). But man has other gods. He worships himself and lives as if there were no God. He worships his nation, his race, money, pleasure, power, and many other things. Man is supposed to make God the center of his life, to live in and for God. Instead he is tempted to live for other things.

1. Modern Influences on the Sin Concept

Once "sin" was a powerful and lucid word but in recent times it is lacking in clarity and force. There are various reasons for this. *First*, there is the implication of naturalism that all knowledge is emperical and that the key to understanding man is not his relationship to God but to nature. Man is thought to be just another animal and whatever he does is therefore natural. One does not speak of the sinful behavior of dogs or horses, so naturalism assumes it is just as senseless to speak of the sinful actions of man. This runs counter to the Christian conception of man, which holds him to be uniquely responsible to God. Naturalism has obscured the difference. If man is only a highly developed animal the idea of sin does not make much sense.

A second factor which has contributed to the difficulty for modern man to understand what is meant by sin is the current idea of relativism. The concept of relativity is no doubt meaningful. but it can also be carried too far. In the popular notion of relativism moral standards are inclined to be subverted. Sin is hard to explain when the idea is current that right and wrong are always only arbitrary standards. Sin is revolt against God but this concept is difficult to grasp when certain behavior is considered right in one setting and wrong in another. Moral relativism makes it difficult for modern man to take sin very seriously.

A third factor which adds to the difficulties of communicating the Christian idea of sin to this age is superficial psychologizing and psychoanalyzing. Sigmund Freud (1856-1939) and his associates, by stressing the subconscious, have made great contributions to the understanding of man. But when accepted by modern man as a substitute for religion, offering salvation, depth psychology can make it difficult for man to understand that sin describes the broken relationship between man and God.

Naturalism, relativity, and psychiatry have made real contributions to the understanding of man and it is only their superficial and extreme interpretations that give us trouble with the Christian concept of sin and its consequence by denying man's proper relationship to God.[20]

2. *The Biblical Witness Regarding Sin*

The biblical writers are very definite on this matter of sin. Here are a few quotations:

> There is no man who does not sin (I Kings 8:46). Surely there is not a righteous man on earth who does good and never sins (Ecclesiastes 7:20). The fool says in his heart "there is no God." They are corrupt, they do abominable deeds, there is none that does good . . . They have all gone astray, they are all alike corrupt; there is none that does good, no, not one (Psalm 14:1, 3). If thou, O Lord shouldst mark iniquities, Lord, who could stand? (Psalm 130:3). Enter not into judgment with thy servant; for no man living is righteous before thee (Psalm 143:2). All we like sheep have gone astray; we have turned every one to his own way (Isaiah 53:6). We have all become like one who is unclean, and all our righteous deeds are like a polluted garment (Isaiah 64:6).

The Apostle Paul opens his Epistle to the Romans by arguing for nearly three chapters, that all men, Jews and Gentiles alike, are sinners in God's sight and concludes "there is no distinction; since all have sinned and fall short of the glory of God" (Romans 3:22-23). John is even more explicit and declares, "If we say we have no sin we deceive ourselves . . . if we say we have not sinned we make him a liar" (I John 1:8, 10).

Sin is a fact of our everyday experience. We read about it in history and in newspapers. We meet it as we travel or mix with others. We see it in our own homes and in our own lives. Nearly all of our legislation has come about because human beings cannot be trusted to settle their disputes honestly. A promise is not enough; we need a contract. Doors are not enough; they must be locked and bolted. Payment of fares is not enough; tickets have to be punched and collected. Law and order are not enough; police are needed to enforce them. These and many other things that we have grown accustomed to and do not even notice, are due to man's sin.

The perversion of the best becomes the worst and it is in the sins of the spirit that man sins most deeply. It is through imagination that man accomplishes the tasks that differentiate him from animals and it is through the imagination that it is possible for him to revolt in the most sophisticated ways.

---

20. G. W. Forell, *The Protestant Faith*, Prentice-Hall, 1960, pp. 159-164.

Jesus said: "out of the heart come evil thoughts, murder, adultery, fornication, theft, false witness, slander" (Matthew 15:19). And Paul lists the following:

> Now the works of the flesh are plain: immorality, impurity, licentiousness, idolatry, sorcery, enmity, strife, jealousy, anger, selfishness, dissension, party spirit, envy, drunkenness, carousing, and the like (Galatians 5:19-21).

In spite of any attempt to deny or explain away the existence of sin as old-fashioned and irrelevant, the results of sin are nevertheless demonstrable, observable, and painfully apparent. However much modern man may deny the existence of sin, he has been unsuccessful in avoiding the consequences of it.

3. *The Genesis Story of the Fall*

Man was created for free fellowship with God. Instead he uses his freedom to revolt against his Creator. Man wants to be God and have everything revolve around himself. He wants to be the center of the universe. He resents the fact that he is finite, that he is dispensable, and that life goes on without him. He envies God for being God and so revolts against Him. This is implied in the Genesis story of the fall (Gen. 3:1-6).

The temptation to "be like God," sufficient unto themselves, was so beguiling that man succumbed and disobeyed the Divine command. As a result Adam and Eve were conscious of guilt and shame which led them to hide themselves from God. As penalty for this disobedience they were expelled from the garden of inner peace and happiness and sent forth discredited into an unhospitable world as outcasts from the presence of God.

This symbolic story has religious meaning and significance. It is a picture or parable of the entrance of sin into man's life in every age and every person, rather than a definite historical event in the life of two individuals in the dim past. Just as the value of the story of the Prodigal Son in the teachings of Jesus depends not on one definite event but rather represents an episode or chapter in all individual human lives.

(a) *Some abiding spiritual truths* in this Genesis story are: *First,* it represents sin as a transgression of a Divine command. Though the command indicates a connection of the temptation with the more physical side of man's nature, the essence of the situation lies in the fact that man is represented as acting contrary to what he felt to be the higher authority outside and above himself, namely

God. Sin is represented as something done against God. Wrong done against others is a crime; wrong done against our own selves is a vice; but wrong against God is sin. Naturally, insofar as crime and vice are also against God they are also sin. David confesses: "Against thee, thee only, have I sinned and done that which is evil in thy sight" (Psalm 51:4). The Prodigal Son upon his return home says "Father I have sinned against heaven and before you" (Luke 15:21). Sin is something with infinite dimensions. The sense of sin deepens with the more intimate knowledge of God revealed in Jesus Christ. It is only in the Cross of Calvary that we see the gravity of sin for there we have the crucifixion of the love of God as revealed in Christ Jesus.

A second truth expressed in this pictorial story of Genesis pertains not only to the nature of sin but to its origin as well. Man's sin was not so much his physical desire for the fruit but rather in his disobedience. The root of the trouble was not so much in the body but rather in the mind, the spirit, and the will of man. He had the power of self-determining choice and decision. The motive of sin is represented as being the desire on man's part to be a law unto himself and to run his own life as he pleases. That means self-centeredness, pride, self-love, self-interest, in short selfishness is the origin of sin.

In the *third place* the results of sin in this story portray the consequences as the judgment of God. God is holy and righteous and can not ignore the revolt of man. He would and could not be God, if evil and sin were not abhorrent to Him. The prophets were convinced of this. Listen to Amos:

> Seek the Lord and live, lest he break out like fire in the house of Joseph, and it devour, with none to quench it for Bethel, O you who turn justice to wormwood, and cast down righteousness to the earth! . . . They hate him who reproves in the gate, and they abhor him who speaks the truth. Therefore, because you trample upon the poor and take from him exactions of wheat, you have built houses of new stone, but you shall not dwell in them; you have planted pleasant vineyards, but you shall not drink their wine. For I know how many are your transgressions, and how great are your sins . . . (Amos 5:6-12).

God has not abdicated as ruler of the universe and man's disobedience and revolt result in consequences. The results of sin are evident and cannot be denied even by those who would deny the cause. Every person and all human society are affected and feel the consequences of sin.

(b) *Some Results of Sin,* we must briefly look at also.

First, we note a sense of guilt and shame as a result mentioned in the Genesis story (Genesis 3:7-10). So deeply were the guilt and shame felt that the "man and his wife hid themselves from the presence of the Lord God" (Genesis 3:8). They had abused the privilege and honor God had given them and so had disgraced themselves and now felt deeply mortified by it all. The more this depressing situation is brooded upon the more serious and dangerous to the well-being of the respective person it can become until it culminates in a deranged mental condition. Self-accusing guilt and shame need correction in order to restore the health and happiness of the individuals involved.

Second, we note that far-reaching physical results also occur as an outcome of sin. There is mentioned the depressing fact of increasing and multiplying "your pain in childbearing," and to have the ground cursed so that

> ". . . . thorns and thistles it shall bring forth to you and . . . In the sweat of your face you shall eat bread till you return to the ground for . . . you are dust, and to dust you shall return" (Genesis 3:18-19).

Third, the Spiritual consequences are even more serious than the physical. There follows the ever widening development of sin in the relationships of life. Adam accuses Eve, Eve accuses the serpent, and Cain slays Abel. So from denying the fatherhood of God and the brotherhood of man all other ills have come. The deepest penalty of sin is more sin. So that the subsequent life of individuals and society is permeated with the poison of sin and its results. Sin becomes a state or condition of sinfulness so that we need to repent not only of what we have done but of what we are, and pray not only for the forgiveness of particular acts but for deliverance from sinful nature.

Fourth, estrangement, strife, disagreement, and war are other results of sin. Sin is at the bottom of all family and personal quarrels. Jesus when speaking of a man wanting to worship but is angry with his fellowman, said:

> "So if you are offering your gift at the altar, and there remember that your brother has something against you, leave your gift there before the altar and go; first be reconciled to your brother, and then come and offer your gift" (Matthew 5:23-24).

Estrangement from our fellowman implies estrangement from God. This applies also to estrangement between families, communities, and nations. Interracial and international conflicts are the result of sin. Here sin is both a cause and a result. Sin is the cause of hatred between nations that embitter our international life, and hatred in turn causes more sin resulting in war. There is nothing subjective about Hiroshima.

Fifth - Meaninglessness is another result of sin. This estrangement from God and man finally leads to recognition of the self as a hypocrite and so man finally even finds it impossible to accept and live with himself. For him life becomes meaningless and is "only a tale told by an idiot full of sound and fury, signifying nothing." This is the story of Shakespeare's *Hamlet,* Goethe's *Faust,* and Ibsen's *Peter Gynt.* Man is inclined either to love himself with an idolatrous love, or hate himself with demonic hatred, which may drive him to suicide. For the persistent sinner life loses its meaning and finally he insists that "vanity of vanities, . . all is vanity" (Ecclesiastes 1:2).

Sixth - Death also is a result of sin. "For in the day that you eat of it you shall die" (Genesis 2:17). "The wages of sin is death" (Romans 6:23). There are various views as to the meaning here of "death." One view is that physical death is a law of organic nature and that man as a part of it would in any case also undergo physical death. But when scripture speaks of death as a penalty for sin it refers not only to physical death. Spiritual death is real also and even more significant. Modern man does not like to think or speak about death. Our mortuaries and graveyards indicate how far we are willing to go to persuade ourselves that death is after all not real.

The entire world as we know it is involved in sin and its results. In war, we do not only destroy each other, we also destroy nature. In poisoning air and water, we affect not only man but all creatures. This is not man's earth, he is only the steward thereof. The selfishness with which man in innumerable ways deals with the riches of the earth which he is supposed to administer is the result of sin. Paul says, "the whole creation has been groaning in travail together until now" (Romans 8:22).

4. *The Sin of Self-Righteousness*

No sin is so subtle as the sin of "goodness" illustrated by Jesus in His story of the Pharisee and the Publican (Luke 18:10-14). Righteousness so easily covers the sin of self-righteousness and there is no sin so subtly dangerous as self-righteousness. Even all our righteousness is tainted. Egotism of the will to power asserts itself as idealism. The old imperialism was considered as the "White man's burden." Present communism considers itself a crusade for social justice. The militarist regards war as a just cause. The pacifist considers his objection to war as a matter of conscience.

These high claims may be sincere but often there are also other motives along with the good ones. "For even Satan disguises himself as an angel of light" (II Corinthians 11:14). Even at its best, man's goodness is poisoned by the sin of pride. It is so easy for a person of moral rectitude not even to be conscious of his egocentricity. This legalistic self-sufficiency is the core of sin. We only come to understand "Grace" when we come to see this legalistic relation to God as sin. In the parable of the Prodigal Son, Jesus illustrates this truth by the older son's reception of the younger brother's return: "he was angry and refused to go in" (Luke 15:38). Jesus says: "there will be more joy in heaven over one sinner who repents than over ninety-nine righteous persons who need no repentance" (Luke 15:7).

5. Total Depravity and Original Sin

Sin has a long history. Man's deeds of injustice are conditioned to a large degree by deeds done long ago by someone else. Sin proliferates and gives birth to more sin. The doctrine of "Total Depravity" has been misinterpreted as meaning that man is totally corrupted and is as bad as he can possibly be. If that was the case there would be no hope for the future of the individual or society. What this doctrine really means is that sin has permeated the whole of life. That there is no part of man's nature that is not to some degree affected by it. It does not mean "that the stream of human history, instead of being crystal clear, is solid mud; but that it is impure, corrupted in every part of its course."[21] Even our ideals and disinterested achievements are tainted by self-interest and pride. Ethically considered man is a mixture of good and bad.

The term "original sin" describes the fact that man is born in revolt and sin. The rebellion is not only something which he gradually learns but which has also become the pattern of human nature. Because mankind collectively has been in revolt against God since the dawn of history, sin surrounds and embraces man at birth in the respective culture he is born into. This sin permeated culture affects everything the child learns.

Our personal and social life is perverted by sin. It affects our relationship with our enemies and our friends. When we think we

---

21. J. S. Whale, *Christian Doctrine,* Cambridge Press, 1950, p. 42.

have completely escaped it, then is really when it is most pernicious. ✗
This is illustrated by the Pharisees. They were good people and proud
in the conceit of their goodness. If pride is the core of sin, nothing
is so deadly as pride of one's humility. Man is involved in personal
and current as well as historical collective guilt. All of man's troubles
stem from this source. They can only be solved by establishing the
proper relationship with God that has been broken by sin.

E. SUMMARY AND CONCLUSION

In this chapter on "Man: His Majesty and Misery" we have considered: The Origin of Man; Various Views of Man; The Spiritual
Nature of Human Personality; and Man as a Sinner.

In the Christian view of man, his origin and his future possibilities
belong together. His majesty is already indicated in his origin, when
God created him in His own image. True, man is still far from that
goal but his potentialities are indeed majestic. Man has made great
advances in many areas and recently even found his way to the moon
—however through sin man has also brought great misery upon
himself and mankind. He is plagued with guilt because of his
disobedience to his Creator in many respects. He has failed to fulfill
his mission to become an effective spirit of freedom and love as
an individual person and society as a whole.

Man's misery is great and real, but there nevertheless is hope.
Man's task is to be co-worker with God and help promote the doing
of God's will here on earth. Man cannot do this alone but with God's ✓
help in Jesus Christ he can make great contributions toward that end.
Yes, man is a sinner, but he can be saved, and he is worth saving.
That is where Jesus Christ comes in, so we turn to the next chapter.

For Further Reading on Man

Adler, A., *Understanding Human Nature,* Fawcett Pub. Co., 1957.

Brace, C. L., *Stages in Human Evolution,* Prentice-Hall, 1967.

Brunner, Emil, *Man in Revolt,* trans., Westminster, 1947.

Buber, Martin, *Between Man and Man,* trans., K Paul, London, 1947.

Eichrodt, W., *Man in the Old Testament,* Allenson, 1951.

Frank, Waldo D., *The Rediscovery of Man,* Braziller, N.Y., 1958.

Frankel, Charles, *The Case for Modern Man,* Harper, 1956.

Frankl, V. E., *Man's Search for Meaning,* Washington Sq., 1966.

Howells, W. W., *Back of History,* Doubleday, 1963.

Kaufman, G. D., "The Christian Understanding of Man" Part III, *Systematic Theology,* Scribners, 1968.

Kuemmel, W. G., *Man in the New Testament,* Westminster, 1963.

La Barre, Weston, *The Human Animal,* Univ. of Chicago Press, 1954.

LeFevre, Perry, *Understanding Man,* Westminster, 1966.

Medawar, Peter B., *The Future of Man,* Basic Books, 1960.

Miller, Alexander, *The Renewal of Man,* Doubleday, 1955.

Miller, Samuel H., *Man the Believer,* Abingdon, 1968.

Monle, C. F., *Man and Nature in New Testament,* Fortress, 1967.

Montegu, Ashley, *The Biosocial Nature of Man,* Grove Press, 1956.

Mork, D. W., *Biblical Meaning of Man,* Bruce, 1967.

Niebuhr, Reinhold, *The Self and the Drama of History,* Scribners, 1955.

Owen, D. R., *Body and Soul,* Westminster, 1956.

Poteat, Edwin, *Jesus' Belief in Man,* Abingdon, 1956.

Roberts, David, *The Grandeur and Misery of Man,* Oxford Univ. Press, 1955.

Shedd, R. R., *Man in Community,* Eerdmans, 1964.

Shinn, R. L., *Man, The New Humanism,* Westminster, 1968.

Teilhard de Chardin, Pierre, *The Future of Man,* Harper, 1964.

Trueblood, D. Elton, *The Predicament of Man,* Harper, 1944.

Winkler, Franz E., *Man, the Bridge Between Two Worlds,* Harper, 1960.

Wolstenhohne, Gordon E., *Man and His Future,* Little, Brown & Co., Boston, 1963.

Wright, G. E., *The Biblical Doctrine of Man and Society,* SCM, 1954.

BASIC CHRISTIAN CONVICTIONS

CHAPTER V

JESUS CHRIST, LORD
AND SAVIOR

"I am the way, and the truth, and the life" (John 14:6).
*For no other foundation can any one lay than that which
is laid, which is Jesus Christ* (I Corinthians 3:11).

A. THE NEED FOR MEDIATION

The doctrine of Christ as mediator between God and man is the
most unique element in Christianity and distinguishes it from all
other faiths although some notion of mediation is also found in
other religions. Without mediation no divine-human intercourse can
take place. Tillich points out that in religion there are two great
demands which he calls "ultimacy" and "concreteness." Only an
"ultimate" divine being (God) can hold man's adoration and worship;
and only a "concretely mediated" divine being (Jesus Christ) can
touch man's life. If ultimacy overshadows concreteness then deity
becomes distant and inaccessible; if concreteness overshadows ultimacy, then idolatry takes place. Only a divine-human mediator can
meet these two demands, and only by some trinitarian formula including the Holy Spirit can the role of such mediator be consistently
presented.[1]

The nature and character of a mediator will of course vary according to the conception of God and man. A crucified Christ is "foolishness to the Greeks" and those who do not see God in history. A
crucified Christ is a "stumbling block to Jews" (I Corinthians
1:23) because, although they see God in history, they look for a
Messiah to triumph immediately, physically and militarily instead
of being crucified.

Pantheistic and monotheistic deities have a tendency to be thought
of as reaching down toward concreteness in various ways; while

---

1. Paul Tillich, *Systematic Theology*, Vol. I, Univ. of Chicago Press, 1951,
pp. 221 ff.

Omit
125–
155

humanistic deities have a tendency to be thought of as reaching upward toward ultimacy. Egyptian Pharaohs, Alexander the Great, Augustus Caesar and his successors, the Emperors of China and Japan, and in our time Hitler, Mussolini, Lenin, and even Mao Tse-tung are considered not only as supermen but as divine-human beings by many of their adoring followers.

The danger of self-deception and disillusionment here is real and great. Yet it is no greater now than it was at the time when Caesar was thought to be the Roman Savior and when in Israel every few years a new political Messiah appeared. We have difficulty in putting ourselves back in historical imagination to the time before Jesus was first called the Christ, the Son of God (Matthew 16:16) and considered to be the divinely anointed Mediator to bring about reconciliation between sinful man and the Holy God.

Man has broken the father-child relationship by his revolt against God and he cannot reestablish the former relationship by himself. The illustration has been used of a man being held by a friend while climbing a high mountain. He can hold on to the helping hand or push it away and free himself from this helping hand. But once he has done so, he falls into the yawning abyss below, and has no way of again grasping the helping hand. He was free to push the helping hand away, but having done so he cannot again get hold of it. Now he will fall to his death unless something unforeseen happens from outside his own power. So the sinner is lost after having revolted against God unless God does something to save him.[2]

Kierkegaard has a similar illustration of a knight, whom two armies invited to fight on their respective side. He makes his choice, but his side is defeated and he is taken prisoner by the victor. Now he foolishly offers his services to the victor. Naturally, the victor tells him he had an opportunity to choose before the battle but went with the enemy, who was defeated and now he is a prisoner of war. So, too, man has broken the relationship with God and made the wrong decision by revolting. Now the sinner can do nothing to restore himself. It all depends upon God.[3]

The Christian faith asserts that God has become man in Jesus Christ so as to bridge the gap caused by man's revolt, and so save him. God coming in human form is called "incarnation" (becoming

---

2. G. F. Forell, *The Protestant Faith*, Prentice-Hall, 1960, p. 166.
3. Soren Kierkegaard, *Philosophical Fragments,* trans. by D. F. Swanson, Princeton Press, 1942, p. 11.

126

flesh). It is a translation of God himself into human language. God is infinite and ultimate, man is finite and limited, so cannot understand God as God. Therefore, God translated himself into terms man can understand. This is what happened in the coming of Jesus Christ through whom God speaks in simple language of action and words and a life that man can understand but the total of which nevertheless is beyond complete human comprehension.

The Christian faith holds that Jesus Christ was both "very God of very God" and truly human, subject to limitations and temptations of human beings. As true man and true God He is the mediator between man and God. As Paul says "For there is one God, and there is one mediator, between God and men, the man Christ Jesus," (I Timothy 2:5).

B.   THE HUMAN LIFE OF JESUS

There is little doubt about the historicity of Jesus. Most of what we know about Him comes from the surviving records of the early Christian community, which we know today as the New Testament. But there also are references to Jesus and His career in non-Christian writings of that period. The Jewish historian Josephus, who was born in Jerusalem about A.D. 37, refers to Jesus in Volume 18 of his massive work, *Jewish Antiquities,* as "a wise man . . . a doer of wonderful works, a teacher of such men as receive the truth gladly." He goes on to say that Jesus "drew to him many of the Jews" but was "condemned to the cross" by the Roman procurator Pontius Pilate at the instigation of certain Jewish leaders.

The Roman historian Tacitus, in Volume 15 of his *Annals,* covering the reign of Nero, reports that the emperor "punished with the utmost cruelty a class of men whom the crowd called Christians." He goes on to relate that the sect got its name from its founder, who "had undergone the death penalty in the reign of Tiberius Caesar, by sentence of the procurator Pontius Pilate."

There are also references to Jesus in the *Talmud.* One passage in "Tractate Sanhedrin of Babylonian Talmud 43a, speaks of Jesus having been executed "'on the eve of the Passover" because He had "enticed Israel to apostasy."[4]

Jesus was born at Bethlehem, a few miles south of Jerusalem, around 6-4 B.C. He grew up in the devout Jewish home of Joseph

---

4. Louis Cassels, *The Real Jesus,* Doubleday, 1968, pp. 7-8.

and Mary in the northern province of Galilee in Nazareth. He had four brothers and at least two sisters (Matthew 13:55-56). The father of the family was a carpenter and Jesus for a time apparently also followed this trade. The facts of His human life are found in four short books at the beginning of the New Testament, by Matthew, Mark, Luke, and John, all written some decades after the human life of Jesus. In them we see Jesus already understood as the Christ of faith.

1. *The Nativity*

Two of the gospel writers, Matthew 1:18-25 and Luke 1:26-35, say that Jesus was born of a virgin mother. This tradition is not mentioned by the other two gospel writers, Mark and John, or anywhere else in the New Testament. Some New Testament scholars consider the virgin birth story an inspired myth which conveys, more vividly than any dry dogma could, the essential Christian conviction that Jesus was a unique person in whom God revealed the very essence of His nature through the medium of a human life. "Myth" is not a synonym for "untrue." It is a literary form in which profound truths are expressed symbolically. In the parables of the Good Samaritan or the Prodigal Son timeless truths, and great moral lessons, are in no wise affected by the fact that Jesus was describing hypothetical rather than actual events.

Matthew reports the virgin birth only from Joseph's experience, while Luke reports it only from Mary's experience, which may indicate that they got it from two different sources. These writers also tell stories regarding wise men, a guiding star, shepherds, and singing by angels. More elaborate stories are to be found in so-called apocryphal gospels.

The genealogies of both Matthew and Luke trace Jesus' ancestry through Joseph and not Mary (Matthew 1:16; Luke 3:23). Luke refers to Joseph and Mary as Jesus' parents five times (2:27, 33, 41, 43, 48) without indicating that Joseph was not really Jesus' father. In the Gospel of John, Joseph is referred to as the father of Jesus (1:45). Paul speaks of Jesus as "descended from David according to the flesh" (Romans 1:3). And David's line ran through Joseph, not Mary.

In the polytheistic world of the Greeks, Egyptians, Persians, and others, it was common to consider a person of outstanding character and achievement as having been fathered by a god of similar character. Plato, Alexander the Great, Augustus, Perseus, Achilles, and Hercules are outstanding examples of men for whom virgin birth was claimed. Besides, Jewish scholars of Jesus' day, interpreted the Old Testament in such an allegorical way that they saw the miraculous child conceptions in the Old Testament as virgin births. Philo of Alexandria thought the conceptions of Sarah, Leah, Rebekah, Zipporah, were examples of this.[5]

In view of such readiness of Greeks and Jews of Jesus' day to believe in virgin births of outstanding men, some scholars hold that the idea of Jesus' virgin birth probably came out of natural reflection upon the amazing greatness of Jesus. The people who flocked to Jesus saw and heard things that surpassed anything they had seen or heard before. Thus Matthew and Luke represent the manner in which one strain of the Christian tradition explained how the fullness of God dwelled and acted in Jesus.

The virgin birth story is a testimony to Jesus' godlike impact upon the people of His day. It points to Christ's origin in God. He came from God and in Him God's advent and epiphany (presence and manifestation) have taken place. In both gospels which mention the virgin birth, reference is made to the Holy Spirit whose function it is to bring divinity and humanity together (Matthew 1:20; Luke 1:35). Karl Barth rightly maintains that the doctrine of the virgin birth upholds the divine initiative in the incarnation.[6]

2. *The Youth in the Temple*

The only story that we have of the boyhood of Jesus relates to His experience in the Temple when His parents took Him along to the passover feast at Jerusalem (Luke 2:41-51). On the way home, the parents missed Him and so

> returned to Jerusalem, seeking him. And after three days they found him in the temple, sitting among the teachers, listening to them and asking them questions; and all who heard him were amazed at his understanding and his answers . . . (Luke 2:45-47).

---

5. De Cherubim 12:13, cited by J. Schoneberg Setzer, *What's Left to Believe,* Abingdon, 1968, p. 103.

6. *Church Dogmatics* I/2, p. 177. Jesus died in about 30 A.D. The earliest written gospel - Mark - dates from around 70 A.D. During the 40 years intervening, the deeds and sayings of Jesus were remembered by Christians in the form of oral tradition. Hence some scholars assume that various stories must have gotten mixed in with the authentic history of Jesus before it was written down. Rudolph Bultman is one of the foremost exponents of "Form Criticism" and "Demythologizing." Some of his books are: *Jesus and the Word,* trans. Scribners, 1934; *Theology of the New Testament,* trans. Scribners, 1955; *Primitive Christianity,* trans. Meridian Books, 1956; *History of the Synoptic Tradition,* trans. Harper, 1963; *Jesus Christ and Mythology,* Scribners, 1958.

Jesus recognized His parents' concern and His own immaturity and so obediently went home with them and "increased in wisdom and stature, and in favor with God and man." The entire incident indicates dedication to God and a growing consciousness of a special mission in life.

3. *Baptism*

An important incident in the life of Jesus was His baptism. For this He went to John who hesitated

> saying, "I need to be baptized by you and do you come to me?" But Jesus answered him, "Let it be so now; for thus it is fitting for us to fulfill all righteousness." Then he consented (Matthew 3:14-15).

And here again, the Holy Spirit plays a part as He attests the divine Sonship. In Mark, the earliest gospel, this experience can quite naturally be read as belonging to the inner experience by Jesus of vision and audition but in Luke and Matthew they are reported as publicly observable events (Mark 1:9-11; Matthew 3:13-17; Luke 3:21-22).

It may well be that Jesus had not only responded to the teachings of John but perhaps even became a member of his group. No doubt the baptismal experience was one of vocation indicating spiritual growth and commitment, the beginning of which was already evident in His temple experience at the age of twelve.

The incarnation, is not best understood as something that happened only in a moment of conception, birth, or baptism, but rather something that included the total human experience of Jesus, from birth through life. Consciousness of vocation does not necessarily come in a moment. It is rather a growing commitment of continued development and increasing conviction. Baptism no doubt was the pivotal and decisive moment in the commitment of Jesus to His career. But this moment no doubt was both preceded and followed by a growing understanding of all that this vocation of being the Messiah implied, finally including the terms of the suffering servant (Isaiah 53).

4. *The Temptations*

There must have been repeated times of temptation in Jesus' career. But now, after the baptismal experience and commitment to the vocation as God's "beloved Son," He "returned from the Jordan, and was led by the Spirit for forty days in the wilderness" and in a special way to wrestle with, and think through, the methods

him a great feast at his house where, to the objection that Jesus eats "with tax collectors and sinners," Jesus answers:

> "Those who are well have no need of a physician, but those who are sick; I have not come to call the righteous, but sinners to repentance" (Luke 5:31-32; Mark 2:13-17; Matthew 9:9-13).

All three Synoptic Gospels relate how finally the twelve were chosen and give their names.

> he appointed twelve to be with him, and to be sent out to preach and have authority to cast out demons: Simon whom he surnamed Peter; James the son of Zebedee and John the brother of James, whom he surnamed Boanerges, that is, sons of thunder; Andrew, and Philip, and Bartholomew, and Matthew, and Thomas, and James the son of Alphaeus, and Thaddaeus, and Simon the Cananaean, and Judas Iscariot, who betrayed him (Mark 3:14-19; cf. Luke 6:12-19; Matthew 20:2-4).

Not only were the twelve sent on missions (Matthew 9:36-11:1; Mark 6:7-13; Luke 9:1-6), but larger groups, as many as seventy, were also sent forth (Luke 10:1-24). All this resulted in many followers, large crowds and widespread fame (Matthew 4:23-25; 12:15-21; Mark 3:7-12; Luke 6:17-19). All of which also caused increased opposition on the part of Jewish authorities.

7. *The Transfiguration*

The story of the transfiguration is one of considerable christological significance. The question has been raised if this was not really an experience after the resurrection.[8] Jesus himself calls it "a vision" (Matthew 17:9). In all three Synoptic Gospels the story comes after the disclosure that the Christ was to suffer (Mark 9:2-8; Matthew 17:1-8; Luke 9:28-36). This the disciples just could not understand. Somehow a transition had to take place from the disciples' acquaintance with the human Jesus, to their faith in Him as the suffering Christ. To make this more clear Jesus takes Peter, James and John apart to a mountain.

The story begins with the human Jesus, who has recently disclosed that He will suffer, or who had recently suffered if the transfiguration experience is taken as post-resurrection. The humanity of Jesus is stressed by His association with Moses and Elijah, indicating His continuity with the prophets. Then He is said to shine like the sun,

---

8. Note similarity to some details in Acts 1.

the divine presence is further experienced in the overshadowing cloud and the voice attesting His Sonship.

The story is telling, in pictorial language, how in the man Jesus, the disciples found and saw God. On the one hand Jesus is human, even to the extent of suffering and dying, yet in this human and suffering Jesus the revelation of God takes place for the disciples. Hence Peter's suggestion to "make three booths" had missed the point altogether. Jesus was not only human, but also the Christ and not in need of a material dwelling place. This experience helped the disciples more fully to grasp the meaning and mission of Jesus as the Christ and the revelation of God. This transition of their view of Jesus was in truth a "transfiguration" of their concept of Jesus and His mission as the Christ.

8. *Arrest and Crucifixion*

That Jesus was crucified under Pontius Pilate is the most fully attested fact in the human life of Jesus. The story of the passion is the strongest possible affirmation of the humanity of Christ. To be human means that one will die. Hence in every Docetic or Gnostic heresy, when speaking of Jesus, His death is explained away - and it is held, that He only *seemed* to die. By holding fast to the centrality of the passion, the Church has recognized the full humanity of Jesus and steered clear of any Docetic heresy. The passion and death of Jesus are the events whereby the human Jesus is revealed as the Christ of faith, or whereby the presence of God manifests itself in Him in a special way.

The full account of Good Friday is given in Matthew 27:32-60; Mark 15:21-47; Luke 23:26-56; John 19:17-42. The fast moving events of that last week include: the triumphal entry into Jerusalem with crowds hailing Jesus as King; teaching in the temple and driving out the profiteers; the Last Supper with His disciples; the agonizing prayer in Gethsemane; the betrayal by Judas; arrest and trial before the Jewish Sanhedrin, and Pilate, and Herod, and again Pilate; the sentence of death; the mocking soldiers; the walk out of the city to Golgotha where crucifixion took place.

Jesus himself made many references to His coming crucifixion before it actually happened, such as in: Matthew 20:17-19; 26:1-2, 31-32; Mark 8:31; 10:32-34; 14:8, 21, 27, 32-34; Luke 9:44; 13:33. The earliest recorded interpretations of the crucifixion are in the letters of Paul and he gives it more attention than does any other New Testament writer, with the possible exception of the writer of Hebrews.

The Jews expected the Messiah to bring liberation from the Roman yoke but Jesus did not do that. In fact, the very crucifixion was evidence enough to the Jews that God's favor was not upon Him. So Paul persecuted the Christians until the living Christ met Him on the Damascus Road and convinced him that Jesus was God's chosen one after all. But if so, why did God allow Him to be crucified? That needed an explanation and Paul spent three years in the Arabian desert rethinking his theology (Galatians 1:17-18).

9. *The Burial Story*

The burial story is recorded by all four gospel writers. Matthew says:

> When it was evening, there came a rich man from Arimathea, named Joseph, who was also a disciple of Jesus. He went to Pilate and asked for the body of Jesus. Then Pilate ordered it to be given to him. And Joseph took the body, and wrapped it in a clean linen shroud, and laid it in his own new tomb, which he had hewn in the rock; and he rolled a great stone to the door of the tomb, and departed. Mary Magdalene and the other Mary were there sitting opposite the sepulchre (Matthew 27:57-61).

Mark adds that Joseph was "a respected member of the council, who was also himself looking for the kingdom of God," and that Pilate asked the centurion "whether he was already dead," before "he granted the body to Joseph," and that "Mary Magdalene, and Mary the mother of Jesus saw where he was laid" (Mark 15:42-47).

Luke's story is very much like Matthew's except that "The women who had come with him from Galilee followed, and saw the tomb, and how his body was laid, then they returned, and prepared spices and ointments" (Luke 23:50-56).

From John we further learn that,

> After this Joseph of Arimathea, who was a disciple of Jesus, but secretly for fear of the Jews . . . Nicodemus also, who had at first come to him by night, came bringing a mixture of myrrh and aloes, about a hundred pounds' weight.

And after wrapping the body of Jesus in "linen cloths with the spices, as is the burial custom of the Jews" they laid the body of Jesus in "a new tomb" in the nearby Garden (John 19:38-42).

In the Gospels, about one-third of the space is given to the events of the last week of the human career of Jesus. This says much as to the importance of these events. The following figures indicate the percentage of space given to the last week in each Gospel.[9]

Gospel	Section	Percentage of Total Book
Matthew	21:1-28:20	28%
Mark	11:1-16:8	37%
Luke	19:28-24:53	23%
John	12:12-21:25	41%

10. The Resurrection and its Mystery

In the Christian faith the resurrection has come to be considered as God's validation of all the claims of Jesus as the Son of God and Savior of men. Hence the resurrection, however it may be interpreted, is considered the cornerstone and foundation of the Christian faith. With the resurrection the Christian faith stands or falls.[10]

Evidences of the resurrection can be considered of two kinds. First we look at some evidences related to the resurrection event as such.

(a) *Jesus said* He would rise again. The fact that whenever Jesus spoke of His impending suffering, He also often referred to His resurrection, is significant.

(b) *The enemies remembered this* and had the grave sealed and the tomb watched by a guard (Matthew 27:26-66). But all this could not prevent the resurrection and the guard reported to the chief priests what had happened. After the leaders consulted with each other,

> they gave a sum of money to the soldiers and said, "Tell people, 'His disciples came by night and stole him away while we were asleep.' And if this comes to the governor's ears, we will satisfy him and keep you out of trouble." So they took the money and did as they were directed (Matthew 28:12-15).

(c) *The tomb was found empty* when on the morning of the third day certain women came with spices to complete the anointing of the body of Jesus. Some of them had seen where Joseph and Nicodemus laid the body (Mark 15:17; Luke 23:55) and watched the process of burial "sitting opposite the sepulchre" (Matthew 27:61). John and Peter coming to the tomb soon thereafter also found it empty (John 20:2).

---

9. J. R. M. Scott, *Basic Christianity*. Inter-varsity Fellowship, London, 1963, p. 45 ff.

10. R. H. Fuller, *The Formation of the Resurrection Narratives*, Macmillan, 1971.

(d) *That the graveclothes were left in the tomb undisturbed* is important. John describes his own experience:

> Simon Peter and the other disciple, the one whom Jesus loved . . . ran, but the other disciple outran Peter and reached the tomb first; and stooping to look in, he saw the linen cloths lying there, but he did not go in. Then Simon Peter came, following him, and went into the tomb; he saw the linen cloths lying, and the napkin, which had been on his head, not lying with the linen cloths but rolled up in place by itself. Then the other disciple, who reached the tomb first, also went in, saw and believed (John 20:2, 4-8).

Just what did they "see" that made them believe? The way John tells the story suggests that it was not only the absence of the body, but also the presence of the gravecloths, and especially, their undisturbed condition.

When Joseph asked Pilate for the body of Jesus, Nicodemus also

> . . . came bringing a mixture of myrrh and aloes, about a hundred pounds' weight. They took the body of Jesus, and bound it in linen cloths with the spices, as is the burial custom of the Jews (John 19:39, 40).

A separate cloth was no doubt used for His head, as in the case of Lazarus (John 11:44). Thus they wrapped the body and head, leaving the face and neck bare. Then they laid the body on a stone slab, hewn out of the side of the cave-tomb.

Can it be assumed that in the resurrection Jesus did not begin to move, yawn, stretch and then get up as though He recovered from sleep or a fainting spell? This was a resurrection not a "resuscitation." Could He have passed through death into an altogether new kind of existence? Could His body just have disappeared, vaporized, as it were, transmuted into something new and different, passing through the undisturbed cloths? Naturally the body cloths, with the weight of 100 pounds of spices, would collapse once the body was gone, and would now be lying flat on the stone slab. There would be a gap between the body cloths and the head napkin.

A careful reading of the above passage suggests that there were certain characteristics of the empty gravecloths that John noticed. He saw "the napkin, which had been on his head, not lying with the linen cloths." And he saw that the head napkin was "rolled up in a place by itself," not bundled up or tossed in a corner, but still on the stone slab, only separated from the body cloths. So when Peter and John went into the tomb they noticed the stone slab, the collapsed gravecloths, the shell of the head napkin and a gap between the two. Was it this combination that convinced them not only of the reality of the resurrection, but also indicated its nature as well? The cloths had been neither touched nor folded. They were like the discarded chrysalis left by the butterfly as it emerges. The presence of the undisturbed cloths and the absence of the body were concurrent witnesses to His resurrection.

(e) *The Lord was seen* by various persons on different occasions after the resurrection. Including Paul's experience, the record has twelve separate appearances to those "chosen by God as witnesses." Here is the list: (1) First He appeared to Mary Magdalene (Mark 16:9; John 20:11-18); (2) Then to the women returning from the empty tomb (Matthew 28:8-10); (3) To Peter (Luke 24:34; I Corinthians 15:5); (4) To two on the road to Emmaus (Mark 16:12, 13; Luke 24:13-35); (5) To the ten gathered in the upper room without Thomas (Luke 24:26-42; John 20:19-23); (6) To the eleven, including Thomas (Mark 16:14; John 20:24-39); (7) To seven by the Sea of Tiberias (John 21:1-23); (8) To eleven on a mountain in Galilee (Matthew 28:16-20); (9) To James (I Corinthians 15:7); (10) To more than 500 persons at once (I Corinthians 15:6); (11) To eleven on the Mount of Olives, at His ascension (Luke 24:50-53; Acts 1:6-12); (12) To Paul on the Damascus Road (Acts 9:1-9; I Corinthians 15:8).[11]

Luke tells us that Jesus "presented himself alive after his passion by many proofs, appearing to them during forty days" (Acts 1:3), so there may have been other appearances of which we have no record.

The appearances did not all happen in a few sacred places that were hallowed by their memories of experiences with Jesus before the crucifixion, such as the upper room. They were in a variety of circumstances, places, persons, and moods. Three appearances were to individuals (Mary Magdalene, Peter, and James), one was to two persons on the road to Emmaus, at one appearance seven were present, at another ten, at another eleven, and at still another "more than five hundred" (I Corinthians 15:16).

The places where He appeared also varied: the garden of the tomb, between the garden and the city, the upper room, the road to Emmaus, the mountain in Galilee, the shore of Tiberias, the Mount of Olives near Bethany, and the road to Damascus.

---

11. E. Torline, *Finding God Through Christ*, Abingdon, 1947, p. 113.

The moods of people to whom He appeared also varied: Mary Magdalene was weeping, the other women were afraid, Peter was remorseful, Thomas incredulous, the Emmaus two were puzzled, and Saul was on a mission of persecution. But still through doubts, fears, and unbelief, the Lord made himself known to them as the living Christ, however interpreted.

(f) *The enemies never produced the body*. Some would explain the disappearance of the body of Jesus as having perhaps been taken away by the Roman or Jewish authorities themselves, to forestall trickery. However, shortly after the crucifixion the disciples began to preach the resurrection, the news spread rapidly and threatened to undermine the authority of Judaism and to disturb the peace of Jerusalem. The Jews feared conversions and the Romans feared riots. In this situation the authorities, if they had taken the body of Jesus, had a simple remedy to quiet things down. They could produce the body of Jesus and announce what they had done, thereby indicating that this claim of resurrection was all a fraud. But instead they were silent and resorted to violence, arresting the apostles, imprisoning them, and finally killing some of them. If the authorities could have produced the body of Jesus that would have disproved the resurrection.

(g) *The transformation of the disciples* by these experiences is probably the best evidence for the resurrection, however interpreted. They did not expect and were greatly surprised when Jesus appeared after burial. Again and again we read that they did not believe it (Mark 16:11, 13, 14; Matthew 24:11). They considered Jesus dead and buried. When the women came to complete the anointing and found the tomb empty

> they went out and fled from the tomb; for trembling and astonishment had come upon them; and they said nothing to any one, for they were afraid (Mark 16:8).

And when the women reported their experience to the disciples, "They would not believe it" (Mark 16:11), and their words "seemed to them an idle tale" (Luke 24:11). When Jesus stood in their midst "they were startled and frightened" (Luke 24:37), and Jesus "upbraided them for their unbelief" (Mark 16:14). Thomas refused to believe unless he could feel and see the wounds in His hands and in the side of His body (John 22:24, 25). And later when Jesus met the eleven and others on a mountain in Galilee, "they worshipped him; but some doubted" (Matthew 28:17). The disciples were cautious and skeptical. They were "slow of heart to believe" (Luke 24:25). Only gradually did they come to accept the resurrection as a fact, but once convinced nothing could shake them. Their faith was grounded upon personal experience.

Not only did the apostles center their preaching on the resurrection but they were willing even to suffer for such preaching. If the disciples really stole the body as the authorities wanted people to believe, then they certainly would not have been willing to become martyrs for the cause. Hypocrites and martyrs are too different for that combination.

During the crucifixion, Peter three times denied with cursing that he even knew Jesus. After Jesus was dead and buried, Peter joins the other disciples in the upper room behind barred doors "for fear of the Jews" (John 20:19). But after he is convinced that Christ is living, he is boldly preaching to a large crowd, and so powerfully that three thousand people accept Christ and are baptized. Now he is defying the very Sanhedrin which had condemned Jesus to death, and is glad when he is counted worthy to suffer shame for his Lord, even though it might mean his execution (Acts 2:14-41; 4:1-22; 7:1-6). Now Peter had become a rock, fearlessly declaring "this Jesus, . . . you crucified and killed. . . . But God raised him up, . . . and of that we all are witnesses" (Acts 2:23, 24, 32).

Or look at James, one of the brothers of Jesus, who throughout the Gospels is represented as not believing. We read "Even his brothers did not believe in him" (John 7:5). But after the resurrection when Luke enumerates the assembled disciples in the upper room for prayer, he concludes the list thus: "together with the women and Mary the mother of Jesus, and with his brothers" (Acts 1:14). And soon this James, the brother of Jesus, becomes the head of the Jerusalem church. The difference in James, no doubt, is accounted for by the fact that he had seen the resurrected Jesus, as Paul points out in his list of appearances when he says: "Then he appeared to James" (I Corinthians 15:7).

The resurrection changed Peter from a man of fear into one of courage, James from a person of doubt to one of faith, it changed Saul the persecutor into Paul the apostle. The living Lord was seen and experienced and the disciples were transformed thereby. They were convinced that Jesus was not dead but alive, and that they were "chosen by God as witnesses" to this fact (Acts 10:39-42). The disciples of the four Gospels are new and different men in the Acts. They were despondent, disillusioned and near despair at the crucifixion but after the resurrection they emerge as men of great courage who "risked their lives for the sake of our Lord Jesus Christ" (Acts 15:26). Now they became known as "men who have turned the world up side down" (Acts 17:8).[12]

The Resurrection Influence on History was very great and far-reaching. The seven items listed above are related directly to the resurrection event as such. We turn now briefly to five results as they developed in later history.

(a) *The Christian Church* began with a Jewish remnant looking for the Messiah. After the resurrection this remnant gradually was transformed into the beginning of the Christian Church. Jesus and His early followers were Jews. This was also true of the apostle Paul who took the Gospel to the Gentiles where the movement spread until today the Christian Church encircles the entire globe.

(b) *The production of the New Testament* was one result of the resurrection faith of the early Church.

(c) *The Christian Sunday* replaced the Jewish Sabbath Saturday. The Sabbath was deeply rooted in Jewish history and tradition, as the sacred day of weekly rest and worship. Although the early Christians were Jews the change from the last day of the week as the holy day to the first day of the week came about because of the resurrection on that day.

(d) *The Lord's Supper* has become a sacrament of joy and thanksgiving, whereas without the resurrection faith, it would be one of sorrowful remembrance.

(e) *The B.C. and A.D. division* of history recognizes the resurrected Christ as Lord of History.

These five continuing processes in history are not proofs but quite incontrovertible evidences of the resurrection.

The Mystery of the Resurrection is beyond human comprehension. Scholars differ in their interpretation. In answer to the question why Jesus appeared only to friends of His and not also to enemies, it

---

12. For fuller discussion see *Basic Christianity*, J. R. M. Scott, Inter-Varsity Fellowship, London, 1963, pp. 45-49; James A. Pike, *A Time for Christian Candor*, Harper, 1964, pp. 116-119; Paul Hessert, *Introduction to Christianity*, Prentice-Hall, 1958, pp. 200-203. The "Demythologizers" have been referred to earlier in this chapter in relation to the birth of Jesus. The books by Rudolph Bultman listed there also pertain to questions of miracles, the resurrection and the ascension of Jesus.

can be said that this was in line with His spirit before the resurrection. He never compelled anyone to believe.

If all this was deliberate invention there would be more consistency evident and the doubts and fears of the apostles would not be so prominently reported. Then, too, there would have been more description given in a dramatic account of the power and glory of Jesus as He broke the power of death and burst from the tomb in triumph. But according to the report no one saw it happen.

Naturally there are questions which remain unanswered. For example: What does it mean that the post-resurrection appearances in John and Luke take place at Jerusalem while those of Matthew and Mark in Galilee? In Luke 24:12 Peter alone comes to the empty tomb, while in John 20:3-8 it is Peter and "that other disciple." The Synoptics speak more in physical terms of the resurrection which is not so much the case in John and Paul. In the four Gospels, Jesus eats and is touched. With Paul this is not the case; here a light is seen and a voice is heard but not always by the same persons in the various accounts (see Acts 9:3-7; 22:6-10; 26:12-18). In Mark 6:5 we read of a young man at the grave, in Luke 24:4 of two men, in Matthew 28:2 of an angel, and in John 20:12 of two angels. In the synoptics the women are frightened while in John, Mary indicates no fear. In John 20:17 Jesus says "do not touch me," while in Matthew 28:9 the disciples "took hold of his feet."

Evidently the post-resurrection body of Jesus was not subject to normal physical conditions, yet it could be made manifest to the physical senses. The body of the risen Christ was evidently different from that of the historical Jesus. Mark 16:12 says "he appeared in another form." He came through closed doors (John 20:26), and showed the wounds of the nails in His hands and that of the spear in His side. He ate with them (Luke 24:43, John 1:13) to indicate that He was not a mere ghost. Some of His bodily characteristics were the same and some were different from His being before His death. The disciples were not always sure that it was Jesus. The view of the risen Jesus as having "a spiritual body" coincides with Paul's description of the general resurrection:

> But if there is no resurrection of the dead, then Christ has not been raised; If Christ has not been raised, then our preaching is in vain and your faith is in vain. . . . If in this life we who are in Christ have only hope, we are of all men most to be pitied. . . . But some one will ask "How are the dead raised? With what kind of body do they come?" . . . What is sown is perishable, what is raised is imperishable . . . It is sown a physical body, it is raised

142   BASIC CHRISTIAN CONVICTIONS

a spiritual body . . . flesh and blood cannot inherit the kingdom of God, nor does the perishable inherit the imperishable . . . we shall be changed. For this perishable nature must put on the imperishable, and this mortal nature must put on immortality . . . then shall come to pass the saying that is written: "Death is swallowed up in victory." "O death where is thy victory? O death where is thy sting?" (I Corinthians 15:13, 19, 20, 42, 44, 50, 53-55).

As finite human beings we can only speak of infinite reality in symbolical and allegorical language. Paul's letter was written before the Gospels and he, as does the entire New Testament, makes a distinction between the bodily appearance of Jesus after the resurrection from what it had been during His earthly life. Whatever the resurrected Christ may have looked like, it is clear that the experience of the risen Christ was the most real and lasting experience of the entire life for the disciples and Paul. It became the basis of their faith and gave life new meaning; they banded together, formed the Church, and set out on a lifelong mission as ambassadors of the God revealed in Jesus Christ.

For later Christians the external object of Christ's body is not present, but the internal content of the experience of meeting the Living Christ seems to be the same. Their lives are also changed, integrated and dedicated to His cause. The resurrection means that God did not lose, that the good finally did triumph, that evil and death were overcome. The resurrection makes life meaningful. It indicates that life need not ultimately be tragic but in Christ can be triumphant. Jesus said "Be of good cheer, I have overcome the world" (John 16:33).

Our own interpretation about the experience of the disciples will ultimately depend upon our own experiences of God and Christ. Our own belief in Christ as the Incarnation of God, is a matter partly of fact, partly of experience, and partly of interpretation and faith. It is never only one to the exclusion of all other factors.

The Christian symbol of the resurrection, par excellence, is the emergence of the glorious butterfly from the lowly caterpillar, in the shape unpredictable on the basis of preceding structure.[13]

---

13. A butterfly is only one of four stages in the life of an insect starting as a *tiny egg* laid on a leaf, then becoming a *larvae or caterpiller* which eats leaves and plants for food and turns into a soft object called a *pupa* or chrysalis covered with a shell. After the transforming of the pupa inside, the chrysalis bursts and a bright beautiful *butterfly emerges,* slowly spreads its wings and flies away. The butterfly will feast on the nectar of flowers and find a mate. The females will lay eggs and start the cycle over again. See Encyclopedia Americana, Vol. V, p. 88.

The doctrine of the Resurrection, like the doctrines of Revelation and Incarnation, cannot be properly evaluated in isolation. The three doctrines are bound together and all three stand or fall together. Holding to one virtually commits one also to hold to the other two. If Jesus Christ was in some sense a unique revelation of God, then He was in that sense God incarnate and it is not plausible to expect God in Christ to be defeated on the cross. If God was present in the whole drama of the life and death of Christ, it is only reasonable that He would be victorious in the end by way of the resurrection.

It was the series of experiences of the disciples and early Christians that convinced them that God, and not evil or death, was Lord. Those experiences have been shared by millions since the New Testament period. The whole testimony of the Christian witness is an experience of the living God as He revealed himself through the resurrected Christ then, and the living Christ ever since.

11. *The Ascension*

The ascension, as the resurrection, can be interpreted in different ways. It can be taken as a literal, physical happening. But as a purely historical event it implies a cosmology that modern science has abandoned. Yet as a symbol it expresses the significance of Christ with appropriateness and truth as the culmination of the earthly life of Jesus. In Luke's words Christ "was lifted up, and a cloud took him out of their sight" (Acts 1:9). This suggests that He had become the exalted Lord in the hearts and minds of His disciples, the Christ of faith and one with the Father. It suggests further that the offering of His life was received by God as the smoke of the old sacrifices had gone up into the sky.

The ascension is not a separate event. As a part of His mission on earth it is a symbol of the larger event beginning with His coming and including His entire life and teaching as well as the various items listed above relating to His earthly life. In other words, the ascension is the final symbol of the fact that "the Word was made flesh, and dwelt among us" (John 1:14), namely the incarnation.

The above items in the life of Jesus, highlight the understanding of Jesus that is presented by the whole Gospel story. His entire life, including His teaching, healing, miracles, along with other outstanding events were all signs of the inbreaking Kingdom of God. The total purpose of the entire gospel material then is to present us with one who is unquestionably human, but in whom God also had become incarnate and manifest in a very exceptional degree and manner.

BASIC CHRISTIAN CONVICTIONS

C. Jesus and His Contemporaries

What did the contemporaries of Jesus think of Him? By contemporaries we mean His immediate family and relatives, His neighbors and friends, the general public, His enemies, and finally His disciples. Repeatedly during the teaching and ministry of Jesus here on earth the question was asked: *"Who is this?"*

When Jesus said to a helpless paralytic "your sins are forgiven you" the scribes and Pharisees began to question, saying "Who is this that speaks blasphemies?" (Luke 5:20-21). When Jesus stilled the tempest on the Sea of Galilee, His astonished disciples asked, "Who then is this, that even wind and sea obey him?" (Mark 4:41). One day Jesus was a guest at a Pharisee's house and a woman "which was a sinner" came in and washed His feet with tears, wiped them with her hair, and then anointed them with precious ointment. Jesus said to her, "Your sins are forgiven." Then those who were at the table with Him began to say among themselves, "Who is this, who even forgives sins?" (Luke 7:48, 49). When Herod, after he had beheaded John, heard reports of Jesus' ministry, he was perplexed and exclaimed, "John I beheaded; but who is this about whom I hear such things?" (Luke 9:9). Finally when Jesus rode into Jerusalem on a docile donkey, we are told that, "all the city was stirred, saying 'Who is this?' " (Matthew 21:10).

1. *Relatives, Friends and Neigbhors*

Let us begin with His mother Mary. Although she never quite understood Jesus, she kept her faith in Him. After the heart searching experience with the twelve-year old Jesus, we read that "his mother kept all these things in her heart" (Luke 2:51).

She was also concerned for His welfare during His ministry (Matthew 12:46) and was even present at the crucifixion (John 19: 26, 27). Although often puzzled, the mother never lost faith in her son and remained loyal to Him.

About His brothers we read,

> After this Jesus went about in Galilee . . . So his brothers said to him, "Leave here and go to Judea . . . For no man works in secret if he seeks to be known openly. If you do these things, show yourself to the world." For even his brothers did not believe in him (John 7:1-5).

Even if they did not believe in Him they were nevertheless concerned about Him. On one occasion, "While he was still speaking to the people, behold, his mother and his brothers stood outside, asking to speak to him" (Matthew 12:46).

The neighbors and friends of Jesus were greatly puzzled by Jesus.

> Then he went home; and the crowd came together again, so that they could not even eat. And when his friends heard it, they went out to seize him, for they said, "He is beside himself" (Mark 3: 20-21).

And again, we read:

> coming into his own country he taught them in their synagogue, so that they were astonished, and said, "Where did this man get this wisdom and these mighty works? Is not this the carpenter's son? Is not his mother called Mary? And are not his brothers James and Joseph and Simon and Judas? And are not all his sisters with us? Where did this man get all this?" And they took offense at him (Matthew 13:54-57; cf. Mark 6:1-3).

2. *The General Public*

The general public naturally took various attitudes toward Jesus.

> There was again a division among the Jews because of these words. Many of them said, "He has a demon and, he is mad; why listen to him?" Others said, "These are not the sayings of one who has a demon. Can a demon open the eyes of the blind?" (John 10: 19-21).

There were also those who wanted to make Him king. After feeding the 5000 we read,

> When the people saw the sign which he had done, they said, "This is indeed the prophet" . . . Perceiving then that they were about to come and take him by force to make him king, Jesus withdrew . . . (John 6:14, 15).

He was recognized as teaching with authority. People were astonished. We read:

> "Where did this man get all this? What is the wisdom given to him?" (Mark 6:2). "How is it that this man has learning, when he has never studied?" (John 7:15). "No man ever spoke like this man!" (John 7:46). They were astonished at his teaching for his word was with authority (Luke 4:32 cf. Matthew 7:28).

During the last week when Jesus entered Jerusalem riding a donkey the multitude

> began to rejoice and praise God with a loud voice . . . saying "Blessed is the King who comes in the name of the Lord!" (Luke 19:37-38).

And during the crucifixion

> Pilate also wrote a title and put it on the cross; it read, "Jesus of Nazareth, the King of the Jews" (John 19:19; cf. Luke 23:38).

No doubt the general public thought of Jesus in connection with the expected Messiah who was to serve as King and free them from the yoke of Rome.

3. *The Enemies of Jesus*

The enemies of Jesus had very definite ideas about Him. His relatives, friends and neighbors might have been biased in His favor but certainly His enemies could not be accused of that. "They watched him" (Mark 3:2). They tried "to entrap him in his talk" (Mark 12:13). As is usually the case, when enemies cannot win by argument they resort to personal abuse. One of their accusations was blasphemy. Jesus had forgiven a man's sins. This the enemies considered blasphemous arrogance (Mark 2:5-7). Repeatedly, scribes, Pharisees, and others accused Him of blaspheming (Matthew 9:3; 26:65; Mark 14:64; Luke 5:21).

A second accusation of the enemies was that He associated with evil characters, which horrified them. He fraternized with sinners and ate with publicans (Matthew 9:11).

> "John came neither eating nor drinking, and they say 'He has a demon'; the Son of man came eating and drinking, and they say, 'Behold, a glutton and a drunkard, a friend of tax collectors and sinners!' . . ." (Matthew 11:18, 19).

They considered His religion as rather frivolous. He would not fast like the Pharisees, or even like the disciples of John. Jesus was a joyful person but there is no doubt that He took religion seriously.

In the third place the enemies were incensed by what they called His sabbath-breaking. He healed on the sabbath day. His disciples walked through the fields on the sabbath, plucking, rubbing and eating grain. This to the Scribes and Pharisees was reaping and threshing, and was forbidden. In answer Jesus affirmed that "The sabbath was made for man, not man for the sabbath" (Mark 2:27). On another occasion when the Scribes and Pharisees watched whether He would heal a sick man on the sabbath, we read:

> he knew their thoughts, and he said to the man who had the withered hand, "Come and stand here." And he rose and stood there. And Jesus said to them, "I ask you, is it lawful on the sabbath to do good or to do harm, to save life, or to destroy it?" And he looked around on them all, and said to him, "Stretch out

your hand." And he did so, and his hand was restored. But they were filled with fury and discussed with one another what they might do to Jesus (Luke 6:8-11).

A fourth accusation the enemies had was that "He is possessed by Beelzebul, and by the prince of demons he casts out the demons" (Mark 3:22; Matthew 12:24; Luke 11:15). Interestingly enough the demons, or those possessed by them, are reported as recognizing Jesus as the Son of God. One, whose name was Legion,

> When he saw Jesus he cried out and fell down before him, and said with a loud voice, "What have you to do with me, Jesus, Son of the Most High God?" (Luke 8:28; Mark 5:7).

When the end came and Jesus was on trial for His life, His detractors hired false witnesses against Him but even they did not agree with each other. The only charge the enemies finally could trump up against Him was not moral but political, namely, that He claimed to be "king of the Jews" (Luke 23:2-4). When Pilate heard that Jesus was a Galilean he sent Him to Herod, who found no fault in Him either, and upon His return to Pilate, he

> said to them, "You brought me this man as one who was perverting the people; and after examining him before you, behold, I did not find this man guilty of any of your charges against him, neither did Herod, for he sent him back to us. Behold, nothing deserving death has been done by him" (Luke 23:14, 15).

Even Pilate's wife, after her troublesome dream sent word asking Pilate to "have nothing to do with this righteous man" (Matthew 27:19). After several attempts to extricate himself from this situation, Pilate

> took water and washed his hands before the crowd, saying, "I am innocent of this man's blood; see to it yourselves" (Matthew 27:24).

Judas, filled with remorse "brought back the thirty pieces of silver to the chief priests and the elders, saying 'I have sinned in betraying innocent blood' " (Matthew 27:3, 4). The penitent thief on the cross rebuked his confederate for his abuse and added, "this man has done nothing wrong" (Luke 23:41). And finally the centurion, having watched Jesus suffer and die, exclaimed, "Certainly this man was innocent!" (Luke 23:47).

4. *The Disciples' Evaluation of Jesus*

Before calling in the disciples let us look at the testimony given Jesus by John the Baptist who was also a relative of His. While John was baptizing at the Jordan,

> . . . the Jews sent priests and Levites from Jerusalem to ask him, "Who are you?" . . . John answered them, "I baptize with water; but among you stands one whom you do not know, even he who comes after me, the thong of whose sandal I am not worthy to untie." . . . The next day he saw Jesus coming toward him, and said, "Behold, the Lamb of God, who takes away the sin of the world. This is he of whom I said, 'After me comes a man who ranks before me, for he was before me.' . . . And I have seen and have borne witness that this is the Son of God" (John 1:19, 26-27, 29-30; cf. Matthew 3:13-15).

Now to the disciples who are most important witnesses for they lived in close intimacy with Jesus for some three years. They ate, worked, slept together and had a common purse. The disciples often found fault with each other but never found the sins in Jesus that they found in themselves. Often, familiarity breeds contempt, but not in the close relationship of the disciples with Jesus.

The disciples all were Jews who knew the Old Testament Scriptures from their childhood. One of the outstanding doctrines of the Old Testament is the universality of human sin, "All we like sheep have gone astray; we have turned every one to his own way" (Isaiah 53:6). Or listen to the Psalmist:

> The Lord looks down from heaven upon the children of men, to see if there are any that act wisely, that seek God. They have all gone astray, they are all alike corrupt; there is none that does good, no, not one (Psalm 14:2, 3).

Having imbibed this teaching from their youth, the disciples would not easily have attributed sinlessness to anyone. But this is what they and Paul as New Testament writers say about Jesus.

Peter describes Jesus as "a lamb without blemish or spot" (I Peter 1:19), and goes on to say that "He committed no sin; no guile was found on his lips" (I Peter 2:22). John, after indicating that "if we say we have no sin, we deceive ourselves" (I John 1:8), then goes on to say, "You know that he appeared to take away sins, and in him there is no sin" (I John 3:5). Paul describes Jesus as One "who knew no sin" (I Corinthians 5:21). The author of Hebrews speaks of Jesus as

> . . . one who in every respect has been tempted as we are, yet without sinning . . . holy, blameless, unstained, separated from sinners, exalted above the heavens. He has no need, like those priests to offer sacrifices daily, first for his own sins and then for those of the people; he did this once for all when he offered up himself (Hebrews 4:15; 7:26, 27).

On the question of Jesus being the Son of God, Peter's confession is outstanding. When Jesus

> asked his disciples, "Who do men say that the Son of man is?" And they said, "Some say John the Baptist, others say Elijah, and others Jeremiah or one of the prophets." He said unto them, "But who do you say that I am?" Simon Peter replied, "You are the Christ, the Son of the living God" (Matthew 16:13-16; cf. Mark 8:27-29; Luke 9:18-20).

Peter's judgment on another occasion is also significant. When Jesus likened himself to the manna the fathers had in the wilderness

> . . . many of his disciples drew back and no longer went about with him. Jesus said to the twelve, "Will you also go away?" Simon Peter answered him, "Lord, to whom shall we go? You have the words of eternal life; and we have believed and have come to know that you are the Holy one of God" (John 6: 66-69).

Others also considered Jesus to be the Son of God. When Philip asked Nathanael to come and meet Jesus and he came and was so surprised that Jesus seemed to know him, even before Philip came to Him, he exclaimed, "Rabbi you are the Son of God! You are the King of Israel" (John 1:49). The reference to the "King of Israel" probably indicates that as yet Nathanael hardly thought of Jesus as "the Son of God" with the same implication that is contained in Peter's confession.

At the death of Lazarus Jesus said to Martha:

> "I am the resurrection and the life, he who believes in me, though he die, yet shall he live . . . Do you believe this?" She said to him, "Yes, Lord; I believe that you are the Christ the Son of God" (John 11:25-27).

Here, too, one wonders just what she meant.

Probably as strong and meaningful as any answer to the question who Jesus was that we have in Scripture is that of doubting Thomas, although this was after the resurrection. We read:

> Eight days later, his disciples were again in the house, and Thomas was with them. The doors were shut, but Jesus came and stood among them, and said, "Peace be with you." Then he said to Thomas, "Put your finger here, and see my hands; and put out your hand, and place it in my side; do not be faithless, but believing." Thomas answered him, "My Lord and my God" (John 20:26-28).

Others had used the phrase "Son of God" but Thomas says more by acclaiming Jesus as his Lord and God.

BASIC CHRISTIAN CONVICTIONS

Many asked who Jesus really was. That He was an extraordinary person is clear from the range of testimonies of different persons who came in contact with Him. We have referred to His mother and His relatives, friends and neighbors; His enemies and even the demons or those possessed by them; the general public; John the Baptist; and the disciples of Jesus himself. Jesus himself depended upon the Holy Spirit to make the answer to this question clear after the resurrection and that then His disciples would be His chief witnesses. He said:

> "But when the Counselor comes, whom I shall send to you from the Father, even the Spirit of truth, who proceeds from the Father, he will bear witness to me; and you also are witnesses, because you have been with me from the beginning" (John 15: 26-27).

This the disciples did, when with Paul, under the guidance of the Holy Spirit they began building the Christian Church. We close this section by two quotations from John that have a bearing on this point:

> For God so loved the world that he gave his only Son, that whoever believes in him should not perish but have eternal life (John 3:16). Now Jesus did many other signs in the presence of the disciples which are not written in this book; but these are written that you may believe that Jesus is the Christ, the Son of God, and that believing you may have life in his name (John 20:30).

D.   Jesus' Own Claims About Himself

Brief consideration is here given to Jesus' words, His deeds, and His character, as indicating who He was.

1.   *His Words*

In some ways Jesus seems rather self-advancing as compared with other great religious leaders. They point from themselves and say "that is the truth, follow it," but Jesus said:

> "I am the bread of life; he who comes to me shall not hunger" (John 6:35). "I am the light of the world; he who follows me will not walk in darkness, but will have the light of life" (John 8:12). "I am the door; if any one enters by me, he will be saved" (John 10:9). "I am the good shepherd. The good shepherd lays down his life for the sheep" (John 10:11). "I am the resurrection and the life; he who believes in me, though he die, yet shall he live" (John 11:25). "I am the way, the truth, and the life; no one comes to the Father, but by me" (John 14:6). "I am the vine, you are the branches" (John 15:5). "I said, 'I am the Son of God' " (John 10:36).

He affirmed that Abraham rejoiced to see His day (John 8:56), that Moses had written of Him (John 5:39) and that in the Old Testament there were "Things concerning himself" (Luke 24:27, 44). When He was visiting His home village Nazareth He was given a scroll of Scripture and He stood up and read the passage from Isaiah 61:1-2:

> "The Spirit of the Lord is upon me, because he has anointed me to preach good news to the poor. He has sent me to proclaim release to the captives and recovering of sight to the blind, to set at liberty those who are oppressed, to proclaim the acceptable year of the Lord" (Luke 4:18-19).

Then He closed the book, sat down, and after a while broke the silence with the amazing words, "Today, this scripture has been fulfilled in your hearing" (Luke 4:21). Meaning: "Isaiah was speaking of me."

So convinced was He of His central place in God's program that He promised to send the Holy Spirit to take His place after He would return to heaven. The Holy Spirit (Paraclete) would be the Comforter, that is, an advocate whose task would be to plead the cause of Jesus before the world (John 15:26; 16:12-15).

Jesus clearly believed himself to be the Messiah of the Old Testament expectation. However, He did not think of this in a materialistic or military way as the Jews were inclined to interpret the Messiah. After John was arrested, Mark tells us Jesus came into Galilee preaching "The time is fulfilled, and the kingdom of God is at hand" (Mark 1:15). He accepted and assumed the title "Son of Man" but also accepted the description "Son of God" when challenged by the high priest (Mark 14:61, 62). He interpreted His mission in the light of the suffering servant portrayed by Isaiah. He was not just another prophet but the one to whom the prophets pointed. He told His disciples

> "But blessed are your eyes, for they see, and your ears, for they hear. Truly I say to you, many prophets and righteous men longed to see what you see, and to hear what you hear, and did not hear it" (Matthew 13:16, 17; cf. Luke 10:23, 24).

This Messiahship can also be seen in His reference to His close relation to His Father. He said:

> "Did you not know that I must be in my Father's house?" (Luke 2:49). "My Father is working still, and I am working" (John 5:17). "I and the Father are one" (John 10:30). "Do you not believe that I am in the Father and the Father in me?"

(John 14:10, 11). "All things have been delivered to me by my Father: and no one knows the Son except the Father, and no one knows the Father except the Son and any one to whom the Son chooses to reveal him" (Matthew 11:27).

This claim of intimate relation with God aroused the Jews "because he has made himself the Son of God" (John 19:7). Men's attitude toward himself He equated with man's attitude to God. To know Him was to know God (John 8:19; 14:7); to see Him was to see God (John 12:45; 14:9); to believe in Him was to believe in God (John 12:44; 14:1); to receive Him was to receive God (Mark 9: 37); to hate Him was to hate God (John 15:23); to honor Him was to honor God (John 5:23).

When Jesus told the Jews, "Truly, truly I say to you, if any one keeps my word, he will never see death," that was too much for His critics. They pointed out "Abraham died, as did the prophets . . . are you greater than our father Abraham, who died? And the prophets died! Who do you claim to be?" The Jews were still more perplexed when He answered them "Your father Abraham rejoiced to see my day; he saw it and was glad." And when they pointed out that He was not yet fifty years old, how could He have seen Abraham, He answered: "Truly, truly, I say to you, before Abraham was, I am" (John 8:51-59). Now the Jews were going to stone Him, for this "Before Abraham was, I am," to them meant that He claimed deity, for this "I am who I am" was the name God had given to himself when speaking to Moses at the burning bush (Exodus 3:14).

Jesus repeatedly assumed prerogatives which are divine. He declared that "the Son of man gives life to whom he will" (John 5:21). He never hesitated, apologized, withdrew or modified anything He said, so far as the record goes. He asserted that His words were eternal, "heaven and earth will pass away, but my words will not pass away" (Mark 13:31). Repeatedly He said "it was said to the men of old . . . but I say to you" (Matthew 5:21-22, 27-28, 31-32, 33-34, 38-39, 43-44). He warned His hearers that their destiny depended upon their response to His words (Matthew 7:24-27; John 7:48).

According to the record Jesus was aware that He had much to suffer and would be killed, but promised that He would rise on the third day thereafter. After Peter's great confession, we read:

> From that time Jesus began to show his disciples that he must go to Jerusalem and suffer many things from the elders and chief priests and scribes, and be killed and on the third day be raised (Matthew 16:21; 17:12; Mark 8:31; Luke 9:22).

Jesus knew also that Jewish and Roman authorities would misunderstand and so asked His disciples not to talk about it, although He knew that finally He would need to meet the power-structure of vested interests head-on. This He voluntarily chose to do. He said:

> "For this reason the Father loves me, because I lay down my life, that I may take it again. No one takes it from me, but I lay it down of my own accord. I have power to lay it down and I have power to take it again: this charge I have received from my Father" (John 10:17, 18).

He claimed that He will come to judge the world. He will arouse the dead (John 5:28, 29). All nations will be gathered before Him and the Father will commit all judgment to Him (John 5:22). He will separate men as sheep from the goats and invite them to come and inherit, and condemn the others (Matthew 25:31-46). Not only will He be the judge, but the criterion of judgment will be what men did or did not do "to the least of these my brethren" (Matthew 25:31-46; Mark 3:35), or their response to His word (John 7:47, 48; cf. Matthew 7:23; Matthew 10:32, 33).

2. *His Deeds*

His miracles must not be forgotten in this connection. Their value lies less in their supernatural character than in their spiritual significance. They are "signs" and "wonders." They are never performed selfishly. Their purpose is not to show off or to subdue people. It can be argued that they are mainly illustrations of moral and spiritual authority. They are works that dramatize His words. Feeding the five thousand illustrated His ability to satisfy man's spiritual hunger as the "bread of life" (John 4:35). Having said that He was "the light of the world" (John 6:35) and restoring sight to the man born blind illustrated His power to help men see and know God. He brought Lazarus back from the dead as a sign that He was "the resurrection and the life" (John 10:25).[14]

Jesus was not merely a great teacher. If that is all He was, then surely He was mistaken on one of the chief subjects of His teaching, namely himself. It is also difficult to believe that He was an impostor and that He knew He was not what He claimed to be. Another possibility is that He was sincere but mistaken and deluded about himself. But He does not give the impression of an impostor nor that He

---

14. J. R. M. Scott, *Basic Christianity,* Inter-Varsity Fellowship, 1958, p. 31.

suffered from delusion. The only reasonable conclusion is that He was what and who He claimed to be. It is important to note that His character also supports His claims.

3. *His Character*

The character of Jesus greatly strengthens the Christian's conviction that Jesus was who He said He was. There is no discrepancy between His character and His words. His character was unique and cannot be compared with any other character in history. He is the One and only One, standing apart from all others. We are all contaminated with sin, even the best and the greatest of us. But according to the record, Jesus was sinless. The writer to the Hebrews says that Jesus "in every respect has been tempted as we are, yet without sinning" (Hebrews 4:15; cf. Matthew 4). Jesus himself confirmed this when He asked His critics, "Which of you convicts me of sin?" (John 8:46), and no one dared answer Him. By being tempted as we are and yet remaining sinless His character is really most wonderful. He lived a life of obedience to the Father, "he who sent me is with me; he has not left me alone, for I always do what is pleasing to him" (John 8:29).

He had no sense of guilt or estrangement from God. This is significant in view of His very keen moral judgment. He discerned "the thoughts and intentions of the heart" (Hebrews 4:12), and "knew what was in man" (John 2:25). He had no difficulty in reading inner questionings and perplexities of individual persons or the crowd. Yet His penetrating eye saw no sin in himself.

E.   JESUS CHRIST, LORD AND SAVIOR

In the history of the Church various doctrines of atonement or reconciliation have been advocated, but not one of them has ever been officially adopted.[15] Did Jesus live and die to influence Satan, God, or man? In the New Testament we find a variety of terms used in expressing the saving significance of the life, death and resurrection of Jesus Christ. Paul writes:

---

15. Gustav Aulen, *Christian Victor,* translated by A. G. Hebert, New York, Macmillan Co., 1951; William Hordern, *New Reformation Theology,* Philadelphia, Westminster Press, 1959 pp. 142-151; W. N. Clarke, *An Outline of Christian Theology,* New York, Scribners, 1914, pp. 315-321; L. Harold De-Wolf, *Theology of the Living Church,* Harpers, 1953, pp. 256-269; Ed. G. Kaufman, *Living Creatively,* Faith and Life Press, Newton, Ks., 1966, chapter 13.

they are *justified* by his grace as a gift through the *redemption* which is in Jesus Christ, whom God put forward as an *expiation* by his blood, to be received by faith (Romans 3:24, 25). Since therefore we are now *justified* by his blood, much more shall we be *saved* by him from the wrath of God. For if while we were enemies we were *reconciled* to God by the death of his Son, much more, now that we are *reconciled,* shall we be *saved* by his life. Not only so, but we also rejoice in God through our Lord Jesus Christ, through whom we have now received our *reconciliation* (Romans 5:9-14). God was in Christ *reconciling* the world to himself . . . and entrusting to me the message of *reconciliation* . . . We beseech you on behalf of Christ, be *reconciled* to God (II Corinthians 5:19, 20). Christ *redeemed* us from the curse of the law (Galatians 3:13) (italics added).

These are all figures of speech native to the Jewish and Greek thought of the time in which Paul lived. Behind the term "redemption" is the idea of the emancipation of a slave by purchase; behind "justification" is the idea of acquittal of an accused person in a court of law; behind "expiation" is the idea of an offering with expiatory value; and behind "reconciliation" is the idea of restoring friendly relationship with an enemy.

1. *The Ransom Theory*

The Ransom or "classic" theory of cosmic combat came first in point of time. This was the dominant interpretation of salvation for the first one thousand years of Christendom.

The age of the Greek and Latin Fathers of the early Christian Church covered a period from New Testament times to about 1000 A.D. The dominant characteristic of life during that period was incessant conflict between civilization and barbarism. Although the Roman Empire had in general established universal order, yet in many parts of the Empire unrest, brigandage, and piracy still were disturbing forces. Robber bands made travelers captive and demanded a *ransom* as the price for their release. Hence "captivity and ransom" were dominating ideas of that age and had a strong influence upon contemporary thinking on the nature of Christ's saving work.

Various Scripture passages are to be interpreted in the light of this social condition, as for example:

> . . . the Son of man came not to be served but to serve, and to give his life as a *ransom* for many (Matthew 20:28). For there is one God and one mediator between God and men, the man Christ Jesus, who gave himself as a *ransom* for all (I Timothy 2:5, 6).

> You know that you were *ransomed* . . . with the precious blood of Christ (I Peter 1:18). (Italics added).

Origen of Alexandria (185-254 A.D.) was a storng advocate of this theory. His interpretation was that the ransom paid by Christ's death on man's behalf was paid to Satan - the brigand who had taken mankind captive through sin. Satan was willing to release mankind only on the provision that God gives Christ in death. So the life of Christ is a ransom taken by Satan through crucifixion by evil men. But Satan and the grave could not hold Jesus for God raised Him from the dead. But now Satan must forfeit his claim upon sinners who accept Christ.

The weakness of this interpretation is that it sets things into a commercial framework. This framework later became so crude that Gregory the Great, even spoke of the flesh of Christ used by God on His hook to catch Satan. Which means that God used a rather shady method to win the battle, for He knew all along that Satan would be unable to hold Christ in the grave. Furthermore, in this view man is left merely as a spectator of the great cosmic drama—not an actor but a pawn over whom God and Satan were engaged in a cosmic battle.

This doctrine always had considerable appeal because of man's deep sense of being imprisoned by fate. The ancient stoic met this situation by accepting things as they came whether it made him happy or sad, rich or poor, a king or a slave. Man was imprisoned by demonic forces and now Christ had defeated these forces of Satan, sin, and death and so man was free again—redeemed and ransomed.

This feeling of helplessness again makes itself felt in our time. Contemporary literature, art, drama, and poetry are permeated with this deterministic point of view. Existentialist writers hold our anxiety before us and man is overcome with the meaninglessness of life. Like the stoic of old, the modern existentialist challenges man to defy the undefiable and resist the irresistible. Man is inclined to feel things are closing in on him and his spirituality is being suffocated. The meaning of life seems to have evaporated and fate rules supreme. In such a situation man needs and welcomes the good news that the enemy has been defeated and that these demonic intruders do not have the last word. It is good news to know that God is still working out His purposes in spite of demonic opposition.

2. *Substitutionary Theories*

The Satisfaction, Vicarious and Substitution theories are a second type of interpretation of salvation and are associated mainly with the Medieval and later with the post-Reformation period of Western history. As the age of the Latin and Greek Church Fathers was a period of brigandage and captivity, so the Medieval age was characterized by feudalism and chivalry, with dominant ideas of "honor" and "satisfaction." An injury or insult was considered as a blow to a man's honor and could be rectified only by some form of satisfaction. In such a time, Christ's atoning work tended to be thought of mainly as a satisfaction paid to God to safeguard His honor which had been violated through man's sin.

Saint Anselm (1033-1109) was a great advocate of this theory. This view holds that because of God's justice He could not forgive man and retain His divine honor, unless somehow man's guilt was taken care of first. Man could not do anything to pay for his guilt, because he already owes everything he is and has, to God. There is hope however if this God-man, Jesus Christ, who is innocent and sinless, would give himself in payment for man's guilt, and vicariously take the punishment that man deserves, upon himself. According to this theory, that is what Jesus did in His death on the cross. He was punished in man's place even to the point of being forsaken by God as He cries out on the cross: "My God, My God, why hast thou forsaken me?" (Mark 15:34). Our sin now has been punished and paid for by the crucifixion of Jesus, and so now God can maintain His justice and honor but also forgive man and again accept him.

The objection to this theory is that here we have the framework of a law court instead of a family picture of God and man. God is the stern judge and man is the prisoner. The judge demands that every "pound of flesh" be paid before He forgives and sets man free. Although this theory claims to save God's justice, it is hard to see what is just about punishing an innocent person for a guilty one. Furthermore, how can there be forgiveness when everything is paid for anyhow? In this theory, God represents justice and Christ represents love, but can God's justice and love be separated? Another weakness is, that, here also man is only a spectator and not a participating actor in the drama.

A similar interpretation of the Atonement is associated with the Reformation and post-Reformation Protestant age of Christian history. As the Patristic age was dominated by the ideas of captivity and ransom, giving rise to the *Ransom* theory of salvation; and as the Medieval or Scholastic age was dominated by the ideas of honor and satisfaction, giving rise to the *Satisfaction* theory of salvation; so the post-Reformation age was dominated by ideas of law and justice

BASIC CHRISTIAN CONVICTIONS

and gave rise to what is called the *Vicarious* or *Substitutionary* interpretation of salvation. According to this view the atoning work of Christ consisted essentially in undergoing substitutionary or vicarious punishment for man's sin, taking the guilt of the sinner upon himself and suffering in his stead.

Already Saint Augustine in the fifth century emphasized the need of a mediator between God and man, who can satisfy Divine justice and thereby appease God's righteous wrath against sin. He taught that Christ suffered the punishment, due to man for sin, and so substitutionally or vicariously, on man's behalf Christ offered the satisfaction demanded by the justice of God. This position of Augustine was taken up and reaffirmed by Luther, Calvin and other Reformation leaders.

The great weakness of this view of the Atonement is its very legalistic character, which is ethically objectionable. This view of God is pre-Christian. It represents Christ as coming in between a holy God and sinful men, and by undergoing substitutionary punishment satisfied the justice of God and so changed God's attitude toward the sinner. But God is not an oriental despot.

However these Satisfaction, Vicarious and Substitution theories also have biblical support. (See Romans 3:25; II Corinthians 5:21; I Peter 2:24.) These interpretations take guilt seriously. Modern physicians and psychiatrists tell us that guilt can actually make people sick. Just to ignore it, is only to drive it into the subconscious to fester and poison the whole being. Self-centered man faces the problem of guilt. Man is not pleased with himself and cannot accept himself, hence the feeling of guilt. The preacher calls it "self-love" and the psychiatrist calls it "self-hate," but they both mean the same thing. Man cannot accept what he is, nor can he live up to his hopes, hence the feeling of guilt plagues him. To overcome this guilt man is tempted to compensate in various ways—becoming a religious zealot, an alcoholic, a restless busybody, resort to illness, or even think of suicide.

The Christian idea of God is not that of a stern judge demanding payment for all our sins, not even vicariously. God is a righteous and loving Father who himself bears the full penalty of guilt for His prodigal children. However the problem of guilt is serious and must be taken care of. Man, as an admitted sinner, stands guilty before a holy God, confessing his sinfulness and as he accepts God's gracious forgiveness the burden of guilt falls from him. Constantly to berate oneself for past sins, indicates a lack of faith in God's love and forgiveness. When a person knows himself accepted and forgiven by God even though a sinner, only then can he also accept himself. He is no longer filled with self judgment and so is also freed from judging others in self-defense. Having been forgiven he now can love his neighbor and even his enemy.

3. *The Moral Influence Theory*

The Moral-influence theory is a third interpretation of reconciliation and atonement. Peter Abelard (1079-1142) was a great advocate of this theory. Abelard was Anselm's contemporary and foremost antagonist. We do God wrong, he maintained, if we think that Christ had to appease God's anger or satisfy God's honor, before He could forgive man. He held that the supreme principle in interpreting Christ's saving work is the New Testament teaching of the love of God for man.

Sin has indeed produced alienation between God and man, but this alienation has been on man's side rather than on God's. All that is required is to remove man's distrust about God's attitude toward man. And this Christ accomplished by the crowning exhibition of God's love on the cross. Hence the efficacy of Christ's saving work lay not in its influence upon Satan or upon God, but rather in its influence upon man. The incarnation, the whole life and teaching, as the suffering and death of Christ, are a supreme manifestation of the Divine love for the unworthy sinner that kindles gratitude in man's heart and wins him back to obedience to God.

The God and Father of our Lord Jesus Christ is always willing to forgive, but forgiveness cannot be unilateral; it is a two-way street and only so can be complete. If my friend has injured me I cannot forgive him and restore him to the former relationship, unless he also wishes to be forgiven and restored. So God's forgiveness can only be complete if the sinner wants to be forgiven, asks for it, repents and changes his ways. The Son of God lived a perfect and sinless life and in contrast man can see his own sin all the more clearly. When man sees the love of God revealed in Jesus finally going to the cross, the sinful heart of man melts and he repents. The cross does not cause a change in God's relationship to man; its aim is to change man's attitude to God.

This theory is weak where the others are strong. God having acted, He now leaves it up to man to accept or reject. In this theory there is no good news that Satan and his evil forces have been defeated, or that man's guilt has been assumed by another. On the other hand, this theory is strong where the others are weak. It does not consider the atonement or salvation as a drama that man watches from a distance. Man, here is involved himself. He must accept or reject. The cross speaks to man of God's redeeming love, and man must accept or reject it. Scriptural basis for this doctrine is also available (Luke 15; John 3:16-21; II Corinthians 5:18-20; Colossians 1:19-29; I John 4:13-21).

The Moral-influence theory emphasizes that forgiveness works a change in man. Psychiatrists tell us that a person cannot love until he has been loved. To love we must cease to make ourselves the center of our lives. By the love of another, a person is lifted out of the love for only himself. Man really forgets himself only when he is in love. This does not make forgiveness easy or cheap. God is mindful of sin, but mindful of it in a redemptive way. God's love neither neglects sin nor merely condemns it, but finds creative ways of dealing with it. God's love goes beyond tolerance on the one hand, as well as vindictiveness on the other hand, and is truly redemptive. With forgiveness there comes opportunity for a new beginning. One can give up in despair or begin again. Thanks to God's forgiveness, the Christian life in a sense consists of ever new beginnings in faith, hope and love.

However, salvation is too great and wonderful to be interpreted by any one theory. All three theories—*Ransom, Vicarious-Substitution,* and *Moral Influence*—are helpful in understanding the meaning of salvation.

F. SUMMARY AND CONCLUSION

In this chapter on Jesus Christ as Lord and Savior we have considered: The Need for Mediation; The Human Life of Jesus; Jesus and His Contemporaries; Jesus' Own Claims About Himself; and Jesus Christ as Lord and Savior.

For the Christian, Jesus Christ is Lord and Savior. In the Old Testament the word Lord is used for God. The Greek word translated Lord, was a title given to a god. As the early Church increasingly was composed of former gentiles it is understandable that the simple creed "Jesus is Lord" was very meaningful to them. By this they meant to say that Jesus is divine. God was in Jesus. When Jesus spoke, God was speaking. His Spirit was God's Spirit. When they followed Jesus they did not follow a mere man but tried to fall in step with God. He was their divine Master in thought, words and deeds of everyday life.

The name Jesus means Savior. "And you shall call his name Jesus, for he will save his people from their sins" (Matthew 1:21). He not only saves us from something but also saves us for something. When driving through a strange country, a good guide can save us much time, worry and perhaps disappointment—indeed he can keep us from getting lost—simply by pointing out the right way. Jesus does this for us. Life is a strange territory and there are many roads, some lead downward to destruction and others lead upward to usefulness and happiness. Jesus is the good guide. He knows the way. But more than that—He is the way. If we go with Him and in Him, we shall not get lost but arrive safely at our destination.

But this is not all. When we get on the wrong road He helps us to get back on the right road—not only by telling us but by actually showing us what the love of God for us is like. By accepting Jesus as the revelation of God's love we are forgiven and get help to avoid the same sins in the future.

It is only through the Spirit of Jesus Christ that man is reconciled to God and again comes to at-one-ment (atonement) with Him. This is true of the individual and of the world. In this atomic age, when peril hovers over us constantly, our world and we can only be saved by accepting the Spirit of Jesus and yielding ourselves to the love of God as we see it in Jesus Christ. He is Lord and Savior.

For Further Reading on Jesus Christ

Ainger, G., *Jesus Our Contemporary,* Seabury, 1967.
Anderson, Hugh, ed., *Jesus,* Prentice-Hall, 1967.
Arendzen, J. P., *Christ in God,* Sheed, 1958.
Baillie, D. M., *God was in Christ,* Scribner, 1948.
Barclay, Wm., *The Mind of Jesus,* Harper, 1961.
Beck, D. M., *Through the Gospels to Jesus,* Harper, 1954.
Bornkamn, Guenther, *Jesus of Nazareth,* trans., Harper, 1960.
Braden, Charles S., *Jesus Compared,* Prentice-Hall, 1957.
Brunner, H. E., *Meditor,* Westminster, 1965.
Bultman, R. K., *Jesus Christ and Mythology,* Scribners, 1958.
Cassels, Louis, *The Real Jesus,* Doubleday, 1968.
Colwell, E. C., *Jesus and the Gospel,* Oxford Univ. Press, 1963.
Connick, C., *Jesus: The Man, the Mission, and the Message,* Prentice-Hall, 1963.
Cullman, O., *The Christology of the New Testament,* Westminster, 1964.

Dodd, C. H., *Founder of Christianity,* Macmillan, 1970.

Farmer, H. H., *Word of Reconciliation,* Abingdon, 1967.

Ferre', Nels F. S., *Christ and the Christian,* Harper, 1958.

Filson, F. N., *Jesus Christ, the Risen Lord,* Abingdon, 1956.

Fuller, R. H., *Formation of Resurrection Narratives,* Macmillan, 1971.

Gogarten, F., *Christ the Crisis,* John Knox, 1970.

Goodspeed, E. J., *A Life of Jesus,* Harper, 1950.

Grant, Robert M., *The Earliest Lives of Jesus,* Harper, 1961.

Johnson, R. C., *Christ,* Westminster, 1968.

Kaufman, G. D., *Systematic Theology,* "God the Son," pp. 167-234. Scribners, 1968.

Knox, John, *Jesus: Lord and Christ,* Harper, 1958.

Laymon, Chas. M., *The Life and Teachings of Jesus,* Abingdon, 1955.

MacGregor, C., *The Hemlock and the Cross,* Lippencott, 1963.

Morton, T. Ralph, *Jesus: Man for Today,* Abingdon Press, 1970.

Pannanberg, Wolfart, *Jesus: God and Man,* trans. Westminster, 1968.

Preston, Harold, *The Shining Stranger,* The Wayfarer Press, 1967.

Rowlingson, D. M., *Jesus the Religious Ultimate,* Macmillan, 1961.

Saunders, E. W., *Jesus in the Gospels,* Prentice-Hall, 1967.

Smart, James D., *The Radical Impact of Jesus,* Westminster Press, 1969.

Stewart, James S., *The Life and Teaching of Jesus Christ,* Abingdon Press, 1958.

Thielicke, Helmut, *The Waiting Father,* Harper & Row, 1959.

Whale, J. S., *Victor and Victim,* Cambridge Un., 1960.

CHAPTER VI

THE HOLY SPIRIT
AND THE TRINITY

"I have yet many things to say to you, but you cannot bear them now. When the Spirit of truth comes, he will guide you into all the truth . . . He will glorify me, for he will take what is mine and declare it unto you"

(John 16:12-14).

CONSIDERATION OF THE HOLY SPIRIT NATURALLY FOLLOWS THE study of Jesus Christ and His work, for it is by the Holy Spirit that the work of Christ is carried on in the world. The Holy Spirit can be thought of as God at work in the individual person as well as in human life as a whole.

There are many Christians to whom God the Father and Jesus Christ the Savior mean much, but to whom the Holy Spirit means very little. Christmas and Easter are celebrated by all Christendom, but Pentecost is generally allowed to pass rather unnoticed. This reminds one of Paul's experience when he came to Ephesus and found some disciples who admitted that "we have never even heard that there is a Holy Spirit" (Acts 19:2).

A.   THE SIGNIFICANCE OF THE HOLY SPIRIT

The doctrine of the Holy Spirit helps to conserve and constantly reassert some important truths and religious values. Christianity is a historical religion. It emphasizes the acts of God in history. This is one factor that makes Christianity a living force in ongoing history. In this there is, however, also the danger of only remembering the wonderful events of the past and forgetting that Christianity also has constant relevance to, and power in, an ever ongoing and changing world. God is not only the one who once created the world and who long ago revealed himself in Jesus Christ. He is also the God at work here and now. The doctrine of the Holy Spirit keeps Christianity an active and dynamic religion.[1]

The revelation of God in Jesus Christ should not be regarded as the only Word of God nor as the last word that God ever would speak to men. The disciples could not be true to the memory of Jesus and only look backward. But in time many Christians became much concerned with guarding certain practices and ideas against any changes and forgot to seek fresh understanding of God's ways and purposes. Monuments are still raised for past prophets, while stones are being cast at those who might speak a prophetic word to contemporary times. Jesus indicated that the leaders of His generation were also guilty of this (Luke 11:47-48; Matthew 23:29-32).

The doctrine of the Holy Spirit is a protection of every man's right and obligation to look beyond tradition. Jesus said the Spirit would guide them on, and that there is still much undiscovered truth available to the conscientious seeker under the guidance of the Holy Spirit. In our own time, we have not yet fully assimilated the meaning of the ongoing scientific revolution of the last century and are already facing a new worldwide social revolution with far-reaching implications. It is not enough in such a time to see what the ancients have thought, valuable as that is. In such a time as ours, how grateful we should be for the guidance of the Holy Spirit and truth seeking men, who, under His guidance, can lead us into fuller understanding and a more complete realization of the divine will and purpose.

B. THE HOLY SPIRIT IN THE SCRIPTURES

The first reference in the Old Testament to the Spirit is at the very beginning of creation:

> The earth was without form and void, and darkness was upon the face of the deep; and the Spirit of God was moving over the face of the waters (Genesis 1:2).

In the Old Testament the term holy spirit (without capitals) is used at least three times: "take not thy holy spirit from me" (Psalm 51:11); "grieved his holy spirit" (Isaiah 63:10); and "he who put in the midst of them his holy spirit" (63:11). The agency here mentioned is none other than the Holy Spirit known in the New Testament. Repeatedly in the Old Testament He is simply referred to as "The Spirit of the Lord";

---

1. W. N. Clarke, *An Outline of Christian Theology*, Scribner's, 1914, p. 369 ff.; A. R. Vidler, *Christian Belief*, SCM Press LTD, London, 1950, p. 56.

> And the Spirit of the Lord shall rest upon him, the spirit of wisdom and understanding, the spirit of counsel and might, the spirit of knowledge and the fear of the Lord (Isaiah 11:2); "Not by might, nor by power, but by my Spirit, says the Lord of hosts . . ." (Zechariah 4:6).

In the vision of Ezekiel, men likened to dry bones are promised a new kind of life and relationship with God and each other, and that life would be peaceful, fruitful, and crowned with divine blessing (Ezekiel 37:22, 27, 29). Although this higher life of the Spirit is manifested and experienced only occasionally by rare individuals, mainly prophets, it is also promised that the time will come when it will be made available for all.

> "And it shall come to pass afterward, that I pour out my spirit on all flesh; your sons and your daughters shall prophesy, your old men shall dream dreams, and your young men shall see visions. For upon the menservants and the maidservants in those days, I will pour out my spirit" (Joel 2:28, 29).

This promise, according to Christian belief, was fulfilled in the events of Pentecost to which the New Testament bears witness.

There are a number of references to the Holy Spirit in the Infancy stories of both John the Baptist and Jesus. John's mother, Elizabeth, was filled with the Holy Spirit (Luke 1:41), and her son, it was promised, would "be filled with the Holy Spirit" (Luke 1:35). Of Simeon in the Temple we read, "the Holy Spirit was upon him," and "It had been revealed to him by the Holy Spirit," and that he was "inspired by the Spirit" (Luke 2:25-27).

John preaching and baptizing at the Jordan, in answer to the question as to who he was, says there is one coming "he will baptize you with the Holy Spirit and with fire" (Luke 3:17). After Jesus was baptized we read that "full of the Holy Spirit (He) returned from the Jordan, and was led by the Spirit for forty days in the wilderness" (Luke 4:1-2).

Throughout the ministry of Jesus, it is in the power of the Spirit that He performs His mighty acts of healing and restoration. Toward the end of His ministry He repeatedly spoke of "another Counselor," "the Spirit of truth" that He would send (John 14:16, 17; 15:26). He said:

> "it is to your advantage that I go away, for if I do not go away, the Counselor will not come to you; but if I go, I will send him to you . . . I have yet many things to say to you, but you cannot bear them now. When the Spirit of truth comes, he will guide you into all the truth; for he will not speak on his own authority,

but whatever he hears he will speak, and he will declare to you the things that are to come. He will glorify me, for he will take what is mine and declare it to you" (John 16:7-14).

And again:

after he had given commandment through the Holy Spirit to the apostles . . . he charged them not to depart from Jerusalem, but to wait for the promise of the Father, which, he said, . . . "before many days you shall be baptized with the Holy Spirit" (Acts 1:2-5; cf. Luke 24:25-49).

1. *Pentecost*

Pentecost signifies the new age then beginning (Acts 2). The importance of Pentecost is not the strange, temporary, and sensational phenomena that are said to have occurred, such as tongues of fire, speaking in many languages, rushing wind, and others, but the permanent transformation of human life that took place. As to the more sensational appearances described, these are probably best understood as symbolic of the promise and power of the event. The coming of the Spirit enlightened the minds of the disciples and gave them insight as to the real meaning of what Jesus had taught and done by His suffering and triumph. It changed the disciples, from a group of perplexed and fearful individuals, into a confident community of apostles with a single purpose compelling them to proclaim with great courage and eloquence, all that they had learned of the mighty acts of God. The wind, fire, and linguistic appearances symbolize the fact that henceforth the Holy Spirit will convey the good news of Christ to all nations, races, and tongues with conviction and power.

The outpouring of the Spirit resulted in effervescence, as well as permanent transformation, which remained after the effervescence had subsided. Speaking with tongues is a familiar accompaniment of revivals even today, and is to be distinguished from speaking in foreign languages. Paul was acquainted with this, and although he probably valued it more than we in this day are likely to do, he nevertheless finally rebuked those who thought it is something that really mattered. He wrote two long chapters to the Corinthian Christians to give this subject its proper place, in which he said:

If I speak in the tongues of men and of angels, but have not love, I am a noisy gong or a clanging cymbal . . . I thank God that I speak in tongues more than you all; nevertheless, in church I would rather speak five words with my mind, in order to instruct others, than ten thousand words in a tongue . . . earnestly desire to prophesy, and do not forbid speaking in tongues; but all things should be done decently and in order (I Corinthians 13:1; 14:18, 39-40).

The importance of Pentecost is its emphasis on the new kind of life now available to all mankind. The characteristic quality of that new life is the kind of love that the New Testament calls *agape* rather than *eros* or *phileo* in the Greek. All three words can be translated love but *eros* has reference to affection between the sexes. From it we get our word erotic. *Phileo* refers to love between equals or brothers, as indicated by words like Philadelphia, or philanthropic; while *agape* expresses the kind of divine love which Jesus revealed, namely the love of God for even the unlovely and unworthy. The Holy Spirit imparts that to the Christian. This love is not something that simply evolved out of inherent potentialities of human nature, but is the result of a new kind of personal relationship between God and man and of human beings with each other, due to the activity of the Holy Spirit.

What happened at Pentecost, was not that God for the first time began to be present in the hearts of men. Man was created in the image of God, so was inextricably connected with Him from the beginning and in all his waywardness could not altogether sever this connection. Holy men of every nation have honestly reached out toward God, to know and to do His will, and God gave them a vivid inward sense of His presence. But at Pentecost a whole community began to know God by direct experience as only prophets and sages had known Him before.

This group of fishermen and peasants, who a short while ago had been in headlong flight from the Jerusalem authorities, now stood boldly in their presence to claim the world for their crucified Messiah. This is one of the very extraordinary events in history. Their own explanation of it was not that they were especially bold or heroic but that they were a group who had known and loved the Lord Jesus whom

> "God raised up, and of that we all are witnesses . . . and having received from the Father the promise of the Holy Spirit, he has poured out this which you see and hear" (Acts 2:32, 33).

Individually, they might be unimposing people, but collectively they formed a body of which each member was designated to some useful function by the Spirit of Christ which informed, controlled, united, and sustained them all. Now being baptized with the Holy

BASIC CHRISTIAN CONVICTIONS

Spirit the group began to function as the church, the body of which Jesus Christ is the head.[2]

2. Old and New Testament Differences Regarding the Spirit

There are some differences in the concept of the Spirit before and after the coming of Christ. The Spirit was sometimes spoken of as not yet having come at all. For example, John writes, "as yet the Spirit had not been given, because Jesus was not yet glorified" (John 7:39). This only indicates how really great the difference before and after Christ was. These differences are evident in several areas.[3]

a). *Outward and Inward.* Before Pentecost the activity of the Spirit in general had been more outward, whereas thereafter it has been more inward. In the Old Testament God's will was made known to man largely through the ordinances of the Law and the Torah, or the utterances of the prophets who were moved by the Spirit. The principles of the Law were good but in time these external ordinances tended to become more detailed and elaborate, until complete compliance became burdensome and even impossible.

Even so, the hope was maintained that God would again speak prophetically and inwardly transform His people through the Spirit, so they would do His will spontaneously, and not as a matter only of legal constraint. For example the Lord through Jeremiah and others had promised:

> "this is the covenant which I will make with the house of Israel after those days, says the Lord: I will put my law within them, and I will write it upon their hearts; and I will be their God, and they shall be my people. And no longer shall each man teach his neighbor and each his brother, saying, 'Know the Lord,' for they shall all know me, from the least of them to the greatest, says the Lord" (Jeremiah 31:33, 34; cf. Deuteronomy 18:18; Malachi 3:1; 4:5; II Corinthians 3:3-6).

This promise the early Christians considered was fulfilled in the coming of Christ and the outpouring of the Holy Spirit (Acts 3:22). The early Christians felt liberated from the Law and emancipated from legalism. So now, hereafter the activity of the Holy Spirit is more inward than formerly.

b). *Periodic and Permanent.* Another difference between the Old and the New Testament is that then the activity of the Spirit was

---

2. Walter M. Horton, *Our Christian Faith,* The Pilgrim Press, 1945, p. 40 ff.
3. A. R. Vidler, *Christian Belief,* SCM Press LTD, London, 1950, pp. 62-66.

more periodic while now it was more permanent and steady. Now He is considered to be the very presence of God in the life and heart of the believer. Vidler points out, that in the New Testament the Christians do not pray for the coming of the Holy Spirit but rather live in the Spirit who teaches them how to pray. Christians however, occasionally need to be reminded about their being in the Spirit and that they need only "be still and know" that He is the present and permanent source of their life and joy. Christians live in the Spirit, and so need not call down an absent Spirit but only remember that they have been received into relationship with God through Jesus Christ.

c). *Individual and Community.* A third difference is that in the Old Testament the activity of the Spirit is evident only occasionally in certain individuals, such as artists, warriors, prophets, and others. For example, in connection with the building of the tabernacle we read:

> Moses said to the people of Israel, "See the Lord has called by name . . . and he has filled him with the Spirit of God, with ability, with intelligence, with knowledge, and with all craftsmanships, to devise artistic designs, to work in gold and silver and bronze, in cutting stones for setting, and in carving wood, for work in every skilled craft. And he has inspired him to teach . . . and every able man in whom the Lord has put ability and intelligence to know how to do any work in the construction of the sanctuary shall work in accordance with all that the Lord has commanded" (Exodus 35:30-34; 36:1).

This special gift of the Spirit was also thought to be in great warriors. Of Samson we read:

> the boy grew and the Lord blessed him. And the Spirit of the Lord began to stir him . . . and the Spirit of the Lord came mightily upon him, and he tore the lion asunder as one tears a kid (Judges 13:24-25; 14:6).

Or in one displaying great wisdom in judgment, like Solomon,

> And all Israel heard of the judgment which the king had rendered and they stood in awe of the king, because they perceived that the wisdom of God was in him, to render justice (I Kings 3:28).

Above all, the Spirit of God was the source of inspiration for the prohpets which enabled them to speak fearlessly of God's righteousness, judgment, and deliverance, in matters of personal or national affairs. The prophet is spoken of as "the man of the Spirit" (Hosea 9:7).

In the earlier periods of the Old Testament the work of the

Spirit was considered rather occasional and irregular. But gradually the Spirit came to be considered as invisibly present throughout the universe. For example, the Psalmist asks:

> Whither shall I go from thy Spirit? Or whither shall I flee from thy presence? If I ascend to heaven, thou art there! If I make my bed in Sheol, thou art there! (Psalm 139:7-8).

In *the New Testament* the primary work of the Holy Spirit is to create and sustain the corporate life of a community - the church, the body of which Christ is the head. When the risen Lord took leave He asked His disciples not to leave Jerusalem until they had received the promise of the Father (Acts 1:41). And "When they were all together in one place" (Acts 2:1), the Spirit descended and welded them together into a community that even shared and pooled its property.

> Now the company of those who believed were of one heart and soul, and no one said that any of the things which he possessed was his own, but they had everything in common (Acts 4:32).

The inspiration of the individual was now subject to the common life in the Spirit. This did not mean that individuality was suppressed but rather given a fuller expression of personal talents in the common life of the group. As Paul later puts it:

> Now there are a variety of gifts, but the same Spirit; and there are varieties of service, but the same Lord; and there are varieties of working, but it is the same God who inspires them all in every one. To each is given the manifestation of the Spirit for the common good. To one is given through the Spirit the utterance of wisdom, and to another the utterance of knowledge according to the same Spirit, to another faith by the same Spirit, to another gifts of healing by the one Spirit, . . . All these are inspired by one and the same Spirit, . . . For just as the body is one and has many members, and all the members of the body, though many, are one body, so it is with Christ. For by one Spirit we were all baptized into one body - Jews or Greeks, slaves or free - and all were made to drink of one Spirit (I Corinthians 12:4-13).

The Christians are members of Christ's body, allegorically speaking, each with his own function. The Holy Spirit is the life blood, as it were, that circulates through the body. The full measure of the Holy Spirit can therefore be obtained only in fellowship with other Christians, rather than in isolation.

d). *Israel and the World.* Formerly it was thought that the Spirit was a rather exclusive prerogative of Israel, although this does not mean that He was altogether inactive in other nations. Even the ministry of Jesus, with few exceptions, was limited to Israel. However, after Pentecost the Holy Spirit taught the disciples, in spite of their prejudices, that Christ was the Head not only of one nation but of all nations. After some struggle, the Holy Spirit drew men and women into the newly created community on the ground of their common humanity without respect of race, class, or nationality. At first the disciples and early Christians "were amazed, because the gift of the Holy Spirit had been poured out even on the Gentiles" (Acts 10:45). The Holy Spirit revealed Christ as interested in all mankind.

e). *A Neutral Spirit and the Spirit of Christ.* The word translated "spirit" in the Old Testament is the same as for "wind" or "breath." It means any manifestation of power. Often, this power is not holy or even moral. It seems closely related to what in primitive religions is called "mana," indicating something mysterious and powerful. It may be good, bad, or just neutral. Surprisingly enough even an evil spirit was considered as being sent by God on occasions. This is the case in the stories of the later life of Saul. We read that "an evil spirit from the Lord tormented him" (I Samuel 16:14, 15, 16, 23), and again "Then an evil spirit from the Lord came upon Saul" (I Samuel 19:9).

However, in the New Testament the Spirit of God is only referred to as the Holy Spirit; and now the Holy Spirit is known as the Spirit of Christ. He is to bring illumination to all men and convince them of their sinfulness and that the Christ revealed Agape-love of the Eternal God is available for everyone who repents and believes the Good News.

The Holy Spirit also is the interpreter of Christ who gradually unfolds the fuller meaning of Christ's universal work for the human race. Jesus himself said:

> "I have yet many things to say to you, but you cannot bear them now. When the Spirit of truth comes, he will guide you into all the truth; for he will not speak on his own authority, but whatever he hears he will speak, and he will declare to you the things that are to come. He will glorify me, for he will take what is mine and declare it to you" (John 16:12-14).

This has been the work of the Holy Spirit ever since Pentecost. It is still going on and is far from finished. Christian thinkers and leaders acknowledge that we are only at the beginning of more complete realization, and application of the revelation, of God through Jesus Christ to the individual and corporate life of mankind.

C. The Work of the Holy Spirit

The Greek term used for Holy Spirit is *Paraclete* - which is translated in various ways: "Helper," "Friend," "Comforter," "Counselor," "Walking Besides One," and others. John (chapters 14-16) indicates the rich content of the words that Jesus spoke to His disciples, in view of His impending departure. Jesus indicates that He has been a "Paraclete" to His friends and promises another to take His place (John 14:16). This "Spirit of truth" would be a personal presence (16:13), but He also spoke of himself as present in that presence (16:18, 22). He indicated it was best for His friends that He should leave them and send this Counselor (16:7), who would abide always (16:16). Hence the promise was not limited to the apostles nor to that age. He was coming to remain.

This Counselor was to be the "Spirit of truth" (John 14:17), a Spirit of remembrance and enlightenment concerning Christ himself and to indicate new meanings and applications of His teachings in times to come (14:26; 16:14). This was a Spirit of progress and guidance, leading gradually to fuller understanding of Christ and His kingdom (16:12-13), a Spirit of joy and childlike intimacy and communion with God in prayer (16:22-27), a Spirit of testimony concerning Christ and enabling His friends to become joyful witness bearers of His (15:26, 27).

In other words the Holy Spirit was coming to carry on the work of Christ to its fulfillment. He had earlier encouraged His disciples to ask for the Spirit (Luke 11:13). Pentecost was a turning point in the spiritual history of man but the agent of the spiritual life of man was not altogether new to the world. The faith of Abraham, the penitence of David, the endurance of Jeremiah, the inspiration of Isaiah, were all wrought by the same Spirit that motivated John, Paul, the early Church, and is still working for conviction and renewal in the world today.

At the inauguration of His public ministry at Nazareth Jesus read from Isaiah: "The Spirit of the Lord is upon me . . ." (64:1-2), indicating that He was "anointed" to do certain things, and closing by telling them "Today this scripture has been fulfilled in your hearing" (Luke 4:21). So when His work in the flesh was finished the time was ripe for a fresh outpouring of power in an open world of possibilities to touch the conscience and win the heart of man. Now the Holy Spirit might work as never before for conviction and salvation. Now followed the age of the Holy Spirit, not because He did not work before, but because Christ had opened the way for greater possibilities in the world, the Church, and in the individual.

1. *The Spirit's Work in the World*

The Holy Spirit "will convince the world of sin and of righteouness and of judgment" (John 16:8). This activity of the Spirit is only natural when we remember that

> God so loved the world that he gave his only Son . . . not to condemn the world but that the world might be saved through him (John 3:16, 17).

It was in sin that men were perishing when God so loved them that He gave His Son that they might not perish. Righteousness is the opposite of sin and to understand and appreciate the great difference between the two takes judgment. The first task of the Spirit is to convince the world of sin by awakening its consciousness of and conscience on sin.

The Holy Spirit gradually implants, purifies and deepens the convictions in men as to what sin is, what righteousness is, and what the judgment of men should therefore, also be. This implies the broadest view of the Holy Spirit's work. He is the teacher of humanity concerning good and evil, right and wrong, and the relationship between the two.

God has never left the world, nor any part of its great life, uninfluenced by His Spirit. This is clear from the character of God as revealed by Jesus Christ. Good does not come about without God. All good that appears among and in men is the result of the fostering care of the Holy Spirit. The awakening of the public conscience on various questions, the deepening of general convictions concerning right and wrong, more refined views of good and evil, reforms for better and richer human life, and the general social progress of the race, are the result of the work of the Holy Spirit. This includes general human attitudes on such issues as poverty, racism, drugs, alcohol, sex, democracy, slavery, war, etc.

2. *The Spirit's Work in the Church*

In the Christian Church the Holy Spirit naturally would have deeper and more comprehensive influence. By Church here is meant the inclusive body of Christian people everywhere, including the organizations that have been formed to express and promote the cause of Christ. Jesus promised that "where two or three are gathered in my name, there am I in the midst of them" (Matthew 18:20).

The work of the Spirit in Christians differs from His work in the world because here there are those who know Him and are dedicated to His cause. Naturally the Spirit can impart himself in a richer and more intimate way to those who know Jesus Christ as Savior and are committed to His cause.

The words of Christ were brought to remembrance of the disciples as they later composed the great writings of the New Testament. But that reminding did not end there but continues in all ages as men forget or neglect certain Christian truths. This is what happened during the Reformation and the Wesleyan Revival. There is enough truth in Christ to enrich all ages but it needs to be brought to mind in living form as the Church is able to appropriate it. Jesus promised

> "When the Spirit of truth comes, he will guide you into all the truth . . . He will glorify me, for he will take what is mine and declare it to you" (John 16:13-14).

Neither the individual Christian nor the Church is perfect. The work of the Spirit still continues. He is still leading them to fuller comprehension of the truth in Christ and a more perfect character in fellowship with God through Christ Jesus. His leading does not impart infallibility to individuals or Councils. Yet His leading is an experienced fact and the hope of the Church.

3. The Spirit's Work in the Individual

In individuals the Holy Spirit becomes most specific and effective in His work. He promotes, sustains, and makes the divine life in man more real and more perfect. Since God is love, this divine life in man, that the Holy Spirit promotes, consists of holy love. Holy agape-love was the very substance of the spiritual life and character of Jesus. He said:

> "A new commandment I give to you, that you love one another; even as I have loved you, that you also love one another. By this all men will know that you are my disciples, if you have love for one another" (John 13:34, 35).

John greatly emphasized the importance of love as the core of the Christian life.

> Beloved, let us love one another; for love is of God, and he who loves is born of God and knows God. He who does not love does not know God; for God is love. In this the love of God was made manifest among us, that God sent his only Son into the world, so that we might live through him. . . . Beloved, if God so loved us, we also ought to love one another. No man has ever

seen God; if we love one another, God abides in us and his love is perfected in us. . . . God is love, and he who abides in love abides in God, and God abides in him. . . . There is no fear in love, but perfect love casts out fear. For fear has to do with punishment, and he who fears is not perfected in love. We love, because he first loved us. If any one says, "I love God," and hates his brother, he is a liar; for he who does not love his brother whom he has seen, cannot love God whom he has not seen. And this commandment we have from him, that he who loves God should love his brother also (I John 4:7-21).

This holy love in man finds expression in two ways. First comes the love for God. Christ's human life was permeated by intimate and joyful fellowship with God. God first loved us and in the divine life in us that is awakened and fostered by the Holy Spirit, our love for God will spring up as an answer to His love for us. His boundless grace awakens our gratitude toward Him.

Love by nature is self-sacrificing and this brings us to the second form of expression that this divine love in us takes. The divine life expresses itself in unselfish helpfulness toward others, even as it led Christ to live and die for men. All other graces and virtues are included in this one grace of holy love. Love is the fulfillment of all duty toward the neighbor (Romans 13:19), the bond of perfection, binding all other graces into one, (Colossians 3:14). This is the life that the Holy Spirit awakens, nourishes, trains and increasingly perfects. Still this love in us is always imperfect. Constant growth in the Christian life is growth in love toward God and man, including our enemies.

4. Harmony and Reconciliation

Harmony and reconciliation always is the purpose of the Holy Spirit in working in the world, the Church, or in individual persons. The human being by nature is subject to many conflicting impulses, —good, bad, and indifferent. He is drawn and torn this and that way, and often is subject to turmoil within. In the extreme case he is like the man in the Gospel who, when asked his name by Jesus, called himself "Legion" (Mark 5:9). Jesus brought him to his right mind, integrated and unified his personality. So it is the work of the Holy Spirit to give health, harmony, and singleness of mind. The various impulses, desires and ambitions are integrated when the individual is reconciled to God through Jesus Christ. He then becomes subject to the all embracing purposes of God.

In the Church, and in the world at large, the work of the Holy Spirit also is reconciliation and brings communities and society at large into harmony with themselves and with God. This work cannot be accomplished by the strongest imposing his will on others and forcing them to submit. The Holy Spirit will bring a group, church, or even mankind, to one mind by free interchange of thought and pooling their insights, as well as helpful criticism and goodwill. Only so, can a community, or church, or even a world society be built. In our day the working of the Holy Spirit in this direction is evident by forming and working in the World Council of Churches. On an even broader but less distinctly religious basis, this work of the Holy Spirit is evident in the United Nations and the work it is doing toward world peace and the general welfare of all mankind.

5. Disturbance and Conviction

Here on earth individuals as well as groups, whether of a religious or secular nature, always need to learn and change. Individuals and institutions are always tempted to settle down and be satisfied. It is the work of the Holy Spirit to disturb individuals and society. Only then can one move on to something better and more perfect. The Holy Spirit works like an acid to all complacency. Individuals and society constantly need to be disturbed, awakened and led on to further growth.

As human beings, we so easily become impatient and tired. But it is our privilege to become renewed and refreshed by the Lord through the Holy Spirit, for we have the promise, that

> they who wait for the Lord shall renew their strength, they shall mount up with wings like eagles, they shall run and not be weary, they shall walk and not faint (Isaiah 40:31).

When is a Church not a Church, or when is a Christian not a Christian? The answer is, when they do not have the Holy Spirit. That is, the Spirit of God as revealed in Jesus Christ. When Jesus was asked about being "born anew" by Nicodemus, His answer was:

> "The wind blows where it wills, and you hear the sound of it, but you do not know whence it comes or whither it goes; so it is with every one who is born of the Spirit" (John 3:8).

The Holy Spirit does not merely mean "God in us," which might imply that He was resting, or at least be quietly passive. It rather means God in motion through us, like a current of wind, or water, or electricity flowing through a channel.

6. Humility and Strength

Some translations use Comforter for Holy Spirit. The word comfort has in it the word *fort,* implying fortification and strength. The Holy Spirit gives strength. When an individual or a group becomes disturbed and convinced of the need for further growth, then only can the Holy Spirit do the work of humility, comfort, and assurance of growth and progress. This is a need not only of the poor and ignorant but also of the rich, intelligent, and powerful.

Some of the favorite words of Jesus were such as "the last," "the least," and "the lost." Only when an individual, group, or institution recognizes its need and humbly asks for help can the Holy Spirit work most effectively. Only then can the Holy Spirit purify, reveal and illuminate, give wisdom and counsel, guidance and enabling power that leads to higher integration and reconciliation of the individual or group, with oneself, with the neighbor, and with God.

A Spirit-filled Church or individual, in order to serve as a transmission channel, must, on the one hand be connected with the divine power-house, and on the other hand must also be in touch and contact with the needs of the world. Only so can there be a constant intake of light and energy from God that is to be transmitted and delivered to needy places in the world that God wants to get at, both in individuals and society as a whole.

D. The Standard for Testing the Spirits

In the enthusiasm of the early Christians it seemed that the gift of the Holy Spirit to guide and sustain the Christian fellowship would solve all problems without much human thought or effort. But soon difficulties arose as to which of the many voices speaking in the Church were the real utterances of the Holy Spirit. In what was probably the earliest of all New Testament writings, Paul says to the Thessalonians:

> Do not quench the Spirit, do not despise prophesying, but test everything; hold fast what is good, (I Thessalonians 5:19, 20).

This implies that doubt had already arisen concerning the rather wild ecstatic utterances to which the new recruits from paganism sometimes gave way in Christian meetings. Claims to inspiration must be tested by the character and teaching of Christ. Jesus said "You will know them by their fruits" (Matthew 7:16). In his letters, Paul lays down ethical and religious standards by which the true utterances of the Holy Spirit are to be tested. He writes:

Basic Christian Convictions

But I say, walk by the Spirit, and do not gratify the desires of the flesh. For the desires of the flesh are against the Spirit, and the desires of the Spirit are against the flesh, for these are opposed to each other, to prevent you from doing what you would. But if you are led by the Spirit you are not under the law. Now the works of the flesh are plain: immorality, impurity, licentiousness, idolatry, sorcery, enmity, strife, jealousy, anger, selfishness, dissension, party spirit, envy, drunkenness, carousing, and the like. I warn you, as I warned you before, that those who do such things shall not inherit the kingdom of God. But the fruit of the Spirit is love, joy, peace, patience, kindness, goodness, faithfulness, gentleness, self-control; against such there is no law. And those who belong to Christ Jesus have crucified the flesh with its passions and desires. If we live by the Spirit, let us also walk by the Spirit (Galatians 5:16-25).

A person who is a worthy instrument of the Spirit must be in right relation to God, to his fellowmen, and be of sound personal character.

By the time the First Epistle of John was written the consensus of the early Christians could be very simply stated. He writes:

Beloved, do not believe every spirit, but test the spirits to see whether they are of God; for many false prophets have gone out into the world. By this you know the Spirit of God: every spirit which confesses that Jesus Christ has come in the flesh is of God, and every spirit which does not confess Jesus is not of God. This is the spirit of antichrist, of which you have heard that it was coming, and now it is in the world already (I John 4:1-3).

John has reference here to the Gnostic heresy prevalent in those days, that Jesus was only divine and not human and that He therefore was not really in the flesh. According to this heresy the physical needs of Jesus were considered not to have been real at all but only appearances, including His suffering and death.

The best test of whether a spirit is of God or not is to see if it conforms to the life and teachings of Jesus while He was in the flesh. A movement may not even have the Christian label on it, it is of God if it is in line with the life and teaching of Jesus while He was in the flesh. And the opposite is just as true - in spite of carrying the Christian label a movement or a person is not of God if the things that are worked for are not in line with the life and teaching of Jesus Christ while He was in the flesh.

Mere emotional stir and enthusiasm are not enough. Protestant Reformers faced this problem and laid down the principle that God cannot contradict himself. It is one and the same God revealing himself (1) in all nature, as our Creator, (2) in all history of mankind, especially that of the Jews and the Church, (3) in our individual hearts and personal conscience, and (4) especially in the life, teaching, death, and the entire attitude and Spirit of Jesus Christ while He was in the flesh. The internal *revelation* of God in our hearts must be in harmony with the *external* revelation of God in nature, history and Jesus Christ in the flesh.

There is some danger that this view of the Spirit might be used to suppress all new innovations. This danger, however, is reduced when we remember that Jesus himself was considered a false prophet since His teaching seemed to contradict, or at least go beyond the Old Testament understanding of God at more than one point. In practice the Quakers have worked out a group discipline in trying the spirits which would tend to eliminate fanatical willfulness daring to speak in the name of God. When

> that of God in me and in thee sits down together, God's light in thee makes my own inner light burn more brightly, and helps to overcome my darkness.[4]

E.   THE DOCTRINE OF THE TRINITY

The New Testament speaks of the Father, the Son, and the Holy Spirit, but does not refer to them as "Trinity." Jesus is recorded as instructing His disciples to baptize "in the name of the Father and the Son and of the Holy Spirit" (Matthew 28:29). However there is nothing here that would indicate whether each one of the three was a different God, or if they were three manifestations of the only one God. The Church is using this trinitarian formulation as its baptismal formula.

Paul also speaks of three in his famous benediction when he writes:

> The grace of the Lord Jesus Christ and the love of God and the fellowship of the Holy Spirit be with you all (II Corinthians 13:14).

The Church is also using this trinitarian formula as one form of benediction at the close of religious services. Here the word "Father" is not used at all and the word "God" is substituted for it. Does this mean that there is a distinction between God, on the one hand, and Jesus Christ and the Holy Spirit on the other? John also speaks of God, the Son, and the Spirit in one context (I John 3:6-9).

---

4. Walter M. Horton, *Our Christian Faith*, The Pilgrim Press, Boston, 1945, p. 44.

1. The Origin of This Doctrine

The root of this doctrine lies in the experience of the early Christians related in the New Testament. The early Christians presupposed belief in one God, the Creator of the universe and Lawgiver of the Jews. Their lives were steeped in this ancient faith and they saw His living presence in every natural wonder, in the voice of conscience, in the struggle for freedom and justice, in personal experiences, and in events of history. However they were also aware of the impact of Jesus Christ in their lives. His words, works, death, and resurrection were a transforming reality in their personal experience. At the same time they held fast to the Old Testament revelations of one God. This new revelation of God in Christ was identified with the God and Creator known of old.

But this was not all. After Jesus had gone and His life on earth had become a sacred memory, there was found in the Church, a new life continuous with His life. This new life was not in the form of a man teaching and healing, but rather in the whole Church community bound together in fellowship and victorious faith. To them, this new life in their community and fellowship was more real than anything else. This new experience however was associated with, and considered as a continuation of their experience with Jesus Christ himself. This new experience they called the Holy Spirit. Even though it seemed new - yet God was *one,* of this there could be no doubt.[5]

2. The Meaning of the Trinity

In speaking of the Trinity, Christians have two great concerns. One is to preserve the reality of, and the testimony to, the rich and significant new powers which have come to men and produced the Christian Church, namely Jesus Christ and the Holy Spirit. The other concern is to maintain the monotheistic faith. For, the Hebrew *Shema* also belongs to the Christians. "The Lord our God, the Lord is one" (Deuteronomy 6:4; Mark 12:29).

Christians have always believed in some form of the three-fold revelation of God. God is the Father, the maker of heaven and earth. God is the Son, that is, He was in the life, teaching, death, and resurrection of Jesus Christ. God is the Holy Spirit, as He lives in the heart of man and society. He gives inspiration and courage for

---

5. L. Harold DeWolf, *A Theology of the Christian Church,* Harpers, 1953, p. 276.

the daily individual tasks and the great social causes of mankind as a whole.

The Jews who became Christians brought with them an uncomplicated monotheism. God was thought of as one person. The Gentile converts however came from a different background. The more sophisticated few, influenced by Greek philosophy, were also monotheistic but their conception of God was less personal than that of the Jews, more of a divine principle. But the majority of the Gentiles that came into Christianity had been polytheistic, believing in many deities.

The early Christians regarded Jesus as God. They proclaimed the mighty acts of God in Christ without any reconstruction of their God idea. As the Church became more Gentile in its membership, its prevailing mode of thought also gradually changed from action or verb-Jewish thinking to analytical or noun-Greek ways of thinking. The concepts behind the action or verb-way of thinking presupposes a different world view from the analytical or noun-way of thinking. This raises questions regarding such words as "descended," "ascended," "incarnation," "resurrection" and others. Are they to be taken literally or figuratively? In our space age we have difficulty in taking them literally. We need to remember that language as such is always symbolic, but that these word-symbols nevertheless carry profound truth and real meaning. Paul wrote:

> But we have this treasure in earthen vessels, to show that the transcendent power belongs to God and not to us (II Corinthians 4:7).

This also applies to the Bible and the Creeds.

As the Church grew and moved from Jewish ways of thinking to Greek ways, and then to Roman or Latin thought forms, the problem of doctrinal expression and definition became ever more complex. Much metaphysical speculation has been associated with attempts to explain the Trinity. Various theories have been proposed which can not be harmonized with the truth as actually experienced. One theory compromised monotheism, another compromised the divinity of Christ, and another compromised the ultimacy of the Holy Spirit.

Gradually formulations of diversity and unity, in terms of ancient and medieval metaphysics, gave rise to the teaching that in the Godhead three *hypostases* (Greek) or *personae* (Latin) were united in one substance. The phrase read "Three Persons in one God." However the word "person" in time has undergone great change as to its meaning. Originally it meant the mask of an actor on the stage. With masks an actor could impersonate more than one person.

So the word "person" originally did not mean an individual center of consciousness as it does today. To speak of three persons in the Godhead as three separate individuals, would be tri-theism and lead to polytheism. Originally it only meant one God manifested and revealed in three different ways.

Because of this change of meaning in the word "person," some scholars suggest that the phrase "God in three persons" should be dropped altogether as now it suggests polytheism. The use of the word "mode" or "manifestation" is suggested instead.[6]

Others go even so far as to suggest that the word "Trinity" is confusing rather than helpful and therefore should be dropped altogether.[7]

One suggestive modern approach to describe what is meant by the Trinity from the existentialist point of view, speaks of the Father as "primordial" Being, the Son as "expressive" Being, and the Holy Spirit as "unitive" Being.[8] The expression "primordial" Being points out the ultimate act or energy of letting-be as the source, not only of what is but also of all possibilities of being. Thinking of "primordial" Being (the Father) in isolation would tend toward an utterly distant and unknown transcendent God, or toward a God as undifferentiated Being, hardly distinguishable from the void or nothing. Hence "primordial" Being is thought of as the source of outpouring, which is inseparable from the structure of Being itself. This makes for unity in trinity or a triune God. We can only know something of this mystery of God as He pours himself out in the dynamics of Being, and so is revealed in and through manifestations (Christ and Holy Spirit) that are joined with Him in the unity of Being.

According to this view the Son, or "expressive" Being is energy of "primordial" Being poured out and giving rise to the world and particular beings in space and time. These have a temporary character and can only be understood in terms of time. In identifying Jesus Christ with "expressive" Being we are reminded that in Christian theology, He is the Word or Logos, the agent of the Father in creating and re-creating. The Logos is "expressive" Being and is not to be identified with the Being through which it is given ex-

---

6. Karl Barth, *The Doctrine of the Word of God,* p. 403; Donald Baillie, *God Was in Christ,* p. 136; DeWolf, *op. cit.* p. 277.

7. James A. Pike, *A Time for Christian Candor,* Harpers, 1964, pp. 120-130.

8. John Macquarrie, *Principles of Christian Theology,* Scribners, 1968, pp. 182-183.

pression. The Logos is generated by the Father, and expresses Being which otherwise would remain hidden but now flows out through "expressive" Being into the world. Although the incarnate Logos in Jesus lived at a particular time and place it is nevertheless co-eternal with the Father. As Christians we do not think of the Father as dwelling in isolation and then moving out into "expressive" Being. If the Son is eternally begotten, then there never was a time when the Son was not, then Being has always been dynamic, and "primordial" Being has always been united with "expressive" Being. There is unity and stability of Being through all its diversity and dynamism.

It is of the essence of God (primordial Being) to "let-be." God does not hoard Being within himself. We call Him God and recognize Him as worthy of worship because He pours out Being by moving out from "primordial" Being through "expressive" Being into a world of change, multiplicity and possibility. This involves "risk" because in this process, Being could become split and fragmented. The "risk" becomes acute when such beings as man are brought into existence, who have some freedom and some responsibility to determine their own lives and to manipulate nature. Men can become alienated from Being, although they have received their being from the "letting-be" of Being. Man can be faithful or unfaithful and instead of becoming fuller being, slip into less being. This is not in line with the purpose of the "letting-be" of Being.

Here is where the Holy Spirit or "unitive" Being comes in. It is the function of the Holy Spirit to maintain, strengthen, nurture and restore the unity of beings with Being which is always threatened. The unity which the Spirit now brings about is a higher unity than would have been possible if Being had never moved out of "primordial" Being through "expressive" Being (Jesus Christ). This new unity is one of freedom in diversity of responsible beings. This "unitive" Being (Spirit) maintains the unity of creation on the lower levels of beings also.

In the case of man, Being has itself grasped man and communicated itself to him. The operation of the Holy Spirit then is that of unifying, reconciling and relating beings to Being. Beings such as men are not self-subsistent entities but are beings in which Being is itself manifest. Man is himself not an autonomous being, but a guardian of Being. The function of the Holy Spirit is to promote a new and higher level of unity between beings and Being. This arises from two sides, the Father (primordial Being) and the Son (expressive Being) both of whom also promote reconciliation.

To help understand trinity, many illustrations have been suggested as symbols. The clover plant has three leaves but it is still only one plant. The triangle has three sides but it is only one geometric figure. An idea may be expressed in action, in written words, and finally in the influence these actions and written words have, but it still is only one idea. Or, there is the thought of a house, then the blueprint, and finally the constructed house, but still all three are one. The same person can be a father, a son, and a husband. All sorts of analogies have been used but none altogether meets the case and it is not expected that it should.

The Trinity is probably best understood today as three different kinds of revelation of God experienced by man in history. God has shown himself in three roles. Man has known Him as eternal Father, Creator and Judge, whose very Being is the ground of all existence in the universe, all order and beauty, the moral law, and all truth. Man knows Him also as the Son, or the God who humbled himself in love and gave himself for His children as revealed in Jesus Christ, His transforming Word. Man also knows Him as the Holy Spirit, the sacred presence within ourselves, binding us in love to our brethren and to God, opening our eyes to God as Creator and Judge, reminding us of His acts in nature and history, calling us to faith in Christ Jesus, and enabling us to follow and obey Him.

These revelations are not the work of three individuals but of one God. These are not merely roles of an actor. They are manifestations of His harmonious purposes and will. He does not merely appear as Creator, revealing himself in history in Jesus, and as self-giving presence of the Holy Spirit. He really *is* all of these and these manifestations are true expressions of himself.

3. *The Trinity and World Religions*

Three features of Christianity, namely God as Father, Son, and Holy Spirit, have no parallel in other world religions. These three features on the other hand, have always been regarded as essential in Christianity.

The idea of God as Father has been thought of in three other religions besides Christianity. Zoroaster speaks of Ahura Mazda as Father of Justice and Right, also as the Father of Good Mind (Yasna 31:18; 44:3; 45:4; 47:2). But it is never suggested that human beings might regard God as their Father. In the Scriptures of Judaism there are twenty-eight passages where Yahweh is referred to as a Father, but always as the Father of Israel or of "them that fear him" (Psalm 103:13). Only once is Yahweh referred to as Father in universal terms (Malachi 2:10).

In early documents of Hinduism the most important deity among many is Indra who is referred to as pitar or father (Rig Veda, 4:17.17). Yet Indra is also represented as drunk and indifferent to human worship (Rig Veda, 19::119.5). In other places Indra is boasting of numerous and treacherous destructiveness. One of the two deities of the sky in early Hinduism is designated six times in the Rig Veda as Dyaus-Pitar (Heaven-Father). He is generally coupled with his female counterpart Prithivi-Mater (Earth-Mother). These two are designated as the parents of mankind. However, so minor is this Dyaus-Pitar in the Hindu pantheon that out of over 1,000 hymns of the Rig Veda not one is addressed to him alone, and gradually he disappeared altogether from the Sanskrit literature.[9]

The idea that God is a loving, spiritual, wise, holy Father of all mankind who even experiences suffering for the sins of His human children, and who is patiently helping to redeem them from their sins into the likeness of His own perfect character is developed only in Christianity.

A second unique differentiation of Christianity is the characterization of its founder as Son of God, Savior, and Elder Brother of all men. Nine founders of the eleven major living religions attracted many followers during their lifetime, and many more during subsequent centuries.[10] All nine, except Jesus Christ, are reported in their respective scriptures, as having gone through an early period of searching and uncertainty. All founders of non-Christian religions had some inconsistencies in their personal character; some even changed their program for changed circumstances.

Jesus Christ alone is reported as having had a consistent God-consciousness, a consistent character, and a consistent program for His religion. According to the record He grew up as a human being should grow up. "He increased in wisdom and in stature, and in favor with God and man" (Luke 2:52). Christians believe that He was normal, yet also ideally typical. He was the unique, but also exemplary combination of a son of man but also the Son of God. He grew physically but also participated consciously in the Eternal. He has

---

9. R. E. Hume, *The World's Living Religions,* Scribners, 1950, pp. 272-277.
10. Listed chronologically: Moses 1200 B. C., Zoroaster 606 B. C., Laotze 604 B. C., Mahavira 599 B. C., Buddha 560 B. C., Confucius 551 B. C., Jesus Christ 4(?) B. C., Muhammad 570 A. D., Nanak 1469 A. D.)

made the supreme revelation and manifestation of God to the world. He was unequalled by any other person who ever lived on earth, yet His qualities of personality should be those of all men. He is the pioneer of the Christian faith, and the Lord and Savior of all who accept Him.

A third unique and essential element in the Christian belief and experience is the work of the universal Holy Spirit. All three items: God as Father, Son, and Holy Spirit, were taught by the founder of the Christian religion as recorded in their Scriptures. They are summarized in the formula the Christian Church is using in admitting new members when "baptizing them in the name of the Father and of the Son and of the Holy Spirit" (Matthew 28:19). They have been regarded as essentials of Christianity from its beginning as a separate religion.

It must however be admitted that other religions have also made some approximations in the direction of these three essential and radically unique features of Christianity. Zoroastrianism teaches that Ahura Mazda, its chief deity is a bountiful spirit and works through one designated Spenta Mainyu (Bountiful Spirit). But in either case Zoroastrianism holds that the good Spirit is not really supreme, for from the beginning there was also a co-equal evil spirit, Angra Mainyu, who constantly is seeking to counteract Ahura Mazda. Confucianism holds that man is divinely good and so had no need for help from God for improvement. Judaism comes closest to Christianity in regard to the Holy Spirit but this doctrine has a very subordinate place in Jewish scriptures and has been greatly neglected in their religious life.

Christianity alone teaches the practical importance of the work of the Holy Spirit in the individual, the Church, and in the world. The Holy Spirit disturbs, convicts, reprimands, suggests, inspires, transforms, comforts, strengthens, illuminates, encourages, and is available as an indwelling reality and power to every individual or group whose heart and life is open to His influence. He is ever active, seeking to apply the principles of Christ, and is always leading to fuller discovery and greater appreciation of Truth.

These three essential and unique features of the Christian concept of God in His unity and diversity can be thought of as the *Eternal, Historical,* and *Progressive* manifestation of himself.[11] (a) God has

---

11. Hume, *op. cit.,* p. 277.

manifested himself as loving Father in His perpetual creation, providence, and sustaining of all that is. In God there is something eternal. (b) In God there is also something historical, which He has manifested most fully in the compass of the human life and character of Jesus Christ, our Lord and Savior. (c) In God there is also something progressive, for as a continual companion He is leading human life forward by the manifestation of himself through the Holy Spirit to the individual and society as a whole.

These three features of Christianity are highly theoretical and involve far-reaching theological implications, but they are also thoroughly practical and are best understood when experienced in human life. Together they constitute a comprehensive summary of what Christianity really means and is. On the other hand, they also represent the finest aspirations among the various other religions of the world, and together constitute a prophetic fulfillment of the religious history of all mankind. Compactly stated the essence of Christianity and the blessings which it seeks to give unto the world, has been formulated in the New Testament as the well-known benediction

"The grace of the Lord Jesus Christ, and the love of God and the fellowship of the Holy Spirit be with you all" (II Corinthians 13:14).

F.   SUMMARY AND CONCLUSION

In this chapter we have considered the Significance of the Holy Spirit, The Holy Spirit in the Scriptures, the Work of the Holy Spirit, the Standard for Testing the Spirits, and the Doctrine of the Trinity. In conclusion we again quote Jesus and Paul. Before His death Jesus said to His disciples:

"I have yet many things to say to you, but you cannot bear them now. When the Spirit of truth comes, he will guide you into all the truth . . . He will glorify me, for he will take what is mine and declare it unto you" (John 16:12-14).

And Paul's admonition for Christians to remember that "the fruit of the Spirit is love, joy, peace, patience, kindness, goodness, faithfulness, gentleness, self-control; against such there is no law" (Galatians 5:22, 23).

FOR FURTHER READING ON THE HOLY SPIRIT AND THE TRINITY

ON THE HOLY SPIRIT

Bales, J. D., *The Holy Spirit and the Christian,* Lambert, 1966.

Barclay, Wm., *The Promise of the Holy Spirit,* Westminster, 1960.

Berkhof, *The Doctrine of the Holy Spirit,* John Knox, 1964.

Bruner, D., *Theology of the Holy Spirit,* Eerdmans, 1970.

Calkins, Raymond, *The Holy Spirit,* Abingdon, 1930.

Criswell, W. A., *Holy Spirit in Today's World,* Zondervan, 1966.

Dana, H. E., *The Holy Spirit in Acts,* K. C. Central Seminary, 1943.

Dillistone, F. W., *The Holy Spirit in Life Today,* Westminster, 1947.

Draper, M. R., *The Gifts of the Spirit,* Herald Press, 1969.

Hollenweger, Walter J., *Handbook of the Pentecostal Movement,* eight volumes, in German, copy in Yale University Divinity School Library.

Jones, E. S., *A Study of Pentecost,* Abingdon, 1930.

Joy, D. M., *The Holy Spirit and You,* Abingdon, 1965.

Kaufman, G. D., *Systematic Theology*: "God the Holy Spirit," Scribners, 1968, pp. 223-254.

Kagawa, Toyohiko, *Meditations on the Holy Spirit,* Cokesbury 1943.

Streeter, B. H., ed., *The Relation of God and Man,* Macmillan, 1919.

Walker, A., *Rediscovery of the Holy Spirit,* Abingdon, 1969.

Yates, J. E., *The Spirit and the Kingdom,* Allenson, 1963.

ON THE TRINITY

Bickersteth, E. H., *The Trinity,* Kregel, 1950.

Bowie, W. R., *Jesus and the Trinity,* Abingdon, 1960.

Callahan, D. J. ed., *God, Jesus and Spirit,* Herder, 1970.

Cantwell, L., *The Theology of the Trinity,* Fides Pubs., 1969.

Cooke, B. J., *Beyond Trinity,* Marquette Univ. Press, 1969.

Franks, R. S., *The Doctrine of the Trinity,* Allenson, 1953.

Hedley, G., *The Holy Trinity*, Fortress, 1967.

Rahner, K., *The Trinity,* Herder, 1970.

Richardson, C. C., *The Doctrine of the Trinity,* Abingdon, 1958.

van Duson, H. P., *Spirit, Son and Father,* Scribners, 1958.

Wainright, A. W., *The Trinity in the New Testament,* London, S.P.C.K., 1962.

Welch, V. C., *In This Name,* Scribners, 1952.

CHAPTER VII

THE KINGDOM
AND THE CHURCH

"The Kingdom of God is in the midst of you" (Luke 17: 21). *"I will build my church, and the powers of death shall not prevail against it"* (Matthew 16:18).

THE HUMAN NEED FOR FELLOWSHIP AND INSPIRATION IS UNIVERSAL and all historic religions in some way try to meet it. No religious movement can reach its goal unless it is perpetuated and constantly renewed in and by an inspiring fellowship. In the long run no limited fellowship can fully meet this need, for what man really seeks is participation in the true destiny of mankind, such as the Church at its best.

From ancient times loyalties that have solicited man's full commitment are either of mystical or prophetic nature. Mystical fellowships seek to elevate their members above the world and gather them into union with the divine even while they are still here on earth. Prophetic fellowships unite their members in dedication to a cause and train them for more effective service toward the realization of that cause. At one extreme we have mystical cults without any social concern, and at the other extreme we have ethical cults without any concern for worship or any metaphysical ultimate. Christianity takes the prophetic role whereby fellowship in mystical union with Christ is expressed in prophetic social concern and action of the brotherhood. The Kingdom of God and the Christian Church are of this nature.

A. THE KINGDOM OF GOD

Jesus gave supreme importance to the Kingdom of God. It was already prominent in the lives of people with whom He came in contact. John the Baptist preached it. The disciples frequently asked questions about it. Jesus cast aside the materialistic, militaristic, and nationalistic interpretation of the Kingdom, involving a rebellion against Rome. Although He made reference to the apocalyptic interpretation, He emphasized a personal, responsible, ethical, spiritual, social, and universal interpretation.

1. *The Kingdom Defined*

The Kingdom of God is the rule of God, not only in nature and history, but also in the minds, hearts, and wills of individual persons and society. It is man's acknowledgement and promotion of God's sovereignty in every thought and act, expressed in voluntary submission of his will to God's will. It is a divine gift and at the same time there is something to be achieved by human cooperation. In origin it is individual and spiritual, planted in the mind and heart of man by God. But in its ultimate development it is destined also to transform society and bind men together in a common brotherhood. It has both individual and social aspects, here and hereafter.

The crowning description of the Kingdom was given by Jesus in answer to the question of the Pharisees as to when and how the Kingdom would come. Some expected it to come suddenly, blitz-like, catastrophic, as a militaristic revolution instituted by God without man's help. With this expectation Jesus took direct issue. He declared:

> "The kingdom of God is not coming with signs to be observed; nor will they say, 'Lo, here it is,' or 'There' for behold, the kingdom of God is in the midst of you" (Luke 17:20-21).

This means the Kingdom is not merely to be looked for in the future, but was already in the process of coming. God's Spirit was not only transforming and controlling the minds and hearts of certain individuals and groups, but they were also joyfully acknowledging His role as supreme in their individual and community lives, here and hereafter.

2. *Jesus' References to the Kingdom*

In the New Testament the expression "The kingdom of God" or its equivalent "The kingdom of heaven," is used more than 120 times. It was the burden of Jesus' message. Matthew alone records the use of this phrase by Jesus in forty-eight instances. The Gospel writers use this phrase in many ways, such as:

> "the kingdom of heaven is at hand" (Matthew 3:2), The gospel of the kingdom (Matthew 4:23; 9:35; 24:14), "theirs is the kingdom of heaven" (Matthew 5:10), "Thy kingdom come" (Matthew 6:10), "seek first his kingdom" (Matthew 6:33), "enter the kingdom of heaven" (Matthew 7:21), "sons of the kingdom" (Matthew 8:12; 13:38), "secrets of the kingdom" (Matthew 13:11; Mark 4:11), "coming in his kingdom" (Mat-

thew 16:28), 'inherit the kingdom' (Matthew 25:34), "my Father's kingdom" (Matthew 26:29), "the kingdom of God is at hand" (Mark 1:15), "To such belongs the kingdom" (Mark 10: 14), "You are not far from the kingdom" (Mark 12:34), looking for the kingdom of God (Mark 15:43), "of his kingdom there will be no end" (Luke 1:33), bringing the good news of the kingdom of God (Luke 8:1), "fit for the kingdom of God" (Luke 9:62), "the prophets in the kingdom of God" (Luke 13:28), "sit at the table in the kingdom of God" (Luke 13:29), "The kingdom of God is not coming with signs to be observed . . . the kingdom of God is in the midst of you" (Luke 17:20-21), "eat and drink at my table in my kingdom" (Luke 22:30), "unless one is born anew, he cannot see the kingdom of God" (John 3:3, 8), "My kingship is not of this world" (John 18:36).

Jesus talked much about it. He expected it, prayed for it, and worked to promote it. To no subject did Jesus devote more attention. He talked about it in some twenty parables, such as: the sower, the tares, the mustard seed, the leaven, the treasure, the pearl, the net, the vineyard, the ten virgins, the prodigal son, the great supper, and others. All to make it plain that the Kingdom is one of light and life, truth and righteousness, gladness and peace, self-denying love and sacrificial service, a Kingdom where God reigns.

Jesus was in earnest about the Kingdom. It was bad news for the complacent who thought themselves justified by the right deed or the right creed but refused the right relationship. But it was good news for those who repent and accept the childlike relationship to God with a childlike faith. It was good news for them, not only for the future - after death or after the Kingdom has been established completely - but also good news for here and now.

The first petition in the prayer that He taught His disciples is "Thy kingdom come" (Matthew 6:10). According to His teaching the supreme purpose of life is "to seek first his kingdom and his righteousness" (Matthew 6:33). He spoke of the Kingdom as the one pearl of great value (Matthew 13:45), for which all else should be sacrificed.

> Jesus went about . . . teaching in their synagogues and preaching the gospel of the kingdom . . . (Matthew 4:23). And the people sought him and came to him, and would have kept him from leaving them; but he said to them, "I must preach the good news of the kingdom of God to the other cities also; for I was sent for this purpose" (Luke 4:42, 43).

3. *Love, the Uniting Principle of the Kingdom*

We are told "God is love" (I John 4:6, 16). Paul says that of three abiding values "the greatest is love" and exhorts his readers to

"Make love your aim" (I Corinthians 13:13; 14:1). When Jesus was asked about the greatest commandment, He replied:

> "You shall love the Lord your God with all your heart, and with all your soul, and with all your mind. This is the great and first commandment. And a second is like it. You shall love your neighbor as yourself" (Matthew 22:36-39; cf. Mark 12:29-31).

Christian love is sharing God's own life, "the unsearchable riches of Christ" (Ephesians 3:8) even with the unworthy. "We love, because he first loved us" (I John 4:19). At the very heart of Christian sharing is the divine gift of sharing by God himself. This is the love which is the uniting principle in the Kingdom of God.[1]

In the world at present there is still much injustice and cruelty. Often the wicked prosper while the righteous suffer. Jealousies and greed, pride and hate, unbelief and sorrow, hunger and disease, ignorance and superstition, injustice and war; all are evidences that the Kingdom has not yet fully come and God's will is not yet fully "done on earth as it is in heaven" (Matthew 6:10). Group life in some respects is even much worse than individual life as Niebuhr has pointed out. National life displays pride and selfishness much more extremely than is the case with individuals. In our political, social and economic institutions there is still much evil.[2]

The Christian home, comes nearest to being a Kingdom model on a small scale. But even in the family, wherever tension exists the Kingdom has not yet fully come. The Church is committed to teaching, obeying, and promoting the will of God and it does render great service of love in the world. But even here there still are flagrant contrasts to the spirit of the Kingdom. The striving for place and power, racial and denominational pride and strife, and in many other areas the Kingdom has not yet fully come even in the churches, or even in individual Christian lives.

4. The Coming of the Kingdom

There are different views as to just how to expect God to manifest His power and how men are finally to be made perfect in obedience and love. The one view holds that God will suddenly and cataclysmically intervene in the affairs of the world and in power and glory establish His Kingdom. The other view holds that the Kingdom is already partly present in the world where God's will is done and

---

1. L. H. DeWolf, *Theology of the Living Church,* Harpers, 1954, pp. 299-302.
2. Reinhold Niebuhr, *Moral Man and Immoral Society,* Scribners, 1932.

that it will grow "as a grain of mustard seed" (Matthew 13:31), and like "leaven" (Matthew 13:33). It spreads as His spirit increasingly is recognized, accepted, and practiced in individual and group life.[3]

The Kingdom, however, is not limited to this world. It neither began nor will it end with men or institutions on earth. It does not consist of governments, economic orders or ecclesiastical organizations. It consists of a community of persons to which earthly institutions may contribute or be a hindrance. Institutions of the world are like the forms within which cement is poured to fashion houses of wickedness or temples of worship. The forms are temporary, yet the shape of the structure remains. The Kingdom is favored or hindered by what is done in politics and commerce. Economic injustice and international war do not promote the Kingdom and Christians need to do everything possible to abolish them. Christ's Kingdom is not of this world (John 18:31) but it also is here in our "midst" and Christians seek to promote and advance that reality of greatest value. Its program is to let God reign in all that men do and are, as individuals and as a human society at large. To promote the Kingdom is the task of the Church.[4]

B.   The Christian Church

By the time the Gospels were written the Church was already an established reality. The evangelists were churchmen and so they naturally were inclined to interpret traditions in terms of church life. The word "church" does not appear in any of the Gospels except Matthew and there it is mentioned only three times (Matthew 16:18; 18:17). In contrast the Pauline letters, written even before the earliest Gospels, use the word "church" more than forty times. In Acts, Luke uses the word eighteen times, although it is not used at all in Luke's Gospel.

1.   The Beginnings of the Church

(a) *Pentecost.* In speaking of the origin of the Church reference is often made to the remnant in Israel that welcomed Jesus as the Messiah, or one can even go back to Abraham as the father of faith. However, Pentecost, as a more definite event in history, is usually

---

3. Both of these positions are discussed in more detail in chapter X dealing with "The Christian Hope."

4. John Bright, *The Kingdom of God*, Abingdon, 1953; Paul S. Minear, *The Kingdom and the Power,* Westminster, 1950, Part III.

looked upon as the beginning of the Church. Luke describes this beginning in the first chapters of Acts.

> When the day of Pentecost had come, they were all together in one place. And suddenly a sound came from heaven like the rush of a mighty wind, and it filled the house . . . And they were filled with the Holy Spirit . . . (Acts 2:1-4).
> But Peter, standing with the eleven, lifted up his voice and addressed them (v. 14) . . . Now when they heard this they were cut to the heart, and said . . . "Brethren what shall we do?" And Peter said to them, "Repent, and be baptized every one of you in the name of Jesus Christ for the forgiveness of your sins; . . ." (v. 37-38).
> So those that received his word were baptized, and there were added that day about three thousand souls. And they devoted themselves to the apostles' teaching and fellowship, to the breaking of bread and the prayers . . . (v. 41-42)
> And day by day attending the temple together . . . praising God . . . And the Lord added to their number day by day those who were being saved . . . (v. 46-47)
> And as they were speaking to the people . . . many of those who heard the word believed: and the number of the men came to about five thousand (Ch. 4:1-4).

Soon persecution took place and the Christians spread in all directions. However their numbers steadily increased as they located in the surrounding cities.

(b) *Early Church Characteristics.* Decisive events took place in the first century of our era. In some respects events can be most plainly seen when looked at backward as A. R. Vidler points out.[5] So beginning with about the year 100 A.D. and looking backward one can see certain facts that were not in existence when the century began.

Being *small groups in large cities* is the first fact we note. A network of new societies or brotherhoods, that went by the name "Christian" had come into existence in the cities around the Mediterranean Sea. These were small groups in large cities such as Rome, Ephesus, or Corinth, which perhaps were not even noticeable to the average person. They were at first regarded as only a particular sect of the Jews. Although in fact the two groups had soon become quite different from each other and in reality were in competition with each other.

Being both *exclusive and inclusive* is a second item to note. The Christian group refused to conform to traditions and customs of the

---

5. Alec R. Vidler, *Christian Belief,* SCM Press LTD., London, 1950, Ch. III.

Roman world. They would not participate in Emperor worship, which involved only casting a pinch of incense before his statue. This separated them from other people. They did not mix in society more than necessary. They took no part in popular games and festivals. Their manner and morals were rather strict. Each church was a small isolated unit, meeting regularly on the first day of the week in an obscure place on some back street, perhaps upstairs to be less obvious. There was much contact with other Christian groups in other cities. They felt they all belonged to a single family and really formed a new race of people.

Although in a sense they were rather exclusive, in another sense they were very inclusive. They included different types and classes of people, who formerly would not mix and were rather opposed to each other. Now here were Jews and Gentiles, Greeks and barbarians, freemen and slaves, men and women, different nationalities, classes, and races, all given an equal status. Although, exclusive as far as outsiders were concerned, they were very inclusive and intimate as far as the Christian brotherhood was concerned.

Being *powerless yet powerful* was a third characteristic of these brotherhoods. They were a rather unimportant social group and had no influence on political or economic affairs. At this time it was still unthought of that in a few centuries the whole Empire would become Christian, at least in name.

Even though politically powerless yet it was clear that they did possess spiritual power and lived radiant lives. They were simple uneducated folk and yet must have been intellectually keen and alert to appreciate and preserve the letters of Paul, written to them. The same letters in our day challenge some of the keenest intellects. They had a sense of vitality and hopefulness that was in sharp contrast to the weariness of the Roman world around them. In the decaying Roman Empire the Christian communities represented a new world breaking into life.

Being *authoritarian but free* was a fourth characteristic of the early Christians. "Obey" was an idea that was not only frequently on their lips but they actually thought of themselves as bond-servants and slaves of Jesus Christ. They were people under authority and tried to acknowledge the authority of civil government, but only so far as conscience would allow.

At the same time they also emphasized liberty and rejoiced in it. Paul admonished them: "For freedom Christ has set us free; stand fast therefore, and do not submit again to the yoke of slavery"

196   BASIC CHRISTIAN CONVICTIONS

(Galatians 5:1). Christians were to consider themselves delivered and free from sin and its power as well as from the Jewish ceremonial practices and rites. This does not mean that these communities were free from all stains and strains. They had their shortcomings but still were a new, vital and promising people, not known of in history before.

(c) *Explanation for the Existence of the Church.* At this time there was as yet no official creed, they had no catechism and no pope. Their only sacred book was what we know as the Old Testament, although most of the Gospels and Epistles were already written and later were joined with the Old Testament. The answer Christians would have given in explanation of their existence, would probably have differed somewhat but in essence they would have agreed, namely: that God Almighty, the creator and ruler of the universe had fulfilled the promises He had made to His people, Israel. Long ago when men wandered in darkness and refused to follow the light of their conscience, God had chosen Abraham and his descendants, Israel, to bring all nations to the light and life with God.

But Israel was disobedient and also went astray, rejecting God's messengers and prophets. So God finally sent His son Jesus Christ as the Messiah. He went about doing good and summoning the people to repent and get ready for the new age, the Kingdom of God. But Jesus also, they rejected and crucified. However, God raised Him up and made Him the head of the new people, a new race. Jesus, the Messiah was now the Lord of all, and finally the time would come when the veil which at present concealed His lordship over all would be removed and then He would be universally acknowledged as the deliverer and judge of the living and the dead.

But already the new age had dawned. This was indicated by the coming of the Holy Spirit at Pentecost. This Holy Spirit was a new power of love which enabled them to live a new kind of life together. This fact was witnessed to by the brotherhood of churches which had sprung up all over the Roman Empire. God their Father, Jesus Christ their Savior, and the Holy Spirit their Counselor, they would have said, were at the bottom of these Christian communities and only so could they be accounted for.[6]

---

6. Op. Cit., pp. 42-50.

2. *The Church in History.*

At first the followers of Jesus and the members of the early Church were Jews, but soon it was recognized that the bond of Christians was one of faith and not blood. The recognition that non-Jews would also respond to the Gospel in faith brought on a crisis in the early Church (Acts 10; Galatians 2:11-14). Through personal experience Paul, Peter and others were finally convinced and the matter was definitely settled at the first Conference of Christian leaders at Jerusalem when it was decided that membership in the Christian fellowship did not require being, or first becoming a Jew (Acts 15:1-19). The Christian community thereafter transcended social and racial barriers and included all who came to faith in God through Christ Jesus. The Church increasingly became the meeting point of the Gospel and the world. In other words, the Church became God's special agent in history.

(a) *Assimilation of Hebrew, Greek and Roman Qualities.* To re-examine and reinterpret the Old Testament prophesies in the light of their experience with Jesus Christ was of prime importance to the early Christian leaders. The Jews thought that the Messiah would come to save them from the Roman yoke in a materialistic, military and national manner. However, the Church saw that Jesus fulfilled other prophecies such as that of the suffering servant in Isaiah 53. Christians accepted the Old Testament but in many respects reinterpreted it. In time the Old and the New Testament were put together to form our present Bible.

Greek philosophy was also examined and used by the Church. Many Greeks admired Jesus and His teaching. Many joined the Church. This was true not only of Hellenized Jews but also of Greeks as such. For centuries the Greeks had Hellenized everything they contacted in the spread of their culture. But Jesus Christ, they somehow could not reduce to mere speculation. On the other hand the Church took Greek culture and thought-patterns and clothed its own faith in Greek vocabulary and used Greek philosophy in formulating its own theology.

Roman contributions were also made use of. Not only was it necessary for early Christianity to reinterpret Hebrew prophecy and claim it as its own, to accommodate itself to Greek philosophy and use it to express its own deepest convictions, but early Christianity also had to face the power and opposition of the Roman Government.

In the inevitable collision, Rome undertook to stamp out Christianity. Christians were compelled to flee into the sewers and catacombs; they were outlawed, outcast, furiously hated, and mercilessly persecuted. This only helped to spread the new faith which could not be beheaded, burned, or devoured by ferocious beasts. In the end the Roman Empire gradually disappeared and the Church lived on and continued to grow. Roman roads were used to spread the Gospel and Roman organization was adapted to church organization. Where Christians of early times suffered most, there stands today the most wonderful church building in the world.

In the first three centuries the Christians carried the Gospel one thousand miles north and south and fifteen hundred miles east and west, made seven million converts, and placed a Christian emperor on the throne in Rome who embroidered the cross of the Nazarene on his battle flag with the inscription, "By this sign we conquer." For sheer romance the story has no parallel in history.

(b) *The Dark and Middle Ages* were already preceded by division in the church. After Rome was conquered, the Church had honor heaped upon it. Prosperity is always dangerous. It is difficult to live up to one's best in times of affluence. Seemingly when Christians thought they had nothing to fight against, they started to fight among themselves. Soon they fell apart into East and West—Greek and Latin—Constantinople and Rome—and the Church was divided.

The Dark and Middle Ages followed. This period is often thought of as a tragic era in western history. The northern tribes overran Europe, and it seemed as though civilization had turned on itself. The Goths and the Visigoths crossed the Danube. Two centuries later Attila with his Huns, followed. Somehow the Church weathered the storm. In turn it also crossed the Danube and carried the cross to the Slavs. Under the leadership of St. Boniface, Christians went north into the land of the Teutons, supplanting pagan practices with Christian worship and so giving birth to the Church in that area. Augustine of Hippo, with a small group of disciples, crossed the North Sea and set up the banner of the cross in England.

Then came the Middle Ages when the Schoolmen undertook to combine the vigor of the northern tribes with the Christian Church. In all this, somehow Jesus Christ stood out as supreme and gave a new quality to feudal life and the thinking of the Schoolmen. The Church revived, grew and was strengthened.

Centuries passed. Once again, what was won in adversity was in danger of being lost in times of prosperity. Power is dangerous and easily corrupts. Various compromises were introduced. Pagan customs and heathen traditions were tolerated. Peter Waldo (1176) a retired businessman, began to cry out against the corruption of the clergy. Others followed.

(c) *Reformation* was a crying need. In 1505 young Martin Luther (1483-1546) and his friend Alexis while out walking were overtaken by a thunderstorm and smitten by lightning near the Erfurt gate. Alexis was killed and Luther was knocked to the ground. Struggling to rise he cried out, "St. Anne help me, I will become a monk." He was a law student at the time, planning on a civil career. Soon thereafter he abandoned these plans and joined the monastery.[7]

In his search for peace of soul he went through extreme spiritual agony and finally in penance went to Rome. At last he found peace and later served as priest at Wittenberg, Germany. Here he however increasingly began to question the position of the Pope and the Roman Catholic Church, especially on the matter of "indulgences" and the remission of sin upon financial contributions to the Church. In 1517 he nailed his ninety-five theses on his church door at Wittenberg and the Reformation was born. John Calvin, John Knox, Huldrych Zwingli, Menno Simons and others followed.[8]

After the Reformation came the industrial revolution which further complicated economic, social and political matters and helped to bring about conditions far from ideal. Years passed and John Wesley appeared and helped his generation to an understanding of more meaningful Christianity.

---

7. R. H. Bainton, *The Reformation,* Beacon Press, 1952, p. 28; S. T. Stuber, ed., *The Christian Reader,* Association Press, 1952, p. 207.

8. Before leaving the Reformation something should be said of the Anabaptist and Free Church movement which today is again receiving increasing consideration.

The Mennonite Encyclopedia, Vol. I - IV, Mennonite Publishing House, Scottdale, Pa., 1955, on the back cover of each volume says: "Arising in the Reformation period as a fourth major type of Protestantism alongside of Lutheranism, Calvinism and Anglicanism, Anabaptism was in the words of Rufus M. Jones, 'one of the most momentous and significant undertakings in man's religious struggle after truth . . . It is the spiritual soil out of which all non-conformist sects have sprung.' Professor Walter Koehler of Heidelberg wrote, 'The Anabaptists may claim a place in world history as the pioneers of the modern world view with its freedom of faith and conscience.' Almost crushed by persecution Anabaptism nevertheless left a significant spiritual legacy . . . As lineal descendants of the Anabaptists, the Mennonites . . . have played a significant role in religion and culture . . . They have been Biblical pacifists . . . have entered extensively into Protestant foreign missions, as well as . . . service of relief in 20 foreign countries. *The Mennonite Encylopedia* reports comprehensively on their history in various countries . . . their principles, activities, institutions, culture, and practices . . . as well as outstanding

(d) *The Modern World* begins with Pilgrims and Puritans coming to America in the hope of establishing a Government of free people who could worship God according to the dictates of their conscience. Soon followed the Christian missionary expansion, touching all parts of the world. Still later came the scientific struggle, reinterpreting and enlarging many of our concepts, the end of which is not yet.

Today the Church lifts its banner throughout the world. There are great problems facing it which are also opportunities. With automation and the increase of leisure time; with modern means of

---

leaders, and over 200 family histories. Accounts of over 2,000 individual martyrs are given."

For the Anabaptists the major reformers did not go far enough. Becoming a Christian, for the Anabaptists, was an intimate concern of each individual and the church was considered to be a voluntary society of the regenerate who were living obediently to Christ's principles. After much Bible study and repeated public disputations on questions of baptism, freedom of conscience, sacraments, separation of church and state, the Christian attitude toward war, and related questions, finally on January 21, 1525, actual adult re-baptism took place and the conflict was on. Adult baptism and refusal to bear arms were crucial issues and could not be tolerated by either church or state.

Anabaptism spread rapidly, especially among the depressed and the poor. The utter ruthlessness of the persecution is more understandable in view of extremely fanatical parties that developed among the Anabaptists, who however were a great aberration from the position of the main movement.

Menno Simons (1496-1561) a converted Roman Catholic priest, gathered the remnants of the scattered Anabaptists of the Low Countries. The Mennonites, nicknamed after Menno, thus became the lineal descendants of the original Swiss Anabaptist Brethren. Later the English Baptists and the Quakers show obvious influence of Anabaptist ideas transmitted by way of Anabaptist refugees who fled to England and English refugees who fled to the Low Countries. In Menno Simons' writings we probably have the most balanced picture of the Anabaptist position.

The growing interest in the Free or the Believers' Church today is evidenced by various trends in Europe and America, such as: The Free Church movement in Germany, the 1967 Louisville Believers' Church Conference, and the Believers' Church Conference held at The Chicago Theological Seminary, June 29-July 2, 1970.

Some of the more widely accepted Anabaptist ideas today are: (1) For a Christian it is most important to seek the will of Christ for each life situation and engage in action accordingly. The Kingdom of God is considered more important than anything material, social, political, and even personal, and to promote it is the Christian's chief concern. The Anabaptist way of putting this would be the stress on obediently following Christ (Die Nachfolge Christi). (2) The separation of Church and State that is taken for granted in America and is rapidly spreading to other parts of the world. (3) All this implies Freedom of Conscience. (4) Infant Baptism is increasingly looked upon as superstitious and to be replaced by Infant Consecration and Adult Baptism on confession of faith. Baptism and Communion or The Lord's Supper are both increasingly considered outward symbols of an inner experience. (5) That participation in war is unchristian and to survive, mankind must find

communication and transportation; with population explosion and starvation threatening great masses of people; with unrest and disorder throughout the world; with the colored races gradually taking over more dominance and power; and with the danger now in man's hands, to destroy civilization and nearly all human life through an atomic world war—with all this, and more, what a challenge the Christian Church is facing! The day of the Christian Church is not past; it has not yet fully come, provided it is true to its Lord and Master, Jesus Christ.

---

some other method to settle international questions. The Christian lives by nonviolence and promotes the way of peace, avoiding violence of spirit as well as action, serving men rather than seeking to rule them. The current anti-war position of college students is encouraging. (6) The emphasis on the "Simple Life" is Christian and applies to economic as well as social, personal and group life. By "simple living" more stewardship can be practiced with time, strength, and money. The present student generation stress on the need for new value priorities in individual, social, as well as international life, is important. Human and spiritual values must be given priority over individual and corporate economic and property rights, which increases the poverty of the poor and the wealth of the rich.

For further reading on Anabaptists, Mennonites, or The Believers' Church, see:

Bender, H. S., *These are My People*, Mennonite Pub. House, 1960.

Dyck, C. J., ed., *Introduction to Mennonite History*, Herald Press, 1967.

Durnbaugh, D., *History of the Believers' Church*, Macmillan, 1968;

Estep, W. R., *The Anabaptist Story*, Broadman Press, Nashville, Tenn., 1963;

Garrett, J. L., Jr., *The Concept of the Believers' Church*, Scottdale, Pa., 1968;

—————, *Report, 1970 Believers' Church Conference*, Scottdale, Pa., 1970;

Gingerich, M., *The Christian and Revolution*, Herald Press, Scottdale, Pa., 1968;

Hershberger, Guy, (ed), *The Recovery of the Anabaptist Vision*, Scottdale, Pa., 1957;

Kaufman, Ed. G., *The Mennonite Missionary Interest*, Book Concern, Berne, Ind., 1931;

Kaufman, Gordon D., *The Context of Decision*, Abingdon Press, 1961;

Krahn, C., *Dutch Anabaptism*, Nighoff-Hague, Holland, 1969;

Littell, F. H., *The Free Church*, Star King Press, Boston, 1957;

Smith, C. H., *The Story of the Mennonites*, revised, Menn. Pub. Office, Newton, Ks., 1957;

Strayer, J. M., *Anabaptists and the Sword*, Coronado, 1972.

Trueblood, Elton, *The Company of the Committed*, Harper, 1961;

Unruh, J. D., *In the Name of Christ*, Mennonite Central Committee, 1952.

Wenger, J. C., *The Complete Writings of Menno Simons*, Scottdale, Pa., 1956;

Williams, G. H., *Wilderness and Paradise in Christian Thought*, Harper, 1962.

Yoder, J. H., *The Christian Witness to the State*, Faith and Life Press, Newton, Ks., 1964.

3. *The Nature of the Church*

(a) *The Historic Creeds* speak of the Church as One, Holy, Catholic and Apostolic. The Apostles' Creed says: "the Holy Catholic Church." The Nicene Creed says: "one Catholic and Apostolic Church." Let us briefly look at each of these characteristics.

The *Unity of the Church* comes first. Divided as the Church seemingly is, Christians still affirm that it is one in spirit. The many outward and organizational divisions do not affect the ultimate spiritual unity of the Church. Paul repeatedly speaks of the Church as the one body of which Christ is the head:

> There is one body and one Spirit, just as you were called to one hope that belongs to your call, one Lord, one faith, one baptism, one God and Father of us all, who is above and through all and in all (Ephesians 4:4, 5). He is the head of the body, the church (Colossians 1:18; cf. 3:14-15).
>
> For as in one body, we have many members, and all members do not have the same function, so we, though many, are one body in Christ, and individually members of one another (Romans 12:4-5; cf. Ephesians 5:29-30; I Corinthians 12:12-13; 24-27).

The Church's unity is not dependent upon a unified organization. No super-organization ever controlled the entire Church. Already in the early New Testament Church there were divisions (I Corinthians 1:10-17). As persecution broke out the Christians spread. Soon there were Syrian, Indian, Armenian, and Coptic churches. Later even more divisions developed. But still there is a unity of the Church which is based on the oneness in the spirit and life of Christ and not on organization. The Bible used by all Christians is an embodiment and an expression of the unity of the Church. In deciding upon the canon of the Bible the Church helped to protect the unity of its faith.

Holiness is a second quality of the Church. The Church is holy because it shares in the holiness of Christ, its head and Lord. Paul tells the Christians at Corinth and Rome they are "called to be saints" (I Corinthians 1:2; Romans 1:7). Holiness does not mean otherworldliness by avoiding contamination with earthly things. Holiness means dedication to the cause of Christ. The Church is an agent of Christ in the world. The Church is especially set aside to reincarnate the Christ in individuals and in society. It is not perfect but even in its weakness it is working at the task of promoting the cause of Christ. The Church is holy, that is, consecrated to the cause of making whole or healing.

3. *Catholic* is a third quality of the Church. This means it is universal and worldwide. The Church is for all men. There is no distinction of class or race—all social distinctions are meaningless in the Church. Paul writes:

> There is neither Jew nor Greek, there is neither slave nor free, there is neither male nor female; for you are all one in Christ Jesus (Galatians 3:28).

To the degree to which the living Christ is the Lord of the Church, the universality of the Church will also be realized. Paul also recognized that "there are varieties of gifts . . . varities of services . . . varieties of working" (I Corinthians 12:4-6), in the Church. It is this inclusive unity with diversity that constitutes the catholicity of the Church.

But catholicity also means authenticity. This refers to the consensus of the Church. The authentic faith is based on the universal faith. Whenever some weighty matter needs decision it is done by summoning a council and ascertaining the consensus of the Church. These councils seek to express the considered mind of the universal Church under the guidance of the Holy Spirit. This is how we got our creeds. They express the mind of the Church and the only requirement for joining the Church is to share its faith.

4. *Apostolic* is a fourth quality of the Church. One mark of the early Church was its faithfulness to the apostles. We read "They devoted themselves to the apostles' teaching" (Acts 2:42). To insist that the apostolicity of the Church is based upon a two thousand year "supergeneology" seems shallow and superficial. Apostolic succession, instead of referring to an ordination ceremony, refers to the preaching of the apostolic message. If the apostolic proclamation is absent, no geneology can possibly make up for it.

An apostle is one sent forth with a special message and mission. "He called his disciples and chose from them twelve, whom he named apostles" (Luke 6:13), "to be with him, and to be sent out to preach" (Mark 3:14). The disciples were followers and learners at first, and then became apostles sent forth with a special message and mission. To be apostolic the Church must be a missionary Church in behalf of her Lord and Savior. "Missionary" is from the Latin and "apostolic" from the Greek.

(b) *Some complementary qualities* of the Church are significant.

At first glance these seem to be contradictions, but if taken together, they help to understand the nature of the Church.[9]

An Institution and a Fellowship—the Church is both. As an institution it transcends its individual members. It is made up of individuals but no one individual is the institution. The reality of the Church as an institution is greater than the sum of the individual members. At the same time, the Church is also a fellowship and communion, never merely an institution. It is people living together in fellowship. Whenever the Church is only an organization apart from people, it is no longer the Church and whenever it is only a group of people who meet because they like each other it is no longer the Church either. The Church is both an institution and a fellowship.

A Means and a Goal—the Church is both. It is God's instrument to proclaim the Gospel. Through the Church, Christian love expresses itself in mission and relief work. Through the Church as a means people are instructed in the Gospel and given opportunity to worship together. But the Church is also an end and a goal. Through this teaching and preaching, people become members of the Church, the body of Christ. This fellowship with God is the ultimate purpose of life. Only when the Church is both, a means and an end, a tool and product, is it truly the Church.

A Proclamation and a People—the Church is both. It is a community of people proclaiming a message. If the Church is not witnessing, it has become only a social club. The life of the Church depends upon its proclamation. But the Word is not disembodied, it is spoken and it is lived by people, and for people, to bring about transformation. This transformation in others is brought about by those who themselves have been transformed, and who by doing this proclaiming, themselves also become more fully transformed. The story of Jesus is told in words, but it also is lived by people. The Church is not only a message nor only a people—it is a people with a message and a message that creates a people. Both are requirements.

Visible and Invisible—the Church is both. The Church as a visible ecclesiastical institution is not coextensive with the Church as the people of God. Mere membership in a visible Church does not assure membership in the Kingdom of God or invisible Church. On the other hand the fact that a person does not belong to any visible Church, does not necessarily exclude him from membership

---

9. G. W. Forell, *The Protestant Faith,* Prentice-Hall, 1960, pp. 203 ff.

in the Kingdom of God. Judas belonged to the visible group of disciples but was not really a member of the Kingdom—while the criminal on the cross to whom Jesus said, "today you will be with me in paradise" (Luke 23:43), certainly belonged to the invisible Church although he was not formally a disciple. This does not mean that membership in the visible Church is unimportant.

Aggressive and Triumphant—the Church is both. The Church in this world must be aggressive against all evil. It cannot be at rest where there is hate, injustice, and strife. It must be about its Father's business in the struggle against disease, hunger, ignorance, and war. The Church is not only aggressive against the enemies without, but also against the evils and imperfections still within the visible Church. This militancy sometimes is divisive, but it is meant to be corrective.

Christians also speak of the Church triumphant, referring to that part of the Church on the other side of the curtain of death, and which is now in glory participating in the triumph won by its Lord and Savior. The Church as a whole consists not only of those members now on earth but of all faithful believers from the beginning. We are admonished:

> Since we are surrounded by so great a cloud of witnesses, let us lay aside every weight, and sin which clings so closely, and let us run with perseverance the race that is set before us (Hebrews 12:1).

The Church militant is greatly encouraged by the Church triumphant. The concept of the Church includes both realities.

The Church then, can be thought of as an institution and a fellowship, a means and a goal, a proclamation and a people, visible and invisible, aggressive and triumphant, and with these characteristics the Church nevertheless is *One* in the spirit of Christ; *Holy,* or dedicated to make whole and heal; *Catholic* or universal, welcoming everybody into the Christian community who accepts Jesus as Lord and Savior; and *Apostolic,* or in line with apostolic teaching and spirit, zealous as those sent forth with a special message and mission by and for their Lord.

4. *Organization and Function of the Church*

Some organization for the continuation and growth of the Christian fellowship was inevitable. At first it was the kind of organization that exists in an orchestra. They all play together organized around one leader. While the orchestra tunes up, there is disorganization. As soon as the leader steps on the platform there is organization like iron filings gathering around a magnet. However, soon some physical organization was inevitable as an expression of the faith.

Christian love implies earnest effort to share the meaning and experience of the Gospel. Such efforts demand formal organization. This is needed for the responsible collection and handling of funds; for the designation and training of leaders; for the holding and managing of needed property for education, worship and fellowship; and other Christian purposes. Only so can the Christian message and faith be made effective near and far. Just as the physical body is a help but also can be a temptation for the individual person, so the organization can help or hinder the Church. To have spiritual life in the Church without any concern for its organized expression is difficult if not impossible.

(a) *The Ministry of Preaching and Teaching.* There are two main concepts of the ministry. One thinks of ministers as those who exercise the authority of God in the congregation, ordained by unbroken succession from Christ and the Apostles. Such tasks as administering the sacraments, teaching and pronouncing the forgiveness of God to penitent sinners can only be done by His special representatives and not by ordinary laymen. In the main this is the Catholic view.

The other view considers the ministry as a delegated function of the congregation as a whole. According to this view there is nothing about leading a worship service that a layman could not do, but naturally a person who has been trained for it should be able to do it better. In general this is the Protestant view. A person entering the ministry does so upon feeling a special call of God for this work and the action of the congregation confirming that call. The minister is responsible to both God and the congregation.

Churches organized on the Episcopal pattern depend on a semi-independent clerical government to supply their ministers; others are more democratic and expect each congregation to choose their own. Usually both procedures are combined by permitting congregational selection within overall standards and through processes approved by higher authority. Types of church government, therefore, vary from the Episcopal—with authority vested in the highest office—to the independent form where each congregation governs itself. The Presbyterian is in between with its pattern of local authority combined with a higher governing body.

Qualifications for the ministry are steadily rising. The minister must have a grounding in the Christian faith, the traditions, and the forms and practice of his own church. He should be able to relate Christianity to contemporary life, understand business management as well as psychology. Above all there must be evidence of his religious faith in his own personal and family life. Catholics hold that ordination is a sacrament that puts an indelible mark on a person so that he will always stand in special relation to God even if he becomes unfaithful. Protestants hold that the ministry is a functional office to proclaim the Gospel and to guide the congregation, but being a minister does not place him any closer to God than other Christians. Protestants hold to the priesthood of all believers. Hence the ministry for the Protestant has many forms. Paul says:

> And his gifts were that some should be apostles, some prophets, some evangelists, some pastors and teachers, for the equipment of the saints, for the work of ministry, for building up the body of Christ (Ephesians 4:11-12).

The care and guidance of the Church being the primary task of the ministry whether that be deacon, presbyter, or bishop—the words of Paul still apply to all seeking to serve the Church in any office of leadership:

> If any one aspires to the office of bishop, he desires a noble task. Now a bishop must be above reproach, the husband of one wife, temperate, sensible, dignified, hospitable, an apt teacher, no drunkard, not violent but gentle, not quarrelsome, no lover of money. He must manage his own household well, keeping his children submissive and respectful in every way; for if a man does not know how to manage his own household how can he care for God's church? (I Timothy 3:1).

In the service of the Christian ministry these personal qualifications are more important than the specific manner of selection and appointment to the office.

Jesus instructed His disciples to "Go into all the world and preach the gospel to the whole creation" (Mark 16:15). However they were not to stop with preaching but to go on "teaching them to observe all that I have commanded you" (Matthew 28:20). The foremost function of the Church, as the body of Christ, is to preach and teach, to express and nurture the message of love of God revealed in Christ Jesus. This message is to be proclaimed by word and deed.

Each new generation needs instruction. The Holy Spirit is still at work, and much that needs to be taught is new in every age. To be true to its preaching and teaching function, the Church must also be true to its truth-seeking function. Every preacher must also be a teacher, and every teacher must also be a learner.

Exhortation naturally goes with preaching and teaching if people are to be "doers of the word, and not hearers only" (James 1:20). Encouragement is needed to act upon the truth disclosed. Exhortation is the task of all Church members and not only the preacher and teacher. The apostle says: "therefore encourage one another and build one another up . . . admonish the idle, encourage the faint-hearted, help the weak, be patient with them all" (I Thessalonians 5:11, 14).

Evangelism and missions are included in the preaching and teaching function of the Church. These can be called the growing edge of the Church. This phase of the work also includes healing, agriculture, social reform, and everything else that the Christian spirit can devise to help people. This phase of the work of the Church is still far from finished. A Church that is not evangelistic and missionary is not in truth a Church.

(b) *Communal worship and prayer* is a function of the Church. Here the congregation together is meeting God by means of hymn singing, Scripture reading, prayer, and meditation. Dignity and beauty of this service gives the feeling of fellowship with the saints of the past, and present. By means of the worship service God becomes more real and thereby the individual is more enabled to meet his problems in the spirit of Christ.

(c) *Social action* is another area where the Church must function. Members need direction to useful service at home and abroad. The Church has always tried to take care of its own widows and orphans. But there are also racial tensions, unfair economic conditions, unwholesome amusements, problems of peace and war, all need attention. The Church is to serve as the conscience of the community, the state and nation, reaching out to international affairs. The Church has increasingly mobilized its resources to provide food, clothing, shelter, medicine, education, and other help to distressed areas the world over. Now, even governments have entered this area with various AID and relief programs. Instead of the old pagan ethics regarding enemies, the Church must help to implement the command of Jesus when He said,

> "Love your enemies and pray for those who persecute you, so that you may be sons of your Father who is in heaven . . ." (Matthew 5:44).

(d) *The Christian Ordinances.* Words have their limitations and actions are more communicative. An obvious example of a visible word is the kiss. When a parent kisses a child, or a man kisses his wife, we have an act that is a visible word. A hearty handshake is another visible word. Sacraments or ordinances are such visible words, mediated through fellowship in the Church, by which God and man speak to each other.

Christians differ on the number of ordinances and as to their interpretation. Protestants in general practice only two: Baptism, and the Lord's Supper. Roman Catholic and Greek Orthodox churches have seven: Confirmation, Penance, Extreme Unction, Holy Orders, and Matrimony, besides Baptism and the Lord's Supper. Protestants limit themselves to these particular two because only they were practiced by Jesus himself.

Ordinances guard the faith against false intellectualism. The God of the Bible is not like the Unmoved Mover of the philosophers but is thought of in personal terms as one who acts. The ordinances involving physical elements of water, bread and wine, guard the faith against a false spiritualization which depreciates matter. The God of the Bible is Spirit who created matter and it is therefore, good. The sacraments with their use of the material to symbolize the conveyance of God's grace to man, emphasize the significance of matter and protects against an empty spiritualism which would make matter evil and opposed to God. Man is spirit and body and in the ordinances this fact is recognized.

Protestants in general hold that the efficacy of the ordinances depends upon the moral and spiritual condition of the individual participant. By the observance of the ordinances man's bodily senses are enlisted on the side of the spiritual and an appeal is made to his whole self, spirit and body, when by the observance of these material symbols the impression of the spiritual is deepened and made more vivid.[10]

(1) *Baptism* in various forms has been used as a rite of cleansing in many religions. The Jews used it in their ceremony of admission of proselytes into the Jewish nation. The mystery cults used it as an initiation rite. The baptism by John was "a baptism of repentance for the forgiveness of sins" (Mark 1:4).

All three synoptic Gospels report that Jesus was baptized (Mark 19:1-10; Luke 3:21; Matthew 3:3-16). John on the other hand does not report that Jesus was baptized, but refers to the use of baptism in

---

10. G. W. Forell, *The Protestant Faith,* Prentice-Hall, 1960, p 230 ff.

BASIC CHRISTIAN CONVICTIONS

His ministry (John 3:22; 4:1-3). After His resurrection appearances, Jesus in His Great Commission is reported to have commanded the disciples to "Go therefore, and make disciples of all nations, baptizing them in the name of the Father and of the Son and of the Holy Spirit" (Matthew 28:18-19).

Acts and the letters of Paul have repeated references to the fact that baptism was used as an initiation ceremony for new converts. At Pentecost, after Peter's preaching, people asked what they should do. He said,

> Repent, and be baptized every one of you in the name of Jesus Christ for the forgiveness of your sins . . . (Acts 2:38; cf. Acts 8:16; 19:5; Romans 6:3-4; Galatians 3:27).

The symbolism of baptism first of all is that of cleansing and acceptance of forgiveness upon repentance. In the case of Infant Baptism it would symbolize "pervenient" grace already asked for by the parents and the Church, and assured by God's love. It also symbolizes joining a new community, the Church, with its privileges and responsibilities. The individual is welcomed "into the body of Christ." It is also the symbol of death to the old and resurrection to the new life in Christ. Paul says: "you were buried with him in baptism, in which you were also raised with him through faith . . ." (Colossians 2:12-13).

The Mode of baptism has been a cause of division in the Church. Baptists emphasize immersion. However, many Christians would say that it is of no importance whether immersion, sprinkling, or pouring is used—the outer act is only a symbol of an inner experience. Christ and His disciples meant to set man free from the bondage to prescribed external forms and would have objected to using their example on such matters to forge new bonds.

The early Church was quick to develop a flexible adaptability in the mode of baptism. This is known from pictures in the catacombs and instructions given in the *Didache*:

> But if thou hast not living water, then Baptize in any other water; and if thou art not able in cold, in warm. But if thou hast neither, pour water upon the head thrice in the name of the Father and of the Son and of the Holy Spirit.[11]

---

11. Didache, Chapter 7 - This is a treatise of the second century, called "The Teaching of the Twelve Apostles."

In Christian freedom, liberty should be given to use whatever method is most meaningful to individuals concerned.

Infant or Adult Baptism is another issue upon which Christians do not agree. There is no statement reporting explicitly that infants were baptized. However, on several occasions whole households or families were baptized. About Lydia of Thyatira we read: "The Lord opened her heart . . . she was baptized, with her household" (Acts 16:14-15). In Philippi the jailer "was baptized at once, with all his family" (Acts 16:33). Paul writes "I did baptize also the household of Stephanas" (I Cor. 1:16). Children or infants may have been included in such cases.

Churches practicing Infant Baptism thereby acknowledge the unity of the family and by baptism welcome the child as a member of the Kingdom, however, with the understanding that the parents and the Church will also assume their proper responsibility, and that the child later will, of its own choice, *confirm* its membership in the Church. Some churches practice Infant Baptism and later have Adult Confirmation services. While other Christians just reverse the order and have Infant Consecration and later Adult Baptism, while still others practice only Adult Baptism.

The objection to Infant Baptism rests on the conviction that it cannot be based on the conscious choice of the receiver. According to this view the ordinance should be confined to adults who themselves are able to exercise faith in Jesus Christ as Lord and Savior. Infant Baptism smacks of magic and superstition.

In recent times the question of Infant Baptism has been raised anew by such scholars as Karl Barth and Emil Brunner. They both call for the abandonment of the practice although they both belong to churches which have always practiced it.[12]

---

12. Karl Barth, *The Teaching of the Church Regarding Baptism*, 1943, English translation, 1948, p. 40, "Infant Baptism can hardly be preserved without exegetical and practical artifices and sophism" (p. 49). "What is wanted is a very simple, instead of the present Infant Baptism, a baptism which on the part of the baptized is a responsible act" (p. 54). He calls it "clouded Baptism," "a wound in the body of the Church."

Emil Brunner, *The Divine-Human Encounter*, 1938, English translation, 1944, (p. 132). He writes "The contemporary practice of Infant Baptism can hardly be regarded as anything short of scandalous. . . . It undervalues and obscures the fundamental assertions of the Reformation."

There is also, what has been called a Baptismal Reform Movement within the Church of England, discouraging the traditional practice of Infant Baptism. See R. E. White, *The Expository Times*, January 1950, article "Some

Taking the various arguments of both sides into consideration it would seem that Child Consecration and Adult Baptism would conserve the values both parties are interested in and therefore should be acceptable to all concerned. Human nature being what it is, it will take some time before such a compromise can be achieved.

(2) *The Lord's Supper,* also called Holy Communion or Holy Eucharist is the other ordinance established by Christ. This He did in connection with the last meal before the crucifixion.

> Now as they were eating, Jesus took bread, and blessed and broke it and gave it to the disciples and said, "Take eat; this is my body." And he took a cup and when he had given thanks he gave it to them, saying "Drink of it, all of you; for this is my blood of the covenant which is poured out for many for the forgiveness of sins. I tell you I shall not drink again of this fruit of the vine until that day when I drink it new with you in my Father's kingdom" (Matthew 26:26-29; cf. Mark 14:22-25; Luke 22:14-19; John 6:48-58 and 13:1-35).

Besides this report in the Gospels there is also the earlier account written by Paul to the Corinthians before any of the Gospels were in existence (I Corinthians 11:23-26).

The Lord's Supper became the center of worship in the primitive Church. About it clustered all the precious memories of the Lord as well as the love and faith that He had engendered. Naturally at first the Lord's Supper was observed as a whole meal. This is clear from Paul's complaint that some ate and drank too much and so were really "guilty of profaning the body and the blood of the Lord" (I Corinthians 11:17-34).

The Old Testament antecedent of the Lord's Supper is the Jewish feast of the Passover. Every spring they celebrate their deliverance from Egypt, when Pharaoh finally permitted them to leave after the Lord had slain the firstborn in every Egyptain family but "passed over" the Hebrew homes, where the blood of a sacrificial lamb was painted on the doorposts. Jesus instituted the Lord's Supper in con-

---

Important Issues for Baptismal Theology," a critical discussion of Infant Baptism in which the abandonment of the same is urged for historical, theological, and practical reasons.

Authorities in favor of Infant Baptism are: Gustaf Aulen, *The Faith of the Christian Church,* Muhlenberg Press, Philadelphia, Pa., 1948, pp, 379-385; L. H. DeWolf, *A Theology of the Living Church,* Harper, 1953, pp. 346-348.

See also Edmund Schlink, *The Doctrine of Baptism,* translation, Concordia Press, 1971.

nection with this celebration and Christians have considered Jesus as the passover lamb for them (cf. John 1:29).

The Lord's Supper is an expression of divine love and mercy as well as of the communion of Christians with each other and their Lord, but the interpretation of it also separates Christians very deeply. In the main there are three basic positions, known as transubstantiation, con-substantiation and symbolic memorial.

Tran-substantiation, the Catholic interpretation, holds that as the priest blesses the elements of the Eucharist, the substance of the bread and wine miraculously changes into the actual flesh and blood of Christ, only the appearance of the bread and wine remains. The doctrine is based on metaphysical conceptions of Thomistic-Aristotelianism which are difficult to express in modern terms.[13]

Con-substantiation is a second interpretation. It holds that the body and the blood of Christ are coexistent in and with the bread and the wine of the Eucharist, although the latter retain their form and nature. The Lutherans and some other Protestants believe in this real presence of the flesh and blood of Christ in or along with the elements of the Lord's Supper. This also seems rather mystical and superstitious. Jesus said "God is spirit, and those who worship him must worship him in spirit and in truth" (John 4:24). He is everywhere and His unique presence is found "neither on this mountain nor in Jerusalem" (John 4:21).

A third view considers the Lord's Supper only a symbolic memorial. This is the position of the so-called left-wing Protestants, Anabaptists, and some others. According to this view the elements are in no wise affected by anything that is said or done by a priest or anyone else. The language of Jesus and Paul when they spoke of the bread and wine being the body and blood of Christ is considered metaphorical. This view considers the Holy Communion an ordinance that Christians celebrate to remember who Jesus was and what He did for them. Paul emphasizes "remembrance" when he says:

---

13. Aristotle assumed that everything consists of substance and accidents. Either one can be changed without effecting the other. Chalk may be white and round, but if it were blue and square it would still be chalk. In other words, the wine still looks and tastes like wine but the substance, with the priest's blessing, has been changed into blood, and the substance of the bread into flesh. Not only do these notions run counter to modern science but they also smack of priest craft and superstition.

. . . the Lord Jesus on the night he was betrayed took bread, and when he had given thanks, he broke it, and said, "This is my body which is for you. Do this in *remembrance* of me." In the same way also the cup, after supper, saying, "This cup is the new covenant in my blood. Do this, as often as you drink it, in *remembrance* of me." For as often as you eat this bread and drink the cup, you proclaim the Lord's death until he comes. (I Corinthians 11:23-26). (Italics added)

The meanings of this ordinance are many, reaching through the whole range of the Christian Gospel. Here the Word of God as presented in Jesus Christ and all that He taught, and did, and was, is illustrated in object, word, and act.

Although the ordinance *memorializes* the Christ who was crucified and buried, we do not think of Him as dead but alive and present with us as we participate in the Lord's Supper. He is not only present but presides at the table. We *remember* not only Thursday night and Good Friday but also Easter Sunday. The resurrection was not only *remembered* once a year but every first day of the week they gathered to celebrate the victory of Christ over death. So it happened that the Lord's Supper was observed on every Sunday. For the early Christians, death was often just around the corner, so at this Sunday-night-supper they entered in to the depths of sorrow with Christ, but also were lifted to victory and joy in thanksgiving for the living Christ.

Furthermore when Christians go to the Lord's table they also *thoughtfully recommit themselves* to Christ and His service. Following Him involves work, possibly suffering but also love, joy, peace, and freedom. When the sons of Zebedee with their mother sought places of honor and privilege in the Kingdom, Jesus said: "You do not know what you are asking. Are you able to drink the cup that I am to drink?" (Matthew 20:22). Participating in Holy Communion means a recommitment to the cause of Jesus Christ, no matter what the cost.

Sharing in the Lord's Supper also carries with it the meaning of *fellowship* with Christ and His people. Here we fellowship with the Christians of all classes, all races, all ages, those living and those called to glory—all are here, seen and unseen, in the company at the table of the Lord. As Paul writes:

The cup of blessing which we bless, is it not a participation in the blood of Christ? The bread which we break, is it not a participation in the body of Christ? Because there is one loaf, we who are many are one body, for we all partake of the same loaf (I Corinthians 10:16-17).

There are other meanings that come to the thoughtful person as he returns again and again to participate in this ordinance. Christ changed the cruel cross into the world's most noteworthy symbol of victory, love, joy, and hope. This illustrated word moves man in faith to receive the divine spirit.

(3) *Marriage* is also regarded as a sacrament by the Roman Catholic and Greek Orthodox churches. Protestants do not regard it as such but nevertheless consider it very important. Marriage does not have the specific command of Christ as do Baptism and the Lord's Supper. However, marriage also indicates that in complete mutual self-giving of husband and wife to each other in love and wholesome home life, something of the essence of the Kingdom of God is revealed. Therefore, the traditional relationship of husband and wife in which the husband was regarded as superior, is reinterpreted in Christian terms. The husband's authority should not rest upon accepted social practice, but upon Christian love and should be exercised like the authority of Christ over the Church. The pattern is not that of domination but of self-giving.

Similarly the obedience of the wife is patterned on self-giving love and gratitude and not on fear and law. In this unique relationship the welfare of each partner is identified with the welfare of the other. This unreserved self-giving is similar to the relationship between Christ and the Church. In the words of Paul:

> Be subject to one another out of reverence for Christ . . . Husbands, love your wives, as Christ loved the Church and gave himself up for her . . . even so husbands should love their wives as their own bodies. He who loves his wife loves himself. For no man ever hates his own flesh, but nourishes and cherishes it, as Christ does the church, because we are members of his body. "For this reason a man shall leave his father and mother and be joined to his wife, and the two shall become one." This is a great mystery, and I take it to mean Christ and the church; however, let each one of you love his wife as himself, and let the wife see that she respects her husband (Ephesians 5:21-33).

Before leaving the subject of ordinances it should be pointed out that some Christian groups, such as Quakers, have dispensed altogether with outward ordinances, believing that God's spiritual blessings are given in entirely spiritual ways and that outward observance of ordinances comes near to superstitious practices. Yet even the Quaker Friends have practices that are to nourish and help uphold their faith. Having physical bodies man finds outward physical signs helpful in understanding and receiving inward spiritual grace. Even our knowledge of God himself depended upon His incarnation of himself in Jesus Christ.

5. *The Ecumenical Movement*[14]

The two major groups in Christianity are the Catholic and the Protestant bodies. The Catholic group is divided into Eastern (Orthodox), Western (Roman), and Coptic (Egyptian). The Protestants are divided into many denominations. In recent decades Protestants as well as Catholics have been involved in reexamining the reasons for their differences and trying to discover some basis for more cooperation and unity.

Jesus Christ, when in the flesh, already anticipated the danger of division and not only warned against it but also earnestly prayed for the unity of His followers:

> "I do not pray for these only, but also for those who are to believe in me through their word, and that they may all be one; even as thou, Father, art in me, and I in thee, that they also may be in us, so that the world may believe that thou hast sent me. The glory which thou hast given me I have given to them, that they may be one even as we are one, I in them and thou in me, that they may become perfectly one, so that the world may know that thou hast sent me and hast loved them even as thou hast loved me" (John 17:20-23).

In this prayer for unity Jesus also gives the reason for it, namely, "so that the world may believe that thou hast sent me." Unity of the Church is imperative if it is to do its work and fulfill its mission in the world.

St. Paul also stressed the importance of unity,

> . . . you have been called, with lowliness and meekness, with patience, forbearing one another in love, eager to maintain the unity of the Spirit in the bond of peace. There is one body and one Spirit, just as you were called to the one hope that belongs to your call, one Lord, one faith, one baptism, one God and Father of us all . . . for building up the body of Christ until we all attain the unity of the faith and of the knowledge of the Son of God, . . . (Ephesians 4:1-6; 12-13).

(a) *Background of the World Council.* The World Council of Churches is the result of more than fifty years of interracial, interdenominational, and international cooperation along various lines.

---

14. Norman Goodall, *The Ecumenical Movement,* Oxford Press, 1965.

Many Christian leaders consider the Council "The great new fact of our era." The word "ecumenical" comes from the Greek *ecumene* and means "the inhabited earth" and is synonymous with "universal." This is a movement of Christians to strengthen the bonds of unity throughout the inhabited earth.

The First World Missionary Council held at Edinburgh in 1910 is usually considered the beginning of the modern ecumenical movement, although its roots go back much farther. The Evangelical Alliance was organized in 1840, but this was a union of individuals rather than church bodies. Missionary societies, Bible societies, youth organizations, Sunday school associations, and peace movements were formed during this early period. The greatest single factor that brought the churches of the world together was mission work, and it was here that the bad effects of disunity among Christians was first realized.

The 1910 conference at Edinburgh was called to plan overall missionary strategy and to explore ways for Christian bodies to work together. A continuation committee was created. By 1921 it was possible to form the International Missionary Council representing twenty-eight cooperating missionary agencies.

Two outstanding Missionary Council meetings after 1910 were the Jerusalem Conference in 1928 and the 1938 Madras Conference in India. Gradually leaders from the "younger churches" took places of responsibility which greatly helped the movement.

The Life and Work movement constitutes a second approach to unity. The underlying thought of this movement was that Christians would unite in common tasks of service and action with closer fellowship with each other. This movement also eventuated in a series of world conferences. The first one was held at Stockholm in 1925. This brought together The Federal Council of Churches, organized in 1908, and the World Alliance for International Friendship organized shortly before World War I. A permanent organization was formed and the next world conference was held at Oxford in 1937.

A third influence toward unity was the Christian concern of Faith and Order already kindled at the Edinburgh Missionary Conference in 1910. The underlying thought here was to promote unity by considering the differences of doctrine and ceremony. A World Conference of Faith and Order was held at Lausanne, Switzerland, in 1927, immediately following the Oxford Conference on Life and Work.

All three above mentioned movements found some areas of agreement, but for more than twenty years they flowed in separate channels although it became increasingly clear that they would eventually merge. In 1937 the Oxford and Edinburgh conferences were held on successive dates so that the same delegates could attend both. This was a way of saying that theology, ethics, and missions belong together. A committee of fourteen was created to develop a plan to merge the three movements into one.

(b) *Organization and Later Assemblies.* In 1938 a group of seventy-five representatives of these movements met at Utrecht to draft a constitution for the new organization, merging the Life and Work Movement with the Faith and Order Movement in what was called the World Council of Churches. The International Missionary Council did not merge with the other two at this time as it was more an organization of mission boards rather than denominations. The World Council, however, because of World War II, did not meet again until 1948 at Amsterdam. This was the First Assembly of the World Council of Churches at which time its constitution was also officially adopted.

The Second Assembly of the World Council met at Evanston, Illinois, in 1956, and in *1961 the Third Assembly* was held in New Delhi, India. Here the merging of the International Missionary Council with the World Council took place. This avoided some overlapping and further promoted Christian unity in service and faith. Here also a revision of the basis of membership was adopted to read:

> The World Council of Churches is a fellowship of churches which confess the Lord Jesus Christ as God and Savior according to the Scriptures and therefore seek to fulfill together their common calling to the glory of the one God—Father, Son and Holy Spirit.

The Russian Orthodox Church, with twenty delegates representing a membership of over fifty million also joined here.

The Fourth Assembly of the World Council of Churches was held at Uppsala, Sweden, in 1968, giving major consideration to "The Renewal of the Church." The World Council of Churches, according to *Ecumenical Courier,* March, 1972, now "unites 252 Anglican, Orthodox, and Protestant communions in some 90 countries" with a combined membership of over 250 million persons. Together these Christians, through their representatives, try to achieve fuller mutual understanding of the Christian faith and a clearer expression of the same in "the unity of the Spirit and the bond of peace" (Ephesians 4:8).

Various commissions of the Council are giving much time and

thought to the study of the following areas: Faith and Order, Evangelism, Social Questions, International Affairs, Intergroup Relations, and the Place of the Laity. In these studies and efforts of the World Council of Churches gradually greater mutual understanding and appreciation is a natural by-product which in turn encourages and promotes the unity of the Church and thereby makes it more effective in its mission on earth.

(c) *Agreements and Differences* regarding the Church are considered important. The following six points of agreement are quite evident: (1) The origin of the Church goes back to God's calling a chosen people in Abraham and Israel; (2) The decisive act of God in forming the Church was Jesus Christ, of which act the Church is a continuation in history; (3) The Church is the community of the Holy Spirit and Pentecost was the birthday of the church; (4) The Church is both human and divine; (5) The Church and the Kingdom are not identical, but the former works for a fuller realization of the latter; (6) The Church has a World Mission entrusted to it by Jesus Christ to carry the Gospel to the ends of the earth and promote His Kingdom everywhere.[15]

Differences regarding the Church in general fall into three main areas: (1) How to *identify* the Church—Catholics, Orthodox, and some smaller sects, claim they are the only true Church, while others hold that the Church does not really exist as long as unity is lacking, but most Protestants believe the Church is not a physical but a spiritual reality and exists wherever God's saving grace in Christ is operative; (2) Should the *form* of the Church be episcopal, presbyterian, or congregational? Some insist on one or the other, while many hold that the early Church probably had all three, as influenced by historical development, but they are of secondary importance and should be determined by the needs of circumstances. (3) How about the *continuity* of the Church? Catholics, Orthodox, and Anglicans hold to what is called "Apostolic Succession" regarding ordination of ministers and consider all other ordinations as invalid because of breach in continuity. Protestants put less stress on physical continuity and emphasize the spiritual relation with the Lord, leaving the Church free to be guided by the Holy Spirit.[16]

---

15. H. Horton, *Christian Theology, An Ecumenical Approach*, Harpers, 1955, Chapter VII.
16. C. T. Craig, *The One Church*, Abingdon Press, 1951, pp. 27 ff.

The work and influence of the World Council of Churches is in the direction of stressing existing agreements and reconciling the differences of various groups and denominations and thus increase the unity of the Church in faith and practice.

6. *The Need for Church Renewal*

In general the future of the Church in the world will depend upon its willingness to grapple with the great social issues facing mankind in our day. The so-called "Social Gospel" advocated by former leaders did not enlist the Church as a whole.[17] Today the Church has practically come to terms with society at the expense of its radical and inclusive Gospel of Christ Jesus. The Church has been tamed by society and rejects social obligations as it increasingly becomes secularized and even assumes the position of guardian of the status quo of the social order.

The Church is not to rule the world but serve it, not to reject it but to transform it, not to withdraw from it but to penetrate it with redeeming love. The Church is too much preoccupied with itself and the internal life of its members as it withdraws from issues where men collide, struggle and die.

(a) *Some Reasons for the present ineptitude of the Church*, which must be corrected for the sake of the future of the Church and the world should be recognized.[18]

Christians have been inclined to look at the world which "God so loved" and into which Jesus sent His disciples, in geographic rather than sociological terms. So, foreign missions have been promoted while social action at home has been discouraged. The attempt has been made to cover rather than penetrate the world with the Gospel. Somehow the earth has been mistaken for the world, and the missionary expanse for redemption.

The notion that God lives only in and is concerned only for the Church is still too commonly held by Christians. We forget that God sent His Son to the world, not to the Church. He was born in a stable, not in a church. Christ is at work in the secular world, not only in the sanctified part of it. Man can serve God best by helping his needy fellowmen. The Incarnation, the Word becoming flesh, has not only personal but also social meaning. The Incarnation broke

---

17. Hazelton and Marty, *What's Ahead of the Churches*, Sheed and Ward, New York, 1964, pp. 197 ff.
18. *Op. cit.*, p. 203 ff.

the wall between time and eternity, temple and market, church and shop, sacred and secular, personal and social affairs. Christ seeks the redemption of the whole man and that cannot be done without also redeeming the whole of society.

Christians have looked at history as separate, personal, racial, and national strands rather than as one stream of interrelated world events. We have looked upon mankind as separated and isolated groups of Europeans, Indians, Chinese, Africans, etc., and not as one interdependent human race. Individual man cannot be separated into economic, social, physical, intellectual, personal and family parts. Each person is one whole being, and together we are one human race.

Too often salvation is looked upon in highly personalized and even other-worldly terms. White Christians often deny any malice toward Negroes and yet refuse to participate in any social or legislative program to end Negro segregation and discrimination. Collective action is too often condemned and it is insisted that individual salvation is all that is needed. Many social ills continue in our communities because of the belief that collective welfare depends altogether and only on individual conversion.

Too often the church-state issue is confused with the issues of social Christianity. The idea that religion must be kept out of politics and politics must be kept out of religion is not a Christian attitude. The wisdom, devotion, and ability of religious people are needed in the government of county, city, state, nation, and the international situation. This does not mean ecclesiastical control of civil government nor civil infringement upon religious freedom. Justice, welfare, liberty and freedom are religious as well as political terms. They belong neither to the state nor the Church but to man. Injustice and oppression call for the help of both government and religious people. Personal piety that neglects social obligations is civil irresponsibility and religious heresy.

(b) *The Challenge of the Modern World* is increasingly urgent. Social change has been so rapid in recent decades and the churches have moved so slowly that they have been left behind. Changes brought about by automation, urbanization, atomic power, cybernetics, racial development, international conditions and other factors challenge the Church to be alert to its responsibilities, for the future of the Church itself is at stake. Too many Christians are preoccupied with problems that have been settled long ago, such as science versus religion, evolution versus Genesis, historical criticism versus an infallible Bible, personal versus social salvation, liberalism versus fundamentalism, and so on. Whereas the real problems of today are of a social nature, such as: ethnic and racial relations, the affluent society and humiliating poverty, leisure and idleness, exploding populations and family planning, ignorance and superstition, disease and crime, mental and emotional instability, adult and juvenile delinquency, alcoholism and nuclear holocaust, war and peace, and others.

In part the churches' social alertness has been deadened by the very massiveness of the many current problems. In the face of the threat of nuclear war, Christians must not throw up their hands in helpless despair but rather take a position of resolute defiance. The modern Christian must not lose his faith in the God of history, but he must also assume his responsibility to do what he can individually and socially to do God's will and promote His cause of "peace on earth and goodwill among men."

The shift from rural to urban society in recent decades has far-reaching results. The rural Church was friendly and communicative. Urbanization brings about a feeling of isolation and aloneness. Rural mentality stresses heroic individualism while the problems of urbanization call for collective action. Increasingly American society is composed of massive population centers in our big cities. Although the basic problems of man and himself, man and his neighbor, man and his God, are the primary issues of urban as they were of rural life—yet these same problems present themselves in a different manner on the farm as compared to the city. The impersonal and depersonalizing pressures that the city man has to face, differ in degree and intensity from those experienced by the rural person.

All these problems the churches cannot face and solve by only an evangelistic approach and method. The crucial question of the future may not be so much as to what the Church will do to the world, but rather what the world-in-conflict will do to the Church. If the churches do not respond to this present challenge they will be bypassed and remain as harmless cysts in their material grandeur, isolated from the ongoing life. On the other hand the pressures and pleas of the surrounding world may yet also be the catalyst which will revive, reform, and reactivate the Church.

In the first century the Jewish-Christian community, in danger of becoming an obscure sect, received and accepted a powerful challenge to renewal when Paul, Peter, and others took the Gospel to the Greeks and the Romans. In a later period when Rome was disintegrating and many thought Christianity would fall with it, it was the Ostrogoths and Visigoths, converted to Jesus Christ, that furnished life and energy to the future Church. So today those whom we do not want and in various ways reject, such as the Negro and Oriental Christian, may be the hope of a renewed life in the Church. The condition of the modern world drives the Church back to Christ for renewal who in turn again sends His disciples into the world as His apostles.

C. SUMMARY AND CONCLUSION

In this chapter on "The Kingdom and the Church" we have considered: The Human Need for Fellowship; The Kingdom of God; The Beginnings of the Church; The Church in History; The Nature of the Church; Organization and Function of the Church; The Ecumenical Movement; and The Need for Church Renewal.

In our changing world, new forms of Church life will be developed. Actually the demands on the Church are different in an era when the Church is popular from what they are when the Church is persecuted. The most glorious period in the history of the Church was during the first few centuries, when as yet it had nothing of its present bureaucratic institutional organization or financial wealth and power.

An immense task lies before the Church today to bring the Kingdom of God on earth to fuller actualization. This includes the secularized Christian nations engulfed in materialism, as well as areas of the world that have never been Christianized. The ancient enemies of mankind in the form of The Four Horsemen of the Apocalypse will finally be overcome only by Jesus Christ and the cooperative efforts of all men of good will and peace.

In all this, Christians in loyalty and sacrificial devotion, increasingly need to exemplify that the Church really is the body of which Jesus Christ is the head, through which He works for the fuller realization of the prayer He taught His followers: "Our Father who art in heaven, Hallowed be thy name. Thy kingdom come, Thy will be done, on earth as it is in heaven" (Matthew 6:9-10). And in all this, it is very encouraging to remember that Jesus also said: "I will build my church, and the powers of death shall not prevail against it" (Matthew 16:18).

FOR FURTHER READING ON THE KINGDOM AND THE CHURCH
ON THE KINGDOM OF GOD

Bright, John, *The Kingdom of God,* Abingdon, 1953.

Dodd, C. H., *Parables of the Kingdom,* Scribners, 1935.

Grant, Fredrick C., *The Gospel of the Kingdom,* Macmillan, 1940.

Hines, J. E., *Thy Kingdom Come,* Morehouse, 1967.

Ladd, G. E., *Jesus and the Kingdom,* (2nd ed.), World Books, 1969.

Minear, Paul S., *The Kingdom and the Power,* Westminster, 1950.

Pannanberg, W., *Theology of the Kingdom,* Westminster, 1967.

Perrin, N., *The Kingdom of God in the Teachings of Jesus,* Westminster, 1964.

Schweitzer, A., *The Kingdom of God,* Seabury, 1968.

Weiss, J., *Jesus Proclaims the Kingdom,* Fortress, 1971.

ON THE CHRISTIAN CHURCH

Bainton, R. H., *Christendom,* Vol. I & II, Harper, 1966.

Beaver, R. F., *From Missions to Mission,* Association Press, 1964.

Blauw, J., *The Missionary Nature of the Church,* McGraw-Hill, 1962.

Briggs, W. W., *History of the Church,* St. Martin's Press, 1965.

Caemmerer, R. R., *Christ Builds His Church,* Concordia, 1963.

Clower, J. B., *The Church in Jesus' Thought,* John Knox, 1960.

Colin, W. W., *The Church,* Westminister, 1968.

Dyck, C. J., ed., *Mennonite History,* Herald Press, 1967.

Goodall, Norman, *The Ecumenical Movement,* Oxford Press, 1965.

Gustafson, J. M., *The Church as Human Community,* Harper, 1961.

Hadden, Jeffrey, *Gathering Storm in the Churches,* Doubleday, 1969.

Hahn, F., *Beginning of the Church,* Augsburg, 1970.

Hanson, S., *The Church in the New Testament,* Allenson, 1961.

Hunt, G. L., *Rediscovering the Church,* Association Press, 1956.

Hutchison, P., *The New Ordeal of Christianity,* Asso. Press, 1957.

Knox, John, *Limits of Unbelief,* Seabury Press, 1970.

Küng, H., *The Future of the Church,* Scribners, 1968.

Latourette, K. S., *Christianity in a Revolutionary Age,* Harper, 1958.

Littell, F. H., *The Anabaptist View of the Church,* 1952.

Matson, T. B., *Christianity and World Problems,* Macmillan, 1957.

Newbigin, J. E. L., *The Household of God,* Friendship Press, 1954.

Pope, R. M., *The Church and its Culture,* Bethany Press, 1965.

Raines, R. A., *The Secular Congregation,* Harper, 1968.

Ramsey & Suenens, *The Future of the Church,* Mordionse, 1971.

Schweitzer, E., *Church Order in the New Testament,* Allenson, 1961.

Street, W., *The Growing Edge of the Church,* Knox Press, 1965.

Troeltsch, E., *Social Teachings of the Church,* Macmillan, 1931.

CHAPTER VIII

THE BIBLE: THE STORY
OF RECONCILIATION

"You search the scriptures, because you think that in them you have eternal life; and it is they that bear witness to me . . ." (John 5:39).

CHRISTIANS HAVE ALWAYS CONSIDERED THE BIBLE IN A SPECIAL WAY, as God's word to man. Certain religious communities were the instruments through which God produced the Bible. Back of the Old Testament was the Hebrew community and back of the New Testament was the Christian Church. The word Bible in the Greek plural is *biblia,* meaning books. The German word for library is *bibliothek.* The Bible is really a library composed of sixty-six books, thirty-nine in the Old Testament and twenty-seven in the New Testament. It was produced by many authors, over a period of more than one thousand years, and on three continents. This process took place in various cultures which influenced it, such as: Sumerian, Canaanite, Arabic, Egyptian, Syrian, Assyrian, Babylonian, Persian, Greek, and Roman culture.

A. THE MESSAGE OF THE BIBLE

In spite of great diversity in the Bible there is nevertheless also a certain unity in the Scriptures. We speak of it as the *Word* of God, not the words of God. A word is a symbol that transmits a meaningful message from one person to another. The clearest word that God has spoken to man was through His Son Jesus Christ:

> In the beginning was the Word, and the Word was with God, and the Word was God . . . And the Word became flesh and dwelt among us, full of grace and truth; we have beheld his glory, glory as of the only Son from the Father . . . No one has ever seen God; the only Son, who is in the bosom of the Father he has made him known (John 1:1, 14, 18).

The record of the life and teaching of Jesus Christ is in the Bible and so we speak of the Bible as the *Word* of God. Jesus Christ is the center of the Bible. The Old Testament prepares for Him and points to Him; while the New Testament portrays and interprets Him. Jesus himself said:

> "You search the scriptures because you think that in them you have eternal life; and it is they that bear witness to me" (John 5: 39).

The message of the Bible then is, what the Germans call *"Heils-geschichte"*—the story of salvation. The Bible as a unit, is the record and interpretation of the living *WORD*, Jesus Christ, the message of God to man, the story of reconciliation.

In one sense the Bible is the continuous story of the religious growth of Hebrews and Christians. That is, the continuous search of man for God, but on the other hand, it is really a record of the search of God for man. The message in essence is that God is our Father and all men are brothers. This is portrayed both in the life of the individual as well as in the life of society as a whole.

When Adam went astray, God in His concern looked for him and called to him, "Where are you?" (Genesis 3:9). After Cain slew Abel the Lord searched for him and said, "Where is Abel your brother?" (Genesis 4:9). As the condition of mankind went from bad to worse the Lord gave history a new direction through Abraham when He asked him to

> "Go from your country and your kindred and your father's house to the land that I will show you. And I will make you a great nation, and I will bless you, and make your name great, so that you will be a blessing . . . and by you all the families of the earth will bless themselves" (Genesis 12:1-3).

In the story of Moses we see how God prepared an individual through difficult and stormy experiences until at last he stands strong as an oak tree before his people, as the very incarnation of their hopes and dreams. He chides his people in their weakness, challenges them in their fear, repeatedly summons them to new endeavor, and gradually with great difficulty brings them to the very edge of the promised land.

Here is the inspiring story of the Hebrew people, dug out of obscurity, with their patriarchs, under the leadership of Moses, suffering in Egypt, being tempered in the desert, led by Joshua, forged by the judges, welded into a nation by Saul and David, broken into parts by Solomon, scattered in adversity by the exile, but holding together and later a remnant returning to the promised land, where circumstances finally issue in Jesus Christ.

The story of Paul shows how a chosen vessel in God's hand, after long preparation, conversion, three years in the desert to reorient himself and his understanding of the Scriptures in the light of Jesus Christ, finally becomes a great missionary. He is persecuted, imprisoned, nevertheless rejoices although he is troubled by a "thorn in the flesh" that is not taken away, but he is given strength to bear it. He makes three hazardous but successful missionary tours in the assurance that "in all these things we are more than conquerors through him who loved us" (Romans 8:37). Besides this he wrote about one-third of the New Testament and became its great theologian.

And so the story goes on in the formation of the Church, at first small and weak but growing and expanding even under persecution. In this story of the Hebrew people coming to a climax in the life and teachings of Jesus, and from Him moving on into the Christian Church, developing and spreading to this our day, we can see God working in history. He is not in a hurry but patiently uses individuals and nations in His cause and program. God is marching on, and the Bible in its formation and world influence is a partial record of that march.

B. The Bible in the Making

The making of the Bible was a long and complicated process. It cannot be separated from the history of the Hebrews and the history of the Christian Church.

1. *The Making of the Old Testament*

As the Hebrew people developed and moved from place to place, oral tradition of their past was important. The events and stories of their ancestors were passed on by word of mouth from one generation to the next. Later they were put in writing.

(a) *The nature of this literature* was, of course, religious. In about 900 B.C. a southern Palestinian writer of Judah left some documents in which the word for God, Jehovah, or Yahweh is JHVH and YHWH, respectively. These writings have become known as the "J" documents from the name *Jehovah* and because the author was a *Judean*. Later in about 750 B.C. a northern writer uses *Elohim* for God and these writings have become known as the "E" documents, also as Ephraimite. Still later the two writings were combined and referred to as the "JE" documents.

In 722 B.C. the Northern Kingdom was defeated by the Assyrian King Shalmaneser II, and taken into captivity. There were those in the Southern Kingdom of Judah who felt that God had allowed this to happen to the Northern Kingdom, because the people had developed and adopted a wrong kind of worship displeasing to Yahweh. Hence, now another history was written with special emphasis on what was considered the right method of worship. About 100 years after the defeat of the Northern Kingdom this document, or a copy of it, was discovered while cleaning out rubbish in the Jerusalem Temple. This was in 621 B.C. and led to a far-reaching reform under king Josiah. This writing became known as the "D" or Deuteronomic document. This is our present Deuteronomy. In time the above three together became known as "JED" documents.

In 587 B.C. the Southern Kingdom (Judah) was also defeated and taken into the Babylonian captivity under king Nebuchadnezzar. Already before the fall of Jerusalem the Priests began to rewrite Hebrew history with a Jerusalem emphasis. This writing became known as the "P" document from the fact that it was produced by the Priests. So today we have the "JEDP" documents altogether in our Old Testament. Genesis 1:1--2:4 which uses Elohim for *God*, is a sample of the "P" strand; while Genesis 2:4-3:24 is of the "J" strand and uses Yahweh Elohim, *Lord God* for the deity.[1]

The tribes that were taken into captivity earlier by the Assyrians merged with other peoples and became known as "the lost tribes." The Jews, who were later taken as captives to Babylonia, more successfully resisted the ever present danger of assimilation. It was in this bitter Babylonian captivity that they gathered their ancient writings and memories for their people and for us. These are the first five books of the Bible, known today as the "Pentateuch."

As in the New Testament there are four records of the life of Jesus, so in the Old Testament there are four records of the work of Moses, namely the "JEDP" documents, although finally the four accounts are woven into one. It should also be noted that the contents of the "JEDP" documents in the main reflect viewpoints of a much earlier period than the time when they were reduced to writing and that Moses is to be regarded as the architect of the basic structure of thought found in them, although, naturally expressed in the light of the experiences of Israel in four periods of history. Scholars stress the fidelity with which oral traditions perpetuated the material before it could be put into writing after the language was gradually reduced to written form.

---

1. R. M. Brown, *The Bible Speaks to You*, Westminster, 1955, p. 28.

(b) *Canonization* was a gradual process. "Canon" means rule or standard. A book recognized as authoritative would be considered as in the canon. In time certain writings were recognized, gradually others were added. By about 400 B.C. the Old Testament books of the *Law,* comprising the first five books, were generally recognized and accepted. By about 200 B.C. the *Prophets,* both major and minor, were also recognized. While the third part called *The Writings,* containing the remaining books of the Old Testament, were not officially decided upon until after the time of Christ.

It should be noted that originally the written Hebrew language had no vowels and no punctuation. The consonant letters were just strung out together. For example, the verse "I am the Lord your God, who brought you out of the land of Egypt," would look like this in English: mthlrdyrgdwhbrghtytfthlndfgypt. Later vowel points were added over and under consonants, words were gradually separated and later punctuation was included. The Dead Sea Scrolls already have separate words and paragraphs.

In the early Christian era so many Christian writings appeared that the Jewish fathers thought it necessary officially to pronounce certain books as being the only ones acceptable. So in 90 A.D. a council of Jewish Rabbis met at Jamnia in Palestine to decide upon the canon of their Holy Scriptures more officially.[2] The tests applied to the many religious books then in circulation were: (1) Does it conform to the spirit of the Law? (2) Was it written in Hebrew? (3) Is it ceremonially clean or does it defile? (4) Was it written before the time of Esther, that is Artaxerxes II (404-358 B.C.)?

The council hesitated about accepting some books we now have in the Old Testament. The book of *Ecclesiastes* is rather pessimistic and skeptical. It begins with the proclamation "Vanity of vanities, says the Preacher, vanity of vanities. All is vanity" (Ecclesiastes 1:2). Only after some debate and consideration was the book finally accepted and included in the canon. It at least closes on a positive note, "Fear God, and keep his commandments; for this is the whole duty of man" (Ecclesiastes 12:13).

A second book the Rabbis had some doubt about was *Esther,* for in it Yahweh or God is not even mentioned.[3] However, the nationalistic Hebrew spirit of the book was a strong factor in its favor and it was finally taken in. The third book over which there was consider-

---

2. N. K. Gottwald, *A Light to the Nations,* Harper, 1959, pp. 32-33.
3. In the German translation Luther inserted it, chapter 7:4.

able question was the *Song of Solomon* because of its erotic atmosphere. However, this relation between the lover and his beloved can also be interpreted symbolically, as the relation between Yahweh and His beloved Israel and so have real spiritual significance and meaning. On this basis it also was taken in.

(c) *Chronology.* An approximate chronology of the Old Testament writings as generally accepted by scholars is given below.[4]

Century B.C.

XIII	(or earlier?) Exodus from Egypt	⎫
XII	(?) Settlement in Palestine	Oral traditions (laws, legends,
XI	Wars with Canaanites, etc. Foundation of Monarchy (David, 1000 B.C.).	poems) preserved in later writings. ⎬

X   Court chronicles begin (incorporated in later books).

IX   Early laws and traditions written down: Judaean collection "J" and Ephraimite collection "E", later incorporated in Genesis-to-Joshua.

VIII   Amos, Hosea, Micah, Isaiah (Fall of Samaria, 721).

VII   Josiah's Reformation, 621. Deuteronomy, Jeremiah, Zephaniah, Nahum.

VI   Habakkuk, Judges, Samuel, Kings (Fall of Jerusalem, 586), Ezekiel, "II Isaiah," Haggai, Zechariah.

V   "Priestly" laws and narratives of Genesis-to-Joshua "P" written on basis of earlier traditions. Malachi, Job.

IV   Compilation of Genesis-to-Joshua (out of "J", "E", "P" and Deuteronomy).

III   Chronicles, Ecclesiastes.

II   Book of Psalms completed (Largely out of much earlier poems). Ecclesiasticus, Daniel, etc.

I   Book of Wisdom, etc.

From the above it is clear that not one of the books of the Bible, in its finished form, comes to us from an earlier date than the eighth century B.C. Before that, earlier traditions were handed down by word of mouth and various documents, which were used by later writers. The books of the Old Testament are deeply marked with the influences of the prophets. The prophetic teachings provide the key to the meaning of these records. The great prophets wrote roughly during the two centuries from 750 to 550 B.C.

---

4. C. H. Dodd, *The Bible Today,* Cambridge University Press, 1947, p. 33, for a little different and more complete chronology see *The Interpreter's Bible,* Abingdon, 1957, Vol. XII, p. 669; S. A. Cartledge, *A Conservative Introduction to the Old Testament,* Zondervan, Grand Rapids, Mich., 1943, p. 22 ff. 230.

(d) *Extra-canonical Old Testament literature* should not be forgotten. Following the conquest of Alexander the Great (332 B.C.) there was a large emigration of Jews, both forced and voluntary, from Judea to all the countries of the Mediterranean world. This scattering is known as the Diaspora. Of course there also were earlier dispersions of the Jews as in the Assyrian and Babylonian captivities. Gradually the two centers of the Diaspora were in Babylon and Alexandria. Already in 300 B.C. there were more Jews in Alexandria, Egypt, than in Jerusalem.[5]

Greek was the current language and hence many Jews could not read their Hebrew Scriptures. So in 250 B.C., during the reign of Ptolemy Philadelphus, arrangements were made to translate the Hebrew Scriptures into Greek. The work continued over 70 years and was done by 72 scholars hence called Septuagint.[6]

Alexandrian Judaism, because of Greek influence, was more liberal and tolerant than Palestinian Judaism. Besides the thirty-nine books of the Hebrew Bible, the *New English Bible with the Apocrypha*, 1970, also contains the following list as Apocrypha between the Old and the New Testament:

1. The First Book of Esdras
2. The Second Book of Esdras
3. Tobit
4. Judith
5. Chapters of the Book of Esther
6. The Wisdom of Solomon
7. The Wisdom of Jesus son of Sirach
8. Baruch
9. A Letter of Jeremiah
10. The Song of the Three
11. Daniel and Susanna
12. Daniel, Bel, and the Snake
13. The Prayer of Manasseh
14. The First Book of the Maccabees
15. The Second Book of the Maccabees

These books are known as the Apocrypha (hidden, mysterious, or spurious) and were rejected by the Palestinian Council of Rabbis at Jamnia deciding upon the Hebrew canon of scriptures in 90 A. D., partly because many of them are anonymous and written in Greek.

Under the Roman Empire, gradually Latin became the current language. When the Alexandrian Septuagint was translated into the Old Latin version, it also contained the Apocrypha. In 383 A.D. Jerome was commissioned, by Pope Damasus, to revise the Old Latin and use the current (vulgar) language hence called Vulgate.

---

5. F. G. Bratton, *The History of the Bible*, Beacon Press, 1959, pp. 125-127.
6. The Legendary version is that 72 scholars accomplished this in 72 days.

BASIC CHRISTIAN CONVICTIONS

Since there was general questioning about the Apocryphal books, Jerome hesitated to include them but finally did so, but gave them a secondary place. Later, Luther (1534) as well as Tyndale and the King James Version took the Apocryphal books out of the main body of the Old Testament but included them as an appendix. Gradually Protestants have eliminated them altogether. However, in the present Vulgate and Douay versions of the Roman Catholic Church, the Apocrypha are an integral part of the Old Testament. The Greek Church, inheriting the Septuagint also accepts the Apocrypha.

The Pseudepigrapha (false writings, or under assumed names) is a collection of Jewish books even outside the Septuagint canon. They are largely apocalyptic and legendary, coming from the inter-testamental period or the first two centuries of the Christian era. Since they were not included in the Septuagint, Jerome also rejected them in his Vulgate. Today they are called Apocrypha by the Roman Catholic Church and Pseudepigrapha by the Protestant Church. Generally the following books are included in this list:[7]

The Book of Jubilees	The Sibylline Oracles
The Testaments of the Twelve Patriarchs	The Assumption of Moses
	The Apocalypse of Baruch
The Testament of Job	III. Macabees
The Life of Asenath	IV. Maccabees
The Psalms of Solomon	The Letter of Aristeas
The Book of Enoch	The Ascension of Isaiah
The Secrets of Enoch	

2. The Making of the New Testament

Coming to the New Testament we find the writings are concerned with Jesus Christ and the emergence of the Christian Church—a new type of historical religious community. This community began as a small group within Judaism but soon went beyond these bounds, as in principle it was universal. A first and most important task facing the early Christians was the reinterpretation of the Old Testament in the light of Jesus Christ.

(a) *Reinterpretation of the Old Testament.* In the history of the Old Testament we have alternating phases of crisis and development until Israel was shaped into a people of God, which, however, was never completely achieved. The ideal attributes which the prophets applied to Israel are finally understood by the New Testament

---

7. Bratton, *op. cit.*, pp. 138-140.

writers to apply to the Christian Church. The Church is the "Israel of God"(Galatians 6:16). The Church is a

> chosen race, a royal priesthood, a holy nation, God's own people, that you may declare the wonderful deeds of him who called you out of darkness into his wonderful light (I Peter 2:9).

Jesus Christ has made the Christians "a kingdom of priests to his God and Father" (Revelation 1:6). They are Isaiah's "remnant" (Isaiah 10:22-23, Romans 9:27); Jeremiah's "people of the New Covenant" (Jeremiah 31:31-34; Hebrews 8:6-12; II Corinthians 3:4-18), Ezekiel's "new Israel, risen from the dead" (Romans 8:9-11, Ephesians 2:4-10); "they are justified by his grace as a gift, through the redemption which is in Christ Jesus" (Romans 3:24); they are Daniel's "saints of the Most high" (Daniel 7:18; I Corinthians 1:2); and they are to be built up and given "the inheritance among all those who are sanctified" (Acts 20:32). This deliberate application of prophetic language is "an assertion that the people of God has now passed through the supreme crisis, and reached its complete and final form."[8]

The prophets of the Old Testament recognized a pattern in the history of their people which indicated a divine meaning for them. This pattern recurs in the story of Jesus in the Gospels and continues in the history of the Church. From this point of view, history is God confronting man in judgment and mercy, and to this call man must and does respond. The prophetic picture of the suffering that heals comes true in the suffering of Jesus. He bore the suffering without resentment and by doing so set healing forces to work. The two sides of God's judgment and mercy are related to each other. The suffering of Jesus is also judgment of evil, for He who suffers is innocent, hence judges evil by His very goodness and mercy.

At first the crucifixion of Jesus seemed like sheer disaster to the disciples, but, a few days later they see it all in a different perspective. The Gospels end with the resurrection, which meant that the crucifixion could no longer be regarded as meaningless failure. It was the means of God's victory. In death and resurrection judgment and mercy, disaster and renewal, making the pattern of history in which God confronted mankind with a call that could not be evaded. Accept or reject—some few responded in faith and obedience and the new order was begun. The Church came into existence. In

---

8. Dodd, *op. cit.*, p. 70.

one generation it was already strong enough in Rome to attract the unfriendly attention of the government.

(b) *Periods of Production.* Like similar movements, in its early history, the Church went through three successive periods; expansion, conflict, and consolidation. The writings of the New Testament naturally fall into these three periods, which serves as a rough chronological outline.

The first period was that of expansion and began shortly after the death of Jesus at Jerusalem. This period went on rather smoothly for about thirty years. In this first generation, Christian communities were established in many eastern provinces of the Roman empire and as far west as Italy. During these years the foundations were also laid for the later structure of Christian theology and philosophy. The Apostle Paul was the great missionary and theologian during these early years. His Letters and Epistles, written during this time are an expression of enthusiasm, optimism, and expansive energy that characterized this early period of spiritual adventure. The Acts of the Apostles reflect the same spirit although written somewhat later.

The second period begins with the repressive persecution under Nero in the winter of 64-65 A.D. Much of Rome was destroyed by a great fire and as a convenient scapegoat the Christians were blamed for this fire. As a result the Church was outlawed and its members severely persecuted. For the next thirty years the Christians were constantly aware of their situation in a hostile society. Hence the Christian literature of this period has little of the buoyancy of the earlier period, and rather emphasized fortitude and endurance. Examples are the First Epistle of Peter, the Letter to the Hebrews, and Revelation. Here persecution and martyrdom are spoken of as the normal expectation of a Christian.

Persecution flared up afresh under the Emperor Domitian and the Church needed to pause to gather inspiration and confidence from the memory of its founder, Jesus Christ. The inevitable passing on of the first generation Christians, now accelerated by the persecution, made it important that these memories should be perpetuated in writing. So far as known, the first attempt at a connected account of the life and teachings of Jesus was the Gospel according to Mark. Short collections of the sayings of Jesus and perhaps parts of His life story also were already in writing to be used in the missionary work of the Church. In Mark's Gospel there is an emphasis upon Christ's suffering and the call for Christians to also take up their cross and follow (Mark 8:34; 10:21; Matthew 16:24; Luke 9:23).

The Gospels according to Matthew and Luke probably also appeared before the death of Domitian (96 A.D.). Matthew, the former tax collector, based his gospel upon Mark and gave a systematic and comprehensive account of the teachings of Jesus. It thus provided a good basis for internal consolidation of the Christian community. Matthew being a Jew, wrote mainly for Jewish Christians.

Luke has a little different orientation. He wrote two volumes, the Gospel and the Acts. The whole work is dedicated to a friendly official, the "most excellent Theophilus" (Luke 1:3; Acts 1:1). The author is evidently appealing over the heads of the agents of persecution, to intelligent and friendly persons in Graeco-Roman society, with the hope that accurate information on the origin, aims, and principles of the Church would help to disarm the governmental hostility. Luke was a Greek Christian physician and as Paul's traveling companion, he naturally wrote more particularly for non-Jews.

The third period in the early history of the Church begins with the murder of the Emperor Domitian in 96 A.D., which brought more humane rulers to the throne. In New Testament writings after this date there is less reference to actual persecution. By now the Church was well aware of the necessity to consolidate its communal life and present a united front to the world, as well as to maintain the integrity of its membership in faith and morals. Hence the literature of this period is concerned with order and discipline as well as correct belief and practice. Here come the "Pastoral Epistles" of Paul to Timothy and Titus, the "general Epistles" of John and Jude, and the so-called Second Epistle of Peter.

While internal consolidation went on, new attempts were also made to interpret the faith to outsiders. This refers especially to the Gospel according to John, dated between 90 and 110 A.D. He wrote for a public familiar with the best religious thought of the time in non-Christian circles acquainted with Greek thought forms and philosophy. During the centuries following, the power of the Greek intellect gave itself to the task of constructing a Christian theology, largely under the influence of the Johannine interpretation of the Gospel.

This then is the general sequence of the New Testament literature. The time factor here is less important than in the Old Testament. The production of the entire New Testament literature falling approximately within the first one hundred and fifty years. In the Old Testament the process took over one thousand years. In the Old Testament there were repeated crises to meet, while in the New

Testament there is really only one supreme crisis, namely, the shift from the Old to the New Covenant.

(c) *Canonization*. In the early years of Christianity many books appeared and were circulated that dealt with Jesus and the early Church. There were gospels according to Thomas, Peter, Philip, Ebionites, Egyptians and others; and there were Acts of Paul, John, Peter, Andrew, Thomas and others. In fact there is a New Testament Apocrypha as well as an Old Testament one. These were writings of doubtful origin and authority. Gradually the more authentic and valuable ones gained increased recognition.

In 367 A.D. the Church Father Athanasius, Bishop of Alexandria, wrote a Paschal letter to the churches of the East in which he listed the twenty-seven books he recommended to the Christians. This list happens to coincide with our present New Testament. In 397 A.D. the list was also approved by the Church of the West. But it was not until 692 A.D. that the New Testament canon was approved officially by the Council of Constantinople for the entire Church, East and West.

As in the case of the Old Testament canon, here also various tests were used in the decision regarding each book. These were: (1) Does it conform to the accepted rule of faith? (2) Was it written by an Apostle or associate? and (3) Is it vouched for by a leading congregation of that day? Some New Testament writings had difficulty passing these tests. The authorship of some Epistles could not be established very definitely such as Timothy, Titus and II Peter. It is not known who wrote the Letter to the Hebrews. The book of Revelation was considered somewhat hazy and impractical. Finally, however, they were all accepted. Excluded ones are found in "The Apocrapha of the New Testament."

The question of heresy played an important role. Docetism, holding that Jesus was not really human but only "seemed" human caused much difficulty. Marcion, early in the 2nd century A.D., insisted that the God of the Old Testament and of the New Testament were not the same and advocated that the Old Testament be excluded altogether. Even in the New Testament he would accept only Luke of the Gospels and ten of Paul's letters. However, Marcionism was condemned as heretical.

That there were many versions of the story of Jesus, and the early Christian movement, is clear from the first verses in Luke's Gospel when he writes:

In as much as many have undertaken to compile a narrative of the things which have been accomplished among us. just as they were delivered to us by those who from the beginning were eyewitnesses and ministers of the word, it seemed good to me also, having followed all the things closely for sometime past, to write an orderly account for you, most excellent Theophilus, that you may know the truth concerning the things of which you have been informed (Luke 1:1-4).

(d) *Chronology.* An approximate chronology of the New Testament writings and events is given below.[9]

B.C. 6-4? Birth of Jesus
A.D. 29-33? Ministry of Jesus
A.D. 30-33? Crucifixion of Jesus
A.D. 33-35? Conversion of Paul
A.D. 41-49? Claudius banished Jews from Rome
A.D. 50-52 *I, II Thessalonians*
A.D. 53-54 *Galatians*
A.D. 54-56 *I, II Corinthians*
A.D. 56-57 *Romans*
A.D. 58-60 *Colossians, Philippians, Philemon*
A.D. 66-73 War with Rome
A.D. 66-67 Christians flee to Pella

A.D. 70 Jerusalem and Temple destroyed
A.D. 70 *Gospel of Mark*
A.D. 75-100 *James, Ephesians*
A.D. 85-100 *Gospel of Matthew, Gospel of Luke, Acts*
A.D. 90? Council of Jamnia
A.D. 90-95 *I Peter, Hebrews, Revelation*
A.D. 90-110 *Gospel of John, Letters of John*
A.D. 100-130 *Titus; also I, II Tim.*
A.D. 110-130 *Jude*
A.D. 130-150 *II Peter*

(e) *The Apocryphal and extracanonical books* of the New Testament should not be overlooked. Naturally the process of canonization was slow. It took generations as gradually the more authentic and valuable books came to be more generally accepted and used. It is understandable that there were differences of opinion regarding these matters. That out of this confusion there arose our present New Testament is evidence that the Holy Spirit was at work. Below is a list of the Apocryphal New Testament books with names and number of chapters.[10]

---

9. Kee, Young & Froehlich, *Understanding the New Testament*, Prentice-Hall, 1965, p. 472. See also *The Interpreter's Bible*, Abingdon, 1957, Vol. XII, p. 671; George Potts, *Background to the Bible*, Harper, 1964, pp. 47-48.

10. See *The Apocryphal New Testament*, William Hone, Ludgate Hill, London, 1820; also *The Lost Books of the Bible*, Alpha House, Inc., N.Y., 1926.

Other extracanonical New Testament literature included the following.[11]

3. Transmission of the Bible

The story of the transmission of the Bible to later generations is a long and complicated one. No original autograph of the Bible or any part of it exists today. The books of the Bible as at first written—the Old Testament on skins, the New Testament on papyrus—disappeared not long after their composition, relatively speaking. But they were carefully copied, and our knowledge of their contents comes from studying manuscript copies, or copies of copies. Gutenberg (1397?-1468) with his invention of the printing press had two important results: it increased the circulation of any given book a great many times, and it established the accuracy of the original text of that book for subsequent reproductions. Before the fifteenth

---

11. Based on Bratton, *op. cit.*, pp. 198-213, 355 and *The Lost Books of the Bible*, Alpha House, New York, 1926, pp. 287-290, for discussion and listing.

century no two copies of any book were exactly the same. Copied manuscripts inevitably contained errors or intentional changes by the copyists. Once the originals were lost no one could be sure of the exact original text.

(a) *Hebrew Manuscripts.* Until the discovery in 1947 of the Dead Sea Scrolls, our oldest Hebrew manuscripts went back no earlier than the ninth century A.D. Like the Greek, they had no vowels, which made reading difficult. The Hebrew text was not standardized until the seventh century A.D. Word division was introduced in the text in about 500 A.D. The oldest Hebrew manuscript is the tenth century *St. Petersburg Codex,* now in Leningrad. Soon after canonization in 90 A.D. all Hebrew manuscripts were made to conform to one model, and variant texts were destroyed. The first printed editions of the Hebrew Bible appeared at Soncino (1488). The important Rabbinic Bible was published at Venice in 1524-25 which is the standard version of the Hebrew Bible today.[12]

(b) *Greek Manuscripts.* During the fourth and fifth centuries B.C., papyrus gave way to vellum as manuscript material and was more durable. There are some 2,500 of these vellum manuscripts in existence varying in length from the complete Bible to a few verses. Some recently discovered fragments go back to the third century A.D.[13] The two oldest and most valuable Greek manuscripts are known as *Codex Vaticanus* and *Codex Sinaiticus. Codex Vaticanus* contains 759 leaves, has been in the Vatican Library since 1481 and probably comes from Egypt originally. *Codex Sinaiticus* contains 347 leaves, was discovered by Count Tischendorf in the Monastery of St. Catherine on Mount Sinai in 1859. It is now in the British Museum. A third important manuscript is *Codex Alexandrinus* which was in the Library of Alexandria until 1621 and is now in the British museum. *Codex Ephraemi Syri* is now in Paris, and the *Washington Codex* is in Washington, D.C. All these and other manuscripts differ from each other not only in minor matters but even in the books of the Bible they contain. All this, plus the gradual changes of language spoken and written makes scholarly work of translators very difficult.

(c) *Versions and Translations.* The original language of the Old Testament was Hebrew, with a few passages in Aramaic. The original

---

12. Bratton, op. cit., pp. 525-27.
13. Bratton, *op. cit.,* p. 220.

language of the New Testament was Greek with perhaps also some Armamaic. As different world powers took over, different languages became common and to make the Scriptures available they needed to be translated into the current language. So the time came when the Hebrew Old Testament needed to be translated into Greek, and later the entire Bible into Latin and finally into German and English, etc.

The Septuagint represents the first real translation of the Old Testament and Apocrypha into Greek at Alexandria, Egypt (about 270 B.C.). Greek had replaced Hebrew as the language of the Jews and this version was to meet the needs of the day. The work of various parts is not of the same quality, probably because of the many different scholars working on it but also because the *Pentateuch* and the *Prophets* were already accepted while this was not the case with the Writings until 90 A.D.[14]

The Vulgate Bible is a Latin translation of about 400 A.D. When Latin had replaced the Greek language, the Pope of Rome commissioned St. Jerome to translate the Bible into the "vulgar" language of the people, which became known as the *Vulgate*.

Wycliffe's Bible was the first English version of the whole Bible, translated from the Vulgate in 1382. John Wycliffe was an Oxford forerunner of the Reformation who considered the authority of the Scriptures above that of the Church, anticipating this Lutheran doctrine by 150 years. The Church opposed Wycliffe and a year after he died he was condemned for heresy and his bones were dug up and burned.[15]

The Gutenberg Bible in German was the first one printed with movable type. It was in two volumes and was completed in 1456 after five years of work.

Martin Luther's New Testament in German came out in 1522. Returning from the Wartburg Castle, where he defended himself before the authorities, he was spirited away by his friends for his protection. While in hiding he produced the New Testament in German in 1522, later this was followed by the Old Testament in 1534.

Tyndale's English version of the New Testament and parts of the Old Testament, based on the Latin Vulgate, Greek Septuagint, and texts in the original Hebrew and Greek languages came out in 1525.

---

14. Ira Maurice Price, *The Ancestry of our English Bible* (Revised) Harper, 1949, p. 52.
15. *Ibid.*

He had the advantage of the Gutenberg movable type and the Erasmus Greek translation (1516) of the New Testament, hence his work was not based only on the Latin. Because of opposition Tyndale fled to Germany where he produced his Bibles and sent them back to England hidden in cotton bales. Finally, however, he was apprehended, strangled and burned.

Miles Coverdale's Bible, authorized by the church of England came out in English in 1535. This was only ten years after Tyndale's New Testament.

The *Geneva Bible,* also called the *Breeches* Bible because of a peculiarity in the translation of one passage, was a revision of earlier translations prepared by English Puritans in exile at Geneva, Switzerland in 1560. This was the first Bible with numbered verses.[16]

The King James Bible came out in 1611 and is based on the original Hebrew and Greek tongues and former translations. It was authorized by King James and so is also called the Authorized Version. Forty-seven scholars were appointed by King James I of England to do this translation.

The Revised Version, a revision of the Authorized King James Version, based on original texts as restored by scholars of that day, was produced in 1881-85.

The (American) Revised Version, prepared at the same time as the English Revised Version, but departing somewhat more freely from the Authorized Version was not published until 1901.

The Douay Bible, authorized by the Catholic Church came out in 1909-10 and became the most popular version for Roman Catholics.

The Revised Standard Version (American) of 1952 was prepared by 32 scholars with an Advisory Board of 50 representatives of cooperating denominations who worked on it for 14 years. This version is a translation from the original languages, being the version set forth in A.D. 1611, revised in 1881-1885 and 1901, and compared with the most ancient authorities and revised in A.D. 1952[17]

The New English Bible with the Apocrypha, by Oxford University Press and Cambridge University Press, 1970, was produced by a panel of scholars of British universities appointed by a Joint Committee representing major Protestant denominations and Bible Societies of the British Isles. This is not a revision but a fresh and authoritative

---

16. R. M. Brown, *The Bible Speaks to You,* Westminster, 1955, p. 36.
17. Preface - Revised Standard Version.

translation attempting to use the idiom of contemporary English to convey the meaning of the original Hebrew and Greek. It took more than twenty years to complete. The Joint Committee chose three panels of distinguished scholars as translators of the Old Testament, the New Testament, and the Apocrypha. A fourth panel of literary advisors worked closely with the translators. In the later stages the Committee was also joined by observers representing the Roman Catholic Church.[18]

The Anchor Bible is a new translation still in process. In September, 1964, the first two volumes of the *Anchor Bible* started a project that is finally to reach 42 volumes. The whole work is under the editorial supervision of William Foxwell Albright and David Noel Freedman. The publisher is Doubleday and Co., New York. The unusual procedure in this work is that translators include Roman Catholics, Protestants, and Jews. The text is supplied with the latest discoveries in biblical criticism, history and archaeology.

This list is not complete. There are many popular translations that have encouraged a wider reading of the Bible, such as: Richard F. Weymouth, *The New Testament in Modern Speech,* a British publication in 1903, American edition in 1943; Richard R. Moulton, *The Modern Reader's Bible,* Macmillan, 1917; James Moffatt, *The Holy Bible, A New Translation,* Doran Co., N.Y., 1922; Smith and Goodspeed, *The Bible, An American Translation,* The University of Chicago Press, 1935; *The New Testament in Basic English,* Dutton & Co., N.Y., 1941; J. B. Phillips, *The New Testament in Modern English,* Macmillan, 1958; *Good News for Modern Man, The New Testament in Today's English,* The American Bible Society, 1966; and others.

4. *Time Chart of the Bible in the Making.*

900 B.C. "J" Documents - Southern - Judah - Jehovah, Yahweh for God.

750 B.C. "E" Documents - Northern - Israel (Ephraim) - Elohim for God. Combined they became the "JE" documents.

722 B.C. Israel taken captive by Assyria - South assumes God is displeased with Northern religious practices and so "JE" Documents are rewritten.

---

18. Preface - The New English Bible.

621 B.C. "D" Document - Deuteronomy is found when Josiah cleanses the Temple. All these combined now make "JED" documents.

587 B.C. Judah is taken into captivity by Babylon and here Priests rewrite documents and produce the "P" document.

These combined "JEDP" documents are in our present Old Testament which gradually was developed in three parts: The Law, The Prophets, and The Writings.

270 B.C. Septuagint - the Greek translation in Alexandria.

JESUS CHRIST IS BORN AND THE CHRISTIAN ERA BEGINS 6-4 B.C.?

70 A.D. Jerusalem destroyed by Titus - Jews scattered.

90 A.D. Old Testament canon decided upon by Jewish Rabbis at Jamnia.

367 A.D. Athanasius, Bishop of Alexandria in his Easter letter to Eastern churches lists the present N.T. books as most authentic.

397 A.D. Rome at the Council of Carthage decides on the Athanasius list also, for Western churches.

About 400 A.D. Vulgate translation into Latin by Jerome (340-420) authorized by the Pope.

692 A.D. Council of Constantinople - East and West - agree on N.T. Canon.

1382 A.D. Wycliffe translates Vulgate into English - His bones were later burned.

1522 A.D. Luther N.T. translation into German; 1534 O.T.

1525 A.D. Wm. Tyndale translation - in 1536 he was strangled and burned for unauthorized translating of the Bible into English.

1535 A.D. Church of England authorized Miles Coverdale Translation into English.

1611 A.D. King James or Authorized Version in English.

1885 (English) Revised Version.

1901 (American) Revised Version. Thomas Nelson & Sons.

1952 (American) Revised Standard Version. Thomas Nelson & Sons.

1970 The New English Bible with the Apocrypha, Oxford Univ. Press and Cambridge Univ. Press.

Today the O.T. is published in over 200 languages; the N.T. in over 500 languages; parts of N.T. in over 1000 languages, and at least one book of the Bible in over 1500 languages.

C. The Infallibility and Inspiration of the Bible

The Bible is a book of religion. It can be studied as literature but its authors were not primarily interested in literature. It contains high ranking literary gems but to approach the Bible only from the literary point of view is to miss its main purpose. The Bible can also be studied as history with profit, however it is not a book of history but one of religion. It is *The Book of the Acts of God.*[19] The Bible is not a textbook on science either. Its primitive cosmology sees the earth as flat and stationary, with the sky as its canopy through whose windows the rain falls. The chief value of this *Book of the Acts of God* lies in its moral principles and spiritual guidance. As a book of religion its timeless aspirations and deathless convictions are not affected by an outmoded cosmology. The discoveries of Copernicus, Darwin, and Einstein, do not impair the universal validity of faith, hope and love.

1. Scholarly Research and the Bible

Scholars have made great contributions toward making the Bible better understood and more dynamic. There have always been those who distrust the scholars as though they were only negative. Iron ore needs to be refined in fire to make steel out of it. Fire will not destroy gold but only purify it. All Scriptures of the various religions in the world finally must go through this refining process and as Christians we need not fear that any harm will come to our religion by having our Scriptures tested in every possible way.

(a) *Historical study* of the Bible is used by scholars in various ways, more especially as "higher," "lower," and "form," criticism. *Higher criticism* deals with questions of date, authorship, and relation to other documents of the various books of the Bible. *Lower criticism* relates to attempts of restoring the original text of a book, when it has been subject to variations in the course of transmission of manuscripts for many centuries. This is also called "textual" criticism. *Form creiticism* deals with original context and meaning. Biblical study employs the so-called historical method. To get the various documents into the right chronological order is the first step toward studying them intelligently as records of the historical process, of which they are a part, and of which they are a product.

---

19. Wright and Fuller, *The Book of the Acts of God,* Doubleday, 1957.

In recent years we have moved into a new period of biblical study, which has been described as "post-liberal" which however does not mean "post-critical," although the earlier critical views are also being revised.[20] The Bible comes to us as a revelation of divine truth in the form of a history of events, and the principle of succession in time is essential to it. The historical approach to the study of religion has established the principle that no religion can be appraised, nor can its Scriptures be interpreted, apart from the knowledge of the cultural, historical, and religious background of that respective religion.

(b) *The Science of Archeology* has made great contributions in helping to understand the early Hebrew religion and its sacred writings. A circle drawn on the map of the ancient world of the Near East, with Jerusalem as the center and 800 miles as the radius, includes Egypt, Palestine, Mesopotamia, Asia Minor, and Greece. This area is a gold mine for the archeologists.

In Egypt, one of the by-products of Napoleon's invasion, was the discovery in 1799 of the *Rosetta Stone,* so named after the place where it was found. This block of black basalt, measuring forty-five by twenty-eight inches, proved to be the master-key to the story of Egypt, including the monuments of Thebes, Karnak, Luxor, the Pyramids, the tomb of Tutankhamen, etc. The stone is now in the British Museum. It contains a trilingual inscription, one in the then known as hieroglyphics, one in Demotic, and one in Greek. For many years the stone remained a riddle. Finally the French scholar Champollion who knew Greek and Coptic, assuming that the third language of ancient hieroglyphics contained the same message as the other two columns, after long and hard work, at last gave to the modern world an understanding of hieroglyphics, and thereby opened Egyptian antiquities.

In 1888 an Egyptian peasant woman stumbled over some clay tablets in a field of Tell el-Amarna. This was the former capital of Amenhotep IV, (Ikhnaton) the heretic king who instituted monotheistic sun worship. He was a religious genius but no politician and his far-flung empire went to pieces. These tablets were letters written to him by his viceroys in Palestine, Phoenicia, and Meso-

---

20. Martin E. Marty, ed., *New Directions in Biblical Thought,* Association Press, N.Y., 1960. On "Form Criticism" and "Demythologizing" see various books by Rudolph Bultman.

potamia. Some letters are from his vassel king in Jerusalem, appealing for help against the invading Habiru (Hebrews). These letters were written in the 18th Dynasty (Amenhotep IV. Ikhnaton 1360 B.C.), but it is usually held that Israelites left Egypt only in the 19th Dynasty (Ramses II. 1224 B.C.). The solution to the problem is that this was probably another tribe of Habiru which did not go to Egypt at all but invaded Palestine before Joshua. There must have been more than one group of Habiru who conquered Palestine in at least two periods. The Tell el-Amarna letters also give much information regarding Jerusalem 300 years before David's Monarchy.

Tablets also tell of Tutankhamen, whose grave was found unplundered, who was the son-in-law of Ikhnaton, and who returned Egypt to polytheism because of priestly pressure. Worship of the sun-disk, Aton, as the one true God was monotheistic. Ikhnaton wrote a psalm hymn of praise to Aton much like our 104th Psalm.[21] Did all this perhaps influence Moses in his idea of Yahweh monotheism?[22] Other digs indicate how the Hebrews went Canaanitish in Palestine, refer to the Walls of Jericho, the high places of Gezer, Solomon's stables, the house of Ahab, etc.

Babylonians, like the Egyptians, originally used picture language but later developed the cuneiform characters. The Persians simplified this and developed an alphabet. In 516 B.C. Darius, king of Persia, decided to build himself a monument. But instead of transporting stone, as the Egyptians did for their pyramids, he went to the stones and used them in their original setting. He chose the rocks of Behistun, which tower some 1700 feet in the air and on their bare, smooth surface had his scribes chisel in the record of his victories in three languages. For him who could not read, the story was carved in life-sized picture forms, in which Darius gives thanks to Ahura Mazda for his victories, with the left foot on the form of the usurper Gaumata, in front of nine rebel leaders roped together on the ground. This sculpture measures ten by eighteen feet. Below it is the Persian text telling of the king's vengeance. To the left is the Median text and overhanging it all is the Babylonian version.

Henry C. Rawlinson, who had learned Persian in India, was challenged to copy and decipher these carvings and, with great courage

---

21. J. H. Breasted, *The Dawn of Conscience*, Scribners, 1933.
22. H. H. Rowley, *From Moses to Qumran*, Ass'n Press, 1963, pp. 46-48; W. F. Albright, *From Stoneage to Christianity*, John Hopkins Press, 1946, pp. 196 ff.

and daring, finally did so. In 1846 he published his translation of the Persian column which was a decree of King Darius. With his knowledge of Persian cuneiform, he was able to find corresponding characters in the Babylonian column. Eleven years later he had the entire inscription mastered and published. His deciphering showed that the ancient Babylonian language belonged to the Semitic family and was closely related to Hebrew. Thus, Rawlinson provided the key to Mesopotamia and its Babylonian and Assyrian antiquities. Access to Mesopotamian literature illuminates much biblical history. In it there are: two versions of the creation story; various versions of the Deluge; the lengthy Code of Hammurabi, with some fifty articles similar to our Exodus Chapter 21; a Babylonian forerunner to the Hebrew Job; Ur of Chaldea with evidence of human sacrifice; reference to the Ziggurat as probably the Tower of Babel; stories very similar to our Laban and Jacob with Leah and Rachel, including the teraphim that Rachel stole; Esau's sale of his birthright, etc. All these stories are cruder and more polytheistic than their counterparts in the Bible.

(c) *The Dead Sea Scrolls*. In the spring of 1947 an Arab goatherd followed his animals into a cave, and discovered some twenty ancient scrolls hidden in earthen jars. The most important of these was one of Isaiah, from about the second century B.C., which consisted of twenty-four feet of sheepskin, ten and one half inches wide, containing the entire Hebrew text of Isaiah. In a second search of the cave in 1949 some two hundred additional fragments were found. Altogether some 267 caves in the Khirbet Qumran region have been explored. The presence of tens of thousands of scrolls and fragments thereof in one area, indicates that there must have been a library here at one time. Excavations revealed a stone building with some thirty rooms and an adjacent cemetery containing about 1000 graves. This building was probably a monastery, it is now thought, of the Essene sect. In 1947 a Manual of Discipline was found which seems to have belonged to this order.

The Zadokote fragments also speak of a teacher of Righteousness who is the leader of the New Covenant. He is referred to in Messianic titles as "The Elect One" and "the Righteous One." All this seems to indicate the continuity of Messianic ideas through the intertestamental period on into New Testament times. Whether John the Baptist and Jesus had any connections with this Essene sect is an interesting question. The answer to this would have a bearing on the uniqueness of Jesus and His teaching, the origin of Christian sacraments, and the influence of intertestamental Judaism upon the beginnings of Christianity. This Teacher of Righteousness, as Jesus, also spoke of the New Covenant; preached a similar message; each was regarded as a savior, and each was condemned and put to death by reactionary forces of their day.

What bearing the Dead Sea Scrolls have on one's thought on Christian origins depends largely upon one's theological outlook. To those who have always assumed a certain dependence of Christianity upon earlier institutions and teachings, the implications will not be too startling. Just how it all will affect New Testament interpretation only time can tell.[23]

2. Infallibility of the Bible

In the early centuries when many converts to Christianity came from a pagan background the Church did not allow its members to make their own interpretation of the Scriptures. Naturally, converted pagans had no background, such as the Jews had, to whom the Christian message first came. Hence only those competent to interpret the Scriptures were authorized to do this. Thus interpreted, the Bible became one of the authorities of the Church.

For centuries of later history the Bible was unknown by the common people, because it was written in Hebrew and Greek and kept chained in monastic libraries. After the invention of printing (1456) and the coming of the Reformation it was translated and distributed to the people. Ever since, it has been the world's best seller of books. The people read it eagerly and rejoiced in its rich human material. They named their children after its heroes and heroines, and colored their daily conversation with its phrases. Protestants substituted its authority for that of the Pope and the Church. Gradually Martin Luther's German translation and the Authorized King James Version in English, by many people came to be considered authoritative on all questions and infallible.

Later scholarly and critical study questioned the literal infallibility, because of contradictions and inconsistencies, the differences between ancient texts, unscientific assumptions, differences in moral and religious standards of various portions, and the words of Jesus "You have heard it said, but I say unto you" so and so (Matthew 5: 22, 28, 32, 34, 38, 42).

---

23. Bratton, *op. cit.*, pp. 78-81; H. H. Rowley, *From Moses to Qumran*, Ass'n Press, 1963, chap. viii.

(a) *Contradictions and inconsistencies* on many points are easily found in the Bible. For example, in Exodus 37:1-9 we read that the Ark of the Covenant was made by Bezalel, while in Deuteronomy 10:1-5 Moses reports that God commanded him to make the Ark and says, "so I made an ark of acacia wood . . ." When Joab was ordered to take a census, II Samuel 24:1 tells us that it was by the command of God, while I Chronicles 21:1 says it was by Satan's command. In II Kings 24:8, we read "Jehoiachin was eighteen years old when he became king, and he reigned three months in Jerusalem;" while in II Chronicles 36:9 we read, "Jehoiachin was eight years old when he began to reign, and he reigned three months and ten days in Jerusalem."

Regarding the flood story, Genesis 6:19, 20 says that Noah was to take "two of every sort into the ark," while Genesis 7:2, 3 says that he should take "seven pairs of all clean animals . . . and a pair of the animals that are not clean . . . and seven pairs of the birds." In Genesis 7:17 we read, that "The flood continued forty days," while in Genesis 7:24; 8:3 we read, "the waters prevailed upon the earth a hundred and fifty days." Did David or Elbanan kill Goliath? (I Samuel 17:23, 50; II Samuel 21:19). Did Solomon have 4,000 or 40,000 horses? (I Kings 4:26; II Chronicles 9:25).

Now let us turn to the New Testament. In the geneology of Jesus in Matthew 1:16 it says the grandfather of Jesus on Joseph's side, was Jacob, but Luke 3:23 says it was Heli. Matthew 1:6, 7 traces Jesus' ancestry through David's Son, Solomon, while Luke 3:31 traces it through Nathan, another son of David.

How many times did the cock crow when Peter denied Jesus? Mark 14:72 says twice, but Matthew 26:74, 75; Luke 22:60, 61; John 13:38 say once. The inscription on the Cross of Jesus is differ-ént in each of the four Gospels (Matthew 27:37; Mark 15:26; Luke 28:38; John 19:19). Did the chief priests or Judas buy the potter's field? (Matthew 27:6-8; Acts 1:18, 19). Matthew 27:9 says this transaction of the thirty pieces of silver for the potter's field was prophesied by Jeremiah, however the passage is not in Jeremiah but in Zechariah 11:12-13.

Did those with Saul (Paul) at his conversion hear or see anything? Acts 9:7 says "The men who were travelling with him stood speech-less, hearing the voice but seeing no one," while in Acts 22:9 before the Jews, Paul himself says "Now those that were with me saw the light but did not hear the voice . . .", and before Agrippa in Acts 26:13, 14, he says "I saw on the way a light from heaven, brighter than the sun, shining round me and those who journeyed with me. And when we had fallen to the ground, I heard a voice saying to me . . ."[24]

Scholars point out that it is impossible to work out an exact sequence of events surrounding and including the resurrection of Jesus, without contradiction from the various accounts in the Gospels. On the other hand these minor differences or even contradictions speak well for the authenticity of the Bible as regarding its great message and purpose. Witnesses to any great event will always differ as to details and therefore, this characteristic of the Bible as a whole, rather indicates its dependability on the great spiritual issues that it is concerned with.[25]

(b) *There are differences between various ancient manuscripts.* More than two hundred years lie between the earliest writing in the New Testament and the oldest manuscripts now known, which in general date back only to the fourth century. During that lapse of time various errors and other changes crept in, so that among the different copies important variations occur. Critical studies of differences have brought to light ever closer approximations to the earliest forms of the sacred writings.[26]

For example, in Matthew 5:22 the King James Version reads ". . . whosoever is angry with his brother without a cause shall be in danger of the judgment," while the later Revised Standard Version reads ". . . everyone who is angry with his brother shall be liable to judgment." The later version omits the words "without a cause" which changes the meaning of Jesus' words against anger with a brother even if thought justifiable. Evidently the words "without a cause" were added by some scribe to soften the words of Jesus. The earliest manuscripts we now have do not have them, which is also more in line with the general spirit of Jesus.

Some whole passages evidently were inserted at later dates, and for sometime were not accepted in all textual transmissions. Mark 16:9-19 seems to be so poorly attested that the translators of the Revised Standard Version have put it in fine print, along with an alternative passage supported by some ancient authorities. Similar treatment is given John 7:38--8:11 which some ancient manuscripts omit or place in Luke.

---

24. C. F. Potter, *Is That in the Bible?*, Garden City, 1933, pp. 193-202.
25. L. H. DeWolf, *A Theology of the Living Church*, Harpers, 1953, p. 69.
26. DeWolf, *op. cit.*, p. 70.

(c). *In questions relating to natural science* it is clear that biblical writers occasionally make statements based upon scientific assumptions not substantiated by modern science. When Laban agreed that the striped and spotted goats in his flocks were to belong to Jacob as wages for his labor, we are told that Jacob arranged for the stronger goats to have such offspring by keeping striped and spotted sticks in front of the breeding animals at their watering places (Genesis 30:35-43). This ancient superstition that human beings and animals are liable to be marked from birth by the images seen by pregnant mothers has long been discredited.

Similarly biblical writers assume the fixity of the earth, the movement of moon and sun from east to west, a place above the firmament as the dwelling place of God, and demonological causes for diseases.[27]

(d) *Even on questions of morals* there are passages in the Bible that could hardly be accepted as infallible. No Christian can defend writers who gloat over the suffering of their enemies, whom they killed without mercy, including man, woman, innocent children, and even animals, as we are told in the stories of Israel's conquest of the Canaanites, all in the name of Yahweh.

In the Sermon on the Mount, Jesus asks His followers to deal kindly with their enemies:

> "You have heard that it was said 'An eye for an eye and a tooth for a tooth. But I say to you, Do not resist one who is evil. But if anyone strikes you on the right cheek, turn to him the other also, and if any one would sue you and take your coat, let him have your cloak as well; and if any one forces you to go one mile go with him two miles. Give to him who begs from you, and do not refuse him who would borrow from you.
> You have heard that it was said, 'You shall love your neighbor and hate your enemy.' But I say to you, Love your enemies and pray for those who persecute you, so that you may be sons of your Father who is in heaven; for he makes his sun rise on the evil and on the good, and sends rain on the just and on the unjust . . . You therefore, must be perfect, as your heavenly Father is perfect" (Matthew 5:38-48).

There is a far cry between this attitude and that expressed in some of the Imprecatory Psalms. For example,

> . . . The Lord has recompensed me according to my righteousness, according to the cleanness of my hands in his sight . . . He trains

---

27. Andrew D. White, *The History of Warfare between Science and Theology,* Free Press, 1917.

my hands for war, so that my arms can bend a bow of bronze . . .
I persued my enemies and overtook them; and did not turn back
till they were consumed. I thrust them through, so that they were
not able to rise; they fell under my feet. For thou didst help me
with strength for the battle . . . those who hated me I destroyed
. . . I beat them fine as dust before the wind; I cast them out like
the mire of the streets . . . exalted be the God of my salvation,
the God who gave me vengeance and subdued peoples under me
(Psalm 18:24, 34, 37-40, 46-67).

And again:

Appoint a wicked man against him; let an accuser bring him to
trial. When he is tried, let him come forth guilty; let his prayer
be counted as sin. May his days be few; may another seize his
goods! May his children be fatherless, and his wife a widow!
May his children wander about and beg; may they be driven out
of the ruins they inhabit; May the creditor seize all that he has;
may strangers plunder the fruits of his toil. Let there be none
to extend kindness to him, nor any to pity his fatherless children.
May his posterity be cut off; may his name be blotted out . . .
(Psalm 109:6-13; cf. Psalms 35:4-6, 8, 26; 58:6-8; 137:8-9).

These passages can only be understood if we take the Bible as
"progressive revelation," the earliest portions leading up to the later
portions on a higher level of morality and religion. Some of these
portions are not infallible guides as judged by the life and teachings
of Jesus.

(e) *Jesus had a high regard for the Old Testament* but He unhesi-
tatingly and repeatedly changes Old Testament teaching. Regarding
the Old Testament teaching concerning oaths, Jesus repudiated them
altogether, "But I say unto you, Do not swear at all" (Matthew 5:34).
He went on giving reasons for His command which were as valid in
the days of Deuteronomy, Leviticus and Numbers as they were in
His or are in our day (Matthew 5:33-37). He denounced the doctrine
of loving neighbors but hating enemies, and advocated loving enemies,
praying for persecutors, and again gave reasons which are timeless.

The Bible is a collection of intensely human writings by men who
had their own characteristic education, interests, language and
literary styles. Most of the events are activities of obviously fallible
human beings. There are passages that contradict one another, there
are moral and religious ideas, especially in the older documents, that
are distinctly sub-Christian. Although not infallible in sections, all
this does not deny the inspiration and authority of the Bible as a
whole. We turn then to consider in what sense the Bible may be
considered to be the inspired Word of God.

3. *Evidences of Biblical Inspiration*

The Christian community is both a product and a depository of the message transmitted through the Scriptures. The experience of Christians has been rich in the production of ideas which commend themselves as true and valuable which constitute important evidences for inspiration of the Scriptures.[28]

(a) *Frequently heights of rhetorical beauty, dignity and power* are attained and sustained through long passages in biblical writings. There are the soul-searching prayers of penitence, profound expressions of trust in times of adversity, lofty hymns of joy and praise, or the stirring calls to worship of the Psalms; there are the blazing denunciations of hypocritical religion and social unrighteousness of Amos and Jesus; there is Isaiah's description of overpowering awe experienced in the presence of the righteous and holy God in chapter six; or his description of the loving care and sovereignty of God in chapter forty; or his writing about the suffering servant in chapter fifty-three.

There is Jesus proclaiming His message in the Sermon on the Mount including the Beatitudes in the fifth chapter of Matthew; or His many parables, including that of the Good Samaritan and the Prodigal Son; or His high priestly prayer in John 17. There is Paul, with his chapter on love in I Corinthians 13, or his defense of the Resurrection in chapter 15. There is the 21st chapter of Revelation about "a new heaven and a new earth" in which "the dwelling of God is with men . . . and they shall be his people." And so one could go on and on, all witnesses of profound inspiration and in turn inspiring the reader. Artists and musicians have found the Scriptures their inspiration for the great productions in various areas.

(b) *The substance of thought* in the Bible again and again rises beyond the possibility of adequate literary expression. In the golden age of the Greeks under Pericles (495-429 B.C.) when their great philosophers were taking infanticide for granted and showing very little appreciation for the tenderness and loyalty of family ties, the Hebrews since the 8th Century B.C. had already been reading Hosea's account of God's redemptive love for His wayward people under the figure of the prophet's love for his wayward wife and a father's concern for his little child just learning to walk.

---

28. DeWolf, *op. cit.*, pp. 77-79.

While the Romans engaged soothsayers to search the entrails of butchered beasts for signs from their warring gods, Jesus was confidently speaking of a loving heavenly Father who knows and cares for His children's needs. Even today while nations learn ever more efficient methods of war, destruction and waste, the Scriptures speak of another and better way to peace under law, mercy and love, and nations shall not "learn war anymore." The prophets and the Gospels are still far ahead of mankind in our own age. All this indicates inspiration of a high order. For example:

> "Hear, O Israel, the Lord your God is one Lord, and you shall love the Lord your God with all your heart, with all your soul, and with all your might" (Deut. 6:4); But let justice roll down like waters and righteousness like an overflowing stream (Amos 5:24); I desire steadfast love and not sacrifice, the knowledge of God rather than burnt offerings (Hosea 6:6); He has showed you, O man, what is good; and what does the Lord require of you, but to do justice, and to love kindness, and to walk humbly with your God? (Micah 6:8); The Lord is my shepherd, I shall not want (Ps. 23:1); He shall judge between the nations, and shall decide for many peoples; and they shall beat their swords into plowshares and their spears into pruning hooks, nation shall not lift up sword against nation, neither shall they learn war any more (Isa. 2:4); "So whatever you wish that men should do to you, do so to them; for this is the law and the prophets" (Matt. 7:12); "But seek first his kingdom and his righteousness, and all these things shall be yours as well" (Matt. 6:33); So faith, hope and love abide; these three, but the greatest of these is love (I Cor. 13:13); God is love, and he who abides in love abides in God, and God abides in him (I John 4:16); Then I saw a new heaven and a new earth . . . "Behold the dwelling of God is with men, He will dwell with them, and they shall be his people, and God himself will be with them" . . . "Behold I make all things new" (Rev. 21:1, 3, 5).

(c) *The record of great historical events* in the Bible is another evidence of inspiration. The story of the aspirations, falls, and the long difficult struggle and climb of Israel, drawn by the call and vision of God, is an inspiration to every careful reader. Here also would come the story of Jesus and its meaning for the history of mankind. The Christian faith considers this story, by far, the most important in all history. In this story of Jesus, man finds the answer to the great questions of life. Answers dealing with questions of the purpose of existence, divine help available in man's struggles, his final salvation and the hope of life everlasting. In the Bible there is also the story of the founding of the Christian Church and its mission to the world. The stories of these events relating to Israel, the life of Jesus, the Church and its mission, all indicate the guiding hand of God and the leading of His Holy Spirit, or inspiration.

(d) *The Bible has power to inspire.* It is a missionary book. A tree is known by its fruits. Paul took the Gospel from the East to the West by heeding the call to "Come over to Macedonia and help us" (Acts 16:9). Thereafter whatever light and progress have come to modern western civilization were worked out under the inspiration of the Bible. The status of women was elevated, infanticide was abolished, slavery was outlawed, the sick and the weak were given attention, literacy and education were promoted, the laboring classes were given more consideration, modern science flourished, and the recognition of the worth of the individual as in democracy is spreading to all the world. Admitting that only a beginning along these various lines has so far been made, still it was the Bible with its Gospel that was the light and inspiration in this general direction as man under God gradually moves on toward fuller realization of His calling and destiny in Christ Jesus.

4. *Theories of Biblical Inspiration*

All denominations of the Christian Church maintain that the Bible is inspired and that it is the greatest, best, and most useful book in the world. But, just what is meant by inspired? What is the nature of inspiration? There are different theories of inspiration. The various theories can be divided into two main groups.

(a) *First let us consider the "verbal" or "dictation" theory* of inspiration. According to this theory the Bible is a book dictated by God to certain men who in turn have written down His message. To dictate a message use is made of an "amanuensis." This "amanuensis" does not supply any of the ideas or words. The message belongs entirely to the person who does the dictating. In offices today, use is made of dictating machines, tape recorders, and secretaries. According to the "dictation" theory the Bible was dictated to certain "pen men" and it therefore, is not only the "Word of God" as a whole, but it is the very "words" of God, hence without error and infallible.

However, we know that the Bible was transcribed from one skin to another during hundreds of years. These copyists could not help making errors in their copying. Later the Bible was translated from Hebrew and Greek into Latin, German, English and other languages. These translators were not infallible. One way out of this difficulty is to admit the errors of copyists and tranlators but still insist that the original manuscripts were perfect (plenary inspiration). However, this view only suggests that we really do not have God's Word now at all, as we do not have original copies.

This dictation theory makes the Bible of equal value in all its parts. I Kings is considered as authoritative as Amos. No distinction is made between the Old and New Testament. There are dry stretches in Leviticus, Numbers and Chronicles but the reader patiently plods forward, feeling that God must be pleased because reverence is shown in this way to "His Word."

The dictation theory has repeatedly been the cause of great wrong and tragedy. People who took the Bible as the literal and dictated words of God, read that God told Moses "You shall not permit a sorceress to live" (Exodus 22:18), and concluded that was also a command for them, and so, through centuries the most horrible cruelties were perpetuated upon people accused of witchcraft. It is estimated that in a single century one hundred thousand innocent people charged with witchcraft were put to death, and all based on the Bible.[29]

In the Old Testament we read how Elijah brought four hundred and fifty priests of Baal "down to the brook of Kishon and killed them there" (I Kings 18:19, 40). Repeatedly Church leaders have felt that if God told Elijah to kill those of wrong belief then the Church also must put to death everyone not holding the faith of the Church leaders. So we had the Spanish Inquisition, the slaughter of Anabaptists in Reformation times, and other periods of terrible persecution by the Church of other Christians.

During the first half of the 19th century there were Christian men in America trying to prove, from the Bible, that slavery was a divine institution. Even today some leaders in the South hold this idea which is based on the dictation theory of inspiration of the Bible. During World Wars I and II there were ministers in Europe and America putting out articles defining war as "an ordinance of God," clinching their arguments by Bible quotations—all based upon the dictation theory of inspiration.

Whenever one hears someone say he "believes in the Bible from cover to cover," or that he "always takes the Bible as it reads," one may conclude that the person believes that the whole Bible is the authoritative and infallible "Word of God," and that he holds to the dictation or verbal theory of inspiration.

---

29. Charles Jefferson, *Five Present-Day Controversies*, Flaming, 1924, p. 33.

(b) *The Illumination Theory* is another approach to inspiration. According to this view God is Light and when the Holy Spirit comes into a human life that mind is lighted up, or inspired. The very word "inspired" means filled with the Spirit. As a person is inspired he sees things more clearly than others see them, or he may even see some things others do not see at all. The men who wrote the Bible were inspired because their minds were lighted up by the Holy Spirit.

> This doctrine is that the writing of the Bible as a whole was accomplished by an extraordinary stimulation and elevation of the powers of men who devoutly yielded themselves to God's will and sought, often with success unparalleled elsewhere, to convey truth useful to the salvation of man and nations.[30]

According to this theory of inspiration there are degrees of illumination. One can illuminate a room brilliantly, partially, or dimly. In the first case everything in the room will be seen distinctly. In the second case some things will lie hidden in the shadows. In the third case many things will escape one's eyes. So the illumination theory of inspiration allows for some parts of the Bible to have been more illuminated by the Holy Spirit than others. Not all passages are equally inspired nor are they equally authoritative. The patriarchs had some light but not sufficient to be bothered with polygamy or occasionally to tell a lie. The judges had more light, and the prophets had still more, but not as much as the apostles. And when we come to Jesus we find His mind and soul so flooded with light that He could say—"I am the light of the world" (John 8:12; 9:5).

Inspiration must be considered as progressive. Truth comes to men as light comes into the world. The dawn begins with only a tinge of light, low in the eastern sky. Little by little the sun rises and climbs, first crowning the hills with glory, and later also filling the deepest valleys with light. So the Sun of Righteousness came into the consciousness of the human race. In the beginning the light was faint but it grew little by little, until it became clear as the sun at noon. In the earlier history of the Hebrew people there was much crudeness of thought and rudeness of conduct, which gradually have been left behind. Many things in the Old Testament have long since been outgrown. The ritualistic Levitical system does not belong to us. The early political ideas and scientific assumptions are antiquated. Because inspiration is progressive some moral and religious ideas

---

30. L. H. DeWolf, *A Theology of the Living Church,* Harper, 1953, p. 76.

have also been left behind although they may have served well in their day and age. The Bible is the record of progressive revelation of the character and purposes of the Eternal as mankind was ready and able to receive it.

Paul writes "Every inspired scripture has its use" . . . which is not saying that every scripture is inspired.

> Every inspired scripture has its use for teaching the truth and refuting error, or for reformation of manners and discipline in right living, so that man who belongs to God may be efficient and equipped for good work of every kind (II Timothy 3:16, 17 NEB).

All Christians accept this. The Bible is a reliable book and was written by good and honest men led by the Holy Spirit, some more so than others, to be sure. They expressed truth as they had light to see it. They had no intentions to deceive or mislead. The Bible is an inspired, authoritative, and a unique book. There is no book like it in all the world. "Read to me from the Book," said Sir Walter Scott when he was dying. Lockhart, his son-in-law, asked perplexed, "Which book?" Whereupon the dying but clear-minded Scott replied, "There is but one." And so, both the person who holds the dictation, as well as the one who holds the illumination theory of inspiration say, "There is but one!"[31]

D. SUGGESTIONS FOR BIBLE STUDY AND INTERPRETATION

Regarding the importance of learning to know the Scriptures Paul wrote to Timothy:

> But as for you, continue in what you have learned and have firmly believed, knowing from whom you have learned it and how from childhood you have been acquainted with the sacred writings which are able to instruct you for salvation through faith in Jesus Christ (II Timothy 3:14, 15).

In order to get most help from Bible study and properly to interpret the Scriptures as well as apply them, it is essential to follow certain principles. Some of these briefly are:

1. Daily Devotional Reading

To become acquainted with the Bible it is important to undertake a systematic, purposeful, daily reading of great selections that have been found helpful by Christians in all ages. The more faithfully

---

31. Quoted by Charles Jefferson, *op. cit.*, p. 48.

one does this the more one will treasure the Bible and the greater will its transforming teaching affect one's life. The message of its ultimate hope and eternal truths will greatly contribute to a person's happiness and usefulness.

To make this daily Bible reading most effective it is advisable to set apart a definite time each day for this purpose. Read expectantly and read prayerfully, thoughtfully, and without hurry, and welcome the leading given by God's message. Underscore the important verses and re-read them. When His Spirit guides, follow; when He condemns, bow penitently and ask for forgiveness; when He offers light, accept it gratefully, and when He commands, obey unreservedly.

2. *Study a Book at a Time*

To get perspective read an entire book at a time. It should be read as a letter from a friend. It will give comfort in sorrow, strength in adversity, assurance in periods of uncertainty, courage and power in everyday tasks of life. If occasionally an entire book is read in one sitting this will prove to be a very meaningful experience.

3. *Get the Historical Background*

It is necessary to get the historical setting of any book in the Bible when intending to make a more careful study of the same. This means finding answers to such questions as the following in Bible helps: (a) *Who* wrote this book and what sort of person was he? (b) From *where* was it written and what sort of place was this? (c) *When* was it written and what were the general conditions of that time? (d) To *whom* was it written and what was the general situation there? (e) *Why* was it written and what did the author hope to accomplish? (f) *How* did the author hope to achieve his purpose? (g) *What* is the main message of the book in brief summary? Finding answers to these questions regarding any book in the Bible will make it more meaningful.

4. *Recognize Different Types of Literature*

There are different kinds of literature in the Bible, such as poetry, history, legal codes, genealogies, short stories, dramas, parables, sermons, letters, philosophy and prophecy. Each has its particular purpose. Poetry cannot be interpreted as history, drama cannot be interpreted like letters. There is much symbolism used, as was the current practice of those days. Naturally a biblical passage will mean more if it is first identified as to what class of literature it is. Although many of the scientific assumptions in the Bible are outdated, that does not mean that the message of the passage may not still have meaning for personal and social life in our time. Paul writes "We have this treasure in earthen vessels" (II Corinthians 4:7). But even so it is a God given "treasure," but must be handled with discretion.

5. *Distinguish the Temporal from the Eternal*

The temporal and the eternal elements in the Bible need always to be distinguished from each other. For example the temple dimensions given in the Old Testament are of a temporal nature, while some of the truths the Psalms and the prophets speak about are of eternal significance. The genealogies are of a more local concern while the Sermon on the Mount is of timeless nature and meaning.

6. *Evaluate the Lower by the Higher*

The lower and the higher parts in the Bible should be differentiated from each other and the lower interpreted in the light of the higher. The Old Testament should be interpreted in the light of the New Testament. The New Testament should be interpreted in the light of the Gospels. The Gospels should be interpreted in the light of the Sermon on the Mount. Or to put it another way; the judges should be interpreted by the prophets, and the writings of Paul in the light of the teachings and Spirit of Jesus which is the highest and best we know. The admonition to "test the spirits" (I John 4:1) also applies here. Every spirit in line with the spirit of Jesus when He was in the flesh is of God (I John 4:2, 3). "God is love" (I John 4:8, 16) as revealed by Jesus Christ. This testing of the spirits also applies to the proper interpretation of the Scriptures.

E. SUMMARY AND CONCLUSION

In this chapter on the Bible the subdivisions are: The Message of the Bible; The Bible in the Making; Infallibility and Inspiration of the Bible; and Suggestions for Bible Study and Interpretation.

Already an Old Testament author wrote "Thy word is a lamp to my feet and a light to my path" (Psalm 119:105). And later Jesus himself testified, "You search the scriptures, because you think that in them you have eternal life; and it is they that bear witness to me" (John 5:39). The theme of the Bible is *Heilsgeschichte,* the Story of Reconciliation, or the entrance of God into the spiritual life of man to dignify and enrich the same by giving it meaning of eternal significance. In all this Jesus Christ is the central and focal point.

We know the Bible comes from God, because it leads us to God. The authority of the Scriptures lies in the truth they convey. Canonization did not make the Scriptures, but the quality of the Scriptures brought about canonization. Inspiration does not prove the excellence of the Scriptures, but the excellence of the Scriptures proves their inspiration. We do not believe in Jesus because we believe in the Bible, we believe in the Bible because we believe in Jesus.

God is our Father and the Bible is His servant to make Him known to us. Christ is our Savior and the Bible is His servant that He may save us. The Holy Spirit is our teacher and the Bible is His servant to show us Jesus Christ. We are God's children and the Bible is our servant to guide our feet in the way of salvation.

"God in the Gospel of His Son,
    Makes His eternal counsels known,
Where love in all its glory shines,
    And truth is drawn in fairest lines.
O grant us grace, Almighty Lord,
    To read and mark Thy Holy Word,
Its truth in meekness to receive,
    And by its holy precepts live."

(Benjamin Beddome 1787)
(Hymns of the United Church, No. 86)

FOR FURTHER READING ON THE BIBLE

Albright, W. F., *From the Stone Age to Christianity*, Johns Hopkins Press, 1946.
Anderson, B. W., *Rediscovering the Bible*, Association Press, 1951.
Barclay, W., *The Making of the Bible*, Abingdon Press, 1961.
Bratton, F. G., *The History of the Bible*, Beacon Press, 1959.
Brown, R. M., *The Bible Speaks to You*, Westminster Press, 1955.
Bruce, F. F., *Second Thoughts on the Dead Sea Scrolls*, Eerdmans, 1961.
Bultman, R., *Primitive Christianity in Contemporary Setting*, Meridian, 1957.
Burrows, M., *More Light on Dead Sea Scrolls*, Secker & Warburg, 1958.
Debeaux, Fred, *Understanding the Bible*, Westminster, 1958.
Feucht, O. E., *Learning to Use Your Bible*, Concordia, 1969.
Fosdick, H. E., *A Guide to Understanding the Bible*, Harper Torchbook, 1956.

Gottwald, N. K., *A Light to the Nations,* Harper, 1959.

Grant, R. M., *A Historical Introduction to the New Testament,* Harper, 1963.

Harrison, R. K., *Introduction to the Old Testament,* Eerdmans, 1969.

Henderson, R., *Life in Bible Times,* Rand, 1967.

Keck, L. E., *Taking the Bible Seriously,* Association Press, 1962.

Knox, John, *Criticism and Faith,* Abingdon, 1962.

MacGregor, Geddes, *The Bible in the Making,* Lippincott, 1959.

Marty, M. E., ed., *New Directions in Biblical Thought,* Ass'n Press, 1960.

Nida, E. A., *God's Word in Man's Language,* Harper, 1952.

Platt, R. H., ed., *The Lost Books of the Bible,* World Syndicate, 1927.

Pfeiffer, C. F., *Between the Testaments,* Baker Book House, 1959.

Potts, George, *Background to the Bible,* Harper & Row, 1964.

Price, Ira., *The Ancestry of the English Bible,* Harper, 1949.

Rowley, H. H., *From Moses to Qumran,* Association Press, 1963.

Robertson, E. H., *Take and Read,* John Knox, 1961.

Schlier, H., *Relevance of the New Testament,* Herder, 1968.

Swain, J. C., *Where Our Bible Came From,* Ass'n Press, 1960.

Wright, G. E., *Biblical Archeology,* Westminster, 1961.

Wright and Fuller, *The Book of the Acts of God,* Doubleday, 1957.

CHAPTER IX

THE CHRISTIAN HOPE

FOR THE FUTURE

Then I saw a new heaven and a new earth; for the first heaven and the first earth had passed away . . . and I heard a great voice . . . saying "Behold, the dwelling of God is with man. He will dwell with them, and they shall be his people . . . for the former things have passed away" . . . "Behold, I make all things new" (Revelation 21:1-5).

THE DISCUSSION OF THE CHRISTIAN HOPE FOR THE FUTURE NATURALLY falls into two main divisions: A. The Christian Hope for the Future of this World, and B. The Christian Hope for Personal Life after Death.

A.   THE CHRISTIAN HOPE FOR THE FUTURE OF THIS WORLD

In considering the future, whether of this world or life after death, we begin by admitting that man knows very little about it. There have been many who have speculated as to various possibilities of the future. Hence there is also great disagreement in this area. The Bible speaks about the future but often in general terms and in symbolical language. The Bible gives us no detailed map or calendar of future events.

However, in this world of law and order, it is only to be expected that causes will have their effects and that in general man reaps what he sows.

Do not be deceived; God is not mocked, for whatever a man sows, that will he also reap. For he who sows to his own flesh will from the flesh reap corruption; but he who sows to the Spirit will from the Spirit reap eternal life. And let us not grow weary in well-doing, for in due season we shall reap, if we do not lose heart (Galatians 6:7-9).

This general principle applies to all of life, individual as well as national, physical as well as social and spiritual. Often the harvest is multiplied over the sowing.

> For they sow the wind, and they shall reap the whirlwind (Hosea 8:7). He who sows sparingly, will also reap sparingly, and he who sows bountifully will also reap bountifully (II Corinthians 9:6).

So in general the future depends upon the past. And one naturally asks what kind of a future would be indicated by the remote and recent past?

1. *Different Views on Things to Come*

There are different views regarding the future of the world. On the one hand there are those who would admit that there were ups and downs; but would insist that on the whole, progress is being made and that things are getting better. Those holding this view would point to various achievements such as: the span of human life has about doubled in the past century; there is improved communication and transportation, which helps people of the world to understand each other better than was formerly the case; human slavery has largely been abolished; progress is being made in the reduction of exploitation, as well as in the general battle against ignorance, hunger, and disease. And with the United Nations there is even some hope of finally abolishing war as a means of settling international questions and substitute law, courts, and the conference table. This view holds that gradually mankind will learn the foolishness and danger of selfish ways and increasingly come to apply love, justice, and freedom under law in all relationships. Certainly there would be setbacks from time to time, but ultimately society will be ruled by God and His Kingdom will come. All men of peace and goodwill should do what they can to make the world a better place to hand on to future generations.

On the other hand there are those who think that things are going from bad to worse. The "good old days" are in the past and have been replaced by constant world tension threatening atomic warfare. Juvenile and adult delinquency are multiplying in all countries; corruption and decay among people and governments of the world are on the increase; and the way of evil is gaining strength everywhere until the titanic struggle develops between the forces of good and evil in the great and final battle of Armageddon which will take place at the end of the world (Revelation 16:16). Then finally, according to this view, God will intervene with the second coming of Christ who will subdue evil forever and thus inaugurate His Kingdom.

These two views in many respects are poles apart, but both agree that the final victory will be with God and Christ. In this respect these two views greatly differ from a third view that looks upon history as merely repeating itself in a cyclical manner and therefore has no meaning at all, such as the Greek and Indian idea of history would indicate. The Christian Hope looks into the future with confidence and trust in the God and Father of our Lord Jesus Christ who will increasingly reign even on this earth. But how can such different views arise from the same basic conviction?

2. *The Second Coming of Christ*

Christ is reported to have said that after His departure from this earth, He would again return.

> "For the Son of man is to come with his angels in the glory of his Father" (Matthew 16:27). "Immediately after the tribulation . . . they will see the Son of man coming in the clouds of heaven with power and great glory" (Matthew 24:29-30; cf. 25:31 ff.).

As to the time of His coming He is reported to have said that it would occur within the lifetime of the then living generation (Matthew 10:23; 16:28; 24:34). With equal clearness He also said that nothing more definite was known and that even He did not know the exact time himself (Mark 13:32; Matthew 24:36). In other words His coming was near but of unknown date. In the minds of some writers it evidently was associated with the impending destruction of Jerusalem (Matthew 24:26-30). The Synoptics describe His coming in glowing apocalyptic and symbolic language, like some of the Old Testament prophets used.

In the Gospel of John, Jesus speaks of His coming more in a spiritual manner. Sometimes it is the Holy Spirit that is to be present (John 14:16), sometimes it is He himself (18), and sometimes it is the Father and himself (23). He declared that this spiritual presence would begin only after His departure:

> "I will come again and will take you to myself, that where I am you may be also" (14:3). "I will not leave you desolate; I will come to you" (14:18), "I go away, and I will come to you" (28). "A little while, and you will see me no more; again a little while, and you will see me" (16:16). "I will see you again" (16:22).

He also spoke of himself as a judge of men, both present and future (5:22; 9:39; 12:48). In the Fourth Gospel this coming is represented as invisible and spiritual and is to occur when the Holy Spirit comes. In Matthew there are two passages that are similar to this: "Where two or three are gathered in my name, there am I in the midst of them" (18:20), "and lo, I am with you always, to the close of the age" (28:20).

The notion of the physical return of the Messiah was quite in line with the prevailing expectations of the Jews of that day. The disciples naturally shared in this view and interpreted Jesus' words in that light. So the early Church also thought that Jesus would return physically within their lifetime (See Acts 3:19-21; I Thessalonians 4:13-17; I Corinthians 7:25-31; 15:51-52; I Peter 4:7; Hebrews 10:37). Paul, in his early writings, represents both the nature of Christ's return and the time of its occurrence in vivid apocalyptic style and indicates that he expected all this to happen soon (I Thessalonians 4:13-17). This literal interpretation of apocalyptic language has in many quarters given form to the expectation of the Church regarding Christ's return even to our day.

These hopes however were never fulfilled according to the Jewish and early Christian expectations. But the invisible and spiritual presence of Christ in the Holy Spirit took place soon after His departure—on the day of Pentecost. The promise of Jesus "Lo, I am with you always" then began to be fulfilled and has continued ever since. It was in this spiritual way that the Lord Jesus carried on the work for which He came. His Kingdom is not of this world, and His method is not like that expected by the Jews and early Christians. However, our Lord's prediction of Jerusalem's destruction was fulfilled in A.D. 70. He came in the Holy Spirit. He established His Kingdom and has promoted it ever since. The real coming of Christ is not so much a physical event as a spiritual process, begun long ago and still continuing. But of course, it also has physical results as it develops.

3. *The Millennium*

A controversial issue in this area of eschatology is the so-called "millennium." This is thought to be a period of one thousand years at the end of history when, according to the more apocalyptic interpretation, Christ is expected to return to earth in person a second time and with the saints rule the world in righteousness and peace. The idea is based upon a rather obscure passage in Revelation.

> Then I saw an angel coming down from heaven, holding in his hand the key of the bottomless pit and a great chain. And he seized the dragon, that ancient serpent, who is the Devil and Satan, and bound him for a thousand years, and threw him into

the pit, and shut it and sealed it over him, that he should deceive
the nations no more, till the thousand years were ended. After
that he must be loosed a little while. Then I saw thrones, and
seated on them were those to whom judgment was committed.
Also I saw the souls of those who had been beheaded for their
testimony to Jesus and for the word of God, and who had not
worshipped the beast or its image and had not received its mark
on their foreheads or their hands. They came to life again, and
reigned with Christ a thousand years. The rest of the dead did
not come to life again until the thousand years were ended.
This is the first resurrection! Blessed and Holy is he who shares
in the first resurrection! Over such, the second death has no
power, but they shall be priests of God and of Christ, and they
shall reign with him a thousand years (Revelation 20:1-6).

In this passage "a thousand years" is mentioned four times. This
vision obviously gives leeway for various interpretations. Some groups
have become much attached to these verses and emphasize their importance. They eagerly look for a literal, materialistic and even
militaristic fulfillment of this thousand-year rule. Reformation leaders
interpreted this passage in a symbolical way as beginning with Christ's
victory over death. However left-wing Protestants, including some
Anabaptists, interpreted it as a golden age at the end of history. In
more recent times this apocalytic hope has been increasingly substituted by an immanental interpretation of God's rule coming on earth
through the gradual application of Christian and moral insights to
the social order.

During the Reformation it was especially the left-wing Protestants
that were subjected to persecution by Catholics, Lutherans, and Cal-
vinists, as well as by the various state governments. During this time
the militaristic wing of the Anabaptists under the leadership of Mel-
choir Hoffman took this trend. He prophesied that the end of the
world would come in 1533 and that Strassburg would be the New
Jerusalem.

After him the center was shifted to Muenster in North Germany
under the leadership of Jan Matthys and Jan von Leiden who were
even more radical. The Bishop of Muenster opposed the movement
while believers gathered in the city with increasing numbers. Muenster was besieged, great hunger and terrible suffering was the result.
Finally after more than a year the city was taken and the leaders—
von Leiden and Knipperdolling, were captured and sent through
neighboring towns as criminals, tortured and finally hung in cages

on the towers of St. Lambert's church. Here the cages can still be seen today.[1]

Another sad episode of a similar kind took place among the Russian Mennonites. When in 1873-4 many of them migrated from Russia to America because the formerly promised religious liberty, when they came to Russia, was being endangered. A certain chiliastic group decided not to go to America, but set out for Khiva in the middle of Asia where the second coming of Christ was to take place in 1889. Later the date was moved to 1891. After great suffering amidst their Moslem surroundings the disillusioned remaining members of the colony, that once had numbered over one thousand but were now reduced to about 25 persons, gave up this weird speculation and in 1913 came to America.[2]

There are other such sad examples in the history of Christianity. We shall limit ourselves to one more. William Miller (1782-1894) the founder of the Adventist Church found some passages in Ezekiel and the Book of Revelation from which he concluded that the end of the world was coming April 23, 1843. As a gifted preacher he stirred many people and great meetings were held in the New England states. People were convinced he was right. Some gave up their farms, others closed their business.

Immense crowds in New York City gathered at his meetings. Shops were closed and placards were placed in the windows, reading: "This shop is closed in honour of the King of kings, who will appear about the 20th of April. Get ready, friends, to crown Him Lord of All."

But to the great disappointment of many the Lord did not come on April 23, 1843, as Miller had promised. Now he discovered a slight mistake and the new date announced was Oct. 20, 1844. But of course, that was a mistake also and to this day the Lord has not come in any such materialistic and spectacular way.[3]

In the gradual development of Christian thought, three different

---

1. C. Henry Smith, *The Story of the Mennonites*, Mennonite Publication Office, Newton, Ks., Fouth Edition, 1957, pp. 37-39; 69-82; *Mennonite Encyclopedia*, Mennonite Publishing House, Scottdale, Pa., 1956, Vol. II, pp. 778-784; Vol. III, pp. 777-782; C. Krahn, *Dutch Anabaptism*, Martinus Nijhoff, Hague, 1968.

2. C. Henry Smith, *op. cit.*, pp. 456-462; *Mennonite Encyclopedia*, Vol. II, p. 234.

3. Charles Jefferson, *Five Present-Day Controversies*, Fleming H. Revell N.Y., 1924, pp. 35-36.

strains have come to the surface regarding the Millennium: one is
1) known as Pre-Millennialist, that is, the second coming of Christ
would take place before the "thousand years" of His reign. This view
is held by many of the so-called "Fundamentalists." A second view is
2) the Post-Millennialist, holding that the second coming of Christ will
take place after the "thousand years" of His reign. In this case His
reign is usually considered a spiritual one, however also expressing
itself in material ways. Christians, therefore, are to work to establish
His reign in an ever-increasing manner in all areas of individual and
social life as a prerequisite for the "thousand years" of His complete
reign on earth.

3) Then there is a third view called A-Millennialist, (meaning Non-
Millennialist.) This group takes the references to a "thousand years"
in the above passage not so much in a literal, but rather in a symbolical manner. The first two views have been more characteristic of
various Bible Schools, while the Theological Seminaries as a whole
make very little of the millennium. They hold rather to an immanentel
coming of Christ.

The central point of the teaching regarding the second coming is
that conflict with love in this world makes the cross necessary for
Christians as it did for Christ. But that beyond this suffering in love,
is also love's victory. The Christian hope is not merely the expectation
for better times in general, but it is the hope for fulfillment of what
we already know in Christ. There is a goal in the Christian life including its suffering.[4]

4. The Kingdom Present but Also Still Coming

There are two aspects emphasized in the New Testament about
the coming of the Kingdom of God. One strain describes this coming
as sudden and in a rather materialistic and militaristic way. In this
view the Kingdom of God is spoken of as a future event brought
about suddenly by the power of God. This is not a gradual Chris-
tianization of the world but a growing tension between good and evil,
culminating finally in the sudden second coming of Christ in the
clouds and in a physical fashion.

> "Nation will rise against nation, and kingdom against kingdom,
> and there will be famines and earthquakes in various places . . .
> Because wickedness is multiplied, most men's love will grow

---

4. C. H. Dodd, *The Apostolic Preaching,* p. 144; Karl Barth, *Dogmatics in Outline,* p. 132.

cold . . . False Christs and false prophets will arise and show great signs and wonders, so as to lead astray, if possible the elect . . . Then all the tribes of the earth will mourn, and they will see the Son of man coming on the clouds of heaven with power and great glory. . . . But of that day and hour no one knows, not even the angels of heaven, nor the Son, but the Father only . . . Therefore you also must be ready; for the Son of man is coming at an hour you do not expect" (Matthew 24:7-44).

Paul writes in a similar vein and refers to "the man of lawlessness" and "the son of perdition who opposes and exalts himself against every so-called god or object of worship" who will precede the return of Christ (I Thessalonians 4:13-5:11 and II Thessalonians 2:1-11). The book of Revelation elaborates greatly on the increasing chaos on earth and the appearance of the Antichrist before the final victory of God at the battle of Armageddon.

Some have taken these discriptions literally and understood them as a prediction of the future. Attempts have even been made to arrive at the definite dates when these events are to take place. Earthly tyrants from Nero to Hitler and Stalin have been identified with the beast whose number is "six hundred and sixty-six" (Revelation 13:18).

This general line of thought always comes to the forefront during times of great suffering and persecution. The two books in the Bible that become favorites during such periods are the Book of Daniel in the Old Testament and the Book of Revelation in the New Testament. Both deal with the future and the outcome of history and both were written in times of revolution, persecution and great distress.

But there is also an immanental aspect of the Kingdom of God as a present reality and silently growing into greater spiritual maturity. Many of the parables of Jesus about the Kingdom would fall into this class. Here are some quotations from Jesus in support of this view.

"But if it is by the Spirit of God that I cast out demons, then the kingdom of God has come upon you" (Matthew 12:28).
"The kingdom of heaven is like leaven which a woman took and hid in three measures of meal, till it was all leavened" (Matthew 13:33).
". . . The kingdom of God . . . is like a grain of mustard seed, which when sown upon the ground, is the smallest of all the seeds on earth; yet when it is sown it grows up and becomes the greatest of all shrubs, and puts forth large branches, so that the birds of the air can make nests in its shade" (Mark 4:30-32).
"The kingdom of God is not coming with signs to be observed; nor will they say, 'Lo, here it is,' or 'There,' for behold, the kingdom of God is in the midst of you" (Luke 17:20-21).

Although the Kingdom looks small as a grain of mustard seed or a bit of leaven to begin with it will grow and spread until it becomes great. His hearers are exhorted not to watch for signs for the Kingdom will not come with visible signs (Matthew 12:38-39; 16:4). In fact the Kingdom is already in their midst (Luke 17:20-21), and will continue to be, for the risen Christ will remain with them (Matthew 28:20).

This is not only a purely spiritual coming in the hearts of men while the world itself remains unaffected. The new reign of God is evident in history. Things have changed and are changing. The powers of evil have been defeated and a new era has begun. The decisive battle has been fought, although the clean-up campaign is still going on. Hence, an increasing rule of God over human life, until the process is completed, is to be expected. Just as in World War II there was D-day in Europe and V-day in Japan. The decisive turn of the war took place in the former but it was not completed until in the latter. The Kingdom is present but also still to come. This emphasis of Jesus is often repeated in the New Testament.

The two views need not necessarily be considered contradictory with each other. Any movement in history will have both aspects as it develops: sometimes very quietly making steady progress and then there come times of stress and strain culminating in upheaval and great disturbance. These ups and downs, these times of quiet growth and of sudden eruption are different aspects of the same process. A time of disturbance must be followed by a quiet time of consolidation and growth, and vice versa. The Kingdom is present but it is also still coming and this coming implies both aspects of the process as the Lord of History marches on and His Kingdom advances.

5.   Recent Accelerated Changes and the Future

Change is the law of life and the most certain feature about the future is change. Great and far-reaching changes have taken place in our modern world. Although in comparison to the omnipotence, omnipresence, and omniscience, of the Eternal, man is still a very small, weak and limited creature. Nevertheless the revolutions of recent times in power, communication, and transportation, and the increase in knowledge in general are very great and have brought about magnificent changes in many areas of human life.

Formerly the sources of power were limited to beasts, wind, falling water, and tides—while today these sources include steam, electricity, the internal combustion engine, atomic power, and even the solar source of energy. All of which help to lift age-old burdens

BASIC CHRISTIAN CONVICTIONS

of toil from beasts and men. Man is still far from omnipotent, but it is increasingly clear how great the blessing, or the curse, of concentrated power may become in the future, all depending upon how man will use it.

In communication and transportation similar progress has been made. Today one man's words can be heard simultaneously by all men everywhere; the same image, with Telstar, can be transmitted to all viewers at once. Supersonic planes, flying faster than sound, are already carrying human passengers regularly. Astronauts are flying at speeds that make nonsense of day and night measurements of time.

Still far from omniscient, yet the accumulation of knowledge by man in modern times has been tremendous. The rate of growth in this area is staggering. We are told that ninety percent of all the scientists who ever lived are alive today. Still man is aware that the more we know the more conscious we are of the overwhelming amount we do not know. "Let there be light" is the perpetual demand so that truth and love may increasingly change chaos into cosmos, disorder into order, and discord into the music of the spheres. Light is an evocative symbol of the enlightenment that has steadily spread in human experience in the past century and it promises more, yes, much more for the centuries ahead.

Or will this acceleration of knowledge and power gradually subside and things come to a more even keel? Should this increase continue without abatement, the dangers and stresses connected therewith make man anxious and afraid. Or will increase in knowledge gradually also enable man to improve his biological apparatus for living? Can our eyes, ears, hearts and arteries also gradually be made better genetically from the beginning rather than just by doctoring them after they fail in our old age? Plants and animal organisms we have been reshaping into better forms. Can something along that line also be done for and with man?

The problem is not only in the physical area, it is even much more pressing on the social and spiritual front. Can man with God's help, gradually set up social structures that will enable mankind to live in peace without destroying each other? Can man survive the shock of this present roaring waterfall of change? There are those who think that perhaps even now we are approaching an era when this rapid change will of necessity automatically slow down.

We have been isolated human beings, selfish, combative, ignorant and helpless; but in recent times the processes of knowledge and technology have been pressing us into powerful, prosperous national groupings demanding increasing tolerance, vision, choice, and the planning for a more coordinated human kind. Increasing communication and interaction are at last, under God, forcing nations to make a beginning in deliberating and designing the future development of mankind with a growing confidence in its future. Ancient attitudes and social structures have been burst asunder and if we fail to adjust in time we may all be destroyed.

Dr. John R. Platt uses various metaphors to describe the situation. Just as the youngster makes the critical transitions from crawling to standing, to walking, to running, to tricycle, to bicycle, to motorcycle, to automobile, to airplane—so mankind has gone through various crises of shockingly rapid changes which have destroyed former attitudes and structures. These changes cannot go on indefinitely at an increasing pace and even now they are converging to a limit in many areas. As the butterfly is implicit in the caterpillar so recent developments are pressing us toward a more coordinated human-kind. To give a better understanding of this possible transformation, Platt writes:[5]

> If two billion years of life are represented by that 200-foot height of, say, Rockefeller Chapel at Chicago, the million years of man make a one-inch block on top of the chapel. The 20,000 years of agriculture make a thick postage stamp on top of that, and the 400 years of science make the ink on top of the postage stamp. Now, suddenly, we see what all this has been building up to; and it is about to come within a single generation or two—that is, in the thickness of the film of moisture on top of the ink on the postage stamp. In that short time we will move, if we survive the strain, to a wealthy and powerful and coordinated world society reaching across the solar system, a society that might find out how to keep itself alive and evolving for thousands or millions or billions of years, a time as long as all of evolution past. It is a tremendous prospect. Hardly anyone has seen the enormous sweep and restructuring and unity and future of it except perhaps dreamers like H. G. Wells or Teilhard de Chardin. It is a quantum jump. It is a new state of matter. The act of saving ourselves, if it succeeds, will make us participants in the most incredible event in evolution. It is the step to Man.

If man is wise and, under God, learns to understand his own nature

---

5. John R. Platt, *The Step to Man,* John Wiley & Sons, Inc., New York, 1966, p. 203. See also: A. Toffler, *Future Shock,* Random House, 1970. C. A. Reich, *The Greening of America,* Random House, 1970.

and divine purposes sufficiently to reconstruct and control the present dangers threatening him, he may yet develop coordinating forms that will not only preserve him but also be helpful for future progress. The World Council of Churches, the United Nations, and other world organizations, as also the 1972 Summit Meetings at Peking and Moscow are promising indications of mankind beginning deliberate designs of development with increasing confidence in the choice and creation of their own future. All this reminds one of John's vision when he says:

> Then I saw a new heaven and a new earth; for the first heaven and the first earth had passed away . . . and I heard a great voice from the throne saying, "Behold, the dwelling of God is with men. He will dwell with them, and they shall be his people, and God himself will be with them; . . . for the former things have passed away.". . . "Behold I make all things new." (Revelation 21:1-5).

6. *Summary and Conclusion*

In this section on *The Christian Hope for the Future of this World,* we have discussed: Different Views on Things to Come; The Millennium; The Kingdom Present but Also Still Coming; and Accelerated Recent Changes and the Future.

The Hebrew-Christian view of history is that it has a beginning, a purposive process and a goal. From the Christian point of view, Jesus Christ is the center and His Kingdom is the goal of history. He taught His followers to pray "Thy kingdom come, Thy will be done on earth as it is in heaven" (Matthew 6:10). His last command was, "Go therefore and make disciples of all nations" (Matthew 28: 19).

The realization of this vision calls for a long and steady advance of Christ's Kingdom, which is already at hand but also still to come. It is a misinterpretation for Christians to speak of the absent Lord. He is the present Lord, reigning now in His Spiritual Kingdom. Placing the coming of Christ mainly in the future, has drawn attention away from His desire to fill all of life here and now with His Spirit and dominion.

The apostles who knew Jesus best, were nevertheless men of their own age. They could only receive His truth into minds in which the thoughts of their own age also had influence. Here indeed lay their power and strength, for only this fact enabled them to influence their age and send that influence on to our age. The glory of the first disciples is not in the minute correctness of their conceptions on all matters, but in their spiritual fellowship with Christ their Lord and Master.

Even politically we are only very gradually coming to understand that

> There can be no national security without world peace; no world peace without international justice; no international justice without world law; and no effective world law without institutions to make, interpret and enforce it. Only by substituting processes of law for armed conflict can there be peace. It is not necessary for man to be doomed to die by his own hand. Problems created by man can be solved by man. The will of man to live at peace with his fellows can prevail.[6]

Not only are we still far from the goal of a peaceful world but this is also true of needed food, education, health, and every other area of life. However, the Spirit of God is working in individuals and society and His Kingdom is marching on. Slow as this may seem to be, we are gradually coming to realize that it is our mission to help things move in the right direction. Perfection cannot be expected on earth but growth and improvement can and should be.

Regarding this age-old question of the future we must remember, that this world is only the cradle of souls, where nothing comes to perfection; that life is short and human beings are weak and imperfect; that life is complex and victory of the good over evil very complicated; that so far, many people have not even heard of Christ's first coming, and that even if all men would accept Him that would only be the beginning of the long process of the growing Kingdom. Hence complete victory can only be in the far distant future.

On the other hand we must remember that God Almighty is avowedly and visibly working with His people for the advancement of Christ's Kingdom; that Jesus has bidden us to pray, "Thy kingdom come, thy will be done on earth as it is in heaven"; that God gave His Son for the redemption of the world and that "He is marching on"; that the Kingdom of Christ is a missionary project, working from person to person and from group to group; that human experience is disciplinary, and that the struggle between good and evil helps to develop the conscience of the world in preparation for the better; that new times develop new methods and open possibilities for new advances; that God in Christ and the Holy Spirit is here to awaken and renew; that the Gospel "is the power of God for salvation to

---

6. United World Federalists, Inc., *Bulletin,* October, 1968.

every one who has faith" (Romans 1:16); and that the Kingdom of Christ is the glory of God and the crown of humanity, and therefore we should "be steadfast, immovable, always abounding in the work of the Lord, knowing that in the Lord your labor is not in vain" (I Corinthians 15:58).[7] The end of this world we must leave to God who, in His wisdom and love will bring creation to its final consummation after it has served the purpose for which it was brought into being.

B.   THE CHRISTIAN HOPE FOR PERSONAL LIFE AFTER DEATH

Jesus promised, "I will come again and take you to myself, that where I am you may be also" (John 14:3). We know very little about life after death. It therefore is of great help to begin with the above words of Jesus. This is an area of faith and hope. Sometimes people assume that they know something concerning which real knowledge in this life is unattainable. Hence in this area we speak of "hope," for actual knowledge here lies beyond our experience. Nevertheless the Christian revelation speaks in terms of realities, and our own moral and spiritual nature makes some deeply felt assertions. Furthermore Jesus Christ also shed light on the future life that greatly strengthens the faith of His followers.

1.   *Death, and Life Thereafter*

Death is the cessation of the physical life. At death the vital process of physical life ceases and disintegration and decay of the organism begins. Death ends all, so far as living in the body is concerned. It closes life in this earthly environment. Physical activities are ended when death occurs. Death is sure and universal. Finally all of us must meet the reality symbolized by the skeleton and the sickle. Death compels thinking human beings to choose between despair and faith.

Modern science has greatly enlarged man's concept of the universe and thereby tended to decrease the importance of man. Yet, the causes which first led to the rise of the belief in an after-life still exist. Man is still conscious of capacities and ideals for which the brief span of this life allows no satisfaction. There is still that sense of justice demanding some adjustment of the inequalities that are so evident in this life. And there is still the religious experience of a person's communion with God that warrants hope and gives promise

---

7. W. H. Clarke, *Outline of Christian Theology*, pp. 447-448.

of more complete fellowship to come. Then, too, even the enlarged concept of the universe may also serve to exalt, and need not necessarily belittle, the being who is the crown of creation and was made in the image of God himself.

There is air for the wings of the birds, water for the fish to swim in, light-waves so the eye can see, sound-waves so the ear can hear. Why should it be incredible for the moral and spiritual aspirations of man to be satisfied by life after death?

Paul, on trial before his accusers and King Agrippa, asks, "Why is it thought incredible by any of you that God raises the dead?" (Acts 26:8). Why indeed should this be incredible when we believe in God and are aware of the many wonders He has done and is doing in nature and history? Why should future life be incredible when we consider the potentialities of the human spirit? The extent of the trip planned for an airplane is to some extent indicated by the amount of fuel it carries - ten gallons or one hundred gallons would have different implications as to the extent of the proposed trip.

Man is a self-conscious being that asks himself: Where do I come from? Why am I here? Where am I going? and, What can I do to determine my direction? Or, think of the universe in this space age - how grand, and wonderful, and immense it all is. And yet is not the human being, that can at least in part grasp the universe, more wonderful than the universe itself of which he also is a part? Physically speaking, man compared to the universe seems insignificant, but spiritually or even mentally, is not the astronomer of greater significance than the universe, which he can at least partly understand and areas of which he can manipulate?

Tennyson's "In Memoriam," puts it thus:

> Thou willt not leave us in the dust; Thou madest man, he knows not why; He thinks he was not made to die; and thou hast made him: thou art just.

2. *Immortality, Resurrection and Eternal Life*

(a) *Immortality* of the soul has long been a belief of mankind. Primitive man understands dreams as being gone from the body and returning when he awakens; so he is gone in death but does not return. In some primitive cultures, houses, servants, clothing, and other items are burned at burial and so sent along with the deceased for his use in the beyond. Later these items to burn are made of paper. Every so often food is brought to the grave for the benefit of the spirit "over there." The pyramids of Egypt are evidence of belief in immortality.

Faith in immortality of the soul was especially strong among the

Greeks. In the dialogue called the *Phaedo,* Plato (427-347 B.C.) sets out logically to prove it. The body was considered the greatest obstacle to thought and peace. Death was looked upon as release of the soul. Various arguments for immortality are set forth. One is based on the fact of human reminiscenses. According to this some knowledge comes not from learning but from remembering experiences from pre-existence; and pre-existence implies post-existence.

Another argument is based on the aspiration of the soul for another life. The soul longs to be free of the body and fly to God. These immortal longings are taken as evidence of immortality. A further argument is the moral need for retribution and justice. God is just and so there must be another life to even things out. Hence no real evil can befall a good man in life or death, for God is good and just. The *Phaedo* dialogue is especially impressive when we remember that here Plato is repeating the arguments Socrates (469-399) used after he was condemned to die.

In later times many philosophers argued for or against immortality. One of the modern arguments in favor is called the teleological argument. The universe is considered reasonable and has a *telos,* an end and purpose in it. Immanuel Kant (1724-1804) held that obedience to the moral law is the highest good, but in this life it is not completely attainable. Hence the complete good (union of virtue and happiness) can only be realized in the future life. In this life man can never become what reason says he ought to become, and what he is meant to become; therefore another life is necessary so man may complete his *telos,* his end. Man's potentiality cannot be fully realized in this life, so immortality is necessary.

(b) *Resurrection,* or dying and living again, is a Hebrew concept. It took some time to develop this. Early Hebrew writers lament:

> in death there is no remembrance of thee; in Sheol who can give thee praise? (Ps. 6:5; cf. 30:9) As for man his days are like grass, he flourishes, like a flower of the field; for the wind passes over it, and it is gone and its place knows it no more (Ps. 103: 15, 16).

Later Hebrew writers speak of death in more hopeful terms for the righteous, and punishment for the evil:

> "Thy dead shall live, their bodies shall rise, O dwellers of the dust, awake and sing for joy!" (Is. 26:19). "And many of those who sleep in the dust of the earth shall awake, some to everlasting life, and some to shame and everlasting contempt" (Daniel 12:2).

Here one must not forget Job who asks the question "If a man die, shall he live again?" (Job 14:14), and then answers his own question:

> "For I know that my Redeemer lives, and at last he will stand upon the earth; and after my skin has been thus destroyed, then without my flesh I shall see God, whom I shall see on my side, and my eyes shall behold, and not another" (Job 19:25-27).

In Jewish apocalyptic literature the resurrection is considered universal and associated with the coming of the Messiah and the establishment of the Kingdom. The resurrection was one of the distinctive beliefs of the Pharisees as well as the hope of other devout Israelites in Jesus' day. From the Jews it passed over to early Christianity and furnished the form in which this Christian hope first found expression.

Some primitive peoples buried their dead facing west for they had seen their last sunset. They put markings of a human skull and crossbones upon the grave, indicating that this was the hopeless end. On the other hand the early Christians buried their dead facing east, awaiting the sunrise and the dawn of eternity. Easter lilies were placed in the hands of those to be buried, representing eternal spring.

Early Christians seem to have had different views as to what happens immediately after death. Some thought after death there was a time of sleep for the soul before the resurrection. Jesus refers to Lazarus as having fallen asleep (John 11:11). At the crucifixion we are told that "many bodies of the saints who had fallen asleep were raised" (Matt. 27:52). Paul speaks of the Corinthian dead as having fallen asleep (I Cor. 11:30; 15:6, 20). To the Thessalonians Paul also writes about the dead "who are asleep" (I Thess. 4:13-14).

A second view was that of Millenarianism based on Revelation 20, which held that the end of the world will come in two stages. First will be the resurrection of the martyrs who died for their faith. This will last for a thousand years, a millennium, when the Devil will be bound and the saints with Christ will reign. At the end of it the Devil will be released for one final and last conflict after which he will be thrown into the lake of fire. Then will come the general resurrection, the final judgment and separation of good and evil, one going to everlasting blessedness and the other to everlasting punishment. There were those in the early church, and there are those today, who take all this literally, in materialistic and military terms.

A third view was that there is a long period of time between death and the final resurrection and judgment. When Jesus says "In my Father's house there are many rooms" (John 14:2), this can also be translated "many stages," or stations on a journey, which leaves room for progress from one to the other. The Church Father Origen made much of this. Purgatory as a place and time for purification and improvement would also fit in here.[8] The general idea back of this is that no one is good enough at death to go to heaven, nor bad enough to go to hell, and so needs this longer in-between place and time for final decision.

A fourth view was that immediately upon death, with no intermediate state at all, the soul passes at once either to blessedness or shame. To the penitent thief on the cross Jesus says "today you will be with me in Paradise" (Luke 23:43). Paul expresses the desire to depart and be with Christ (Philippians 1:23). "Man must die and after that comes the judgment" (Hebrews 9:27). Here and now we are surrounded by a cloud of witnesses (Heb. 12:1). Paul insists that nothing in life or death can separate us from the love of God in Christ (Romans 8:38,39). These passages seem to indicate no time in between but rather that here and hereafter the Christian lives in the presence of the Lord.

(c) *Eternal Life* is often spoken of in the New Testament. This concept is a bit different from *immortality,* meaning that man never dies, or *resurrection*, meaning that man dies but is again brought to life in the beyond. *Eternal life,* on the other hand is both the promise and the gift of God (Titus 1:2; I John 2:25; 5:11; Romans 6:25). It is altogether bound up with Jesus Christ. It is the free gift of God in Christ Jesus (Romans 6:23; I John 5:11). To the Samaritan woman Jesus says that the water He gives becomes "a spring of water welling up to eternal life" (John 4:14). He is the food that gives eternal life (John 6:27, 54). His words are words of eternal life (John 17:2) but He is eternal life (I John 5:21).

This eternal life comes to us through different channels. It comes through knowledge. "Eternal life is to know God and Jesus Christ whom God has sent" (John 17:3). This means not only to know about Him, but to know Him through fellowship and experience. It also comes through believing or committing ourselves to Him (John 3:15, 16; 5:24; 6:40, 47; I John 5:13; I Timothy 1:16). Our knowledge of Christ comes from personal experience and fellowship with Him, and then accept Him and His claims and believe Him, that is, commit the whole of our life to Him.

---

8. William Barclay, *The Apostles Creed for Every Man,* Harper, 1967, p. 371.

Eternal life is a gift but it also makes certain demands on man. *The first demand* is obedience (John 12:50; Heb. 5:9). The sick cannot get well unless they obey the physician. A person cannot find eternal life unless he is obedient to the Lord of life. *Secondly,* it demands loyalty (I Timothy 6:12; John 10:27, 28). To find eternal life we must link our life with that of Jesus Christ and the consequences of this may not be easy and demand suffering. *A third demand* is an ethical life. It comes to those who are "patient in well doing" (Rom. 2:7; 6:22). It cannot come to one who hates his brother (I John 3: 5). It comes only to those who keep themselves in the love of God (Jude 21). Eternal life is the good life and no one can share it without complying with the ethical demands of the love of God. Eternal life is not found by hoarding life but by spending it for others, not seeking life but losing it for others (John 12:25). This life of God is a gift but it also has its own demands that must be satisfied by man.

So it is in terms of ETERNAL LIFE, rather than mere immortality or resurrection, that the Christian thinks about the life to come. It is clear that we need not wait for it until we are dead but that we can possess it here and now. In this world of space and time we can enter into that relationship with God which is eternal. Human relationships can be broken, but when we enter into a relationship with God and do our part, it cannot be broken because God is love. There is no need to think of a long or short sleep or interim period. It just goes on from here to there.

Jesus Christ made mankind aware, in a new sense, of the value of human personality. This puts the emphasis upon moral and spiritual kinship of man with God. Jesus himself based His confidence in His own victory over death upon His experience of sonship to God the Father. Surely such a life as His could not have gone out in darkness.

Jesus often spoke about life after death. When the Sadducees, who did not believe in the resurrection, came to ask Him whose wife, in the next life, the woman would be, who had seven husbands in this life

> Jesus answered them, "You are wrong, because you know neither the scriptures nor the power of God. For in the resurrection they neither marry nor are given in marriage . . . And as for the resurrection of the dead, have you not read . . . 'I am the God of Abraham, and the God of Isaac, and the God of Jacob'? He is not God of the dead, but of the living" (Matthew 22:29-33).

And again when He spoke of being the good shepherd,

> "My sheep hear my voice, and I know them, and they follow me; and I give them eternal life, and they shall never perish, and no one shall snatch them out of my hand" (John 10:27, 28).

And again in connection with the death of Lazarus,

> "I am the resurrection and the life, he who believes in me, though he die, yet shall he live, and whoever lives and believes in me shall never die" (John 11:25, 26).

And again:

> "And when I go to prepare a place for you, I will come again and will take you to myself, that where I am you may be also . . . I will not leave you desolate; I will come to you. Yet a little while and the world will see me no more, but you will see me; because I live, you will live also" (John 14:3, 18, 19).

Jesus encouraged His followers to put their trust in God.

> "If you then, who are evil, know how to give good gifts to your children, how much more will your Father who is in heaven give good things to those who ask him?" (Matthew 7:11).

Is it conceivable that He will send them into the final dark night of nothingness? It is the quality of the new life in Christ here on earth experienced by Christians that makes eternal life a reality to them. Jesus himself lived victoriously and it is He that "brought life and immortality to light through the gospel" (II Timothy 1:10).

When the disciples returned from the successful missionary journey in which they subdued the powers of evil in which they greatly rejoiced, Jesus reminds them

> "Nevertheless do not rejoice in this, that the spirits are subject to you; but rejoice that your names are written in heaven" (Luke 10:20).

Some of Jesus' sayings quoted above about eternal life imply that resurrection takes place at death. Such words as: "they shall never perish" (John 10:28), or "whoever lives and believes in me shall never die" (John 11:26) or "because I live, you will live also" (John 14:19) or "He is not God of the dead but of the living" (Matthew 22:32), indicate that death for the Christian is similar to the caterpillar emerging as butterfly. Death for the Christian is really resurrection for he already has eternal life.

One difficulty with this view is that resurrection usually, if not always, refers to resurrection of the body, but we know that after death the body disintegrates and decays. The answer to this objection is that the word "body" stood for personality, as when we speak of some-body, no-body, any-body, every-body, we mean personality and not merely the physical body. Barclay points out that the Greek has no word for our English word "personality" but that "body" meant the total personality.

Paul's doctrine of the resurrection was very unlike the Pharisaic doctrine in which he grew up. They believed in a literal and carnal resurrection of the same body laid down in death. Paul expressly denies this and says there will be a spiritual body, incorruptible and glorious. He speaks of the resurrection of Christians as very closely associated with his idea of the resurrection of Christ himself.

> Now if Christ is preached as raised from the dead, how can some of you say that there is no resurrection of the dead? But if there is no resurrection of the dead, then Christ has not been raised; if Christ has not been raised, then our preaching is in vain and your faith is in vain. We are even found to be misrepresenting God, because we testified of God that he raised Christ, whom he did not raise if it is true that the dead are not raised. For if the dead are not raised, then Christ has not been raised. If Christ has not been raised, then your faith is futile and you are still in your sins. Then those who have fallen asleep in Christ have perished. If in this life we who are in Christ have only hope, we are of all men most to be pitied . . .
>
> But some one will ask, "How are the dead raised? With what kind of a body do they come?" You foolish man! What you sow does not come to life unless it dies. And what you sow is not the body which is to be, but a bare kernel, perhaps of wheat or of some other grain . . . It is sown a physical body, it is raised a spiritual body . . . I tell you this, brethren; flesh and blood cannot inherit the kingdom of God, nor does the perishable inherit the imperishable . . . For this perishable nature must put on the imperishable, and this mortal nature must put on immortality . . . then shall come to pass the saying that is written: "Death is swallowed up in victory. O death, where is thy victory? O death, where is thy sting?" . . . But thanks be to God, who gives us the victory, through our Lord Jesus Christ (I Corinthians 15:12-19; 35-37, 44, 50, 53-57).

And again:

> But we would not have you ignorant, brethren, concerning those who are asleep, that you may not grieve as others do who have no hope. For since we believe that Jesus died and rose again even so, through Jesus God will bring with him those who have fallen asleep (I Thessalonians 4:13-14).

And again:

> For we know that if the earthly tent we live in is destroyed, we have a building from God, a house not made with hands, eternal in the heavens. Here indeed we groan, and long to put on our heavenly dwelling, so that by putting it on we may not be found naked. For while we are still in this tent, we sigh with anxiety, not that we should be unclothed, but that we would be further clothed, so that what is mortal may be swallowed up by life.

He who has prepared us for this very thing is God, who has given us the Spirit as a guarantee (II Corinthians 5:1-5).

In the Christian faith the origin and destiny of man belong together. The Christian view of man culminates in life after death. This idea of eternal life for the Christian is one member of a family of ideas that all hang together: God, a friendly universe, the worth of human personality, Jesus Christ, the Holy Spirit, prayer, the Kingdom, the Church, the Bible, Eternal Life—they all hang together, let one go and they all go. But Jesus Christ is the center and foundation of it all. He lived, died, and rose again, victoriously. As Paul puts it, "our Savior Christ Jesus, who abolished death and brought life and immortality to light through the Gospel" (II Timothy 1:10).

3. The Final Judgment

Much of the language about judgment in the Bible refers to a process that goes on in this world. There is a testing and dividing of men according to their character. There is a judgment between good and evil in this life, but there is also a judgment to come, pointed out in the Scriptures. "It is appointed for men to die once, and after that comes the judgment" (Hebrews 9:27).

The judgment set forth in the Scriptures is one in which God determines our future destiny righteously, in accordance with the life that we have lived. Christ indicates that our destiny will be assigned according to the spirit of our previous conduct (Matthew 22:31-46). God is said to judge men by Christ and in Christ (Romans 2:16; Acts 17:31; John 5:27). In Christ, God's requirement upon men is brought near and is illustrated. To Him God committed the administration of the Kingdom; He therefore, is the proper person to execute the divine judgment. This means that Christ is the standard by comparison with which the character of men is to be estimated. The law of His Kingdom is to be the test of the conduct of men by which their moral state is to be determined.

The application of the life of Christ in the flesh, as the test of judgment is illustrated in the great parable of judgment told by Jesus (Matthew 25:31-46). He said that men would be judged by the law of love, which is His own characteristic law. In this parable He points out that those who have done the works of love will be accepted, and the others will be rejected. Christ illustrated His law of love in His life and death and preached it in His gospel. The test of judgment corresponds to the nature of the Kingdom, and the nature of the Kingdom corresponds to the nature of the King, Jesus Christ.

God does not change. The same God who has created mankind, governed and sought to save mankind through Jesus Christ will also be the final judge. Christ is the true expression of God's eternal character, and the standard of judgment will be Christlike love. It is inexpressibly solemn but also very reassuring that it is our heavenly Father, who in Jesus Christ will righteously judge His children. Judgment is awe inspiring because life is serious and the moral issues of life are very important.

Heaven and Hell used to be spoken of as places; one "up there" and the other "down there." In this space age we are coming to think of them more as a "condition" rather than merely a place. A "condition" a person finds himself in already in this life as a result of his character. Jesus spoke of heaven and also of hell, and even in terms of "eternal fire" (Matthew 10:28; 18:9; 25:41; Luke 12:5; Mark 9:45-48). Evidently He thought of both, heaven and hell, as realities resulting from one's way of life. Whether these realities are conceived of literally as physical places or spiritual conditions spoken of symbolically, in either case, these terms point to the seriousness of decisions regarding moral issues of life as these have far-reaching consequences, both here and hereafter.[9]

Here brief mention should be made of various doctrines that have arisen in connection with the Judgment which are intended to reduce the harsher aspects of eternal punishment. Among such doctrines would come *conditional immortality, absolute annihilation* of the wicked, the idea of *purgatory,* and *universalism.*

The doctrine of *conditional immortality* holds that man was not created immortal but is capable of receiving immortality as a gift. If left alone he would become extinct. According to this view the continuance of personality is not the portion of all men but only of those who have attained or received and accepted this gift of God through Christ. Others, which apparently would include the great majority of mankind, would fall back into nothingness.

The doctrine of *annihilation* holds that the penalty for sin terinates in personal extinction. The extinction of personal existence would be the natural end of a life in which sin runs its full course. By sin man gradually reduces himself to nonentity. This law is considered self-executing, if not in this life then in the next. As punish-

---

9. The popular picture of hell comes from the Greek word Gehenna, the ever burning junk-pile outside of Jerusalem in the Valley of Hinnom. For detailed discussion see Barclay, *op cit.,* pp. 207-210.

ment for sin the unrepentant person in the hereafter will, of course, suffer punishment and gradually end in extinction, according to this view.

The question of *purgatory,* or if there is a state between the time of death and the resurrection and judgment has been widely debated. If the scriptural teaching that in God there is no time, is taken seriously the problem disappears. God is

> the same yesterday and today and forever (Hebrews 13:8). A thousand years in thy sight are but as yesterday when it is past, or as a watch in the night (Psalm 90:4). But do not ignore this one fact, beloved, that with the Lord, one day is as a thousand years, and a thousand years as one day (II Peter 3:8).

We must not project human time into our God concept and so subject Him to the limitations of the human concept of time. Time is a creation of God—it had a beginning and will have an end. This is what Christian eschatology is all about.

At death man is confronted by the living God. He faces eternity the moment he dies and is judged at once—that is, he is placed in the next world where he belongs. This eliminates the idea of purgatory as a state in between when and where the human soul is purged and prepared for fellowship with God. Whatever Paul may mean by "being baptized on behalf of the dead" (I Corinthians 15:29), Protestants reject the notion of purgatory. This rejection was one of the live issues that brought on the Reformation. Protestants hold that fellowship with God is solely the result of God's grace and does not in any way depend upon prayers, baptism, or gifts of the living on behalf of the dead.

Universalism teaches that finally salvation is for all men. Anything less, it is held, would be a defeat for God and therefore, in the long run, God in His wisdom, goodness, and power will save all men here or hereafter. However, fellowship with God is a personal relationship. This personal relationship can, therefore, also be rejected by man. Forcing it upon man would abolish him as a free being. Hell is the result of rejecting and refusing God. However, Universalism holds that God's love will finally bring all men to Him. He, as Father, will not be satisfied until all His children come home.[10]

These ideas of *conditional immortality, complete annihilation, purgatory,* and *universalism* have entered human thought as possi-

---

10. Barclay, *op cit.,* chapter 21.

bilities of hope rather than fear. They have been welcomed by some for the relief they offer from the awful idea of eternal punishment. Any one of them, it is argued, would be considered a blessing if the only alternative were unending suffering and misery.

4. *Characteristics of the Life in Paradise*

If it is correct to think that resurrection and judgment follow death immediately, then man goes directly from his life here to his life beyond and enters at once into its realities. The life beyond is a life of the spirit. Will action there be as truly moral, personal, and responsible as action in this life? If man is still to be man, must he not also still be a responsible being? The New Testament indicates that the following conditions will obtain over there.

(a) *Jesus Christ will be there* and be the center of things.

> For now we see in a mirror dimly, but then face to face. Now I know in part; then I shall understand fully, even as I have been fully understood (I Corinthians 13:12), we are God's children now; it does not yet appear what we shall be, but we know that when he appears we shall be like him, for we shall see him as he is (I John 3:2).

(b) It will be a fully *conscious life*. In the parable of the rich man and poor Lazarus we note that the past is remembered and the rich man saw and knew Lazarus. He was even concerned for those left behind (Luke 16:19-31).

(c) *Suffering and Pain will be ended for the saved.*

> They shall hunger no more, neither thirst any more; the sun shall not strike them, nor any scorching heat. For the Lamb in the midst of the throne will be their shepherd, and he will guide them to springs of living water; and God will wipe away every tear from their eyes (Revelation 7:16-17).

(d) The *element of sex* will not be present. When the Sadducees asked Jesus whose wife, the woman who had seven husbands, would be over there; Jesus answered "in the resurrection they neither marry nor are given in marriage" (Matthew 22:30). Sex is out.

(e) It will be a *social life* not mere existence, but victorious living. The author of Hebrews speaks of "being surrounded by so great a cloud of witnesses" (Hebrews 12:1). And Jesus says to the penitent criminal on the cross "Truly, I say to you, today you will be with me in Paradise" (Luke 23:43).

(f) It will be a *happy situation*. Jesus said "Let not your hearts be troubled . . . In my Father's house are many rooms . . . I will come again and take you to myself, that where I am you may be also" (John 14:1-3). Like going home, the happy occasion is beyond description. "What no eye has seen, nor ear heard, nor the heart of man conceived . . . God has prepared for those who love him" (I Corinthians 2:9).

(g) *Activity and growth* will characterize the life there. Certainly one-third of all persons born, die without having lived long enough to become decidedly good or bad and arrive over there as beginners. The Christian faith leads us to believe that they enter the other world in the care of our heavenly Father. Christ said, "let the children come to me, and do not hinder them; for to such belongs the kingdom of heaven" (Matthew 19:14; Mark 10:14; Luke 18:16). As infants come to maturity they need help and guidance and this may afford opportunity over there for more mature Christians to be of service. And how about the many in all parts of the world who never had an opportunity to hear even of the first coming of Jesus? Is it not reasonable to suppose that, just as children, they also will have an opportunity to learn and grow spiritually? And here also would be an opportunity for wonderful activity for more mature Christians to be of help and service.

(h) But *separation* will be there also. A life that God approves as rightly lived or rightly begun, acceptable to Him in Christ, goes to its characteristic results in fellowship with Christ. And a life that God disapproves as sinful will and heart, set upon evil, goes to its characteristic results. These two, beyond death continue in a great separation. We read of the rich man and Lazarus:

> "between us and you a great chasm has been fixed. In order that those who would pass from here to you may not be able, and none may cross from there to us" (Luke 16:26).

This "chasm has been fixed," no doubt, by different living patterns pursued in this life.

This raises the question of the finality of the future life, or will moral change be possible? Christian thought today is inclined toward the possibility of greater freedom in the future life than was once the case. Some of the New Testament writers seemingly also hinted at this possibility (I Peter 3:18-20; 4:6). And it is asked, why should not punishment bring about a change? Would not correction rather than mere vengeance seem to be the Christ-like purpose of punishment? (See John 12:32; Romans 5:12-21; Philippians 2:9-11; I Corinthians 15:28.) However, Jesus said a "chasm has been fixed"

(Luke 16:26). The church has long considered the idea of a possible change after death as dangerous.

5. *Summary and Conclusion*

In this section on the *Christian Hope for Personal Life after Death* we have briefly discussed Death, and Life Thereafter; Immortality, Resurrection, and Eternal Life; The Judgment; and Characteristics of the Life beyond. We remind ourselves again that we know very little about the future but nevertheless are privileged to share the Christian Hope in Christ Jesus. Christians are convinced that the life in Christ is the "life indeed," laid hold of on earth, but experienced in its fulness only in the world beyond (I Timothy 6:19).

Paul writes with confidence:

> What then shall we say to this? If God is for us, who is against us? He who did not spare his own Son but gave him up for us all, will he not, also give us all things with him? . . . . who is to condemn? . . . Is it Christ Jesus who died, yes, who was raised from the dead, who is at the right hand of God, who indeed intercedes for us? Who shall separate us from the love of Christ? Shall tribulation, or distress, or persecution, or famine, or nakedness, or peril, or sword? . . . No, in all these things we are more than conquerors through him who loved us. For I am sure that neither death, nor life, nor angels, nor principalities, nor things present, nor things to come, nor powers, nor height, nor depth, nor anything else in all creation, will be able to separate us from the love of God in Christ Jesus our Lord (Romans 8:31-39).

To the Thessalonians Paul writes: "And so we shall always be with the Lord" (I Thess. 4:17), and Jesus promised: "I will come again and will take you to myself, that where I am you may be also" (John 14:3).

FOR FURTHER READING ON THE CHRISTIAN HOPE

A. ON THE FUTURE OF THIS WORLD

Aurobindo, S., *The Future Evolution of Man,* Humanities Pr., 1971.

Bennett, J. C., *Social Salvation,* Scribners, 1933.

Boros, L., *Living in Hope,* Herder, 1970.

Castel, H., ed., *World Development,* Macmillan, 1971.

Dodd, C. H., *The Coming of Christ,* Cambridge Un., 1954.

Facre, G., *The Rainbow-Sign,* Eerdmans, 1969.

Fulbright, J. W., *The Pentagon Propaganda Machine,* Liveright, 1970.

Kahn & Weiner, *The Year 2000,* Macmillan, 1967.

Keys & Allen, ed., *God and The H-Bomb,* Random House, 1961.

Minear, P. S., *The Christian Hope and Second Coming,* Westminster, 1954.

Moltmann, Juergen, *Theology of Hope,* Harper, 1967.

Musser, F., *Christ and the World's End,* Notre Dame Pr., 1971.

Niebuhr, Reinhold, *Faith and History,* Scribners, 1949.

O'Collins, G., *Man and His New Hopes,* Herder, 1969.

Pauling, Linus, *No More War,* Dodd-Mead, 1958.

Pohle, J., *Eschatology,* Greenwood, 1971.

Schweitzer, A., *Peace or Atomic War?* Henry Holt, 1968.

Teller & Latter, *Our Nuclear Future,* Criterion Pr., 1958.

Reich, C. H., *The Greening of America,* Random House, 1970.

Rosenstock-Heusy, E., *The Christian Future,* Scribners, 1946.

Siwek, P., *The Enigma of the Future,* Phil. Library, 1952.

Williams, J. G., *Christian Faith and the Space Age,* World Pub., 1968.

B. ON THE FUTURE LIFE AFTER DEATH

Baillie, John, *And the Life Everlasting,* Scribners, 1933.

Benoit, P., ed., *Immortality and Resurrection,* Herder, 1970.

Berkof, H., *Well-Founded Hope,* John Knox, 1968.

Braaten, C. E., *The Future of God,* Harper, 1969.

Brunner, E., *The Eternal Hope,* Westminster, 1954.

Edlemann, L. H., *Last Things,* Zondervan, 1969.

Friend, N. E., *The Tapestry of Eternity,* Phil. Lib., 1954.

Grishan, E. W., *Our Home for Eternity,* Carlton, 1970.

Hendrikson, W., *Bible on Life Hereafter,* Baker Bk., 1971.

Jenson, R. W., *Knowledge of Things Hoped For,* Oxford, 1969.

Kantonen, T. A., *Life After Death,* Fortress, 1962.

Pieper, J., *Death and Immortality,* Herder, 1969.

Standahl, C., ed., *Immortality and Resurrection,* Macmillan, 1965.

Trueblood, E., *The Future of the Christian,* Harper, 1970.

THE CHRISTIAN HOPE FOR THE FUTURE

CHAPTER X

THE CHRISTIAN LIFE

"You shall be my witnesses in Jerusalem and in all Judea and Samaria and to the end of the earth" (Acts 1:8).

THE WORD "CHRISTIAN" APPEARS ONLY THREE TIMES IN THE NEW Testament. The author of Acts writes:

And a great number that believed turned to the Lord . . . For a whole year they met with the church, and taught a large company of people; and in Antioch the disciples were for the first time called Christians (Acts 11:21, 26).

Here it is pointed out that people becoming Christians "turned." They turn away from self to Christ, away from bad to the good. Another term for the word *turn* is conversion. A person in becoming a Christian undergoes a real change. In this passage we also note that those that turned to the Lord, joined the Church. One cannot be a Christian alone in isolation. In becoming a Christian one naturally joins other like-minded people, for to be a Christian means to have become a part of the body of Christ. Christians joining together thereby strengthen each other.

A second passage in which the word "Christian" is used relates how Paul appeared before Porcius Festus and King Agrippa and in his own defense made an address. He was so persuasive that Agrippa replied: "In a short time you think to make me a Christian!" (Acts 26:28). This would indicate that the term "Christian" was commonly used and understood.

Besides Luke and King Agrippa, Peter also uses the term. He writes, "yet if one suffers as a Christian, let him not be ashamed, but under that name let him glorify God" (I Peter 4:16). To be a Christian involves a turning, joining Church, and may even result in suffering. Peter makes a distinction between merely suffering and suffering as a Christian. To be a Christian costs something and part of the price may be suffering because of it.

A. The New Birth

The Christian gospel is good news of salvation. Salvation involves a change in three areas: Change within the individual, change in his relation to God, and change in his relation to other persons.

Every human being is caught in a network of evil constraints from his very birth. He is not satisfied or happy to live under these and he does not have the strength in himself to overcome them either. Estranged from God, imprisoned in himself, and out of harmony with his fellowman, he finally comes to the personal question put by Saul of Tarsus on the Damascus road, "What shall I do, Lord?" (Acts 22:10), or the similar question asked by the Philippian jailer, "What must I do to be saved?" (Acts 26:30). There is a turning necessary, a personal response which must be made to Jesus as Savior and Lord, for a person to become a Christian.

> Do not be conformed to this world but be transformed by the renewal of your mind, that you may prove what is the will of God, what is good and acceptable and perfect (Romans 12:2).
> "Unless one is born anew he cannot see the kingdom of God" (John 3:3).

1. Lost and Found

Being lost or saved is what Jesus was talking about in the stories of the lost sheep, the lost coin, and the lost son. When the shepherd who had a hundred sheep found the lost one

> ". . . he calls together his friends and neighbors, saying to them, 'Rejoice with me, for I have found my sheep which was lost.' Just so, I tell you there will be more joy in heaven over one sinner who repents, than over ninety-nine righteous persons who need no repentance" (Luke 15:6-7).

Likewise the woman who had ten coins and lost one, she lights a lamp, sweeps the house and searches and when she finds it,

> ". . . she calls together her friends and neighbors, saying, 'Rejoice with me, for I have found the coin which was lost.' Even so I tell you, there is joy before the angels of God over one sinner who repents" (Luke 15:9-10).

The difference between being lost or saved is even more dramatically set forth in the story of the prodigal son. When he was lost his own will was his only law and he did as he pleased. He paid no attention to his father's wishes and was estranged from him. He lived selfishly and mainly for physical pleasures. He thought he had a good time to begin with but later became very miserable and unhappy.

This is the broad way that leads to destruction. But when this lost son came to himself, repented, and returned to his waiting father, his condition was very different. Now his own will was set aside. His pride was humbled so that he did not think himself worthy to be considered a son and asked only to be a servant. Now the son was responsive to his father's wishes and was forgiven. Now he found satisfaction not in bodily pleasures but in the companionship with his father and others. He was thoroughly happy and saved. This is the narrow way that leads to life everlasting.

To be lost means not to know where you came from, where you are, why you are here, nor which way to take to get home. During younger years the writer worked with a threshing crew to earn money to attend college. My task was to haul water for the steam engine. Late one Saturday night, some fifteen miles west of my home word arrived that my brother was very sick and wanted me to come home at once. So, after midnight my horses were hitched to the buggy I had with me and we started for home. Tired and sleepy, tying the lines around my body, I reclined on the buggy seat, assuming the trotting horses would surely know the way home as that was directly east and they had repeatedly traveled that road before.

After falling asleep, the buggy suddenly turned a sharp corner. I awoke and noticed my horses were following another buggy into a farm yard. Stopping them and turning back onto the main road, it dawned on me that I did not know how long my team had followed the other buggy, nor how many turns they might have made before I woke up. I was lost and did not know where I was, nor which way was home. Driving along slowly, I wondered how to reorient myself. It was after midnight and no farm lights could be seen in the neighborhood. Which way was east and how far off the main road had my horses taken me before I awoke? Then I remembered the North Star and the Dipper. The sky was clear and finally I located, what I thought was the Dipper and North Star, but they seemed to be in the wrong direction.

Slowly I found my directions and turned to what had to be east according to the stars. I did not go to sleep again and finally came to what looked like my uncle's farm home. His name was on the mailbox which gave me assurance. My horses had evidently turned a corner while I was asleep and taken me two miles south without my knowledge. However now I knew where I was and got home just at dawn, as my father was walking toward the barn to milk the cows. Needless to say, both of us were grateful for the North Star.

BASIC CHRISTIAN CONVICTIONS

A similar experience of what it means to be lost I had in China. Late one winter evening a bad blizzard accompanied by dense snow and sleet, severe cold, and high wind furiously raged. We had a milk cow in our yard and under the circumstances thought it wise to take her into the barn. A lantern was lit and as I stepped out-of-doors an anxious voice was heard calling in Chinese "Wo mie lu, wo mie lu; degio wo, degio wo!" (I am lost, I am lost, save me, save me!) I called back but he could not hear me because of the direction of the wind.

As I proceeded toward the barn, a sudden gust of wind extinguished my lantern, and then with new vigor and insistence the calling voice continued. He evidently thought the light going out indicated that I had gone back into the house. However, I continued walking in the direction of the voice and after a while he heard me calling to him, and again with new determination he responded. Finally I reached him. Here was Mr. Wang, a neighbor of ours, under a tree. He recognized me and wondered where I came from. Asking him about his condition, he explained that he was in the neighboring village starting for home as it got dark and the fury of the storm began. It was very difficult to proceed but he finally came to the tree where he halted to rest a bit. Although not quite sure of his directions he nevertheless, after a short while ventured on his way again. Thinking he was going toward home, but after a while, he again arrived at the same tree. He now realized that he was going in circles and was lost, and so decided to go no further but call for help in the hope that someone would hear.

He was grateful I came and could hardly believe me when I told him he was only about a quarter of a mile from home. He gladly took my hand and we proceeded, soon coming to a woven wire fence, when I asked him if he knew now where he was? Before answering me, he asked if this was the fence around the mission compound. After I indicated that it was, he rejoicingly said that his home was at the corner of the fence just a short distance from where we were standing. As we parted he threw his arms around me and with great feeling thanked me for being his "savior." The weather being what it was, he no doubt would have frozen to death under the tree, unless someone else would have heard his call and come to rescue him. After this experience, whenever we met he always greeted me as his "savior."

So man is lost, not knowing where he is, where he came from, nor which way is home, until he sees and takes his directions from the "North Star," or takes the hand of "the savior" who is looking for him to bring him home.

Salvation means a certain way of life. The characteristics of it are: deliverance from our own self-will, along with our own self-conscious fears and worries; yielding ourselves completely to God's will and accepting His forgiveness for our wrongs and sins; finding our greatest satisfaction in fellowship with God and other good people; and a resultant happiness not destroyed by life's ups and downs. As we find this way of life and become that type of person, we are saved. As we miss it, we are lost.

Salvation is not a once-for-all proposition, suddenly becoming our possession never to leave us. It is rather a growth and development in a certain direction. However, a time of decision is necessary. The prodigal son began to be saved when he actually decided to go back to his father and really started. But it probably took him months and years to again grow fully into the life of his father's house. That is a matter of an entire lifetime. St. Paul had been an earnest Christian for a long time when he wrote,

> Not that I have already obtained this or am already perfect, but I press on to make it my own, because Christ Jesus has made me his own. Brethren, I do not consider that I have made it my own; but one thing I do, forgetting what lies behind and straining forward to what lies ahead, I press on toward the goal for the prize of the upward call of God in Christ Jesus. Let those of us who are mature be thus minded (Philippians 3:12-15).

2. *Salvation: A Joint Affair*

Salvation is a joint affair in which God and man work together. God takes the initiative but we must respond. We must decide to take this way. God, in His grace, even gives us the will and the strength to make the decision and act upon it. Paul writes:

> . . . work out your own salvation with fear and trembling; for God is at work in you, both to will and to work for his good pleasure (Philippians 2:12-13).

God has given us laws of nature to show us something of His ways. He has given us a conscience through which He works. He has given us our families, other good people, the Bible, the Church, and most of all He has given us Jesus Christ as the way, the truth, and the life. God leaves no stones unturned. The prodigal son did not realize that his father was anxiously waiting and looking for him. While he slowly and with hesitation walked toward home, to his surprise,

> . . . while he was yet at a distance, his father saw him and had compassion, and ran and embraced him and kissed him . . . (and) said to his servants, "Bring quickly the best robe, and put it on

BASIC CHRISTIAN CONVICTIONS

him; and put a ring on his hand, and shoes on his feet; and bring the fatted calf and kill it, and let us eat and make merry for this my son was dead and is alive again; he was lost, and is found" (Luke 15:20-24).

God's unfailing love for His children is best portrayed by Jesus, and most clearly when on the cross. In the crucifixion Jesus carried God's love for people to the bitter end. The cross opens a window into the nature of God for "God was in Christ reconciling the world to himself" (II Corinthians 5:19). The artist Holman Hunt in his famous picture "The Light of the World" portrays how Christ himself says "Behold, I stand at the door and knock; if anyone hears my voice and opens the door, I will come in to him and eat with him, and he with me" (Revelation 3:20). In Hunt's picture, on the left side we see the door, fast barred, knitted and bound to the stanchions by tendrils of ivy, showing that it has not been open for a long time. A bat hovers about it and the threshold is overgrown with brambles. Christ approaches it at night. He is dressed in a royal robe and wears a crown of thorns. In His left hand is a lantern, while His right hand is knocking at the door.

He comes to our door not because we are worthy but because we need Him and He cares. His hand that knocks is scarred. His feet bear the print of the nails. In humility He is standing and knocking, but the house is really His. He is the architect. He designed it and He made it. He is really the landlord. We are only tenants. He could command us to open, instead He invites us to open. We must make the decision and ask Him to come in. He not only desires to give himself to us, but desires that we should also give ourselves to Him.

If we ask Him to come in, our house will be under new management. To open the door is a definite act on our part. He cannot open it from the outside. In Hunt's picture there is neither latch nor handle on the outside of the door. The door can only be opened from the inside. He knocks, but we must open. We must make the decision. If we take Him in, the cleansing and growing will not be only a matter of seconds but a matter of a lifetime.

3. *Repentance and Forgiveness*

Repentance and Forgiveness are a part of the new birth. Paul, before king Agrippa, describes his work as declaring to both the Jews and the Gentiles "that they should repent and turn to God and perform deeds worthy of their repentance" (Acts 26:20). God is righteous, and true fellowship between Him and the sinner is not possible until the sinner repents. But before one can repent one must be sorry for his transgressions and have hope for forgiveness. This sorrow and this hope, God is working to bring about by all His many blessings; through every human kindness; through the life, teaching, death, and resurrection of Jesus Christ; and through the work of the Holy Spirit in one's heart. But until there is repentance no forgiveness can be accepted by man.

We read of John the Baptist preaching "Repent, for the kingdom of heaven is at hand" (Matthew 3:2). At Pentecost Peter urged "Repent and be baptized every one of you in the name of Jesus Christ for the forgiveness of your sins" (Acts 2:38). And again "Repent therefore, and turn again that your sins may be blotted out" (Acts 3:19). And Paul at Corinth admonishes "The times of ignorance God overlooked, but now he commands all men everywhere to repent" (Acts 17:30).

True repentance accompanied by sorrow and regret for trangression is followed by forgiveness. Right in the center of the prayer that Jesus taught His disciples there is the petition that God may "forgive us our debts" (Matthew 6:12). "If we confess our sins, he is faithful and just, and will forgive our sins and cleanse us from all unrighteousness" (I John 1:9). God is merciful and ready to forgive. However, we must not stop with forgiveness but go on, and do what He wants us to do, and be what He wants us to be. With forgiveness also comes new strength to overcome temptations and do what previously seemed impossible.

During this transforming experience we repeatedly have to say with Paul:

> I do not understand my own actions. For I do not do what I want, but I do the very thing I hate . . . I can will what is right but I cannot do it. For I do not do the good I want, but the evil I do not want is what I do (Romans 7:15, 19).

But when God has done His transforming work then the testimony of Paul is, "For the law of the Spirit of life in Christ Jesus has set me free from the law of sin and death" (Romans 8:2). This change in the self is brought about in an encounter with God in Christ who forgives and sets men free.

In the new relationship there is continual communion with God. His presence and love give support for ever more obedient faithfulness. But man is weak and falls again and again, nevertheless when he seeks forgiveness of God the communion by which he now lives is restored. This divine-human relationship becomes the very center of his life and gives it a new direction. Now he has entered

BASIC CHRISTIAN CONVICTIONS

"the communion of the saints" and in comradeship with others this communion with God is fostered.

4. *Jesus Christ the Center*

Jesus Christ is the center of the Christian's life. This means that He will become the personal ideal and His Kingdom the social ideal. These two will provide the exacting norms for judging all individual questions and all social relationships.

With rebirth come the assurance of forgiveness and the release from the feeling of guilt, fear, anxiety, self-pity and other forms of preoccupation with oneself. These will be replaced by a feeling of confidence, security, sympathetic concern for others and cooperative participation in unselfish service. This comes about because in conversion one puts God at the center of one's life. Paul writes:

> Finally, brethren, we beseech and exhort you in the Lord Jesus, that as you learned from us how you ought to live and to please God, just as you are doing, you do so more and more (I Thessalonians 4:1). Am I now seeking the favor of men, or of God? Or am I trying to please men? If I were still pleasing men, I should not be a servant of Christ (Galatians 1:10).

With Jesus Christ as the center, the convert will find conflicting ideals vanish. His supreme allegiance is to his Lord and Savior which will also widen his concern, from only self-centered interests to include all mankind as God's creatures.

Rebirth may be rather sudden or it may take a longer time. On this matter of being reborn, a difference might be expected in a conscientious youth that grew up in a Christian home, and that of an older and more hardened sinner. In some cases a radical change of direction will result from rebirth while in others it may mean only more conscientious devotion and commitment, but in the same general direction. The Spirit works in different ways in different lives. But fast or slowly, somehow there comes a time of a new awakening to one's responsibility before God and a conscious and unreserved commitment to Him and His cause.

Paul certainly could speak of a definite time and place. But to Timothy Paul himself writes:

> I am reminded of your sincere faith, a faith that dwelt first in your grandmother Lois and your mother Eunice and now, I am sure, dwells in you. Hence I remind you to rekindle the gift of God that is within you (II Timothy 1:5-6).

Evidently Timothy had a Christian grandmother and mother and grew up in the Christian way. But nevertheless needed occasional "rekindling" and rededication. In any case, whether conversion was sudden or gradual, it is a lifetime task to fully accept Jesus as our Lord and Savior. It means repenting, following, yielding to His guidance and love as He makes these ever more completely known to us.

B.   COUNTING THE COST

Jesus never concealed the fact that in His religion there was a demand as well as an offer. In fact, a total demand and a free offer. He offered His salvation and demanded total surrender. Luke tells of three men who had an opportunity to follow Jesus but none of them passed the Lord's test (Luke 9:57-62). Then there was the rich young ruler, morally earnest, and attractive who wanted eternal life on his own terms, but went away sorrowful when he understood the cost (Luke 18:18-24). One day a multitude was following Jesus shouting their allegiance but Jesus knew how superficial their attachment to Him was, so He told them:

> "Whoever does not bear his own cross and come after me, cannot be my disciple. For which of you desiring to build a tower, does not first sit down and count the cost, whether he has enough to complete it? Otherwise, when he has laid a foundation, and is not able to finish all who see it begin to mock him, saying, 'This man began to build, and was not able to finish' " (Luke 14:27-30).

Throughout history many have undertaken to follow Christ without ever counting the cost. The result is the great scandal of Christendom called "nominal Christians." They allow themselves to become involved enough to be respectable but not enough to be uncomfortable.

There can be no following without there being, at the same time, also a forsaking. Simon and Andrew "left their boats and followed him" (Mark 1:18). James and John "left their father Zebedee in the boat with the hired servants, and followed him" (Mark 1:20). Matthew heard Christ's call while he was "sitting at the tax office . . . left everything, and rose and followed him" (Luke 5:27-28). This call of Jesus to follow Him is still the same. He still says "whoever of you does not renounce all that he has cannot be my disciple" (Luke 14:33). Admittedly, for most Christians, this may not mean a physical forsaking of their home and job. However, it includes an inner surrender of all, and does not allow family affection, material possessions, or worldly ambition to occupy first place in our hearts.

1.   *Renouncing of Self*

The self must be renounced. Repentance involves a turning away from thoughts, words, deeds, habits, and attitudes that we know are wrong and displeasing to our Lord and detrimental to us and others. Sometimes true repentance will include restitution. Zacchaeus, the tax-collector said: "Lord, the half of my goods I give to the poor; and if I have defrauded any one of anything, I restore it fourfold" and Jesus answered, "Today salvation has come to this house" (Luke 19:8-9). We must do what we can to redress the past and mend the harm we have done.

Renunciation of the self means to submit our will to His will. "If any man would come after me, let him deny himself and take up his cross daily and follow me" (Luke 9:23). The word "daily" should not be overlooked. Paul puts it thus, "those who belong to Christ Jesus have crucified the flesh with its passions and desires" (Galatians 5:24). Every day the Christian is to renew his unconditional surrender to Jesus Christ. Jesus also described the renunciation of the self in terms of losing one's life. "For whoever would save his life will lose it; and whoever loses his life for my sake, he will save it" (Luke 9:24).

"Jesus is Lord" was the first Christian creed, so far as is known. Imperial Rome was pressing its citizens to say "Caesar is Lord" and it was dangerous to say "Jesus is Lord." In spite of danger the early Christians did not flinch and insisted that their first allegiance was to Jesus as Lord. They believed the time would come when before Him "every knee should bow, in heaven and on earth and under the earth, and every tongue confess that Jesus Christ is Lord" (Philippians 2:10-11).

2. Choice of Career and Education

The choice of a career or a profession is to be made in consideration of the fact that Christ is our Lord. This does not mean that all Christians must be preachers. God has given each person certain talents. He has a purpose for each life. We must discover it and do it. In what vocation and where geographically, will our lives count most for Him? The Christian learns to see God's purpose in his work and labors at it "as serving the Lord and not men" (Colossians 3:23). In connection with the choice of a life work the decision would also need to be made as to how much and what kind of education one should acquire. Here also the Lordship of Christ would be the deciding factor.

3. Marriage and Home

Marriage and the home is another area where the Lordship of

Christ would exert the main influence. A Christian is at liberty to marry only a Christian (II Corinthians 6:14). Marriage is the most intimate human relationship. God intends this to be so, not only in physical matters, but in emotional, intellectual, social, and especially in spiritual areas. In all this we must not forget that although home life is very important and sacred, yet the Lordship of Christ demands loyalty even beyond that. Jesus said, "He who loves father or mother . . . son or daughter more than me is not worthy of me" (Matthew 7:37).

4. *Money and Time*

Money and time do not remain a merely private matter when Jesus is accepted as Lord. Jesus often spoke of riches and its dangers. Possessions are not necessarily sinful in themselves, but when Christ is accepted as Savior and Lord, He will also be above material possessions. This will require a certain detachment from earthly possessions and unselfish use of them for the benefit of worthy causes and the needy, even if it does not require literal renunciation of all property. "You cannot serve God and mammon" (Matthew 6:24). Money, then is no longer ours. We only hold it in stewardship. The question then becomes not "How much of my money shall I give to God?" but rather "How much of His money do I need for myself?" This is also true of *time*. The list of priorities will have to be rearranged. If Christ is Lord one takes time for daily prayer, Bible reading, Sunday worship, fellowship with other Christians and some kind of Christian service in the Church and the community.

5. *Confessing Christ.*

Confessing Christ before others and the world, by words and actions, is a natural result of accepting Him as Lord. We follow Him privately and confess Him publicly.

> "For whoever is ashamed of me and of my words . . . of him will the Son of man also be ashamed" (Mark 8:38). 'So everyone who acknowledges me before men, I also will acknowledge before my Father who is in heaven; but whoever denies me before men, I also will deny before my Father" (Matthew 10:32-33).

The very fact that Jesus asks us not to be ashamed of Him indicates that He foresaw that His Church would be a minority movement and require courage. This public confession, Paul thought was essential to salvation, "For man believes with his heart and so is justified, and he confesses with his lips and so is saved" (Romans 10:10).

Baptism is such a confession. It is an outward sign of inward

BASIC CHRISTIAN CONVICTIONS

cleansing, but it is also a public acknowledgement that one has accepted Christ as Savior and Lord. Of course, open confession does not end with baptism but will continue in word and act whenever opportunity offers. By example and testimony the Christian will try to win others for Jesus his Lord and Savior.

6. *Demands and Incentives*

Demands and incentives are both important when one considers the call of Jesus to accept Him as Lord and become a Christian. Jesus, after all, came into the world, that man "might have life, and have it abundantly" (John 10:10). His purpose is to enrich, and not to impoverish. You lose yourself by committing yourself to Him and so really find yourself. True self-denial for Christ's sake leads to true self-discovery in Christian freedom. Of course, it costs to be a Christian, but it costs more not to be one.

A second incentive to accept Him as Lord and Savior is what one then can do for others. There is no greater satisfaction than to have a share in spreading the peace and love of Christ to others in every way available. The best contribution anyone can make is to live a Christian life, to build a Christian home, to engage in Christian work and thereby radiate the light of Christ and promote His cause.

An even greater incentive to become a Christian is to do it for the sake of Christ himself. We should not follow Him only for what we can get, nor only for what we can give, but supremely because of what He did and gave. He left His Father's glory and humbled himself to take on man's nature, to be born in a stable, to work as a carpenter, to befriend ordinary human beings, and finally to suffer and die on the cross. He came to reveal the love of God for man and so persuade us to repent and return to the fellowship of the Father. The very cross should make us willing to deny ourselves and follow Him. His love for us should be the great incentive to accept Him as Lord and Savior. "We love, because he first loved us" (I John 4:19).[1]

It is indeed wonderful that "to all who received him, who believed in his name he gave power to become children of God" (John 1:12). There are privileges and responsibilities of being Christian. The privileges center around the fact that now one has a more definite relationship to God, "See what love the Father has given us, that we should be called children of God; and so we are" (I John 3:1). He

---

1. J. R. W. Scott, *Basic Christianity,* pp. 109-120.

may need to chasten and correct us too, "For the Lord disciplines him whom he loves, and chastises every son whom he receives" (Hebrews 12: 6). But all this is done by a loving Father. If we sin and are disobedient the fellowship is marred but is again restored if we confess and repent. "If we confess our sins, he is faithful and just, and will forgive our sins and cleanse us from all unrighteousness" (I John 1:9).

This relationship is not only intimate it is also assured and secure. John says "I write this to you who believe in the name of the Son of God, that you may know that you have eternal life" (I John 5:13). There is such a thing as relying too much on superficial feelings. It must be remembered that this is a fact no matter how one feels. Our relationship to God as children is not based so much on our feelings as on the fact that God says that we are His children. "This is the testimony, that God gave us eternal life, and this life is in his Son. He who has the Son has life; he who has not the Son has not life" (I John 5:11-12). The Bible is full of such promises (John 6:37; 10:28; I Corinthians 10:13; Hebrews 8:5, 6; James 1:5; I John 1:9).

The outward witness of the Holy Spirit in Scripture is confirmed by the inward witness of the Holy Spirit in our hearts. "God's love has been poured into our hearts through the Holy Spirit . . . it is the Spirit himself bearing witness with our spirit that we are children of God" (Romans 5:5; 8:16).

Furthermore the same Spirit who bears witness to our sonship in Scripture as well as in our hearts, also completes His testimony in our character. His Spirit dwells within us and inevitably brings about a change in our manner of life. The profession will be accompanied by righteousness of life and practical love to one's neighbors, even including one's enemies.

In considering the cost of discipleship, demands and incentives both enter the picture, but the latter far outweigh the former. As Paul writes:

> For all who are led by the Spirit of God are sons of God. For you did not receive the spirit of slavery to fall back into fear, but you have received the spirit of sonship. When we cry, "Abba! Father!" it is the spirit himself bearing witness with our spirit that we are children of God, and if children, then heirs, heirs of God and fellow heirs with Christ, provided we suffer with him in order that we may also be glorified with him. I consider that the sufferings of this present time are not worth comparing with the glory that is to be revealed to us (Romans 8:14-18).

C. GROWTH IN THE CHRISTIAN LIFE

In this childlike relationship with God, the great responsibility is growth. St. Peter admonishes "Like newborn babes, long for the pure spiritual milk, that by it you may grow up to salvation" (I Peter 2:2). Everybody loves children but everybody also wants them to grow and mature. "Babes in Christ" are expected to become "mature in Christ" (I Corinthians 3:1; Colossians 1:28).

Christian growth is to take place in two areas; in understanding, and in Christian character. When a person begins the Christian life he needs to grow in his understanding of God the Father as revealed by Jesus Christ our Lord and Savior. The Christian is "to lead a life worthy of the Lord, fully pleasing to him, bearing fruit in every good work and increasing in the knowledge of God" (Colossians 1: 10). Peter admonished to "grow in grace and the knowledge of our Lord and Savior Jesus Christ" (II Peter 3:18). This knowledge is partly intellectual and partly personal experience.

The Holy Spirit will lead and guide us in this process of growth. He will help us bring forth the fruits of the Spirit, namely: "love, joy, peace, patience, kindness, goodness, faithfulness, gentleness, self-control" (Galatians 5:22-23). In this matter of Christian growth, the practice of prayer, Bible study, active church membership, and participation in some form of Christian service to one's fellowmen, are important. Not that thereby one might earn anything, but just as an expression of gratitude for the restored fellowship with God.

1. *Prayer*

Prayer is the soul of the Christian religion. The highest privilege a human being can enjoy is communion with God. God is our creator and the source of the renewal of our being. In prayer our spirits are refreshed by His Spirit. There are different types of prayer, such as: petition, thanksgiving, confession, self-dedication, intercession, and communion. Often some of these are fused in a single prayer.[2]

(a) *Petition* is the form of prayer most widely known and practiced. Many turn their attention to prayer only when a personal need is urgently felt and there is no ordinary prospect of satisfying it. Although to limit one's prayer only to petition is evidence of a very immature spiritual life, yet it can serve as a beginning and gradually

---

2. L. H. DeWolf, *A Theology of the Living Church*, Harper, 1953, Chap. 42; Elton Trueblood, *The Lord's Prayers*, Harper, 1965.

develop into a more mature notion of prayer. Regarding petitionary prayer Jesus said:

> "Ask and it shall be given you" (Matthew 7:7; John 14:13). "If you, then, who are evil, know how to give good gifts to your children, how much more will your Father who is in heaven give good things to them that ask him?" (Matthew 7:11).

Jesus experienced great hardship, short life, and the greatest agony, not in spite of prayer but because of it. Because of prayer He became the Savior of men and the Victor over death (Hebrews 5:7-10). The cup which Jesus prayed to have removed was not taken from Him but an eternal crown was added. God is the Creator of the world and its laws. Even human beings can make some things different in this world. Surely God as the Creator, is not more helpless than we are, but His answers may not always be what we expect.

Does God always answer prayer? Should we expect Him to do that in this world of law and order? When we present our petitions to God are we asking Him to set aside the laws of the universe to answer our prayers? The Christian prayer is always in the name of Christ. This is not a magic formula, but means that we ask our prayers to be answered only in so far as they are in accordance with the Spirit of Christ. Unless our prayer is in line with Jesus' prayer when He prayed "nevertheless, not as I will, but as thou wilt . . . thy will be done" (Matthew 26:39, 42), it is not a Christian prayer. So God answers all Christian prayers in His way. He knows better than we do what is best.

(b) *Thanksgiving* and gratitude open the soul to the sunlight of both human and divine love. Hence in coming to God in prayer, it is natural to begin with thanksgiving. Ingratitude to man and God is one of the most blighting of attitudes and will be consciously avoided by the sincere Christian. Since God is good and the source of every good, to know Him is to praise and thank Him. With thanksgiving also go adoration and worship. The prayer Jesus taught His disciples begins with adoration and ends with praise.

(c) *Confession* in the form of prayer indicates a feeling of guilt and unworthiness to even appear before God. The real prayer of confession is accompanied by repentance and the request for forgiveness. All this implies that one will also be specific in confessing certain definite wrongs and sins committed when asking for forgiveness of the same. This further means that such wrongs are also confessed to the person against whom the wrong was committed and

     BASIC CHRISTIAN CONVICTIONS

every effort is made to reestablish former good relationships, make compensation for the wrong done, and avoid similar behavior in the future. Prayers of confession also include a plea for God's help to overcome temptation of the kind involved in the specific confession.

(d) *Self-dedication* to God's will and purpose is another aspect of Christian prayer. Every person is supremely devoted to something. We all have some value at the center of our life—some great value by which every other value is reevaluated. For the Christian that value is God himself, and to make this a real and meaningful experience will take self-dedication. In this prayer we yield ourselves to His purpose and put our very lives into the hands of God to be used by Him as He sees fit. This is the losing of one's life by which the real life is found. The prayer of self-consecration will help overcome that worrisome self-dividing life of compromise which saps our joy and wastes our power. This prayer is for unification and integration of our selves and our wills in His will for us. This consecration will make for concentration, worthwhileness and effectiveness of the Christian life.

(e) *Intercession* has a real place in Christian prayer. Here we take others for whom we are concerned into God's presence—such as children, parents, friends, the sick and hungry. Prayer cannot be only a matter of self-concern. In the Lord's Prayer there is no reference to "I," "me," "my," or "mine." It is always "we," "our," and "us." We need to remind ourselves that God cares for these loved and needy ones even more than we care, but then also do what we can. Then there are community, national, and international problems that we do well to lift into His light and learn to see them as He does and then work at them as we know that He does also.

(f) *Communion* with God in prayer is the highest and most precious experience of the Christian. Above every gift that God can give is His bestowal to us of himself. In this prayer of communion God himself is the object desired, sought after, and enjoyed. The possession of the sense that He is near and cares is most worthwhile to the Christian. Here belongs the mystic's ecstasy which transports him out of the ordinary framework of life into the enraptured association with God and His love.

In prayer Jesus found peace in the midst of agony, and illumination when the way seemed dark. In prayer He found His task which so overwhelmed Him and drove Him into some days of temptation in the wilderness. In prayer He found the cross as well as the strength to die upon it. Most of all in prayer He found such consciousness of God's presence and favor which made His life radiant with the assurance of the Father's love and concern.

(g) *The Lord's Prayer that Jesus taught* His disciples is a model for all prayer. It begins by speaking to God and about Him. That His name is to be revered, that His Kingdom might come and His will be done on earth as in heaven. We are about halfway through the prayer before we come to any petitions for ourselves and these are of a general nature. We ask for our daily bread, thereby meaning all our physical needs. We ask God to forgive us our sins and help us to forgive those who sin against us. And we ask not to be tempted beyond our ability to withstand. Just these three petitions and that is all. Then our thoughts are again turned back to God as we acknowledge that the Kingdom, the power and the glory belong to Him forever.

There is nothing here of detailed requests for things. As children we will naturally also share some of our more intimate and personal needs with our Father, but the main point of prayer does not lie in asking. Nor is it primarily saying words. In public prayer, words are needed to keep the people together in their approach to God. But in personal, private prayer, it may take the form of wordless silent meditation.

Someone described prayer as a time of exposure of the soul to God. In a time exposure the camera is first of all pointed toward the desired object or scene, then the shutter is opened and held open for as long as necessary to get a lasting impression on the film. So prayer is a deliberate turning toward God and holding the attention there long enough for a lasting impression to be made on the soul. So that, after prayer our own life is more like God than it was before. In prayer we consciously and purposefully allow God's image to stamp itself more indelibly on our own entire being. So that our spirit may become more like God's spirit, our will like His will, and our thoughts more like His thoughts. Real prayer is not an attempt to change God but to change ourselves, by getting ourselves more in line and in tune with His will and being.

When Jesus withdrew to pray in the Garden of Gethsemane just before the crucifixion, He prayed "My Father, if it is possible, let this cup pass from me; nevertheless, not as I will, but as thou wilt" (Matthew 26:39, 42, 44). Three times He prayed this prayer, opening His soul wide to God so that His love and purpose might register fully. He was making sure that in this emergency God's will might also be His will and that God's strength might also be His strength in the forthcoming ordeal. Hoffman's well-known painting of this scene is a good portrayal of what happened. Jesus is kneeling, hands and arms resting on a rock, His face turned upward and outward like the face of a camera, with a gentle beam of light representing the Spirit of God streaming down upon Him. This is Christian prayer at its highest and best.

A good analogy of prayer is Nathaniel Hawthorne's story of the Great Stone Face that was looking down strong and gently from the mountainside upon the peaceful valley below. The legend had it that some day a child would be born who in manhood would be the exact image of the Great Stone Face. The boy, Ernest, had heard this legend from his mother and so spent many hours gazing at the human-like stone face on the mountainside and was wondering when the person like it would appear. Three characters in succession born in the valley, return with great fame from the outside world. But Ernest could not see any resemblance in Gathergold, the man of wealth; nor in the famous general Blood and Thunder; nor in the great politician Stony Phiz. By now Ernest himself was old and had become known as the kind and wise leader in the valley with many coming to consult him. Finally a poet with discernment recognized that Ernest himself had become the exact resemblance of the Great Stone Face. He had lived in its presence so steadily and admired it so much that the likeness of it stamped itself upon him. This is Christian prayer.

When waking in the morning we turn Godward to think of Him. The new morning with the sunrise, the beauty of nature, the day ahead with family, friends and usefulness—it is God's day, we think about Him and what He wants us to do and be this day. In what ways could our lives resemble Him more?

And in the evening, again we turn to Him and open our lives and thoughts to Him. We run over the many evidences of His goodness we experienced that day—sunshine and rain, food and clothing, family and friends, truth and beauty, work and play—all these speak of God and make us more aware of Him in whose constant care we are. He is present and within us, never far away and yet also beyond the farthest star. After thinking about God for a while we turn to ourselves. What have we been like this day? Have we reflected His likeness? Is there something that needs to be forgiven? What changes need we undergo to be more like Him?

In prayer we come face to face with the Eternal. We see our own lives and the circumstances about us in His light. We need to remind ourselves that around us and beneath us are His everlasting arms. This is no guarantee against misfortune but it gives confidence that whatever happens, nothing can really harm us if we are in His will. This is not dodging hard decisions but it is facing them with God's help. And so in quietness we rest or work or suffer in confidence and assurance that His will is our peace.

A child's relationship to his parent goes through different stages as the child grows up. At first the child comes running asking his parent "Give me this," or "Give me that." The parent can't give him everything, but nevertheless, welcomes the child and the ties between them grow closer. At a later stage when the son is in his teens, he still comes with requests, but in a different way. He still wants things, or money to buy them, but he also wants guidance in perplexities he now faces. These he talks over with his parent and seeks advice. He needs strength to see things through and does not go away disappointed. Still later the child is a grown person and has entered upon a vocation, maybe the same as that of his father. Gradually the son has more and more become like his father. He often comes to visit the father. They sit by the fire, happy to be together. Now the son may not ask for anything at all. They just visit with each other about matters of common concern, or perhaps simply sit side by side in silence. The son's main desire now is just to be near his father and that is granted and very satisfying.

The best answer we can hope for our prayers is God himself. If we consistently expose our inner being to God, His likeness will be stamped upon our lives more and more. Increasingly we shall resemble Him and enter into closer fellowship with Him. Our lives will become orderly and purposeful while bewilderment and anxiety will disappear. We shall joyfully live in the presence of the Invisible and Eternal. Prayer is essential for Christian growth.

2. *Bible Study*

For the nurture of the Christian life, Bible study is important. The primary message of the Bible has to do with God. The word "God" appears more than four thousand times in the Bible, not including *Lord* or *Father* or other names by which God is known. Here is the record of how God slowly and patiently revealed himself to man.

The secondary message of the Bible has to do with man: who he is, whence he came, what he is here for, how he should live with his fellows, and how he should respond to God's gracious dealings with him.

But in a real sense, Jesus Christ himself is the central message and climax of the Bible. Jesus Christ both tells us and shows us what God is, and what we are and can become through Him. The author of Hebrews writes:

> In many and in various ways God spoke of old to our fathers by the prophets; but in these last days he has spoken to us by a Son, whom he appointed the heir of all things (Hebrews 1:1-2).

To nurture our physical body we have special times, place, position, either alone, with the family or with special company. The inner being of man also merits such regular and daily practice. This applies to both prayer and Bible study.

Whereas, the Bible and how to use it is dealt with more fully in Chapter VIII, we shall not go into detail here, except to emphasize that Bible study is an indispensable necessity for healthy Christian growth.

3. *Active Church Membership*

Active church membership plays an important role in the nurture of the Christian life. To be a Christian is not only a private affair. By being born again we are born into a family with God as father and every other Christian in the world our brother or sister in Christ. One of the commonest names for Christians in the New Testament is Brethren. However, membership in the universal Body of Christ should also be supplemented by active membership in some local congregation somewhere. Baptism is the way of entry into this visible Christian society but this should be followed by active fellowship with other members and regular participation in the work of the Church. This includes the weekly worship service whenever possible, the Lord's Supper, promotion of Christian education, evangelism, missions, as well as the social action program carried on by the Church.

Whereas the Church and various aspects of it have been more fully dealt with in Chapter VI, the discussion of this subject here is terminated by reemphasizing the fact that Christian nurture and growth is a natural by-product in the life of the person participating in the various activities of the Church. Every individual claiming Jesus Christ as Lord and Savior is not only privileged, but obligated actively to participate in the work of the Church—the Body of Christ, and thereby also automatically nurture and promote the growth of his own spiritual life.

4. Faith and Works

Speaking of the Christian Life something should be said about the relation of faith and works. Every Christian should engage in some form of community and world service of so-called secular nature, besides his regular church activities.

Salvation is a process of change and growth from sin to righteousness, beginning with the first stirrings of spiritual awareness and continuing on even until death. In this process some have stressed the importance of faith to the exclusion of works while others have taken a somewhat opposite position and over-stressed works. However, in reality both belong together. By faith we do not mean only a creedal assent to a formula, but rather a commitment to Jesus Christ and His program. When one goes to the physician for an operation one must have faith in him. This means a willingness to lie down on the operating table, go to sleep, and trust him for the outcome of the operation. Faith implies trust and commitment.

Then "works" often also are thought of in too narrow terms— only as ritualistic acts or ascetic practices. No man can buy his salvation with ritualistic rites or even other ordinary good works. In fact man is not saved by works, but by grace. Paul writes:

> For by grace you have been saved through faith; and this is not your own doing, it is the gift of God - not because of works, lest any man should boast. For we are his workmanship, created in Christ Jesus for good works, which God prepared beforehand, that we should walk in them (Ephesians 2:8-10).

The initiative in salvation is taken by God—that is grace. Our response to grace is to have faith and accept it. Some people talk as though they thought they were saved by faith—which is not any more correct than to think we are saved by good works. However both of them are involved in the total process. "For by grace you have been saved through faith . . . for good works." God's Grace comes first; then comes our response of faith, and works come last as an expression of gratitude for salvation and not as an attempt to earn it.

Jesus stressed both, an attitude of trusting obedience to the Father (Matthew 6:25-34), as well as works of gratitude and love (Matthew 25:31-46; Mark 10:17-21; Luke 6:46-49). Jesus also emphasizes both, faith (John 8:24; I John 4:12), along with spiritual union with Christ for works (John 15:1-5), in speaking of the relationship of the branches with the vine.

Paul and James seemingly can be quoted on opposite sides, if not properly understood. Paul says "For we hold that man is justified by faith apart from works of law" (Romans 3:28). While James, on the other hand, writes,

> What does it profit, my brethren, if a man says he has faith but has not works? Can his faith save him? If a brother or sister is ill-clad and in lack of daily food, and one of you says to them, "Go in peace, be warmed and filled," without giving them the things needed for the body, what does it profit? So faith by itself, if it has no works is dead (James 2:14-17).

It is clear that in speaking of works Paul has in mind Jewish rituals. James on the other hand is speaking of works as helping others in need, which faith is bound to produce if it is alive. Taking their total view into consideration they are not so different as it may at first seem. Paul insists that if you have a saving faith you obey God (Romans 6:12-19), and James says "Show me your faith apart from your works, and I by my works will show you my faith" (James 2:18).

The faith by which we accept the saving grace of God is not a mere intellectual assent to a creedal statement for "Even the demons believe and shudder" (James 2:19). We are saved by grace through faith in a person, not a proposition. This includes both the attitude of trust and obedience. Man cannot purchase life nor salvation by good works. God alone grants salvation by grace through faith but this, if it is real, will issue in good works of gratitude. Our very selves must be committed by His grace to life with Him, which is faith and which will in gratitude produce good works.

This means not only good works at home and in the church, but also on a more secular basis in the community and in the world at large to help abolish hunger, ignorance, disease, war and every other condition that militates against the fuller coming of the Kingdom of God, and also help promote all such activities, organizations, and institutions that would advance the Kingdom of God. Such interest and activity will also greatly enrich the growth of the Christian life of the participant.

D. BEING LED BY THE SPIRIT

In a nutshell, to live the Christian life means always to seek the leading of the Holy Spirit in all decisions and activities of life.

> For all who are led by the Spirit of God are sons of God (Romans 8:14). "I am the vine, you are the branches. He that abides in me, and I in him, he it is that bears much fruit, for apart from

me you can do nothing" (John 15:5). "I will put my laws into their minds and write them on their hearts and I will be their God and they shall be my people" (Hebrews 8:10). Have this mind among yourselves, which you have in Christ Jesus, who, though he was in the form of God, did not count equality with God a thing to be grasped, but emptied himself, taking the form of a servant, being born in the likeness of men (Philippians 2:5-7).

These passages indicate that the Christian life means to share the spirit of Christ, that is, share His faith, His values, His work, as well as His methods and attitudes.

Sharing the faith of Christ means absolute trust in, and commitment to, God the Father, who creates, sustains and orders all. The highest in spirit is also the deepest in nature. The universe is friendly to man. Physical laws, social laws, as well as spiritual laws are God's ways of operating. The very stars in their courses are on the side of righteousness. Jesus had faith not only in God but also in man and his possibilities. He had faith that Simon could become Peter, the rock; that John, a son of thunder, could become the apostle of love, that Saul the persecutor, could become Paul the great apostle.

Sharing the values of Christ means to put the kingdom of God first. He said: "But seek first his kingdom and his righteousness, and all these things shall be yours as well" (Matthew 6:33; Luke 12:31). Jesus considered human personality of supreme value.

> "For the Son of man came to seek and to save that which was lost" (Luke 19:10). "What does it profit a man, to gain the whole world and forfeit his life? For what can a man give in return for his life?" (Mark 8:36-37).

Sharing the work of Christ means

> ". . . to seek and to save the lost" (Luke 19:10). "Go therefore and make disciples of all nations . . . teaching them to observe all that I have commanded you" (Matthew 28:19, 20). "He who believes in me will also do the works I do" (John 14:12). "If you love me, you will keep my commandments" (John 14:15). "Do not labor for the food which perishes, but for the food which endures to eternal life" (John 6:27).

Sharing the methods and attitudes of Christ is not to rely upon force but upon love.

> "This is my commandment that you love one another as I have loved you" (John 15:12). "I say to you, Love your enemies and pray for those who persecute you, so that you may be sons of your Father who is in heaven." "By this all men will know that you are my disciples, if you have love for one another" (Matth. 5:45; John 13:35).

As Jesus was crucified He prayed "Father forgive them; for they know not what they do" (Luke 23:34). Both His method and attitude were love.

The apostle Paul so identified himself with Christ that he could speak of "my gospel" instead of only Christ's gospel (Romans 2:16; II Timothy 2:8). A person is a Christian only insofar as he has made the Gospel of Christ his own, for only so can we pass it on. The Christian must know Christ, not only about Christ. The Christian life means to share the life of Christ. In the New Testament we have the Gospel according to Matthew, and according to Mark, and Luke, and John. They gave us the Gospel as they understood and comprehended it. In a real sense there is also the Gospel according to you and me as Christians. My Gospel is me, not only what I say, but even more so, what I do, and especially what I am. Our personal Gospel is being read. We find Christ easiest through persons who represent Him. Some one needs just our Gospel.

The disciples were not all Peters or Pauls. They had different gifts, different personalities and each one gave his particular expression to the Gospel of Christ. And so today, the Lord needs Albert Schweitzers but He also needs ordinary folks, with ordinary gifts, as Christians to represent Him and His Gospel in the world. Christ is the vine and we are the branches. The Christian life consists in sharing Christ's faith, His values, His work, and His methods and attitudes. "For all who are led by the Spirit of God are sons of God" (Romans 8:14).

E. SUMMARY AND CONCLUSION

The discussion on the Christian Life in this chapter has been carried on under the following subheads: The New Birth; Counting the Cost; Growth in the Christian Life; and, Being Led by the Spirit.

In summary one may say that to live the Christian Life one needs to learn to say with Paul:

> For to me to live is Christ, and to die is gain (Philippians 1:21).
> None of us lives to himself, and none of us dies to himself. If
> we live, we live to the Lord, and if we die we die to the Lord; so
> then, whether we live or whether we die, we are the Lord's (Romans 14:7-8). . . . show that you are a letter from Christ . . .
> written not with ink but with the Spirit of the living God, not on
> tablets of stone but on tablets of human hearts (II Corinthians
> 3:3).

Jesus said:

> "You are the salt of the earth . . . You are the light of the world
> . . . Let your light so shine before men, that they may see your
> good works and give glory to your Father who is in heaven"
> (Matthew 5:13, 14, 16). "I am the vine, you are the branches"
> (John 15:5). "As the Father has sent me, so send I you" (John
> 20:21). "But you shall receive power when the Holy Spirit is
> come upon you; and you shall be my witnesses in Jerusalem, and
> in all Judea and Samaria and to the end of the earth" (Acts 1:8).

The Christian life is the life of Christ in the Christian. "For all who
are led by the Spirit of God are sons of God" (Rom. 8:14).

FOR FURTHER READING ON THE CHRISTIAN LIFE

Baillie, John, *The Sense of the Presence of God,* Scribners, 1962.
Barth, Karl, *The Call for God,* Harper, 1965.
Bonhoeffer, Dietrich, *The Cost of Discipleship,* Macmillan, 1960.
Bonnell, J. S., *What Are You Living For,* Abingdon, 1960.
Brunner, Emil, *The Great Invitation,* Westminster, 1955.
Buttrick, G. A., *So We Believe, So We Pray,* Abingdon, 1951.
Fosdick, Harry E., *The Secret of Victorious Living,* Harper, 1934.
Hessert, Paul, *The Christian Life,* Westminster, 1967.
Hutchison, O., *Christian Love in Everyday Living,* Westminster.
Irwin, J. C., *On Being a Christian,* Abingdon, 1958.
Kaufman, Gordon D., *The Context of Decision,* Abingdon, 1961.
Kerr, Hugh Thomas, *Design for Christian Living,* Westminster, 1953.
Kennedy, Gerald, *Go Inquire of the Lord,* Harper, 1952.
King, Martin Luther, *Strength to Love,* Harper, 1963.
Larson, B., *No Longer Strangers,* World Books, 1971.
Miller, Alexander, *The Renewal of Man,* Doubleday, 1955.
Moser, L. E., *The Lonely Road Back,* World Books, 1971.
Nixon, Justin Wroe, *Responsible Christianity,* Harper, 1950.
Meland, Bernard E., *Seeds of Redemption,* Macmillan, 1947.
Nelson, John Oliver, ed., *Work and Vocation,* Harper, 1954.
Pardue, Austin, *Create and Make New,* Harper, 1952.
Peace, R., *Learning to Love People,* Zondervan, 1968.
Reid, A. C., *Invitation to Worship,* Abingdon, 1952.
Shoemaker, S. M., *With the Holy Spirit and With Fire,* Harper, 1960.
Smith, Ralph M., *Living the Spirit-filled Life,* Zondervan, 1967.
Steere, Douglas V., *On Beginning from Within,* Harper, 1964.
Stewart, James S., *A Faith to Proclaim,* Scribners, 1953.
Tillich, Paul, *The New Being,* Scribners, 1953.
Thurman, Howard, *The Growing Edge,* Harper, 1956.

EPILOGUE

IN THE FOREWORD SOMETHING WAS SAID AS TO HOW THIS BOOK CAME to be written and the purpose thereof. The title—*Basic Christian Convictions*—indicates what the general content of the volume is supposed to be. This *Epilogue* is a brief summarization of these Basic Christian Convictions.

Beginning with *Religion and the Religions* it was pointed out that religion is the supreme value of an individual or group in the light of which all other values are constantly being reevaluated. All religions are an expression of the search for the most satisfying supreme value, namely God. This is a constant double search: God's search for man, desiring to reveal himself more fully to man, and man's search for God to understand and serve Him more perfectly.

For the idea of *God, Our Father* we go back to the Hebrew Yahweh of the Old Testament, gradually leading up to "when the time had fully come, God sent forth his Son" (Gal. 4:4), who "reflects the glory of God and bears the very stamp of his nature" (Heb. 1:3). In other words, the most perfect revelation of God that we have is the life, teaching, death and resurrection of Jesus Christ who said "He who has seen me has seen the Father" (John 14:9).

Creation is God's Handiwork was the conclusion of the Psalmist when he says: "The heavens are telling the glory of God; and the firmament proclaims his handiwork" (Ps. 19:1). Although there is much about creation that is a mystery to man, still the *Basic Christian Conviction* is that it is God's Handiwork.

Coming to *Man* as a part of creation we are keenly aware of two aspects, namely, *His Majesty and Misery*. Man is the crown but through sin has also become the shame of creation. He has the potentiality to rise higher but also to sink lower than any other creature. Although a sinner, the *Basic Christian Conviction* about man is that he can be saved and is worth saving.

This brings us to *Jesus Christ, Lord and Savior,* who is the core and center of all Basic Christian Convictions. "For no other foundation can any one lay than that which is laid, which is Jesus Christ"

(I Cor. 3:11). He not only said "I am the way, and the truth, and the life" (John 14:6), but one can also experientially verify that "In him was life and the life was the light of men" (John 1:4). "He is the image of the invisible God" (Col. 1:15).

The Holy Spirit and the Trinity are rather unique *Christian Convictions*. Of all religions, Christianity alone emphasizes the practical importance of the work of the Holy Spirit in the life of the individual and society. This Spirit disturbs, convicts, reprimands, suggests, guides, comforts, inspires, heals, transforms, makes whole, and is available as an indwelling reality to every individual or group open to His influence. The unique trinitarian feature of the Christian concept of God in His *unity* and *diversity* can be thought of as the eternal, historical, and progressive manifestations of himself. God manifests himself as a loving Father in His perpetual creation and sustaining of all that is. He is eternal. But He also manifests himself in history, and most fully in the human life of Jesus Christ. And as a constant companion, God is progressively leading mankind forward by the manifestation of himself through the Holy Spirit in the life of individuals and society. God is ONE, but manifesting himself as Father, Son, and Holy Spirit.

This brings us to *The Kingdom and the Church* as two distinct realities. Jesus said: "the kingdom of God is in the midst of you" (Luke 17:21). The Kingdom of God is where God rules in the life of the individual or society. With man as a free being, this rule of God here on earth is never perfect but can always be improved. Christ "is the head of the body, the church" (Col. 1:18). The work of the Church is to promote the Kingdom but it is not to be identified with it. In the history of the Church there have been periods of great promise but also periods of discouragement and worldliness. Jesus promised: "I will build my church, and the powers of death shall not prevail against it" (Matt. 16:18). The great need of the Church today is *spiritual renewal* as the body of Christ and so become more relevant as a real leaven for Christ in the world.

The Bible: The Story of Reconciliation is basic for all *Christian Convictions*. It is the *Word* of God (not the *words* of God). This Word or message of God to man contains the story of reconciliation culminating in Jesus Christ. The Old Testament leads up to the coming of Jesus and the New Testament springs from the life, teaching, death, and resurrection of Jesus. "God was in Christ reconciling the world to himself" (II Cor. 5:19). The Bible contains the story of that reconciliation. Jesus said: "You search the scriptures because you think that in them you have eternal life; and it is they that bear witness to me" (John 5:39).

The Christian Hope relates to the future of this world and the future life after death. About both issues we know very little but the Christian outlook is hopeful and positive. It has been said, "where there is life there is hope, and where there is hope there is religion." Jesus taught us to hope and pray and work for the increase of God's rule and the more complete coming of His Kingdom. However dark and discouraging conditions may seem, and even if this world finally comes to an end and disappears, still, if not here, then in the life to come the Christian's *Hope* will be realized. For, "Behold the dwelling of God is with men. He will dwell with them and they shall be his people" (Rev. 21:3), and Jesus promised: "I will come again and will take you to myself, that where I am you may be also" (John 14:3).

The Christian Life consists in sharing Christ's faith, values, work, attitudes and methods. He said, "you shall be my witnesses . . . to the ends of the earth" (Acts 1:8), and "By this all men will know that you are my disciples, if you love one another" (John 13:35). Paul urges: "show that you are a letter from Christ . . . written not with ink but with the Spirit of the living God, not on tablets of stone but on tablets of human hearts" (II Cor. 3:3). The Christian life is the life of Christ in the Christian. "For all who are led by the Spirit of God are sons of God" (Rom. 8:14).

To conclude these *Basic Christian Convictions* we quote *An Affirmation of Faith.*[1]

> We believe in Jesus Christ the Lord,
>   Who was promised to the people of Israel,
>   Who came in the flesh to dwell among us,
>   Who announced the coming of the rule of God,
>   Who gathered disciples and taught them,
>   Who died on the cross to free us from sin,
>   Who rose from the dead to give us life and hope,
>   Who reigns in heaven at the right hand of God,
>   Who comes to judge and bring justice to victory.

---

1. Author unknown, *The Mennonite Hymnal,* Mennonite Pub. House, Scottdale, Pa., and Faith and Life Press, Newton, Kansas, 1970, No. 723.

We believe in God His Father,
    Who raised Him from the dead,
    Who created and sustains the universe,
    Who acts to deliver His people in times of need,
    Who desires all men everywhere to be saved,
    Who rules over the destinies of men and nations,
    Who continues to love men even when they reject Him.

We believe in the Holy Spirit,
    Who is the form of God present in the Church,
    Who moves men to faith and obedience,
    Who is the guarantee of our deliverance,
    Who leads us to find God's will in the Word,
    Who assists those whom he renews in prayer,
    Who guides us in discernment,
    Who impels us to act together.

We believe God has made us His people,
    To invite others to follow Christ,
    To encourage one another to deeper commitment,
    To proclaim forgiveness of sins and hope,
    To reconcile men to God through word and deed,
    To bear witness of the power of love over hate,
    To proclaim Jesus the Lord over all,
    To meet the daily tasks of life with purpose,
    To suffer joyfully for the cause of right,
        To the ends of the earth,
        To the end of the age,
        To the praise of His glory, Amen.

FOR FUTHER READING IN GENERAL CHRISTIAN THEOLOGY

Anderson, G. H., *Theology of Christian Missions,* McGraw-Hill, 1961.
Aulen, Gustaf, *The Faith of the Christian Church,* Muhlenberg, 1948.
Barclay, W., *The Apostles Creed for Everyman,* Harper, 1967.

Barth, Karl, *Evangelical Theology,* Doubleday, 1964.

Braaten, C. E., *The Future of God,* Harper, 1969.

Brown, R. M., *The Spirit of Protestantism,* Oxford Univ. Press, 1960.

Brunner, Emil, *The Great Invitation,* Westminster, 1955.

Bultman, R. E., *Jesus Christ and Mythology,* Scribners, 1958.

Burtt, E. A., *Man Seeks the Divine,* Harper, 1971.

Carnell, E. J., *The Theology of Reinhold Niebuhr,* Eerdmans, 1960.

Cousins, E. H., *Process Theology,* Newman Press, 1970.

Cullman, O., *Christ and Time,* Westminster, 1950.

DeWolf, L. H., *A Theology of the Living Church,* Harper, 1953.

Forrell, G. W., *The Protestant Faith,* Prentice-Hall, 1960.

Foster, A. D., *The God Who Loves,* Bruce, 1971.

Guery, E., *God, The Father,* Shedd, 1970.

Guitton, J., *Great Heresies and Church Councils,* trans., Harper, 1965.

Gutzke, M. G., *Christian Words,* Zondervan, 1964.

Hartsock, D. E., *Contemporary Religious Issues,* Wadsworth, 1968.

Hazelton, R., *Contemporary Theology,* Harper, 1960.

Heick, O. W., *A History of Christian Thought,* Fortress Press, 1965.

Hessert, Paul, *Introduction to Christianity,* Prentice-Hall, 1958.

Hordern, E., ed., *New Directions in Theology,* Vol. I-VII, Westminster, 1966.

Horton, W. M., *Christian Theology, An Ecumenical Approach,* Harper, 1955.

Hughes, P. E., *Creative Minds in Contemporary Theology,* Eerdmans, 1966.

Jacob, E., *The Theology of the Old Testament,* trans., Harper, 1958.

Kaufman, Gordon D., *Systematic Theology,* Scribners, 1968.

Knox, John, *Limits of Unbelief,* Seabury, 1970.

Kramer, K. F., *The God Who Saves Us,* Herder, 1971.

Macquarrie, J., *Principles of Christian Theology,* Scribners, 1966.

Moltman, Jurgen, *The Theology of Hope,* trans., Harper, 1967.

Richardson, A., *The Theology of the New Testament,* Harper, 1959.

Richardson, H. W., *Toward an American Theology,* Harper, 1967.

Schilling, S. F., *Contemporary Continental Theologians,* Abingdon, 1966.

Setzer, J. S., *What's Left to Believe,* Abingdon, 1968.

Siddiqi. R. A., *Man, Reality and Value,* Macmillan, 1971.

Tillich, Paul, *Systematic Theology,* Vol. I-III, Univ. of Chicago, 1964.

Weatherhead, L. D., *The Christian Agnostic,* Abingdon, 1965.

Whiteley, D. E. H., *The Theology of St. Paul,* Fortress Press, 1964.

INDEX OF NAMES

AND SUBJECTS

BASIC CHRISTIAN CONVICTIONS

New Israel, 234
Ordinances, 209 f.
Organization, 206, 207
Pentecost the beginning, 194, 195
People, 205
Unity, 203
Visible and invisible, 205
World Council, 217-219
Clarke, W. H., 21, 155, 165, 277
Code of Hammurabi, 248
Coe, G. A., 22, 25
Commitment, 69
Communion, 307, 308
Community, 170
Compton, Arthur H., 81
Conduct, 287
Confessing, 302, 306, 307
Conflict and Cooperation, 78
Confucius, 10, 17, 187
Conscience, 174
Constantine, 64
Con-substantiation, 214
Conversion, 300
Copernicus and Darwin, 79, 80
Cosmic conflict, 157
Counselor, 166
Craig, C. T., 220n
Creation, 71
  Causal Law, 82
  Creation's crown, 72
  It was good, 72
  Miracle, 83
  Prayer and law, 84
Creed, "Jesus is Lord," 161
Creeds, historic, 203
Cross of Jesus, 250
Cyrus, 14

Damascus, 42
Damascus Pope, 232
Dan, 40
Dante, 80
Darius, 247
Dark Ages, 199
Darwin, Charles, 78
David, 40, 227, 250
Dead Sea Scrolls, 230, 248
Dedication, 307
Demands, 303
Demiurge, 59, 89
Demythologizing, 129n
Dervishes, 15
Devil, 280
DeWolf, L. H., 155, 181, 193, 213, 251, 305

Diaspora, 232
Dictation (theory of inspiration), 256
Didache, 211
Disciples, 173, 267
Divine Comedy, 64
Divine mobility, 39
Docetism, 237
Documents of Biblical material
  D.—Deuteronomy document, 229
  E.—Elohim, Ephraim document, 228
  J.—Jehovah, Judaeic document, 228
  P.—Priestly document, 229
  JE.—combined document, 229
  JED.—document, 229
  JEDP.—document, 229
Dodd, C. H., 231, 234, 370
Dominion over creation, 73
Domitian died 96 A.D., - 236
Douay version, 233
Double search (God and man), 317
Dualism, 3
Durnbaugh, D., 202
Dutton, Anthony, 62n
Dyck, C. J., 202

Eastern Church, N.T. Canon, 367, 237
Ecumenical movement, 217
Edinburgh, 218
Education, 301
Egypt, 57, 227
Einstein, Albert, 61
Elder brother, 186
El Elyon, 36
Elijah, 37, 41
Elisha, 42
Elizabeth, 166
Elohim, 36, 228
El Shaddai, 36
Ephesus, 51
Ephramite, 39
Epilogue, 317
Episcopal, 207
Eros (Love), 168
Eschatology, 287
Estep, W. R., 202
Esther, 48
Eternal fire, 287
Eternal life, 281-285
Evangelical alliance, 218
Evangelism, 209
Evolutionary theory, 81
Evil (a problem), 85-95
  a mystery, 93
  An illusion? 89

Hordern, William, 155
Horeb, 37
Horton, H., 220
Horton, Walter M., 100, 180
Hosea, 43
Human being, 176
Hume, David, 20
Hume, R. E., 5n, 89n, 186n

Ikhnaton, 247
Image of God, 72
Immanental coming, 271
Immortality, 278-279
Incarnation, 130, 221
Incentives for Christian, 303
India, 5
Individual concern, 76, 170
Individualism, 47
Industrial impact, 62
Infanticide, 254
Inspiration, 190, 258
Intercession, 307
International problems, 44
Interpreter's Bible, 231
Isaiah, 46
Islam, 47
Israel, 171, 197
I-Thou, 63
I-You, 63

Jainism, 6, 16
James, Jesus' brother, 140
James, William, 22
Jamnia, 230, 232
Japan, 11
Jefferson, Charles, 257n, 269n
Jehoiachin, 250
Jeremiah, 44, 45
Jericho, 38
Jeroboam, 40
Jerome, 232
Jerusalem, 40, 168, 267
Jethro, 37
Jesus Christ, 125-163
  Accusations, 147, 148
  Appraisal, 145
  Arrest, 134
  Ascension, 144
  Baptism, 130, 166
  Burial, 135
  Character, 155
  Claims about self, 151-154
  Contemporaries' opinion, 145, 146
  Crucifixion, 134
  Deeds, 154

Disciples, 132-133, 139, 148-150
Enemies' accusation, 147-148
Evaluation by John the Baptist, 148, 149
Forgiving sins, 145
General public opinion, 146
God consciousness of Jesus, 186
Holy Spirit He would send, 151, 152
Judges the world, 154
Kingdom is message 132, 152
Last week, 135, 136
Lord and God, Thomas' confession, 150
Lord and Savior, 155-161
Mediation, 125-127
Ministry, 131, 166, 173
Miracles, 154
Nativity, 128
Old Testament regard, 253
Resurrection mystery, 136-143
Son of God, 150
Spirit of Jesus, 168
Teaching, 131, 146, 178
Temptation, 130, 155
Transfiguration, 133
Youth in Temple, 129
Jezebel, 40
Joab, 250
Job, 66, 87
John the Baptist, 131, 166, 248
Josephus, 127
Joshua, 36, 47, 227
Josiah, 229
Jung, C. G., 23
Jurgi, E. J., 20n

Kant, Immanuel, 21, 80, 278
Karma, 6, 7
Katija, 14
Kaufman, Ed. G., 155n, 202n
Kaufman, Gordon D., 202
Kautzsch, E., 34
Kee, Young & Froehlich, 238
Kenite theory, 37
Khalsa, 8
Khirbet Qumran, 248
Khiva, 269
Kierkegaard, Sören, 54, 64, 111, 126
Kingdom of God, 66, 190-194, 318
  Church's mission, 194
  Coming Kingdom, 193
  Defined, 191
  Established, 280
  Jesus' reference to Kingdom, 190,

326   BASIC CHRISTIAN CONVICTIONS

192
Parables of Kingdom, 271
Present now, 270
King, Irving, 23
Knipperdolling and von Leiden, 268
Knowing God, 66
Knox, John, 200
Kojiki, 11
Koran, 15
Krahn, C., 202n, 269n
Kroeber, A. L., 98
Kropotkin, P. A., 78

Laban and Jacob, 248, 252
Lahore, 8
Lao-tze, 9
Latourette, K. S., 51n
Law, 169, 229
Law of love, 285
Lazarus, 280, 283
Leah & Rachel, 248
LeFevre, Perry, 98, 114
Leuba, J. H., 20, 21
Levels of knowing, 67
Life after death, 277-290
Light of man, 318
Littell, F. H., 202
Logos, 51, 56, 59
Lord's Supper, 212-215
   Con-substantiation, 214
   Tran-substantiation, 214
   Symbolic memorial, 214
Lost, 293-295
Lost Books of the Bible, 239n
Lost Tribes, 229
Love, 168
   Agape, Eros, Phileo, 168
   Holy, 176
   Loving Father, 318
   Uniting principle, 192
Loyalty, 282
Luke, Paul's companion, 236
Luther, Martin, 110, 200, 233, 249

McArthur, H. K., 132
Macquarrie, John p. 183
McTaggart, J., 21
Man, his Majesty and Misery, 95-124
   As a creative being, 109
   As co-laborer with God, 73, 114
   As Decider, 110
   Different from animal, 103, 104
   Judaeo-Christian view, 98
   Living soul, 106-108
   Naturalistic view, 98

Origin, 96
   Rationalistic view, 98
   Scientific and Christian views, 101
   Sinner, 115
Mana, 172
Manifestation of God, 187 f.
   Eternal as Father,
   Historical as Son,
   Progressive as Spirit,
Marcion, 51, 237
Marriage, 216, 301, 302
Martin, E. D., 23n
Marty, Martin E., 64, 246
Mary Magdalene, 135
Matthys, Jan, 268
Maya, 7
Mecca, 14, 15
Mediation, 125
Medina, 14
Meek, T. J., 37
Melkart, 40
Membership, Church, 311
Mennonite Encyclopedia, 200-201
Mennonites, 201, 202
   Russia, 269
Menzies, Allen, 21
Mesopotamian literature, 248
Messiah, 267, 280
Methods of Christ, 314
Middle Ages, 199
Midianite, 37
Mikado, 11
Millennium, 267, 270
Miller, William, 269
Ministry, 207-210
Miracle and Prayer, 81
Mishna, 12
Missionary, 204
Moab, 42
Modern thought and God concept, 60
Molech, 42
Moltman, Juergen, 64
Monotheism, 3
Montefoire, 53
Moore, G. F., 1n
Moral Influence Theory, 160
Moses, 3, 12, 35, 58, 227, 229
Moslem, 7
   Prayer, 84
Mountain God, 37
Mount Sinai, 35-37
Mueller, Max, 20
Muenster, 268
Muhammadanism, 14, 15, 110
Mutual Aid, 78

Providence of God, 74-75
Pruyser, P. W., 23n
Ptolemy Philadelphus, 232
Pyke, Magnus, 62, 81

Quaker, Friends, 216
Quest for Value, 104

Rain, 41
Ransom Theory, 156-157
Rawlinson, Henry C., 247
Rebirth, 229
Rechabites, 37
Reciprocity, 11
Reconciliation, 54, 156, 176, 226-262
Redemption, 156
Re-evaluation, 25, 29
Reformation, 200, 249, 268
Reformation, God concept, 59
Reich, C. A., 274
Relation with God, 282, 310
Relativity, 81
Religion, 1-33
    Active and dynamic, 165
    Cosmology & religion, 79
    General characteristics, 16-19
    Growth, 1-4
    Main teachings, 16
    Order of origin, 16
    Origin of religions (area)
        East Asia (China, Japan), 8 f.
        South Asia, (India), 5 f.
        West Asia, (Palestine, Persia, Arabia), 12 f.
    Patterns of Religion, 5-16
        Buddhism, 7
        Confucianism, 9, 10
        Christianity, 16
        Hinduism 5-6
        Jainism, 6
        Judaism, 12
        Muhammadanism, 14-15
        Shintoism, 11
        Sikhism, 8
        Taoism, 9
        Zoroastrianism, 13
    Various approaches to Religion, 20-24
        Emotional approach, 21
        Escape approach, 22
        Intellectual approach, 21
        Psychological approach, 22
        Value approach, 23, 25-31
        Voluntaristic approach, 21
        Worship approach, 21

Religious process as re-evaluation of values, 25-31
    Graphic figures of process, 26, 27
Repentance, 297, 298
Resurrection, 251, 279-281, 284
    Not resuscitation, 137
Revelation, 165
Ricoeur, Paul, 50
Roberts, D. E., 23n
Roman Catholic, 198-200
Romanes, G. J., 20
Rosetta Stone, 246
Rowley, H. H., 247n
Russia, 269

Sabatier, August, 21
Sacrificial love, 79
Sadducees, 282
Saint Augustine, 90
Salvation, 222, 296, 297, 312
Samson, 170
Saul, 172
Schleiermacher, F., 21
Schlink, Edmund, 213
Scholarly research, 232, 245
Schweitzer, Albert, 68
Science influence, 181, 252, 277
Scott, J. R. M., 136n, 141n, 303
Scott, Sir Walter, 259
Second coming, 266
Self-denial, 300-303
Separation, 289
Septuagint, 232
Sermon on the Mount, 252-254
Setzer, J. S., 129n
Shakespeare, 121
Shalmaneser II, 228
Shantung, 10
Shaw, J. S., 53
Shema, 12
Shintoism, 11, 17
Sikhism, 8, 16
Simeon, 166
Simons, Menno, 200
Sin, 174
    Biblical view, 117
    Genesis story, 118
    Influence of science, 60
    Naturalistic view, 116
    Original, 122
    Relativity and sin, 116
    Results of sin, 120 f.
    Scientific materialism, 61
    Total depravity, 122
Siva, 5

Williams, G. H., 202
Wilson, Dorothy Clark, 86
Witchcraft, 257
Witnesses, 140
Word (Logos), 183, 184
Word of God, 227
Work of the Church, 318
Works, 312, 313
World, 171
World end, 277
World modern, 202, 222
World Council of Churches, 177, 217-
  220
  Background, 217-218
  Conference of Faith & Order, 218
  Life and Work Movement, 218
  Missionary Council, 218
  Russian Orthodox Church, 219
World Council meeting places, 218
World Council problems, 220
  Evangelism, 220
  Faith and Order, 220
  Intergroup relations, 220

Laity of the church, 220
  Membership statement, 219
  World Peace, 177, 220
Wright, G. E., 34n

Yahweh, Chap. II, 34-39, 228
Yahweh (Father idea), 185
  Post-exilic development, 47, 49
  Pre-exilic development, 43, 44
  Prophets in exile, 45, 46
Yang, 9
Yasna, 185
Yin, 9
Yoder, J. H., 202n

Zebedee, 215
Zadokote fragments, 248
Zerubbabel, 47
Zeus, 3, 53
Ziggurat, 40
Zoroastrianism, 3, 13, 17, 18, 89,
  185-187
Zwingli, Huldrych, 200

INDEX OF BIBLICAL REFERENCES

BASIC CHRISTIAN CONVICTIONS

BASIC CHRISTIAN CONVICTIONS